Rituals of Ethnicity

CONTEMPORARY ETHNOGRAPHY

Kirin Narayan and Alma Gottlieb, Series Editors

A complete list of books in the series is available from the publisher.

Rituals of Ethnicity

Thangmi Identities Between Nepal and India

Sara Shneiderman

PENN

UNIVERSITY OF PENNSYLVANIA PRESS

PHILADELPHIA

Published by
University of Pennsylvania Press
Philadelphia, Pennsylvania 19104-4112
www.upenn.edu/pennpress

Printed in the United States of America
on acid-free paper
10 9 8 7 6 5 4 3 2 1

Library of Congress Cataloging-in-Publication Data
Shneiderman, Sara.
   Rituals of ethnicity : Thangmi identities between Nepal and India / Sara Shneiderman. — 1st ed.
      p. cm. — (Contemporary ethnography)
   Includes bibliographical references and index.
   ISBN 978-0-8122-4683-4 (hardcover : alk. paper)
   1. Thami (Nepalese people) 2. Thami (Nepalese people)—Ethnic identity. 3. Thami (Nepalese people)—Migrations. 4. Thami (Nepalese people)—Government relations—Nepal. 5. Thami (Nepalese people)—Government relations—India, Northeastern. 6. Tribes—Government policy—Nepal. 7. Tribes—Government policy—India, Northeastern. 8. Ethnicity—Political aspects—Himalaya Mountains Region. 9. Emigration and immigration—Political aspects—Himalaya Mountains Region. I. Title. II. Series: Contemporary ethnography.
   DS493.9.T46S56   2015
   305.80095496—dc23

2014028283

Ama apa, bubu pairi, tete jarphu, hu wari, humi damari, ca camaica!
Sakale kai seva!

Mother and father, older brother and sister-in-law, older sister and brother-in-law, younger brother and sister-in-law, younger sister and brother-in-law, son and daughter!

I offer service to all of you!

*   *   *

With this Thangmi greeting that recognizes all present with invocations of kinship, I dedicate this book to those who contributed to this project but did not live to see its end: Rana Bahadur and Maili of Balasode; Ram Bahadur of Kodari; Maili and Jyakha Bhojyu (Buddha Laxmi) of Pashelung; Junkiri of Suspa; Dalaman of Alampu; Singha Bahadur and Khumbalal of Kathmandu; and Basant, Gopal Singh, and Latte Apa (Man Bahadur) of Darjeeling

Contents

List of Abbreviations   ix

Preface   xi

1. Of Rocks and Rivers—Being Both at Once   1

2. Framing, Practicing, and Performing Ethnicity   32

3. Origin Myths and Myths of Originality   61

4. Circular Economies of Migration, Belonging, and Citizenship   98

5. Developing Associations of Ethnicity and Class   128

6. Transcendent Territory, Portable Deities, and the Problem of Indigeneity   169

7. The Work of Life-Cycle Rituals and the Power of Parallel Descent   196

8. Resisting the End of a Ritual   235

Epilogue: *Thami ke ho?*—What Is Thami?   252

Glossary   257

Notes   263

Bibliography   277

Index   293

Acknowledgments   301

AIGL	All India Gorkha League
BLTS	Bhai Larke Thami Samaj
BTWA	Bharatiya Thami Welfare Association
CPI	Communist Party of India
CPI(M)	Communist Party of India (Marxist)
CPN	Communist Party of Nepal
CPN-ML	Communist Party of Nepal—Marxist-Leninist
CPN-UML	Communist Party of Nepal—United Marxist-Leninist
DFID	Department for International Development (U.K.)
DGHC	Darjeeling Gorkha Hill Council
GDNS	Gorkha Duhkha Nivarak Sammelan
GJM	Gorkhaland Janamukti Morcha
GNLF	Gorkhaland National Liberation Front
HPSU	Hill People's Social Union
ILO	International Labour Organization
IPO	Indigenous People's Organization
JANSEEP	Janajati Social and Economic Empowerment Project
JEP	Janajati Empowerment Project
LGES	Lapilang Gau Ekai Samiti
NC	Nepali Congress
NEFEN	Nepal Federation of Nationalities
NEFIN	Nepal Federation of Indigenous Nationalities
NFDIN	National Foundation for the Development of Indigenous Nationalities
NGO	nongovernmental organization
NPTS	Niko Pragatisil Thami Samaj
NTS	Nepal Thami Samaj
NTSS	Niko Thami Seva Samiti

OBC	Other Backward Class
SC	Scheduled Caste
ST	Scheduled Tribe
TAR	Tibetan Autonomous Region
TBTSUK	Thami Bhasa Tatha Sanskriti Utthan Kendra
TEP	Thami Empowerment Project
UCPN(M)	Unified Communist Party of Nepal (Maoist)
VDC	Village Development Committee

Preface

This book is the first comprehensive ethnography of the Thangmi, also known as Thami.[1] They are a Himalayan community of approximately 40,000 who speak a Tibeto-Burman language. Their religion synthesizes aspects of shamanic, Hindu, and Buddhist practice. The Dolakha and Sindhupalchok districts of central-eastern Nepal are home to the largest concentration of Thangmi, with smaller numbers in Ilam, Jhapa, Ramechap, and Udayapur districts.[2] There are also substantial populations in the Darjeeling district of India's West Bengal state and the neighboring state of Sikkim.[3] Cross-border circular migration between these locations, as well as to Nyalam county of China's Tibetan Autonomous Region (TAR), which immediately borders Nepal, is an important feature of Thangmi life. Thangmi experience forms of economic and social marginalization in all of the countries in which they live.

The ensuing chapters flesh out this brief description with ethnographic details that unfold across three countries over more than a decade, complemented by oral and archival histories that extend the narrative back still further. The story is told by many voices, of which mine is just one. It is a story of commonality and difference, specificity and generality, emplacement and mobility. I hope that Thangmi everywhere will recognize something of themselves in it.

I first traveled to Nepal's Thangmi villages in 1998 with Mark Turin, a linguist and anthropologist then conducting doctoral research toward the first comprehensive grammar of the Thangmi language. We married in 2004, and much of the ethnographic research presented here was conducted collaboratively. The scholarly division of labor upon which we agreed means that the linguistic dimensions of Thangmi identity are not addressed comprehensively here; I direct interested readers to Mark Turin's publications, which are cited at relevant points throughout the text.

The village setting of my early work in Nepal lent itself to the traditional ethnographic method of participant-observation, both of daily life and ritual practice. I also conducted many formal and informal interviews. I sought out *guru* (shamans) and village elders, as well as laypeople of all genders, ages, and class backgrounds.[4] Most Thangmi with whom I worked asked explicitly to be recognized by name and place of residence. I therefore do not use pseudonyms in the text, although I occasionally omit personal names to honor the anonymity of those who requested it.

Throughout these encounters, I used photography to document events and to provide a springboard for discussion when I later returned photos to participants. Later, I incorporated digital video into my fieldwork practice. Recording video of practice and performance events in one location and showing it to people in others became a defining methodology of my multi-sited work. I organized small viewings in villages, as well as large public programs in Kathmandu and Darjeeling, at which I presented video footage and elicited comments. These programs, some of which are described in the chapters that follow, became forums for broad-ranging discussions among Thangmi who might not otherwise have met. My own role—and the role of ethnography in general—in "producing" Thangmi identity through such events is a central theme of this book. I can only reproduce a few photographs here, but I direct interested readers to two online portals where more audiovisual material is housed: Digital Himalaya (www.digitalhima-laya.com/collections/thangmiarchive) and the Tibetan and Himalayan Library (mms.thlib.org/topics/2823).

Sources and Languages

Throughout this book, I draw upon four compilations of writing published by Thangmi organizations: *Nan Ni Patuko* (2054 VS), *Dolakha Reng* (1999), *Niko Bachinte* (2003), and *Thami Samudayako Aitihasik Chinari ra Sanskar Sanskriti* ([2056] 2061 VS).[5] I cite these by their titles (using the following one-word abbreviations, respectively: Patuko, Reng, Niko, and Samudaya). Although each publication lists the editor(s), articles are only erratically attributed, making it difficult to ascribe individual authorship in some cases. Several more recent Thangmi-published books and articles exist (notably a regular series of Thangmi language pieces in Nepal's *Gorkhapatra* daily), along with many audio collections on cassette and CD, and documentary films on VCD and DVD—not to mention lively debates via social media. While I cannot analyze these in depth here, they constitute a rich archive for ongoing analysis.

Most speakers of Thangmi are bilingual in Nepali, the lingua franca in Darjeeling and Sikkim as well as the official language of Nepal, and my primary research language. Ritual practice is conducted largely in a special register of the Thangmi language in which I gained basic competence. To understand the details, I worked with Bir Bahadur, a Thangmi man my own age fluent in both Nepali and Thangmi. He provided on-the-fly translation as events or conversations unfolded, detailed transcription and translation of recorded materials, and a wealth of knowledge and analysis. The term "research assistant" does not adequately recognize Bir Bahadur's contribution to this project over fifteen years, but I use it to describe the formal aspect of our relationship in the scholarly context of this book.

Frequently in India, and occasionally in Nepal, informants chose to speak with me in English or sprinkle their otherwise Nepali conversation with English words. Documents were in both Nepali and English. Sanskrit and Tibetan words also appeared occasionally. When possible, I indicate the language in which statements were made or in which a text was published, using single quotation marks to set off English words in otherwise non-English sentences. Non-English terms are presented in phonetic form without diacritics, in italics, with the following abbreviations: (N) Nepali, (T) Thangmi, (T*) Thangmi ritual language, (Tib) Tibetan, and (Skt) Sanskrit. Proper place, ethnic, and personal names (i.e., Kathmandu, Thangmi, Bir Bahadur) are capitalized but not italicized. I hope that specialist readers will understand my eclectic approach as an effort to make the work accessible to a broad interdisciplinary audience.

Terminology and Locations

"Nepalese" was once the commonly agreed upon English term for citizens of the nation-state of Nepal, as well as for the country's lingua franca. However, many Nepali-speaking intellectuals view it as a colonial invention that does not match the ethnonym they use to talk about themselves and their language, "Nepali."[6] Others, however, seek to reclaim "Nepalese" to refer to citizens of Nepal, arguing that "Nepali" only fully includes mother-tongue speakers of the Nepali language, while excluding native speakers of the many other languages spoken within Nepal's borders. For the most part, contemporary scholarship in English follows the convention of using the term "Nepali," as established by Nepal-based writers.[7]

"Nepali" is more open-ended, since like "Tibetan," it refers to the language, as well as to a broad cultural complex, neither of which carries an inherent indication of citizenship. This usage is most widespread in Nepali-speaking areas of India, including Darjeeling and Sikkim, where people identify themselves as linguistically or ethnically Nepali yet are Indian citizens frustrated by assumptions that "Nepali" refers only to citizens of Nepal. In its most extreme form, this frustration manifests in the attempt to do away with "Nepali" altogether in favor of "Gorkha" or "Gorkhali"—the term preferred by those agitating for a separate Nepali-speaking state of Gorkhaland within India.

Many people with whom I worked in India used "Nepali" and "Gorkhali" interchangeably. Some insisted on the exclusive use of "Gorkhali," while others dismissed "Gorkhali" as associated with a political agenda they did not support, opting simply for "Nepali."[8] For those who used "Nepali" to describe themselves, the implication was not "citizens of Nepal" but rather "citizens of India belonging to an ethnic group defined by its shared Nepali linguistic and cultural forms." To describe this large category of people—including many Thangmi in India but also extending beyond them—I use "Indian citizens of Nepali heritage."

To Indian citizens of Nepali heritage, the usage of "Nepali" for people who are presumed to hold citizenship in Nepal but who come to India for short-term labor effectively implies that everyone of Nepali heritage is de facto a Nepali citizen and therefore does not have rights to citizenship in India.[9] This complicated logic emerges out of the terms of the Indo-Nepal Friendship Treaty of 1950, which forecloses the possibility of dual citizenship in the two countries. Indians of Nepali heritage therefore harbor a constant anxiety that they may be expelled en masse, as people from similar backgrounds indeed were in the 1980s and 1990s from the Indian states of Meghalaya and Mizoram, as well as from the neighboring country of Bhutan (Hutt 2003).

For all of these reasons, I do not use "Nepali" as a noun to refer to people. I do, however, use it as an adjective for complexes that transcend national boundaries: language, literature, society, history, heritage, media, and the public sphere. When necessary, I also use "Nepali" to denote entities specifically linked to the modern nation-state of Nepal: "the Nepali state," "Nepali citizenship," "Nepali legislation," "Nepali state policy," and "the Nepali national framework."

The category of "Indian" is equally vexed for different reasons. While Indian citizens of Nepali heritage fight for recognition of their Indianness in India, when they travel to or live in Nepal, they downplay it as much as possible. Only citizens of Nepal may own land in Nepal, and Indians are stereotyped as the imperious big brother next door whom everyone loves to hate. As described in Chapter 4, many Indian citizens of Nepali heritage in fact continue to own land in Nepal and work in the private sector as teachers, doctors, and entrepreneurs. All of these occupations entail the production of Nepali "paper citizenship" (Sadiq 2008), despite the fact that these individuals already hold Indian documents. The possession of dual-citizenship documents puts these individuals in a large, quasi-illicit category. For this reason, although many Thangmi I encountered in Nepal had been born, educated, or otherwise spent much of their lives in India, they preferred not to be set apart from other Thangmi in Nepal as "Indian." The latter term did not have the same connotations of a particular ethnic, cultural, or linguistic heritage that "Nepali" did; so I use "Indian" only in a manner equivalent to the second usage of "Nepali" above: to refer to the "Indian state," "Indian citizenship," "Indian legal framework," and so forth. These issues, which have great implications for how Thangmi identity is conceptualized and produced, are discussed in Chapters 4 and 6.

In Nepal, the majority of Thangmi live in rural hill villages in Dolakha and Sindhupalchok. Some of the largest Thangmi settlements are in Alampu, Chokati, Dhuskun, Dumkot, Lapilang, Piskar, Surkhe, and Suspa (although members of other ethnic groups also usually live in or near these settlements). A small number of Thangmi live in urban Kathmandu—Nepal's only truly metropolitan city—along with a similar number in semi-urban towns in the Tarai districts of Jhapa and Udayapur.[10] Both of these groups are composed largely of individuals who settled in these towns later in life, having grown up either in rural Nepal or in Darjeeling. I refer to such groups as "Kathmandu-based Thangmi" and "Jhapa-based Thangmi" because their locations—and the life experiences associated with them—set them apart from the majority of Thangmi living in hill districts. Each district, village, and hamlet has its own particularities. With the exception of a pronounced dialect difference between the Thangmi language spoken in Sindhupalchok and Dolakha, these are almost impossible to describe schematically.

The majority of the Thangmi population in India lives in urban Darjeeling municipality or adjacent quasiurban settlements, such as Alubari, Jawahar Basti, Jorebunglow, Mangalpuri, and Tungsung. There are also small concentrations of Thangmi in rural areas throughout the district, both on tea plantations like Tumsong, and in such villages as Bijen Bari, Rangbull, and Tin Mile. In the neighboring state of Sikkim, several Thangmi reside in urban Gangtok, while others are dispersed across rural areas. Thangmi residence patterns in India are rarely ethnically homogeneous in the manner that they are in Nepal. Yet there as in Nepal, place is central to the cultural politics of Thangminess, so I pay careful attention to locality. Throughout the book, whenever possible I mention the village or town with which an individual has connections, or where an event took place.

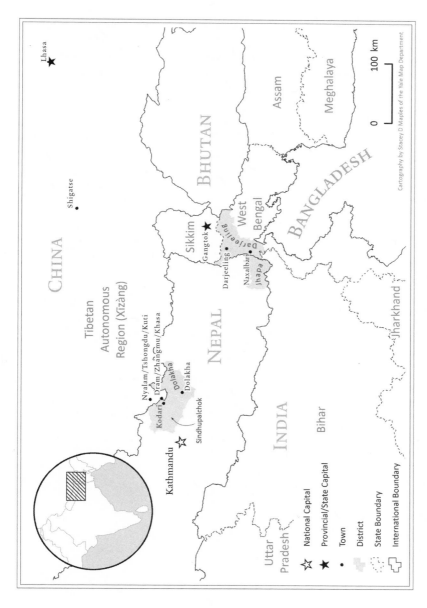

Areas of Thangmi residence and mobility in Nepal, India, and China's Tibetan Autonomous Region (TAR). Map courtesy of Stacey D. Maples.

Chapter 1

Of Rocks and Rivers—Being Both at Once

> We are solid like rocks and viscous like mud. We have offered incense
> to our deities . . .
> Come, deities, strung in a straight line like the necklaces of the
> sparrow, of our ancestors . . . come strung in a straight line . . .
> As the deities rose, the rocks dissolved. It was light and the wood
> dissolved. As it dissolved, everything became fluid. . . . Let's create
> humans, the deities said.

Chanting these lines, the voices of Thangmi shamans rise and fall to the
beat of an animal-skin drum. Monotonous yet captivating, every ritual
event begins with these recitations about the origins of the world. This is
also the soundtrack I always hear in my mind as I write about Thangmi
lives. I can almost smell the incense, recalling myself in the midst of one
ritual after another, some over a decade ago now. Weddings, funerals, sup-
plications to territorial deities for a good harvest, most taking place late at
night, lit first by kerosene lamps and candles and in later years by bare
electric bulbs strung along mud walls. Some Thangmi listen attentively,
some drink grain beer and joke loudly about the shamans' performance,
others coo children to sleep in corners amid the hubbub. I struggle to stay
awake and make sense of what the words, actions, and beliefs behind them
might mean.

These chants are part of the Thangmi *paloke*, a narrative cycle about
origins and being in the world. It is a story that Thangmi tell themselves
about themselves and their relations to others. It is a story heard from
childhood onward that plays a crucial role in shaping Thangmi sensibilities

about who they are, as individuals, members of an ethnic community, inhabitants of particular pieces of territory, and mobile citizens of multiple states. Repeated again and again throughout each ritual cycle, the first line sums up an apparent paradox of Thangmi being. As they propitiate their deities, the speakers are at once "solid like rocks and viscous like mud," both immovable objects and malleable forms. For a group of people who openly acknowledge themselves as peripheral to dominant formulations of national, ethnic, and religious identity, and who practice circular migration between three countries as a primary socioeconomic strategy, this fluid state of being is not only a ritual metaphor but a fact of daily life.

I was listening to academic addresses—eerily evocative of the Thangmi *paloke* in their cadence—at a conference on "Ethnicity and Federalisation" in Kathmandu, Nepal, in April 2011. Leading scholars, activists, and policy makers had gathered to discuss the role of ethnicity in restructuring the Nepali state. After a ten-year civil conflict between Maoist insurgents and state forces ended in 2006, Nepal began the transformation from a unitary Hindu monarchy to a secular democratic federal republic. The country's first Constituent Assembly was elected in 2008, and the process of constitution writing began amid great hope for a more equitable future. By the time of the conference in 2011, however, the deadline for a new constitution had been extended several times beyond the initial two years, and agreement on the shape of the new state was still uncertain. Ultimately, the Constituent Assembly would be dissolved in 2012 without promulgating a constitution. The role of ethnicity in determining new provincial boundaries was at the center of contentious debate.

There were no Thangmi, and few members of other marginalized groups like them, in the hotel ballroom filled to capacity with several hundred representatives of Nepal's political and academic elite. I was invited to present a paper as a "foreign expert" on ethnicity in Nepal but found myself unsure of the implications of my statements in this highly politicized context. Social scientific arguments about the nature of ethnicity were being deployed in novel ways to argue for or against recognizing ethnicity as a valid basis for demarcating Nepal's newly proposed federal units.

An influential sociologist from Tribhuvan University in Kathmandu took the podium. "Ethnic distinctions and boundaries keep shifting and multiplying and coalescing," he said, "'before' and 'after' and in-between are akin to waves on the move rather than to fixed rocks" (Mishra 2012:88).

He was describing ethnicity in terms similar to those I had heard over and over in the Thangmi chants. But here the relationship between the two possibilities was cast in oppositional terms—either a rock or a wave, a fixed object or a mutable flow—while in the shamans' formulation these were complementary properties of a holistic state of being reproduced through ritualized action.

This book considers the implications of each of these points of view for contemporary understandings of ethnicity. Is ethnicity a rock or a river? Fixed or fluid? Both at once? To whom? At what particular places and times? How can interpreting the process of ethnicization as a process of ritualization, which brings disparate individuals together around the shared sacred object of identity, offer new explanations for the powerful persistence of ethnic identities despite the increasing realities of mobile, hybrid lives?

I consider these questions through the story of one putatively singular community, the Thangmi, and their life experiences as they move across the Himalayan borders of Nepal, India, and China's Tibetan Autonomous Region (TAR). But this story raises larger questions about how ethnicity and identity are produced, ritual and politics enacted, cross-border migration lived, and consciousness experienced for many people across the region and the world who have something in common with those who recognize themselves as Thangmi. At the most intimate level, this category of commonality includes those who identify as members of other *adivasi janajati* (indigenous nationality) groups in Nepal, as Indians of Nepali heritage, and as border people in China.[1] At the next level of abstraction, it includes those who define themselves, or are defined by others, as indigenous, tribal, marginal, or "out-of-the-way" (Tsing 1993) anywhere in the world. At the most general level, the category can be expanded to include all those whose lives entail cross-border, transnational, diasporic, or migratory movements and hybrid or synthetic practices. While I tell the Thangmi story for its own sake, this narrative comes to articulate with many others through the telling.

Why Ethnicity?

Mishra (2012) was not the first scholar to use the metaphor of rocks and rivers to describe the nature of cultural processes in the Himalayas. In his ethnography of the Thakali, *Fluid Boundaries*, William Fisher writes of the Kali Gandaki river running through his informants' villages in western Nepal in just such a way:

> Thakali culture . . . is like the Kali Gandaki River. It flows in a wide riverbed that allows it to break up into several meandering streams that merge again downstream. These separations and mergings vary unpredictably over time, but the separated channels always rejoin further downstream. . . . The river changes over time . . . . But it is nevertheless the same river.
>
> Similarly, any description of Thakali culture is at best a representation of a moment in an ongoing cultural process. The difficulty of locating cultural coherence does not mean that Thakali culture has broken down or that it is in a transitional phase between one coherent structure or another. It merely reflects the process in which Thakali culture has been continually renewed. (2001:19–20)

I read this description early in my fieldwork and pondered it often as I struggled to understand the eddies of Thangmi culture swirling around me. I took my cue from ethnographers like Fisher and Arjun Guneratne (2002), whose work was emerging just as I began my research, to define the initial subject of my study as the process of producing Thangmi identity in its totality in a cross-border context.

Yet I entered the field at a very different historical moment, in both scholarly and political terms, than my immediate predecessors in the lineage of Himalayan anthropology. By the late 1990s, cultural critique was at its pinnacle, and much anthropological writing on the region demonstrated the constructedness of ethnic categories and cultural forms. During the same period, both Nepal and India experienced an explosion of public debate over the nature of social difference. This was due in part to national political developments, including the 1990 return of democracy in Nepal, and the subsequent promulgation of a new constitution that for the first time recognized this extremely diverse country as a "multiethnic" nation, but stopped short of attaching entitlements to specific identities. The year 1990 also saw India's implementation of the Mandal Commission report, which revised that country's system of affirmative action—constitutionally mandated since 1950—followed in 1991 by economic liberalization (Gupta and Sivaramakrishnan 2011). The accelerated circulation of global discourses also played a role in fostering debate: multiculturalism, indigeneity, and inclusion, all couched in the broader terms of "rights." These were often given programmatic teeth by international development actors (Shneiderman 2013a).

Taken together, these developments yielded the somewhat paradoxical intellectual environment of the late 1990s in which I first became acquainted with the Thangmi. On the one hand, the constructed nature of ethnicity and its limitations as an analytical tool were becoming taken for granted in the scholarly world. On the other hand, the ability to make political claims in ethnic terms was viewed as an increasingly valuable skill by people I encountered on the ground. I began to feel that the processual interpretation of culture espoused by Fisher and others was incomplete. It was not wrong, but it could not account entirely for the proliferation of ethnic expressions I observed or for the desire among those with whom I worked to possess what we might call the objects, rather than the processes, of culture. I do not mean objects only in the tangible sense but also in the intangible sense in which such concepts as identity, origins, territory, and indigeneity can be constituted as sacred objects through ritualized action.

To pursue Fisher's metaphor, most of the Thangmi I met were not content just to watch the river flow, as a tourist—or a scholar—might be. Rather, they sought to engage with it as an entity in the phenomenal world: to build a bridge across it, to drink from it, to catch fish in it. In other words, many Thangmi were aware at some level that identity was produced through processual action, but this consciousness of identity-as-process did not preclude their desire for identity-as-object. The capacity to engage in ritualized action that produced 'Thangminess' as a recognizable object was the key to community membership. That such ritualized action could take multiple forms, from deity propitiations to political conferences, was understood as a key feature of the synthetic, collectively produced nature of Thangmi identity itself.

The persistence of this fundamental human desire to objectify one's identity in terms recognizable to others is, I argue, why ethnicity still matters, as an analytical construct, a political resource, and an affective anchor for identity. This is the case despite a general agreement by the late 1990s within anthropology and perhaps across much of the social sciences that ethnicity, and even the concept of "the group," was dead. In a 1996 survey of the topic, Marcus Banks concluded that "while ethnicity has an ever more insubstantial place within the narrow world of academia, . . . it appears to be increasingly important in the wider world" (1996:183). "Unfortunately," he continued, "it is too late to kill it off or pronounce ethnicity dead; the discourse on ethnicity has escaped from the academy and into the field" (189). In this formulation, ethnicity exists first as an analytical rubric and only subsequently as a subjective experience.

To ground this discussion in the South Asian contexts in which my ethnography unfolds, consider this 1997 comment from David Gellner: "There is a bitter irony in the fact . . . that just when a scholarly and anthropological consensus is emerging that a Hindu-tribe dichotomy was hopelessly flawed as a tool for understanding Nepalese society, Nepalese intellectuals should begin to take it up with a vengeance" (22). More than fifteen years later, at the time of writing in 2014, Nepal is engaged in a historically unprecedented process of "post-conflict" federal restructuring, stalled due to the political impasse over the demand for ethnically deline- ated states that would take what Gellner calls the "Hindu-tribe dichotomy" for granted. Across the border in Nepali-speaking areas of India, the call for a separate state of Gorkhaland for Indian citizens of Nepali heritage (often called Gorkhas) was newly revived in 2008. An earlier agitation ended in 1989 with the creation of the Darjeeling Gorkha Hill Council (DGHC). Debate over Darjeeling's future remains a key political issue for the Indian state of West Bengal.

Portraying such large-scale political transformations as the ironic result of the "escape" of a scholarly paradigm for ethnicity into "the field" would be analytically insufficient. Rather, we must evaluate what ethnicity signifies for those who claim it. We must investigate anew how such forms of consciousness are produced by all kinds of individuals—not only by self- proclaimed ethnic activists—who see themselves as members of a collectiv- ity and seek recognition as such from others. Acknowledging that ethnicity is inevitably constructed is not the end of the story but rather the beginning of understanding the ongoing life of such constructions. "Tracing the con- tours of this new life" (Banks 1996:189) of ethnicity is important not because scholars necessarily believe it to be the most accurate way of under- standing "the group," "belonging," or "difference" but because many con- temporary ethnic subjects and the recognizing agents with which they must engage—both state and nonstate—do.

Scholarship indicates an emerging realization that ethnicity's case is not yet closed. Whether by highlighting the cross-border nature of ethnogenesis

(Scott 2009) or the power of global market forces (Comaroff and Comaroff 2009), contemporary explorations of ethnicity broaden analyses beyond the frame of the nation-state, while recognizing the power of national borders and state-specific regimes of recognition in shaping ethnic configurations. In this vein, which productively tempers 1990s arguments about the ascendance of transnational, deterritorialized identities, this book argues that nation-states remain a key frame in relation to which ethnicity is produced, even and perhaps especially in contexts of high cross-border mobility. Furthermore, I argue that ethnicity is a result not only of the prerogatives of state control or market forces but also of a ritual process through which identity is produced as a sacred object that binds diverse people together. Such sacred objects serve as shared referents, enabling heterogeneous individuals—often dispersed across multiple nation-states, with multiple class, gender, age and educational experiences—to contribute in diverse ways to collective projects of ethnicity in action.

This argument returns to traditional anthropological formulations by building upon Edmund Leach's supposition that "the maintenance and insistence upon cultural difference can itself become a ritual action expressive of social relations" (1964:17). Leach's insight reveals ethnicity as not only a political project but also an affective domain in which the cultural difference constitutive of social relations is expressed to both selves and others through ritual action. In this spirit, I refocus attention on the objectification of identity as a fundamental human process that persists through ritualized action regardless of the contingencies of state formation or economic paradigm. I hope readers will find here an ethnographic explanation of how ethnicity may be both a rock and a river at once, solid yet also viscous like the muddy flow of a swollen monsoon watershed that carries boulders through Himalayan valleys.

This argument shifts attention away from the representational construction of ethnicity through discourse to foreground instead the expressive production of ethnicity in action (Bentley 1987) and its ongoing pragmatic effects, and affect, for those who enact it. The Comaroffs suggest that in academic studies of ethnicity, the overwhelming "stress on the *politics* of ethnicity above all else has a number of critical costs: it depends on an underspecified, almost metaphorical conception of the political, the primary referent of which is the pursuit of interest; it reduces cultural identity to a utility function, the measure of which is power, again underspecified; and it confuses the deployment of ethnicity as a *tactical* claim to entitlement and as a means of mobilization for instrumental ends, with the *substantive* content of ethnic consciousness" (2009:44). Indeed, much of the last great spell of anthropological work on ethnicity, particularly in South Asia, focused on "ethnonationalist conflict" (Tambiah 1996) and "ethnic violence" (Appadurai 1998). Although these works built valuably upon Frederik Barth's (1969) formative insights to explain why, in certain cases, ethnic boundaries become aggravated sites of contestation, they shifted focus away from the group-specific, culturally contextual, substantive content of ethnic consciousness that lies between and animates such boundaries. Moreover, while many scholars have effectively explored how state paradigms for recognition in South Asia shape ethnic consciousness writ large, much literature presumes that the contents of all such consciousnesses are interchangeable.[2] I contend instead that although the mechanisms of and criteria for state recognition with which all groups must engage may be the same, the substantive content of ethnic consciousness develops in large part through the process of mobilizing specific cultural and ethnographic content, the nature of which varies widely between groups. If we wish to understand the dialectic between ethnic consciousness and legal paradigms for recognition, we must attend to the ethnographic specifics of individual contemporary groups, both within and beyond the political frame.

The Comaroffs are hardly the first scholars to suggest that the political life of ethnicity is not its only one (Leach 1964; Williams 1989; Jenkins 2002). But the Comaroffs newly situate ethnicity under the sign of the market, understood in neoliberal terms. They call upon scholars to investigate the dialectic between "the incorporation of identity and the commodification of culture" (2009:89) as a means of moving beyond the analysis of ethnicity as a purely political construct, and to "fashion a critical scholarship to deal with its ambiguous promises, its material and moral vision for times to come, the deep affective attachments it engenders" (149).

So how do we do that? The fact that academic interests in the "political" aspects of ethnicity often occlude attention to its embodied, affective aspects is a methodological problem as much as a theoretical one. It is relatively straightforward to examine the discursive production of ethnicity through the analysis of texts and media, but understanding "the substantive content of ethnic consciousness" is more complicated. This book takes up the challenge through in-depth ethnography that emphasizes ritualized action, a concept that I take to encompass both "practice" and "performance." These terms are defined and their analytical value explored in Chapter 2.

By recognizing diverse forms of action as constitutive of ethnicity—from private household practices to public political performances—I consider an equally broad range of actors as legitimate cultural producers. In so doing, I move beyond the idea that activists who objectify cultural forms to achieve specific political goals are somehow outside the realm of "authentic" cultural production or must be viewed in conceptual opposition to "the rural poor" (Shah 2010:31). Rather, I consider Thangmi activists within an overarching framework that also includes shamans, elders, housewives, youth group members, schoolchildren, and multiple others as differently agentive but mutually influential producers of the shared social field of ethnicity in action. By the same token, I do not take at face value activist assertions as authentic statements of ethnic consciousness but rather calibrate these with competing claims from other, equally Thangmi, actors.

This dynamic view of ethnicity as a collective production to which multiple, diverse actors contribute shifts the focus away from the concern with authenticity that has preoccupied much earlier work on ethnicity, identity, and indigeneity. Debates centered on the discursive formation of "indigeneity" in particular challenge conventional stereotypes to reveal the diversity of indigenous experiences, not all of which entail social and economic marginality in the same measures (de la Cadena and Starn 2007; Cattelino 2008). Yet as explained in Chapter 6, indigeneity itself is a contested term within the Thangmi community, as well as within the broader public spheres of both Nepal and India. It is therefore only one component of my discussion rather than the primary analytical rubric. Considering the relationship between ethnicity and indigeneity allows us to explore the multiple scales on which contemporary subaltern identities are articulated (Li 2000).

The People Without an Ethnography

When I returned to Kathmandu after my first visits to Thangmi villages in central-eastern Nepal in 1998, I scoured bookstores and libraries for information about the group but could find nothing. It is puzzling that this relatively sizable group failed entirely to make it onto the ethnographic map of Nepal, where several numerically smaller communities have been popular ethnographic subjects, and barely onto that of India, where colonial administrators carefully enumerated and categorized the communities they encountered. This absence, noticeable in both scholarly and political contexts, provided the impetus for my research with the Thangmi.

"*Thami ke ho?*" or "What is Thami?" is a common Nepali language refrain that Thangmi everywhere hear throughout their lives. Nirmala, a young woman from the village of Dumkot in Dolakha, explained how this made her feel: "Everyone in the bazaar asks, '*Thami ke ho?*' I want to tell them '*Yo Thangmi ho,*' or—'This is Thangmi' [*pointing to herself*]. But that is not enough; we need to know our history and culture so we can explain. Some of the books published in Darjeeling which I have read, like this one, are very helpful in that way." Nirmala held up a copy of the 2003 publication *Niko Bachinte* (Our Morning, in Thangmi). Superimposed over a photo of a Thangmi shaman in Sindhupalchok (that I had shot early in my research), the text on the back cover of the publication began with the question "*Thami ke ho?*"

What was often encountered as a flippant query from curious outsiders had become a burning rhetorical question that the community posed to themselves. Unpacked somewhat, it actually means, "How do you fit into familiar systems of classification?" or "Where is your place in the social order?" The Thangmi ethnonym's lack of clear signification derives in part from a history of misrecognition, which many Thangmi exacerbated by intentionally misrepresenting themselves as members of other better-known groups.[3] In social interactions, Thangmi often find that they are mistaken for Kami, a *dalit* (previously "untouchable") blacksmith caste, or Dhami, a socially marginalized group of folk healers, owing to the similar sounds of their names. They are just as frequently misrecognized as members of neighboring ethnic groups, primarily Tamang, Rai, or Limbu, by the general public, scholars, and members of those groups who seek to claim the Thangmi population as part of their own for political purposes.

In both countries, "Thami" is the group's official moniker, appearing on citizenship cards in Nepal or ration cards in India as a surname. Members of the group usually prefer their own ethnonym, "Thangmi." But neither name conveys enough information for outsiders to easily categorize those who bear it, since most people simply do not know what "Thami," and even less "Thangmi," indexes in terms of ethnicity, religion, or region. Despite their different citizenships and life experiences in Nepal and India, members of the current generation of the Thangmi community are drawn together by their desire for "existential recognition" (Graham 2005) of a distinctive presence in practice, which might help fill the discursive absence surrounding their name.

Although the Thangmi recognize themselves as a distinct group, they are not named in Nepal's 1854 Muluki Ain, the legal code that provided the historical basis for political recognition in Nepal (Höfer [1979] 2004).[4] Later scholarly and bureaucratic ethnographies in both Nepal and India compounded the problem. For example, the 1993 update of the *Anthropological Survey of India*, which has existed since the colonial era (Cohn 1987), states, "There is no idea about the origin of the Thami community or the term 'Thami.' Their history is indeed obscure. . . . The Thamis do not have any exclusive ritual worth mentioning" (Subba 1993:184–85).

Indeed, beyond Mark Turin's description of the Thangmi language (2012), which shows that this under-documented Tibeto-Burman tongue is related to both Kiranti (Rai and Limbu) and Newar languages,[5] there is no previous authoritative scholarship in English on the Thangmi. The small body of existing material is largely inaccessible. This includes the field notes of Christoph von Fürer-Haimendorf archived at the School of Oriental and African Studies in London (this founding father of Himalayan anthropology passed through Thangmi villages several times but never made an in-depth study), American anthropologist Creighton Peet's unpublished 1978 dissertation,[6] and the notes of French linguist Genevieve Stein (who worked in the village of Alampu in the 1970s but never published her findings). Other locally published materials are now out of print (Sapkota 2045 VS; Toba 1990).[7] Newspaper articles in the Nepali media are another source of information, but with some notable exceptions (Lall 1966), these are generally based on secondary sources of questionable veracity and tend to represent the Thangmi in a folkloristic idiom, casting them as a quaint, backward group notable for their cultural oddities, such as their supposed belief that they are *yeti-ko santan*, or "the descendants of yeti" (Manandhar 2001).[8]

In several compendia, the Thangmi are classified as a subgroup of other better-known groups, such as Tamang (Bista 1967:48; Gaborieau 1978:107; Majupuria and Majupuria 1978:60, 1980:57), Kiranti (Lévi, as cited in Riccardi 1975:23), or Parbatiya Hindu (Vansittart 1918:70).[9] A 1994 ethnographic survey by Rajesh Gautam and Ashoke Thapa-Magar exemplifies the derogatory language often used to describe the group: "not clean in their habits" (1994:314), "when a Thami is seen it is clear that these people have recently renounced their uncivilized ways" (1994:323). Debates about the meaning of the ethnonym "Thangmi"—which most likely derives either from the Tibetan *mtha' mi* (people of the border) or *thang mi* (people of the steppe)—are literally relegated to the footnotes of Himalayan anthropology.[10] A 1928 recruitment manual for the Gurkha regiments of the British Army recognizes the Thangmi as a distinct group but powerfully sums up their marginal position within national and transnational hierarchies of recognition: "Coarse in appearance, and the inferior of the other races in social and religious matters, they do not merit further description" (Northey and Morris 1928:260).

The point on which most scholars agree, and the one they often refer to in explaining why they did not conduct further research with the Thangmi, is that they are an extremely poor group with little distinctive material culture: no unique artistic or architectural traditions, no colorful crafts or costumes, nothing visible beyond the lowest common denominator features of rural Himalayan life. To an outside eye, there is indeed little to distinguish a Thangmi individual or village from the next person or place.

However, this apparent absence of distinctive ethnic markers from an outsider's perspective is belied by a rich cultural presence enacted through practice within the community itself. Thangmi cultural content is largely contained in the intangible, internally coherent aspects of ritualized action rather than in any tangible, externally recognizable visual form. When I asked what made Thangmi themselves, the answers nearly always pointed to ritualized action, broadly defined. Indeed, as I looked around me, I saw octogenarian shamans propitiating territorial deities, young ethnic activists mounting political performances, and householders offhandedly saluting the deities under whose auspices they went about their daily business. Only through understanding such forms of action could I understand how Thangminess itself was produced.

Why *Rituals of Ethnicity?* Recognition, Complicity, and the Ethnographic Contract

Although desire for political recognition from the state is a relatively new phenomenon for many Thangmi, recognition from other sources, particularly the divine world, has long been a key force in constituting Thangmi social relations. As Man Bahadur, a middle-aged Thangmi man from Dolakha, put it, "If we Thangmi forgot to worship our deities, they would not recognize us. If the deities do not recognize us, how can others recognize our ethnicity?" This compels us to reconsider recognition as a deep-seated subjective desire (Taylor 1992) that drives much of human communicative interaction (Keane 1997). While often fostered through political means, recognition should not be reductively understood only as a regime of control produced by specific sociopolitical formations (Povinelli 2002). Rather, understanding the mechanisms of recognition and the content of the consciousnesses they produce requires an exploration of the full range of "recognizing agents" with which subjects engage. For Thangmi, these have over time included the divine world, the Nepali and Indian states, social scientists, nongovernmental organizations (NGOs), members of other communities, and crucially, other members of the Thangmi community itself, separated by citizenship, distance, class, and other vectors of difference.

Anthropologists themselves may become recognizing agents "complicit" (Marcus 1999) in catalyzing community efforts to achieve recognition from other sources. Ethnography that works to transform the "terms of recognition" can become part of the toolkit groups use to craft their future (Appadurai 2004). This book therefore uses the conceit of ethnography as an organizing principle, with chapters loosely structured around classical anthropological subjects: ritual, myth, economy, political organization, territory, descent and the life cycle, and the dynamics of power and agency. Organizing the book in this way provokes a reconsideration of the relationship between anthropological form and content by demonstrating that reflexive, multisited research with transnational communities need not preclude in-depth description of fundamental aspects of social life, presented in a manner that is meaningful to both scholars and communities themselves. That the rubric "Thangmi" describes a diversity of experiences not easily reconciled within a singular frame is a fundamental premise of this book; yet using the monographic form of ethnography allows me to create the coherent social scientific profile that disparate members of the Thangmi community commonly desire.

The lack of accessible, accurate scholarly material about the Thangmi is not simply an academic concern. It has concrete consequences within the crucible of *janajati* and tribal politics in Nepal and India, as Thangmi attempts to control the terms of their own recognition vis-à-vis the multiple states in which they live have shifted over time from a strategy of state evasion, or "dissimilation" (Geoffrey Benjamin as cited in Scott 2009:173–74), to one of direct, intentional engagement.

Historically, land and labor exploitation under the Rana and Shah regimes compelled Thangmi in Nepal to remain under the radar of state recognition whenever possible.[11] Fear of the state, which primarily manifested in its tax-collecting form, encouraged the insular maintenance of cultural practices. Thangmi intentionally avoided public forms of cultural objectification that might attract curious outsiders. Many Thangmi elders told me that they actually counted themselves lucky to have been left out of the 1854 Muluki Ain legal code. This lacuna encouraged Thangmi to misrepresent themselves as members of better-known ethnic groups in encounters with authority.

But in 2002, the Nepal Foundation for the Development of Indigenous Nationalities (NFDIN) Act first created the legal category of *adivasi janajati* in Nepal, listing fifty-six groups. In 2004, the nongovernmental Nepal Federation of Indigenous Nationalities (NEFIN) introduced a new five-tiered classification system to further categorize these groups as "endangered," "highly marginalized," "marginalized," "disadvantaged," and "advantaged" (Gellner 2007; Hangen 2007; Middleton and Shneiderman 2008; Onta 2006b; Shneiderman 2013a). The government of Nepal ratified International Labour Organization (ILO) Convention 169 on the Rights of Indigenous Peoples in 2007, becoming only the second Asian country to do so. Under these changing circumstances, a recognizable identity encoded in an ethnographic tome began to seem newly important to groups concerned with securing recognition in a state that might be restructured along ethnic lines. What use is remaining intentionally beyond the range of state recognition when the state begins offering options for self-governance, if "autonomy" can only be provided to those groups who are already officially recognized at the point of devolution?

In India, by contrast, there has long been a dialectic between indigenous self-representation and state-sponsored ethnography (Cohn 1987; Dirks 2001). The Indian Constitution of 1950 provides for the "upliftment" of marginalized groups through official recognition (known as "scheduling") and quotas (Galanter 1984; Jenkins 2003). In the early 1990s, in the wake of the Mandal Commission report, which revamped India's affirmative action system, Thangmi in India demanded Other Backward Class (OBC) status, which they received in 1995. Since then, they have campaigned for—but not yet received—Scheduled Tribe (ST) status, which is perceived to offer greater political, educational, and economic benefits. These descendants of Thangmi migrants, who left Nepal as long as 150 years ago, for the most part no longer speak the Thangmi language and grew up in environments where Thangmi ritual practitioners were often not available. In the process of applying for ST status, however, many Thangmi in India have become interested in rediscovering Thangmi "culture." Chapter 5 examines these processes in depth.

Nowhere does the Indian constitution specifically define the criteria for ST recognition. In 1965, the Lokur Committee established these semiofficial guidelines, which remain in place today: "indication of primitive traits; distinctive culture; geographical isolation; shyness of contact with the community at large; and backwardness" (Galanter 1984:152). The first two criteria are almost universally interpreted by aspirant groups to mean that ethnographic materials must be submitted as part of their application.

Much of the onus for presenting ethnographic data lies with the aspirant communities themselves. The potential for social science research to contribute to such campaigns for recognition, as well as to become complicit in them, has been discussed at length elsewhere in the world, particularly in Latin America and Australia. In these regions, scholars have contributed ethnographic knowledge to indigenous land-rights claims, cultural performances, and various other mediations between the communities with whom they work and broader publics. The results of such engagement are always complex and rarely morally clear-cut. The "moral contract for research" (Warren and Jackson 2002:4) is always fraught, as information about and access to community-specific knowledge, actions, and discourse are exchanged for social scientific recognition. Often the ethnographic contract remains unspoken—and certainly unsigned. Yet it evokes expectations and aspirations on all sides from the moment that a scholar first engages with people from whom she wishes to collect "data." In exchange for our data, I believe that scholars conducting ethnographic work have an ethical responsibility to, at the very least, investigate potential avenues for contributing to the agendas of those with whom we work. For me, this belief has led to carefully chosen strategies for raising Thangmi public profiles through the production of social scientific knowledge about them.

Charles Hale (2006) describes how this kind of engagement with subaltern communities, which he calls "activist research," may conflict with the prerogatives of cultural critique (Clifford and Marcus 1986; Marcus and Fischer 1986). Activist research, although always politically compromised, has the potential to create uniquely generative theoretical spaces that move beyond institutional academic commitments. Hale suggests that although cultural critique positions itself as the only approach that can adequately represent subaltern voices in a nonessentialized, politically correct manner, problems arise when subaltern communities themselves choose to use theoretically unfashionable categories: "As long as the heavy weapons of deconstruction are aimed at the powerful, the proposal remains on high ground. But what about the other 'sites' of a multisited ethnography? How do we responsibly address situations in which the relatively powerless are using these same vexed categories to advance their struggles?" (2006:102). This is precisely the situation I encountered. While my initial scholarly impulse was to demonstrate the processual constructedness of Thangmi ethnic identity, I ultimately could not ignore the intensity with which Thangmi from diverse backgrounds—including activists, ritual practitioners, and common people who bumped up against the problem of misrecognition in their daily lives—asked me to provide an essentializing ethnographic portrait of "the Thangmi" as a unified, unique, and historically unchanging group.

Why shouldn't they want this when, for instance, an early application to the government of India for ST status was met with rejection and the directive to "submit total ethnographic material of your caste to the ministry"?[12] It may be the case within academic anthropology that "the production of portraits of other cultures, no matter how well drawn, is in a sense no longer a major option" (Ortner 1999:9). Yet it is precisely this ethnographic portrait, presented in an authoritative academic voice, that many Thangmi desire, as an instrument of both psychological and political recognition. With no holistic portrait produced in the bygone days of anthropology when such work was not yet politically incorrect, why should Thangmi forgo this aspiration when their counterparts in other better-documented communities proudly brandish their ethnographies as important heritage objects?

It would be a sad irony if postcolonial anthropological reflexivity worked to reinforce earlier disciplinary biases—and their entanglements with local relations of power—by rejecting calls from historically understudied people to produce knowledge about them. As one young Thangmi activist writes, "We have a request for all scientists and scholars: please do research about the Thami, please write about us, and we will stand ready to help you" (Tahal Thami, in Samudaya ([2056] 2061 VS:vi). Rather than disengaging from such projects because they make *us* feel uneasy as scholars, we might consider how uneasy it feels to be a people without an ethnography in many contemporary political environments. The fact that ethnography itself is complicit in shaping people's political futures is a part of anthropology's disciplinary legacy that remains to be adequately acknowledged and transformed through collaboration with contemporary communities who are themselves engaged in the ethnographic project.

For many Thangmi, engagement in ethnographic research itself— whether as a researcher, an informant, or both—has become an important mode of ethnic expression. I write candidly about my own role in these processes as an ethnographer and acknowledge that this work is relevant not only to an academic audience but to Thangmi and the various audiences they engage.

Rituals of Ethnicity emerged as the title of choice from my discussions with Thangmi interlocutors about these issues of presence and absence, object and action, complicity and collaboration. It became clear early on that the title of this book must be recognizable in some form to Thangmi themselves (even in English), and foreground the Thangmi-specific ethnography at its core, despite what I hope is the broader applicability of the anthropological arguments contained herein. I asked many Thangmi with whom I worked what I should call the book that would emerge from my long-term engagement with their community. Most of the answers were variations of *"Thangmi jati-ko sanskar ra sanskriti," "hamro jati-ko sanskar,"* or in its most concise form, *"jatiya sanskar,"* all in Nepali. Literally meaning "rituals and culture of the Thangmi ethnicity," "rituals of our ethnicity," or "ethnic rituals," respectively,[13] these phrases indicated to the people who proffered them that the book so named would be a useful compendium of ethnographic information about what constituted them as a community: the ritual practices in which they engaged. *Rituals of Ethnicity* preserves this meaning, while also enabling an anthropological double entendre: it refers to both the specific rituals of the Thangmi community and the general social processes through which both ritual and ethnicity, as well as consciousness itself, are produced.

Cross-Border Mobility and the Feedback Loop

Colonial documents show that people calling themselves Thangmi have been moving across what are now the borders of Nepal and India since at least the mid-nineteenth century.[14] Several pilgrimage accounts authored by traveling Tibetan lamas also suggest that a group called *mtha' mi*, or "people of the border" in Tibetan, lived in the borderlands between what is now China's TAR and Nepal as early as the seventeenth century (Ehrhard 1997). Chapter 4 provides the historical context of these movements, while Chapter 6 argues that the very idea of mobility is a central feature of Thangmi ethnic identity. Yet these patterns of mobility were not at all obvious to me when I began my residence in the Thangmi heartland of rural central-eastern Nepal. Only after several months did I begin to realize that the Thangmi were anything but sedentary inhabitants of bounded villages.

My outlook was conditioned by the trajectory of Himalayan anthropology, defined by a paradigmatic series of ethnographic monographs focused on discrete communities—largely in the highlands—whose members were imagined as residents of bounded localities within a single nation-state. These monographs included works on Gurung (Macfarlane 1976; Pignède [1966] 1993), Limbu (Caplan [1970] 2000; Sagant 1996), Magar (Hitchcock 1966), Newar (Gellner 1992; Levy 1990), Sherpa (Adams 1996; J. Fisher 1990; Fürer-Haimendorf 1964; Ortner 1978, 1989), Tamang (Holmberg 1989; March 2002), Thakali (W. Fisher 2001; Vinding 1998), Tharu (Guneratne 2002; Krauskopff 1989), Yolmo (Desjarlais 2003), and various Rai groups (Gaenzsle 2000, 2002; Hardman 2000; McDougal 1979). Some of these ethnographies hint at the importance of mobility and experiences in India or historical Tibet in constituting ethnic subjectivities, but such stories were ethnographically under-unexplored.

As I conducted more interviews with Thangmi in Nepal, I was surprised by how often conversation turned to experiences of India and the TAR or to family members who were currently there. Many people spoke powerfully of how time spent in these other places had shaped their worldviews. I eventually realized that I would need to travel to India and the TAR to understand what being Thangmi meant.

The ethnographic realities that I encountered in these places demanded a middle path between two popular social scientific approaches to ethnicity. The first suggests that ethnicity is an exclusive product of modern nation-states, emerging only within clearly demarcated national boundaries (Verdery 1994; Williams 1989). The second emphasizes the narrative of deterritorialization (Appadurai 1990; Basch, Schiller, and Szanton Blanc 1994; Inda and Rosaldo 2002), suggesting that locality and national borders are no longer the primary factors in shaping ethnic identity. In the Thangmi case, neither of these interpretations applies. Rather, ethnicity is at once shaped by country-specific discourse and policy, yet is also dependent on a dialogue between members of a community across state borders.

Economic remittances earned largely in the Middle East and Malaysia are increasingly recognized as crucial in sustaining Nepal's contemporary economy, just as transnational mobility is increasingly recognized as crucial to anthropological accounts of rural modernity (Chu 2010). This book adds to such conversations by showing that cross-border labor migration to adjacent countries has been a long-standing component of Himalayan livelihood strategies rather than a new experience emerging from modern processes of economic globalization. I argue that the relative impact of "social remittances" (Levitt 2001) and the "spaces of cultural assertion" (Gidwani and Sivaramakrishnan 2003) opened through migration—the changes in worldview and values that return migrants bring home—have been as, or more, important in the long run than cash earned in India or Tibetan parts of China.

I locate experiences in India and China as central to ethnicity formation in Nepal and, conversely, experiences in Nepal as relevant to related processes in Himalayan areas of India and China. I term this the "cross-border feedback loop": the process of communication and exchange through which ideologies of ethnicity originating in discrete nation-states become embedded in the discursive and practical aspects of cultural production elsewhere. This creates a cyclical process of consciousness formation that on the one hand emerges within each national context but, on the other, transcends national boundaries to create a synthesis independent of any single nation-state. The agents of the feedback loop are Thangmi themselves, as they move back and forth and engage with others across the collectivity.

Being "In" Place: The Himalayas, South Asia, and Area Studies

My focus on the cross-border feedback loop within the Thangmi community shapes a larger conversation across academic area studies. Rather than a project of comparison, which analyzes tit-for-tat the differences in ethnicity formation as experienced in three discrete nation-states, mine is an ethnography of connection (Tsing 2005), which explores the links between those experiences, and the scholarly and political discourses surrounding them, in multiple national and regional frames.

In many academic contexts, South Asian studies in practice refers to the study of India. Nepal and other smaller South Asian states are relegated to the periphery of major debates, or perhaps scholars of the peripheries intentionally keep to themselves. Much of this positioning has to do with the historical effects of what Mary Des Chene (2007) calls Nepal's "condition of non-postcoloniality." Ironically, while the fact that the country was never fully colonized is one of the central tenets of Nepali nationalism, it also accounts for the country's near absence from the English-language historiographic record[15] and Nepal's subsequent marginalization within South Asian studies.

I contend here that processes of state and ethnicity formation in Nepal cannot be adequately understood in isolation. Rather, they must be situated within more expansive transregional conversations that both acknowledge the reality of cross-border mobility on the ground and make use of conceptual categories from South Asian studies to develop comprehensive analytical frames. At the same time, work on Nepal has great potential to deepen the empirical basis and theoretical purchase of analyses emerging from India. Nepal offers an alternative, non-postcolonial South Asian vantage point, at once shaped by similar long-term cultural trajectories as its southern neighbor yet possessing a very different modern political history. The story of Thangmi ethnicity formation engages in South Asian conversations on ethnicity, caste, class, and the politics of marginality, not as an anomalous case from Nepal conceptualized as somewhere "other" but rather by probing how such discourses extend beyond the political borders of India to influence dynamics of subject formation in South Asia writ large.

Beyond South Asia, both political and cultural Tibet (Goldstein 1998:4) have been important points of reference for Thangmi over time. As described in Chapter 4, the border between Nepal and the TAR is only a few miles away from several of the largest Thangmi villages. Many members of the community regularly travel across it, making use of the "border citizen" card issued jointly by the Nepali and Chinese governments that allows them to engage in cross-border travel without a passport or visa (Shneiderman 2013b). In such contexts, contemporary Thangmi generally refer to the political entity north of them as "China," although older individuals at times still use "Tibet." When describing the geopolitical entity, I refer to the territory directly north of Nepal as "China's Tibetan Autonomous Region," or "TAR." I use "Tibetan" to describe broader cultural, religious, or linguistic concepts that relate to the Tibetan cultural world but are not necessarily limited to the boundaries of political Tibet. Chapter 3 explains how the complexes of Tibetan language and Buddhist religion perceived to originate across the border to the north figure prominently in Thangmi ideologies of synthesis, providing an important counterpoint to the Nepali and Hindi languages, as well as Hindu religion, emanating from the south.

My initial intentions to conduct research in an equally balanced manner between Thangmi communities in Nepal, India, and the TAR never came to fruition. I could not secure research permission for more than one month in the TAR. The people represented in this book are, therefore, primarily those whom I describe as "Thangmi in Nepal" and "Thangmi in India" (although "Thangmi in China" make brief appearances, especially in Chapter 4).

Brian Axel pinpoints the potential problem with such terminology in his ethnography of the Sikh diaspora: "One would be hard put to say that, preferring the local to the global, there are no diasporas, rather Chinese *in* New York or, for example, Sikhs *in* London" (2001:1). He opts instead for the doubled "Sikh diaspora *as a diaspora*" (8) to reiterate that it is the diaspora itself that is his object of study, not "exemplary" members of it in any particular location (1). Chapter 6 explains why the Thangmi case complicates such definitions of diaspora. My point here is that focusing on a diaspora, or any other type of multisited community, as the object of one's study does not obviate the need to evaluate carefully how various members of it orient themselves within specific nation-state frameworks at specific historical junctures.

For me, the word "in" locates a set of actions within the ideological framework of a nation, not a body within a bounded physical territory. When I write "Thangmi in Nepal," I mean "Thangmi acting in relation to the nation-state of Nepal as a primary frame, although they may have spent time in India, or at other times have acted in relation to the nation-state of India as a primary frame, and/or may be aware of the relationship between the two frames in shaping their actions, even if they have not actually visited the other country." "Thangmi in India" means the converse. By "Thangmi in Nepal" or "Thangmi in India," I do not intend to imply "Thangmi who have never left Nepal" or "Thangmi who have a certain essential quality because they were born in, or live in, India." Sometimes, I use "Thangmi from Nepal" when referring to "Thangmi acting in relation to the nation-state of Nepal as a primary frame, but who are physically present in India at the point of action," and "Thangmi from India" when I mean the opposite.

Why do I not simply use the more obvious "Nepalese Thangmi" or "Nepali Thangmi," and "Indian Thangmi"? As described in the Preface to this book, for political and legal reasons that must be taken seriously, each of these terms is rejected by some subset of those ostensibly described by it.

Historical, Political, and Personal Contexts

The Thangmi story unfolds against the backdrop of large-scale political transformations, revealing the far-reaching impacts, as well as the limits, of the discourses and practices of democracy and communism in Nepal, India, and the TAR. The ethnographic present of this book spans a decade, from 1998 to 2008, with the broader time frame primarily that of remembered history. I made special efforts to work with older people who could recount details from personal experience dating back to the early 1940s in some cases. This locates the beginning of my narrative at the very end of colonialism in India, the final phase of Rana rule in Nepal, and the years immediately preceding the assertion of Chinese control in Tibet. Supplementing ethnography with documentary evidence occasionally allows me to project further back into the past, locating the roots of political transformations that occurred during the period of my research in ongoing processes of state formation and ethnic classification that began much earlier.

In the wake of Indian independence in 1947, followed by the Constituent Assembly of 1948–1950, democracy became an important vector shaping political subjectivity across South Asia. In a novel application of a core concept of liberal democracy, the Indian constitution enshrined a commitment to the "upliftment" of marginalized communities. However, the implementation of such ideals in administrative practice remains a contentious issue, underlying debates over affirmative action, usually called "reservations" in India, which in turn point to larger questions about the nature of political subject formation.

The year 1951 saw the beginnings of Nepal's first experiment with multiparty democracy, as activists from Nepal used their exile base in India to overthrow the Rana oligarchy in collaboration with King Tribhuvan. This first phase of democracy came to an end in 1959, when King Mahendra acceded to the throne, banning political parties and establishing the so-called *panchayat* partyless democracy. The 1962 constitution legally defined Nepal as a unitary nation with only one culture and one language. Much later, in 1990, the country returned to multiparty democracy, after what is commonly referred to as the first *jana andolan* (N: People's Movement). Only after the 1990 constitution officially recognized Nepal as a multicultural, multilingual state (although still a Hindu one) could ethnicity and other forms of cultural difference be discussed publicly without fear of persecution.

Communism was a simultaneously important ideological and political force in both Nepal and India. It constituted a site of cross-border linkage between the two countries, as well as with China. In South Asia, communism and democracy are not always radically opposed ideologies nor sequential forms of governance, as in much of what is now referred to as the "postsocialist" world. Rather, democracy and communism are parallel, mutually influential political trajectories that intertwine in often unexpected ways over time to shape localized forms of political consciousness.

Founded in the 1920s, the Communist Party of India (CPI) played a crucial role in early nationalist politics. In the 1960s, the Communist Party of India (Marxist), or CPI(M), split from the larger party, rising to prominence in the state of West Bengal, where Darjeeling is situated. By the late 1980s, when the Gorkhaland agitation for a separate Nepali-speaking state in Darjeeling began, reopening calls for autonomy that date to the turn of the twentieth century, the CPI(M) had been in power at the state level for over a decade. The CPI(M) reign continued until 2011. Many analyses of the first Gorkhaland movement suggest that it was in fact a proxy for anti-communist mobilization in a context where it was extremely difficult to challenge the status quo (Subba 1992), highlighting the complex relationships between ethnic and class-based mobilization in this part of the world.

Also in West Bengal, communist party hardliners known as the Naxalites led a peasant insurgency in the late 1960s. Their base in the town of Naxalbari was along one of the primary vehicular routes I traveled between Nepal and Darjeeling during my fieldwork. The legacy of the Naxalbari revolt deeply influenced Thangmi who traveled regularly through the Naxalite heartland as circular migrants, just as it did the trajectories of the contemporary Maoist parties in both India and Nepal today. The former maintains a strong presence in central Indian states like Jharkhand and Chattisgarh, provoking violent responses from Indian state forces, while the latter won the 2008 elections in Nepal and led two of the country's subsequent governments.

The Communist Party of Nepal (CPN) was founded in Calcutta in 1949. After many splits and mergers, the CPN yielded both the contemporary Unified Communist Party of Nepal-Maoist (UCPN-M)—popularly known as the Maoists—and the centrist Communist Party of Nepal-Unified Marxist Leninist (CPN-UML). These entities constitute two of what are commonly referred to as the three major political parties in Nepal at the time of writing. The third is the center-right Nepali Congress (NC), Nepal's oldest party. Established in the late 1940s in northern India, with close ties to the Indian National Congress party, the NC led Nepal's earliest democracy movements. All of these parties were forced underground during the *panchayat* era.

In the late 1970s to early 1980s, there was a brief moment of greater liberalism around a constitutional referendum called by King Birendra. During that period, activists from the CPN-UML traveled to the Thangmi regions of central-eastern Nepal to establish local bases (Shneiderman 2010). Their efforts were brutally quashed in a 1984 police massacre in the Thangmi village of Piskar, which, as detailed in Chapter 5 and elsewhere (Shneiderman 2009), remains a crucial moment in the formation of both ethnic and class consciousness for many Thangmi. This local event was part of the larger trend of state repression across the country through the 1980s, which eventually led to the democratic revolution of the early 1990s (Hachhethu 2002).

By the time I first traveled to Nepal in 1994, the country had the world's only democratically elected communist government under a Hindu constitutional monarchy. This period was short-lived, as the communist government lasted for only nine months before a vote of no confidence led to one of the countless political reshufflings throughout the 1990s and 2000s. The complexity of the country's political landscape baffled me, and my initial research focus was on questions of ethnic and religious identity, not political mobilization. As I began working on what I imagined to be "basic ethnographic research" with the Thangmi while on a Fulbright fellowship in 1999, the linkages between these superficially separate domains became increasingly apparent.

I was not the only outsider visiting Thangmi villages at that time. Maoist activists had launched the People's War in western Nepal in 1996 and by the late 1990s were scoping out prospective base areas in the east. My encounters with them in Dolakha and Sindhupalchok significantly shaped my research. Documenting the early phases of Maoist mobilization in the region became an important project, leading to several publications in which I and my coauthors described the experience of insurgency at the village level, as well as its implications for us as scholars (Pettigrew and Shneiderman 2004; Pettigrew, Shneiderman, and Harper 2004; Shneiderman and Turin 2004; Shneiderman 2009, 2010). Yet I remained committed to the question of Thangmi ethnicity and its absence from the ethnographic record that had drawn me to these villages in the first place. This book therefore does not substantively describe Nepal's Maoist movement, its ideology, or its operations. Yet the Thangmi story presented here tells us much about the context in which that movement emerged and the larger set of ongoing political transformations of which the Maoist insurgency was just one part.

By the time I returned to South Asia in 2004 for doctoral research, civil conflict was at its height. King Gyanendra Shah imposed authoritarian rule through a royal coup in 2005. The combination of Maoist armed insurgency and popular protest led to the second *jana andolan* (People's Movement) in 2006. Later that year, the king was stripped of his powers (although the dynasty was only formally deposed in 2008), and the Comprehensive Peace Agreement officially ended the conflict. The interim constitution of 2007 declared Nepal a secular federal democratic republic, building upon long-standing Maoist demands for both a Constituent Assembly and federal restructuring along ethnic lines. I watched members of the Thangmi community vote in the 2008 Constituent Assembly elections, which yielded a victory if not an outright majority for the Maoists, among whom was the first ever elected Thangmi parliamentarian.

In late 2007, just as Nepal was gearing up for Constituent Assembly elections, a renewed movement for a separate state of Gorkhaland was launched in Darjeeling. This time under the leadership of the Gorkhaland Janamukti Morcha (GJM) rather than the Gorkhaland National Liberation Front (GNLF), which had led the agitation in the late 1980s, activists demanded a separate state within the Indian federation, free from Calcutta's control. Encouraged by the creation of new states like Jharkhand and

Uttarakhand in the early 2000s, the agitators claimed that the DGHC established as part of the resolution to the 1980s movement did not have the teeth to deliver genuine autonomy as promised. The year 2011 saw a sea change in West Bengal's political landscape, as the communist government finally fell to Mamata Banerjee's Trinamool Congress after thirty-three years of rule. Soon after election results were in, the GJM engaged in extended tripartite negotiations with the center and the new state government, which led to the formation of the Gorkhaland Territorial Administration. At the time of writing, the territorial and political limits of this body remain unclear.

Over time, Thangmi have participated in all of the parties and movements described here. As detailed in Chapter 5, the formation of ethnic consciousness has been critically linked with that of class consciousness, but often in unexpected ways that challenge received ideas about the relationships between these two forms of mobilization. Just as communism and democracy have been intertwined on the macro level of national politics in South Asia, ideas about class and ethnicity have been deeply interconnected at the micro level of Thangmi experience. Neither paradigm for understanding social difference and inequality exists in isolation (Lawoti 2003; Tamang 2006), nor is there a teleology in which one leads inevitably to the other. Rather than engaging in over-deterministic arguments about whether class or ethnic mobilization is more effective in challenging ingrained inequalities like those from which Thangmi have unquestionably suffered, here I demonstrate how each of these paradigms has differently deployed "the currency of culture" (Cattelino 2008) for political purposes, in the process contributing to the affective production of identity.

Understanding Thangmi ethnicity formation over the *longue durée* yields important insights into how ethnic claims—whether in the context of demands for identity-based federalism in restructuring Nepal or campaigns for tribal recognition and the state of Gorkhaland in India—come to be lived, embodied, and felt deeply by the people who make them. This window into ethnicity-in-the making for one small group at a particular geographical, historical, and political conjuncture tells us much about how and why the substantive content of ethnic consciousness is produced in general, and suggests that states and policy makers would do well to consider the affective dimensions of this process that make it such a compelling force for mobilization.

A Total Social Fact

My first serious Thangmi interlocutor in Nepal was Rana Bahadur, whose life story is presented in Chapter 3. This senior guru was a vast repository of cultural, historical, and ritual knowledge, but he was at first reluctant to speak with me. Bir Bahadur, who worked with me as a research assistant, told me that Rana Bahadur did not want to talk at all unless I was willing to record the entirety of his ritual knowledge. Rana Bahadur had apparently found his interactions with previous researchers unsatisfying: foreign as well as Thangmi and non-Thangmi from India and Nepal had wanted quick summaries of "Thangmi culture," but did not want to spend the time observing or listening to the dense complex of ritualized action and recitations that comprised it.

Rana Bahadur explained that the problem with writing was that it allowed the writer to pick and choose what to represent, whereas his oral tradition required the full recitation of the entire ritual "line" from an embodied place of knowledge that made it impossible to extract any piece from the whole. (He and other gurus regularly used the English term "line" to denote the fixed trajectory of each invocation.) Therefore, if I was to write or otherwise record (since audio and video technologies were, from his perspective, just embellished forms of writing) anything at all, I had to be prepared to record everything he knew.

I told Rana Bahadur that I was ready to listen to as much as he wished to tell me. After several afternoons following the old guru's schedule and recording whatever he said, I seemed to pass Rana Bahadur's test. He announced that he was ready to "open" his knowledge to me, and every ensuing recording session began with a chanted invocation in the same idiom used to propitiate deities: "[So and so—names and nationalities of previous researchers] came but did not want to listen to all of my knowledge, so I bit my tongue. . . . Then they went back to their own countries, and this American woman came. She wanted to listen to everything, and so I have opened my knowledge to her. I have sent as much as I know in her writing . . . and now the funerary rites can be done for this dead man." I first thought that these lines were simply part of Rana Bahadur's standard invocation. Upon analyzing them closely with Bir Bahadur, I was embarrassed to discover that I had been written into the ritual recitation itself.

Initially I removed this part of the recitation from all of my transcriptions, bracketing out Rana Bahadur's repeated references to me as an anomaly that I did not really know how to handle. If I had become part of the chant, was what I was recording the "genuine" Thangmi culture that I sought, or was it already transformed by my very presence? I was similarly disturbed when Darjeeling's senior guru Latte Apa—whose life story is also presented in Chapter 3—began a funerary ritual with the statement, "Because she's here [*pointing to me*], this time I'll definitely do it by the real, old rules!"

Eventually I came to see that from Rana Bahadur's perspective, I was a useful recognizing agent. I appeared at the end of his life, reassuring him that the knowledge he had gained through years of ritual practice remained relevant in an era when much around him was changing. Even after I thought I had recorded everything he had to tell me in 1999–2000, he contacted me several times in the remaining years before he died in 2003, telling me to come to Dolakha urgently so he could tell me one more thing before he died (an eventuality for which he was carefully preparing). For Rana Bahadur, my recognition of him as a holder of culturally valuable knowledge became a personal obsession, which seemed to have little to do with a desire for political recognition. My recognition of his special relationship with the Thangmi deities who had been the primary recogniz-ing agents throughout his life seemed to augment the feeling of self-worth that he gained from that divine relationship. Rana Bahadur never asked me to publish what I had recorded with him, or to submit it to the Nepali or Indian state (as others later would); he accepted my terms of recognition and in exchange simply asked me to write down what he knew in its entirety—to document his knowledge as a totality.

Despite the superficial differences in their approach to Thangmi culture, it was also in this holistic sense that the Thangmi ethnic activists whom I later came to know wanted me to contribute information to their efforts to portray Thangmi culture as an embodied social fact. As the late Gopal Singh, then vice president of the Bharatiya Thami Welfare Association (BTWA), phrased this sentiment, "Language is our breath, culture is the whole body," Yet Thangmi identity, he continued, as embodied in "our pure language and pure culture," has "not been fully brought to light." In order to achieve these goals, Gopal Singh admonished "all the Thami-loving brothers and sisters to remain honest and loyal to this ethnicity and to collect and publish proven facts relating to the Thami" (Niko 2003:7). This echoes a similar emphasis on "scientific fact" in Thangmi publications from Nepal, where "truth" about the group and its history is depicted as the hard-won fruit of "research" on a positivist "reality." One such essay suggests that such myths are to be discounted as "unscientific" since they are only "stories collected from the elders" rather than the results of "comprehensive research" (Samudaya [2056] 2061 VS:17).

If elders were not a legitimate source of authority on the culture and history of a community, what did this mean for my "research"? In "reality," there was no alternative, more legitimate source of evidence for the claims that Thangmi activists in both Nepal and India wanted me to help them make. My sources—like Rana Bahadur—were the very "elders" whose knowledge was dismissed as "stories" rather than evidence. But I felt compelled to honor my ethnographic contract with such elders by representing the stories they told me in their totality, even when such stories did not yield the "research results" that my simultaneously binding ethnographic contract with activist informants stipulated.

As I waded deeper into the ethical complexities of such multisited complicity (Marcus 1999) during my first in-depth fieldwork in India in 2004, I lost sleep trying to figure out how my "research" fit into the picture. What did the Thangmi activists whom I was coming to know actually want from me? On the one hand, they were skeptical of what the empirical evidence that I had collected told them about themselves. On the other hand, they repeatedly thanked me for sharing my research openly with them, telling me on numerous occasions, "You are our god," or "You are our Sunari Ama," the mythical ancestress of all Thangmi. Such statements made me feel not only uncomfortable, just as Rana Bahadur's incorporation of me into his ritual chant had, but antithetical to the activists' erstwhile requests for me to conduct "scientific" research aimed at demonstrating a "pure" culture. At first I consigned such statements to the same conceptual category of inexplicable fieldwork ephemera in which I had mentally placed Rana Bahadur's invocation of my presence. But as I heard them over and over again, back in Nepal as well as in India, these ascriptions of divine power continued to bother me, and I came back to them later as I strove to understand the relationship between research, ritual, and politics in effecting recognition.

Perhaps the critique of "research" based on the "stories of elders" was not actually a critique of those elders or their stories themselves, but rather of the interpretive frameworks of researchers who, based on short-term encounters, had taken such "stories" at face value. These researchers had concluded that the Thangmi culture, if it could even be called that, was derivative and degenerate. By sticking with the ethnographic project past the point at which others had decided that the Thangmi were "not worthy of future attention" (Northey and Morris 1928), I had demonstrated my commitment to Thangmi agendas, competing and contradictory though they might be. By appearing in the public domain alongside members of the Thangmi community repeatedly over a decade with the trappings of social scientific authority—notebook, video camera, university affiliation, research funding—I was demonstrating to outside others that the Thangmi must have some kind of culture worth recognizing.

It was in this sense that I became a recognizing agent—a catalyst who augmented Thangmi individuals' sense of self-worth and the community's visibility—and that the divine metaphor became comprehensible, if still disconcerting. For the Thangmi activists with whom I worked, "research" was in part a symbolic process that was not only about its empirical content but also about its form as a mode of ritual action carried out in the public domain, the efficacious performance of which could yield pragmatic results from the recognizing agents of the state (and/or the organizations that stood in for it, such as NGOs, particularly in Nepal). In this formulation, I was not so much like a deity as a ritual specialist, capable of mediating between the human and divine, the citizen and his or her state(s).

At first I tried to deny such powers—"I am just a student," "No, I don't have any powerful friends," "No, I am not with any 'project'; I am just a researcher"—but over time I realized this was disingenuous. The reality was that unlike most Thangmi, I could and did command attention when I walked into governmental or organizational offices (or wrote a letter to the editor, made a phone call, or engaged in cocktail conversation) to make a point about pressing issues, be it a badly managed road project, an idea for economic development, or a hurtful misrepresentation of the Thangmi community. It was not just my Thangmi interlocutors who believed that my work could have concrete effects; other ethnic activists, politicians, and bureaucrats lauded me for conducting "research" about a "marginalized group" that no one else could be bothered to do, so that the Thangmi might have a chance at future "advancement."

In the larger scheme of things, it did not matter if my written research presented precisely the empirical conclusions the activists desired. They were more interested in my research as a form of efficacious action and in my role as an outside figure of academic authority—a recognizing agent— whose very attention to the social fact of "Thangmi culture" legitimized the results of their own research, which in the end were the ones they sought to promote to the state, not mine.

In short, I and social science as a whole were useful mediators between divine and political forms of recognition. Thangmi activists did not want to divest themselves entirely from their relationship with the territorial deities who had historically provided a strong sense of recognition; rather they wanted to reinterpret these relationships within the increasingly attractive terms of recognition offered by the states in which they lived. I could help in this process by presenting "data" about Thangmi history and culture as a total social fact that evidenced their "unique" identity.

By telling me repeatedly that I was like a god, Thangmi with whom I worked ensured that I would feel obligated to act as such: if they acted in a ritually correct manner, by providing me access to the information I requested, then, like a deity who responds to rituals conducted according to the appropriate protocols, or like an ethnographer under the binding terms of an ethnographic contract, I was expected to deliver the goods. In a reversal of Bronislaw Malinowski's classic argument for the value of fieldwork—which he claimed was important because only in that context does "the anthropologist have the myth-maker at his elbow" ([1948] 1974:100)—in this case, the "myth-makers" had the anthropologist at their elbow, ready to parlay the partial truths they wanted to tell about themselves into a totality worthy of broader recognition. In this sense, ethnography may be a complicit form of identity-producing action that cannot be fully disentangled from the projects of recognition that it seeks to describe.

Acknowledging the place of ethnography (and ethnographers) in the interplay between contemporary forms of recognition—political, divine, scholarly, and beyond—can enable this complicity to become a productive tool in transforming the terms of recognition themselves. To members of a historically misrecognized group like the Thangmi, that is part of what research is for. For social scientists, as Marisol de la Cadena and Orin Starn argue in their discussion of contemporary indigeneity, "a role for careful, engaged scholarship can be to contribute to understanding and activism that recognizes the paradoxes, limits and possibilities" (2007:22) of indigenous projects of recognition. This vision may be extended to ethnic projects, broadly conceived, and such intentions guide my writing here.

Chapter 2

Framing, Practicing, and Performing Ethnicity

Colorful banners around Gangtok advertised the event: "Tribal Folk Dances of Sikkim, presented in honor of Shri P. R. Kyndiah, Union Minister of Tribal Affairs." It was November 2005, and each ethnic organization registered in India's state of Sikkim, as well as in the adjacent Darjeeling district of West Bengal, had been invited to perform a single "folk dance" that best demonstrated their "tribal culture."

In the rehearsal session before the actual performance, it became clear that the fifty-odd dancers from fourteen ethnic organizations were well aware of the politically charged environment in which they were performing. These groups were seeking recognition from the central Indian government as Scheduled Tribes (STs), and each sought to capture the minister's eye with a carefully framed performance that demonstrated the "tribal" nature of their identity. The rehearsing groups received stage directions from the director of Sikkim's Department of Culture, who told them brusquely, "Shake your hips faster and make sure to flutter your eyelashes! Remember, if you look happy, the audience will be happy. And if they are not happy, why should they watch you? You must make them feel comfortable and familiar with your culture."

The Thangmi performance troupe, sponsored by the Bharatiya Thami Welfare Association (BTWA), was composed of a combination of migrant workers from Nepal who spent several months at a time in India and Thangmi from urban Darjeeling with professional dance experience. Together, they took the director of culture's suggestions to heart in their lively, upbeat performance of what the emcee introduced as a "Thami wedding dance." The participation of the dancers from Nepal made the choreographers from India more confident about the efficacy of their performance. The former knew how to perform the slow, repetitive steps that characterize Thangmi cultural practice in village contexts, while the latter knew how to transform these plodding moves into Bollywood-style numbers that carried the weight of "culture" in the generically recognizable South Asian sense. The end result as danced for the minister (Figure 1) bore little resemblance to anything one would see at a Thangmi wedding or other ritual event, but the performance was greeted with resounding applause. Afterward, the minister sent a message to the BTWA expressing his appreciation. The members of the group from India were hopeful that the performance would serve as a catalyst in getting their ST application approved.

Although they participated in the event with apparent enthusiasm, some of the members of the group from Nepal later told me that they felt uncomfortable with the choreographers' appropriation of elements of ritual practice into another performative context. The dancers from Nepal found the experience unsettling because the audience was not the assembly of deities propitiated through comparable elements of ritual action at home but rather the representatives of a state in which they did not hold full citizenship. This ambiguity could be overcome, since although bureaucratic audiences might require different offerings than divine ones, the overall ritualized form of the event was similar. The larger problem was that the performers from Nepal stood to gain little direct benefit from this transformation of practice into performance since the minister and his colleagues answered to the Indian state alone. Only those Thangmi with fully documented Indian citizenship would be eligible for benefits if the government of India recognized the group as an ST. As will be explored further in Chapter 4, although many Thangmi consider themselves "dual citizens" at the level of belonging and hold some documentary trappings of Indian citizenship, most circular migrants from Nepal cannot prove adequate evidence of the full citizenship required to apply for the special rights offered by an ST or Other Backward Class (OBC) certificate in India.

The Thangmi from Nepal were not outright opposed to the performatization of practice—a process akin to what Richard Handler (2011) has called the "ritualization of ritual," following Erving Goffman (1971:79). In fact, I had seen several of them applaud heartily at a similarly staged performance of a "wedding dance" at a conference in Kathmandu, hosted by the Nepal Thami Samaj (NTS) earlier in the same year (Figure 2). Rather, they felt that the political results had to be worth the phenomenological and ethical trade-offs that such transformation entailed. In other words, the objectification of culture was acceptable—even desirable—as

Figure 1. Thangmi wedding dance performed in Gangtok, Sikkim, India, November 2005. Photo by the author.

Figure 2. Thangmi wedding dance performed at the Nepal Thami Samaj Second National Convention, Kathmandu, Nepal, May 2005. Photo by the author.

long as it was done in the service of a specific goal, and as long as the resulting field of performance was recognized as a complement to, rather than a replacement for, the field of practice out of which it emerged. Once the dust had settled, the Gangtok experience prompted some of the initially uneasy performers from Nepal to consider how they might also deploy cultural performance to bolster emerging claims to the Nepali state about their rights to special benefits as members of a "highly marginalized" *jana-jati* group. Such claims, if recognized, could help create the material conditions necessary to maintain the field of practice itself. These views were forged in the context of ongoing debates within the cross-border Thangmi community about the ownership of cultural knowledge and its power to define ethnic identity. Shifting political paradigms for evaluating and rewarding cultural "authenticity" in India and Nepal compelled Thangmi on both sides of the border to think carefully about the particularities of object and audience that defined practice and performance (two terms I will define shortly), their relative efficacy in each national context, and the need to balance both fields of cultural production in the overall process of reproducing Thangmi ethnicity.

This chapter argues that Thangmi individuals from diverse backgrounds in both Nepal and India possess a high level of self-consciousness regarding the multiple fields of ritualized action in which they engage. They intentionally choose to deploy different types of action within different social "frames" (Goffman 1974; Handler 2011) to achieve a range of results from diverse recognizing agents: state, divine, and otherwise. This self-consciousness emerges in part through the experience of moving regularly between multiple nation-states through circular migration. Familiarity with more than one national frame within which ethnicity is conceptualized and recognized enables Thangmi, as both individuals and members of a collective, to see the framing machinery through which ethnicity is produced and reproduced in each context. They may therefore take self-conscious, agentive roles in employing appropriate framing devices for their own purposes. These may range from assuaging territorial deities through private household propitiations to assuaging skeptical state representatives through public cultural performances, but ultimately all of the ritualized action so framed has a shared sacred referent: Thangmi identity itself.

This argument takes us beyond portrayals of ethnicity as either an evasive response to state control (Scott 2009) or a creation of market forces (Comaroff and Comaroff 2009) to reveal it instead as a ritual process. I show how the objectification of identity cannot always be reduced to a process of "ethno-commodification" (Comaroff and Comaroff 2009) but rather must be seen as a fundamental human process that persists through ritual action regardless of the contingencies of state formation or economic paradigm. Ultimately, ethnicity is a complex collective production, which coheres around the sacred object of identity. This serves as a shared referent that enables heterogeneous individuals—bound together by little more than name across nation-state, class, age, gender, and other boundaries—to contribute in diverse ways to collective projects of ethnicity-in-action. The affective reality of the identity that results from this synthesis draws its power from the very diversity of its component parts.

Defining Practice and Performance

My definitions of "practice" and "performance" diverge from other received definitions. The two are qualitatively distinct, but inextricably linked and mutually influential fields of "ritualized activity," which I follow Catherine Bell in defining as "a particular cultural strategy of differentiation linked to particular social effects and rooted in a distinctive interplay of a socialized body and the environment it structures" (1992:8). I acknowledge at the outset that most practice has a performative aspect (Austin 1975; Bauman 1975; Bauman and Briggs 1990; Butler 1997a), and almost all performance can be seen as a form of "practice" in Bourdieu's sense (1977, 1990). Nonetheless, making a distinction between practice and performance is helpful at the analytical level as we attempt to understand the dynamics of consciousness and objectification inherent in the process of producing ethnicity. At the level of action, there is no question that the edges of these categories blur into one another. However, these distinctions are described as ontologically real by Thangmi themselves, which suggests that they are worth paying attention to.

"Practice" refers to embodied, ritualized actions carried out by Thangmi individuals within a group-internal epistemological framework that mediates between the human and divine world: to stop malevolent deities from plaguing one's mind, for instance, or to guide a loved one's soul to the realm of the ancestors. Practices are addressed to the synthetic pantheon of animistic, Hindu and Buddhist deities that inhabit the Thangmi divine world, and take place within the clearly delimited private domains of the household, or communal but exclusively Thangmi, spaces. Practices then are the actions encapsulated in what Goffman calls social "primary frameworks" (1974).

"Performances," in the contrast I draw here, are framed "keyings," or "transformations," in Goffman's terms (1974), of the practices found within primary frameworks. Performances are ritualized actions carried out within a broader discursive context created by political, economic, or other kinds of external agendas. They are mounted for express consumption by non-Thangmi audiences, which may comprise representatives of the Nepali or Indian states—as at the Gangtok performance with which this chapter began—or members of other ethnic communities, NGO representatives, anthropologists, and various others. Performances take place in the open, in public domains, with the express purpose of demonstrating to both selves and various others what practices are like.

Participation in both of these forms of ritualized action contributes to contemporary experiences of what culture, identity, and ethnicity are from the perspectives of the actors who engage in them. Neither practice nor performance can stand in for the whole of culture or as the sole signifier of cultural authenticity. Instead, practice and performance, as I define them here, are both essential aspects of contemporary cultural production and as such are mutually constitutive. Neither can be substituted or subsumed by the other. Both are necessary for groups and individuals to maintain the pragmatic and emotional well-being that derives from a sense of belonging to a shared identity that is recognized by others within the political context of individual nation-states, as well as within transnational environments shaped by cross-border movements and international discourses of indi-geneity and heritage.

Arjun Guneratne's work with the Tharu of Nepal's Tarai provides an ethnographic touchstone for discussing the dynamics of identity and con-sciousness in Nepal. Guneratne distinguishes between two "levels of group identity":

> The first is implicit or unselfconscious, associated with the tradi-tional, local, endogamous group. . . . In Bourdieu's terms, it exists as doxa or the unreflected upon and "naturalized" process of social reproduction of the community (Bourdieu 1977). . . . The "natural" character of social facts, hitherto accepted as part of the given order, become subject to critique when an objective crisis brings some aspect of doxa—identity—into question. This is a necessary precon-dition for the emergence of the second level of identity I wish to distinguish.
>
> This second or more encompassing level of identity is a self-conscious . . . and politically oriented identity that draws together various local communities and groups and endows them with an imagined coherence (cf. Anderson 1991). It is imagined in the sense that the structural linkages . . . that help to shape the first level of group identity defined above do not exist at this level. (1998:753)

These two levels of identity are in many ways coterminous with the social fields produced by practice and performance as I define them. I extend Guneratne's insights further by suggesting that the two fields of identity coexist and mutually constitute each other. In other words, the shift from one level of identity to another is not a quintessentially modern transformation that moves in only one direction, from a state of "identity as doxa" to a state of "identity as political imagination," with the latter eventually eclipsing the former. Instead, both forms of identity can exist simultaneously and influence each other in a multidirectional feedback loop. This potentiality comes into focus when we turn our analytical gaze to the actions of practice and performance rather than keeping it trained on the more static notion of identity itself. Practice and performance are mutually dependent aspects of the overall processes of cultural production and social reproduction, a relationship augmented but not initiated by the politics of recognition within modern nation-states. Take away practice and there is no cultural content for performance to objectify. Take away performance and there is no means for groups to demonstrate in a public forum their existential presence.

Ethnicity as Synthetic Action

Let us pause to reflect again on one of the central questions of this book: why does ethnicity still matter, and how can a focus on its ritualized nature add value to what sometimes appears to be a fully saturated sphere of scholarly discourse? The answer to this question requires a brief foray into an anthropological notion of "practice" broader than my own, as described above: that which came to the fore in the 1980s and early 1990s in the wake of Pierre Bourdieu's seminal work in outlining a "theory of practice" (1977, 1990). Appropriating Bourdieu's well-known concept of *habitus* as a "system of durable, transposable dispositions" (Bourdieu 1977:72), G. Carter Bentley argued for a "practice theory of ethnicity" through which we might understand ethnicity as a "multi-dimensional habitus [in which] it is possible for an individual to possess several different situationally relevant but nonetheless emotionally authentic identities and to symbolize all of them in terms of shared descent" (1987:35). For Bentley, "the theory of practice provides an efficient means of explaining the conjunct of affect and instrumentality in the phenomenon of ethnicity" (28), but following Bourdieu, Bentley suggests that the dispositions of habitus are "not normally open to conscious apprehension" (27).

The promise of such action-oriented approaches to understanding ethnicity—summarized succinctly by Felicia Hughes-Freeland and Mary Crain's call for anthropologists to "consider identity less as being, and more in terms of doing" (1998:15)—has been to some extent compromised by the Marxist-inflected legacy of Bourdieu's emphasis on the unconscious nature of practice. This influence is also evident in work that treats ethnicity as a "fetish," which conceals the true conditions of its production (van Beek 2000; Willford 2006). As ethnicity began to decline as a fashionable topic of anthropological inquiry by the late 1990s, work like Bentley's, which sought to understand how ethnic subjectivity itself was produced in action, was eclipsed by work that foregrounded the discursive construction of ideas *about* ethnicity (Anderson 1991).

James Scott takes a different position toward the intentionality of ethnic actors in his framing of the problem of "ethno-genesis" in Southeast Asia, while at the same time returning to the insights of earlier scholars who sought to understand ethnicity-in-action long before the turn toward practice theory, notably Edmund Leach. Scott casts ethnic communities—particularly those he defines as "highland peoples"—as key players in shaping the states on whose margins they live. Scott focuses on a meta-level historical discussion of these dynamics, offering only brief but enticing insights into how ethnic consciousness is actually produced on the ground. "A person's ethnic identity . . . would be the repertoire of possible performances and the contexts in which they are exhibited," he writes, but "there is, of course, no reason at all to suppose one part of the repertoire is more authentic or 'real' than any other" (2009:254–55). This assertion hearkens back to Bentley's (1987) description of a multidimensional habitus in which multiple authentic identities may coexist, while also according ethnic action a degree of consciousness that Bentley and others working within the confines of formal practice theory cannot. I seek to carry forward the promise of both these approaches by marrying an analysis of ethnicity-in-action with a focus on intentionality.

Enacting simultaneous, multiple subjective states that are all affectively real requires a substantial degree of self-consciousness and self-objectification on the part of actors who practice and perform ethnic identities. For many Thangmi, this consciousness emerges in the subjective space created by the repeated process of shifting frames between multiple nation-states as circular migrants. For Thangmi settled in one location or another, contact with Thangmi circular migrants and their worldviews can effect different but comparably intimate shifts in frame. The self-consciousness engendered through these regular reframings is evident in the manner in which individuals recognize the gap between practice and performance, and work to synthesize these fields of action into an identity that is both productive, in the affective sense of belonging, and constructive, in the political sense of rights (cf. Ortner 1996). An action-based approach to ethnicity enables us to see how a wide range of different intentions and motivations held by many individuals belonging to a putatively singular ethnic group can in fact work in concert to produce a multidimensional ethnic habitus, of which the recognition of intragroup difference is itself a key feature.

Framing Cross-Border Subjectivities

It is easy to reify the unit of the nation-state itself, as well as "other kinds of groups that spring up in the wake of or in resistance to the nation-state," as primordial "individuals-writ-large . . . imagined to 'possess' cultural properties that define their personalities and legitimate their right to exist" (Handler 2011). Anthropologists have widely recognized the modern nation-state as the primary structure shaping processes of ethnicization. But does this assessment match with the subjective perceptions of those who experience ethnicization? Nation-states may certainly be viewed as "individuals-writ-large" by people who live firmly within the borders of one state or another and whose subjectivity is defined by such a nationalist ethos in a singular manner. However, the views of "border peoples," whose subjectivities have long been defined by interactions with multiple states may be markedly different.[1] In the Thangmi context, the long history of cross-border circular migration and the concomitant in-depth experience of multiple frameworks for defining national and ethnic identities lead to a different view. Nation-states are seen as flexible identity-*framing* devices, in relation to which individuals and collectivities produce meaningful cultural content in each context, rather than absolute identity-*determining* struc- tures, which in themselves dictate that content.

This argument leads to an inversion of nationalist perspectives in which "the group is imagined as an individual" with a homogeneous identity (Handler 2011). Instead, in the cross-border Thangmi context, collective identity cannot exist without the manifold contributions of heterogeneous individuals, each of whom possesses complementary elements of the overall repertoire of ritualized action required to establish the existential presence of the group within multiple state frames. From the perspectives of those who belong to it, the group is not imagined as a coherent "individual" but is readily acknowledged as the product of disparate life experiences embod- ied by multiple individuals in as many locations. As Surbir, a long-term Darjeeling resident originally from Nepal put it, "We Thangmi are like the beads of a broken necklace that have been scattered all over the place. And now it's time to find them and put them back together again." Surbir's statement shows that this sense of fragmentation is not necessarily the desired state of affairs, and many Thangmi activist agendas focus on synthesizing disparate Thangmi practices into a coherent whole. The Nepal Thami Samaj (NTS) Second National Convention Report, for instance, echoes Surbir's metaphor with the assertion that the convention's main objective was "to integrate the Thamis living in various places, . . . to make [our] demands and fundamental identity widespread, and to string together all the Thamis" (NTS 2005:4). Yet it is the self-consciousness of this process of mixture, the ongoing synthesis of disparate experiences, beliefs, and ideologies, all held together under the name "Thangmi," as well as "Thami," which defines collective identity at the most fundamental level.

Mahendra, a Thangmi artist well-known in Darjeeling, explained his views on the collective production of Thangminess with an analogy: "I am an artist; so many people who meet me who have never met a Thangmi before think that all Thangmi are artists. Actually, they should think instead, 'If a Thangmi can be an artist, then there must also be Thangmi writers, cooks, football players, dancers, and everything else.' Each Thangmi should be Thangmi in his own way." Viewing ethnicity as a collective project, to which individuals may make varying contributions in a laterally differentiated manner rather than as a vertically homogenous "individual" that requires group members to articulate belonging in more or less similar ways, diminishes the need to wrestle divergent experiences into neat arguments about group solidarity or singular authenticity. The quality of "we-feeling," which, for instance, the Nepal Foundation for the Development of Indigenous Nationalities (NFDIN) Act (NFDIN 2003:7) lists as one of the defining criteria for membership as an Indigenous People's Organization (IPO), may actually be produced through the interactions and communication *among* members of individual groups, across boundaries of class, gender, and state.

Nonetheless, what happens inside each state at the policy level matters. Conceptualizing ethnicity as a collective process enacted across multiple state borders demands a nuanced analysis of the effects and localized meanings of global discourses like indigeneity (Tsing 2009) and heritage. For instance, the government of India rejects the English "indigenous" as an operative term in its minority legislation. Somewhat ironically, the Indian state prefers to maintain the colonial "tribal" and has to date refused to ratify international instruments like the International Labour Organization (ILO) Convention 169 on the Rights of Indigenous Peoples. In addition, India scrutinizes international organizations working within its borders, with the Indian state itself providing the majority of economic and cultural support to marginalized groups through affirmative action measures. By contrast, as mentioned in Chapter 1, Nepal was one of the first Asian countries to ratify this Convention and integrate the term "indigenous" into its official language. The Nepali state allows a range of international organizations to provide targeted development aid to marginalized groups. These national differences in accepting and implementing the prerogatives of global discourse as propagated by international actors have substantial effects on the ways in which groups like the Thangmi envision their own ethnic identity within each state. This argument will be developed further in Chapter 6.

In short, academic attention to processes of globalization has often overplayed the extent to which Western-influenced ideologies—global discourses—dominate local discourse and practice, leading to analytical models that deemphasize the ongoing power of individual nation-states to imbue identity production with locally specific meanings. We are told that nations become deterritorialized through constant border-crossing movements, including labor migration, conflict-induced displacement, and cosmopolitan jet-setting, with the result that transnational frameworks eventually supersede national ones in shaping identities (Appadurai 1990; Basch, Schiller, and Szanton Blanc 1994; Inda and Rosaldo 2002). Contrary to such assumptions, the Thangmi case shows how transnational life experiences in fact bring into sharp focus the specific properties of individual national frameworks rather than erasing them.

I argue that nation-states remain crucial framing devices in the production of ethnicity but that these framing machineries are now rarely experienced in isolation. They are therefore not taken for granted. Instead, nation-states are experienced as multiple but simultaneously existing frames, which become visible in the process of switching between them. Each frame demands and facilitates different forms of ritualized action, manifested in different contexts to produce recognizable identities. In this formulation, nation-states continue to exercise sovereignty in very real ways. But such state tactics can never become entirely hegemonic in a mobile world where cross-border experiences are increasingly common. Anyone who regularly crosses borders knows that sovereignties do not exist in isolation. Instead, the role of nation-states as framing devices becomes evident at the same time that their previously presumed absolute power becomes relative. Nonetheless, the ability to control such frameworks in order to produce the desired effects within them is a complicated craft, requiring great care and ritualized attention to the nuances of practice and performance to achieve success.

Recognizing the Sacred: On Consciousness and Objectification

The distinction between practice and performance may appear to be academic, but it also has an indigenous ontological reality. Members of the Thangmi community in both Nepal and India differentiate between the aims and efficacy of a practice carried out within Thangmi company for a divine audience and a performance carried out in a public environment for broader political purposes. To distinguish between the two types of action, Thangmi use the Nepali terms *sakali* and *nakali*, which translate as "real, true, original" (Turner [1931] 1997:578) and "copy, imitation" (333) to describe practices and performances respectively.[2] Thangmi individuals talk about how one must get carefully dressed and made up—*nakal parnu parchha* (N)—in order to mount successful performances, while practices require no such costuming.

While viewing video I shot of Thangmi cultural performances in Darjeeling, several audience members at a program in Kathmandu organized by the NTS shouted out comments like, "Oh, how nicely they have dressed up [literally "imitated"]! They look really great!" After the video viewing, one elderly man commented to me, "That *nakali* dance works well to show our Thangmi ethnic culture (*jatiya sanskriti* [N]), but it's a bit different from the *sakali*." In this statement, *nakali* is not necessarily a negative quality but rather a positive and efficacious quality, which in its very contrast to the *sakali* enables an alternative set of objectives to be realized. Through their demonstrative capacity to "show" and make visible "Thangmi culture" to audiences beyond group members and their deities, *nakali* performances do something that *sakali* practices cannot; yet the *nakali* cannot exist without constantly referring to and objectifying the *sakali*.

The difference between *sakali* and *nakali* glosses the distinction between practice and performance well. It was these concepts proffered by Thangmi interlocutors that compelled me to appreciate the different techniques of objectification each form of ritualized action entails. At some level, every expressive action, every ritual, is fundamentally an act of objectification: the process of making deeply held worldviews visible in social space. In the Durkheimian sense, rituals are "the rules of conduct which prescribe how a man should comport himself in the presence of . . . sacred objects" ([1912] 1995:56). As a set of rules enacted in the public sphere, rituals are inherently objectified forms of social action that articulate human relationships with the sacred.

My argument therefore is not that practice—the *sakali*—is somehow unobjectified, raw, or pure doxa lost in the process of objectification that creating the *nakali* entails. Rather, I suggest that the techniques and intentions of objectification operative in the *sakali* field of practice are different from those operative in the *nakali* field of performance. To put it in Goffman's terms (1974), primary social frameworks are still frameworks. *Nakali* performance objectifies in a new and differently efficacious manner the already objectified *sakali* field of practice. Thangmi gurus who go into trance to conduct private ritual practices in homes objectify the set of rules that governs their relationship with territorial deities. In the same manner, Thangmi youth who perform a staged rendition of such shamanic practice to a pop music soundtrack reobjectify the gurus' practice in order to themselves objectify the rules that govern their relationship with the Indian state.

In other words, each field of action entails intentionally different strategies of ritualization, implemented with the help of different framing devices (of which the nation-state is one), in order to make claims upon different community-external entities that will yield different results. Yet one field of action does not supersede the other. Rather, *sakali* practice and *nakali* performance both continue to exist simultaneously and mutually influence each other. Individual Thangmi may employ one, the other, or both in making their own contributions to the collective production of ethnicity.

The constant that links these disparate forms of action together is the enduring presence of the "sacred object" of ritual attention that requires certain rules of conduct to be set out in ritualized form. Handler (2011) follows Durkheim closely by suggesting that the sacred object of heritage performances may be the "social self." I take this notion a step further by proposing that in the Thangmi case, the sacred object is identity itself. Ethnicity then is one set of the "rules of conduct" that govern behavior in the presence of this sacred object. These rules are expressed in a synthetic set of ritualized actions produced by disparate members of the collectivity, which taken together objectify the inalienable but intangible sacred originary in a manner simultaneously recognizable to insiders and outsiders.

Creating Sacred Objects

"The sacred," writes Maurice Godelier, "is a certain kind of relationship with the origin" (1999:169). People's relations with each other across a collectivity—as enacted in moments of practice and performance— objectify as sacred human connections with their origins, along with their concomitant position in social, political, and cosmic orders. This combination of introverted knowledge of one's origins and extroverted relationships with states, markets, and other temporal regimes of recognition is ethnicity itself. It is produced through a range of diverse but simultaneously existing fields of action maintained by the disparate individuals who compose the collectivity.

In Godelier's terms, sacred objects are those that cannot be exchanged (as gifts or commodities) or alienated, and that give people "an identity and root this identity in the Beginning" (1999:120–21). For the Baruya about whom he writes, sacred objects are in fact tangible objects as such. These objects act as an inalienable extension of the human body in their ability to simultaneously contain and represent identity.

For Thangmi, however, such tangible sacred objects have historically been almost nonexistent. There is no easily discernible Thangmi material culture—no icons, art, architecture, texts, or costumes—that might be objectified as sacred. In the absence of tangible signifying items, identity must serve as its own sacred object. Identity itself must be objectified and presented to the representatives of the divine or the state since there is little else in the material world that can stand in for it.

This absence of material culture contributes substantially to the problems of recognition that Thangmi face at the political level in Nepal and India. Moreover, for generations, Thangmi intentionally retreated from the gaze of the state rather than engaging with it, and the Thangmi ethnonym remains largely empty of significance to anyone but Thangmi themselves. Accordingly, to an outside eye, there is little to distinguish a Thangmi individual or village from the next person or place.

There is, in fact, an enormous amount of Thangmi cultural content, but it is all contained in the intangible aspects of practice: origin myths; propitiation chants to pacify territorial deities; the place names along the route that the Thangmi ancestors followed to Nepal and India; the memorial process of reconstructing the body of the deceased out of everyday foodstuff; the way in which offerings to the ancestors are made of chicken blood, alcohol, and dried trumpet flowers.

It is telling that the only notable exceptions to the generally true statement that the Thangmi have no unique material culture are the ritual implements of *take* (T: drum) and *thurmi* (T: wooden dagger). However, these are both pan-Himalayan shamanic implements also used by other groups across the region and as such have little sacred power as identity-signifying objects per se. They only become sacred when used in the specific context of Thangmi ritual language invoked by Thangmi gurus to marshal the power of Thangmi territorial deities (Figure 3). But as soon as such rituals are over, the *take* and *thurmi* become generic objects, not particularly Thangmi nor particularly sacred. In order to work, *take* and *thurmi* must be used by a guru who received these ritual implements from his own father or shamanic teacher. This suggests that in the appropriate context, such objects may also work as signifiers of shared descent—but not in an abstractable manner beyond the guru's lineage itself. This is why the BTWA's use of a *thurmi* image for its logo (Figure 4), along with the more complex diagram of one submitted as part of its ST application, are viewed as *nakali* uses of the object by gurus who use such items in ritual practice. Recall, however, that *nakali* is not necessarily a negative attribute. Rather, it implies the reobjectification of the *sakali* in a new context for a different purpose. As the late Latte Apa, Darjeeling's senior Thangmi guru put it, "I always think it's strange when I see the *thurmi* on the BTWA certificates. It is not a 'real' *thurmi*. But then I think, the government doesn't know us yet, but we must make them know us. If they see the *thurmi*, they will know, 'That is Thangmi.'"

Such statements show how the sacred object of Thangmi identity remains constant, although it may be objectified in a diverse range of *sakali* and *nakali* forms. The *nakali* use of the *thurmi* as a logo for the Thangmi ethnic organization did not compromise its continued *sakali* use by Latte Apa in ritual practice; he acknowledged the value of the former yet continued with the latter. The audiences who reaffirm the sacrality of the *thurmi* in each context may be different, but each plays a comparable and equally

Figure 3. Guru Maila displays his *thurmi* as he prepares to propitiate Bhume, in Suspa-Kshamawati, Dolakha, Nepal, April 2008. Photo by the author.

Figure 4. BTWA member Shova shows the association's *thurmi* logo, as displayed on the banner affixed to the back wall of the BTWA Darjeeling office, November 2004. Photo by the author.

necessary role. Latte Apa was both a practitioner and a performer without a sense of internal contradiction; the sacred object toward which his various forms of ritualized activity were oriented did not change, and both practice and performance reaffirmed the primacy of that sacred object. His practices ensured that deities came to know the Thangmi and validated their special relationship with territorial deities, whereas his performances ensured that state officials and other outsiders came to know the Thangmi as a community worthy of recognition. The mechanisms of recognition in each domain are different, but both realms of ritualized action regulate key arenas of the social world in which the sacred object of Thangmi identity is reproduced.

Recognition and Self-Consciousness

A concern with "recognition" runs throughout Godelier's discussion of the sacred. He asks, "To what extent do humans not recognize themselves in their replicas?" (1999:178), and soon answers, "To be sure he can *see himself* in these sacred objects because he knows the *code*, but he cannot *recognize* himself in them, cannot recognize himself as their author and maker, in short as their origin" (1999:178–79; italics in original). Although Godelier accords his subjects the power to "see" themselves, he stops short of granting them the ability to "recognize" themselves, therefore suggesting that ritual behavior cannot be fully self-conscious. Handler similarly hedges his bets, suggesting first that actors have a certain level of self-consciousness: "Audiences, too, will have differing kinds of awareness of the frame and the contents of heritage rituals. And of course, both actors and audiences will be more or less aware of each others' interpretations of such issues" (2011:52). Soon after, however, Handler returns to a more traditional Durkheimian position by suggesting that "modern social groups worship at the altar of their own identity, but they do not consciously realize that the idea of identity itself, like the idea of god, is a social production" (53).

Such arguments allude to larger anthropological debates over authenticity and the role of objectification in constituting the modern "culture concept." Crediting Bernard Cohn (1987), Handler defines "cultural objectification" as a quintessentially modern process that is "the imaginative embodiment of human realities in terms of a theoretical discourse based on the concept of culture" (1984:56). Along with this argument comes the assumption that engaging in the process of objectification some-how removes one from the realm of pure, un-selfconscious, and, by impli-cation, nonmodern culture. Recall also Guneratne's (1998) separation of Tharu identity into two distinct domains—that of un-selfconscious doxa versus that of self-conscious political posturing—a formulation that draws upon Bourdieu's dichotomous separation of the fields of "practice" and "theory" and their respective identification with worlds of the "native" and the "analyst" (1990).

These arguments entail two paradoxes regarding the self-consciousness (or lack thereof) of cultural actors. The first paradox: on the one hand, those who do not engage in objectification—"natives" in whose world "rites take place because . . . they cannot afford the luxury of logical specu-lation" as Bourdieu puts it (1990:96), or nonmodern actors in Handler's terms—are portrayed as unable to see the frames within which their social world is produced, instead taking "identity" and "culture" for granted as sacred realities without recognizing themselves as the authors of these phe-nomenon. On the other hand, those who do engage in objectification—analysts and modern cultural actors—may be able to see the frames within which social reality and identity are produced, yet they still perceive the resulting cultural objects as real and sacred, without self-consciously recog-nizing the role of their own actions in reifying the frames within which such objects are created.

The second paradox: any sign of consciousness in the manipulation of cultural forms is portrayed negatively as a fall from nonobjectified, genuine grace. Such "calculating, interested, manipulated belief" comprises acts of "bad faith" in Godelier's words (1999:178). At the same time, conscious-ness on the part of those who attempt to identify instances of such manipu-lation is seen as evidence of good social science at work.

There are two problems with such arguments. First, they assume that there is a moment of rupture, an "epistemological break" (Bentley 1987:44, citing Foucault 1977) heralding "epochal difference,"[3] when social groups—conceived of as coherent, homogeneous individuals—make the transition, never to return, from nonobjectified to objectified cultural action, from identity as doxa to identity as politics, from practice (in Bour-dieu's sense of the word, not mine) to theory, from ethnic community to "ethno-commodity" (Comaroff and Comaroff 2009). Consider Guner-atne's description of the Tharu community's transformation: "While the cultural practices of their elders become in one sense marginal to their everyday concerns, in another sense they undergo a reification and reappear as an essential aspect of their modern identity. It is no longer culture as doxa in Bourdieu's sense but culture as performance, a tale that Tharus tell themselves about themselves" (1998:760). Second, regardless of how and when that moment of rupture occurs, individuals are not portrayed as gaining genuine self-consciousness through the transition. Rather, they are portrayed as moving from a state in which they lack self-consciousness entirely to a state in which total belief in their analytical capacities—belief in the power of objectification inherent in the modern culture concept—obscures their real inabilities to comprehend their contributions to the production of sacred objects like identity.

It is time to reconsider these assumptions. First, I question the dividing lines between the types of actors discussed above (modern/nonmodern; native/analyst) since all engage in processes of objectification. Second, I suggest that all such actors (rather than none of them) may act with a substantial level of self-consciousness. Finally, I argue that there is no singular moment of rupture when groups shift from one form of objectification to another. I propose instead that multiple forms of objectifying action, each with different intended audiences and effects, are employed simultaneously in the production of sets of social rules like ethnicity. By refocusing on the entire range of things that individuals belonging to a collectivity—defined by name and the associated implication of shared descent—actually do to objectify various parts of their social world, we can see that culture as doxa, or practice, does not necessarily give rise, in a unidirectional, evolutionary manner, to culture as performance. Instead, people across the collectivity engage in multiple fields of ritualized action that coexist and inform each other.

This argument revisits some of the territory covered by debates over change and continuity, tradition and modernity, that dominate much anthropological work on questions of cultural objectification and authenticity (Briggs 1996; Handler 1986; Jackson and Ramírez 2009; Linnekin 1991). Rather than focusing on cultural objects themselves, foregrounding the diverse forms of sacralizing action people use to produce their cultural world and the constantly shifting interplay between such forms—which are not inherently attached to specific chronological conjunctures—helps move beyond limiting dichotomies. Furthermore, acknowledging that there is a range of simultaneously available objectifying actions that people may employ to express their relationship with the sacred object of identity allows us to see there is a modicum of choice—and therefore self-consciousness—in the decisions that people make about which forms of action to employ in which circumstances, and thus come to recognize themselves as creators of their own social world.

I am not suggesting, as Scott (2009) seems to, that people make fully rational, strategic choices about how they represent their identity for purely expedient political and economic reasons. Rather, actors are conscious of and make choices between various forms of action that articulate different aspects of their relationship with the sacred to different but equally important audiences. Each form of action occasions recognition from a public larger than the individual or the ethnic collectivity itself, whether that be the divine world or the state, and that experience of recognition leads to a powerfully affective affirmation of the social self. For some, this strong experience of validation might come from material evidence that the divine exists and has a special relationship with believers: natural wonders, deities speaking in tongues through possessed shamans, or other "miracles." For others, affirmation might come from evidence that the government notices and has a special relationship with their own community: constitutional provisions for special treatment, political and educational quotas, or other such policies. The desire to gain either one or both of these forms of "existential recognition" (Graham 2005) cannot exist without a minimum sense of self-recognition as a legitimate subject for recognition from others. That basic level of self-consciousness—and the ensuing confidence that external recognition will at some point be forthcoming—is the necessary impetus for individuals to undertake the often expensive, as well as mentally and physically arduous, ritual tasks of propitiating deities (multiday Thangmi rituals often require participants to go without sleep for close to a week) or submitting government applications (a process requiring repeat visits to government offices over several years at great personal expense). The objectifying actions necessary to secure each form of recognition and its evidence are different, but the affective results are comparable. For many, a complete sense of recognition may come from a combination of both.

On the Politics of Heritage and Cross-Border Frames

Building upon the notion that in the performance of heritage, "people become living signs of themselves" (Kirshenblatt-Gimblett 1998:18), the

Comaroffs suggest that the commodification of ethnicity "demands that the alienation of heritage ride a delicate balance between exoticism and banalization—an equation that often requires 'natives' to perform themselves in such a way as to make their indigeneity legible to the consumer of otherness" (2009:142). Is this what the Thangmi dancers with whom this chapter began were doing? If so, who exactly is the consumer of otherness? Most Thangmi rarely come in contact with tourists or other foreigners—the class of people, for lack of a better term, who often provoke the processes of ethnocommodification that the Comaroffs describe. The areas of Thangmi residence in Nepal's hills were never on a tourist trekking route, and the Maoist-state conflict from 1996 to 2006 made it nearly impossible to consider development along those lines. Darjeeling does see a reasonable amount of tourists, but throughout the course of my research, I never documented any engagement with them on the part of the Thangmi community.

The "consumer of otherness" here is instead the state and, especially in Nepal, its associates in international development. But such performances for state consumption are not divorced from practices that are carried out for divine consumption, and understanding both as forms of ritualized action that objectify ethnic consciousness simultaneously to both ethnic selves and others is key. This is not an either/or proposition: at the same time that ethnic actors perform themselves for consumption by temporal or divine others, they also engage in practices that represent themselves to themselves in order to reproduce the content of ethnic consciousness. Scott is quite right that no single part of a repertoire is more "real" than others.

Echoing Kirshenblatt-Gimblett, Godelier asserts that through ritual activity, "People generate duplicate selves . . . which, once they have split off, stand before them as persons who are at once familiar and alien. In reality these are not duplicates which stand before them as aliens; these are the people themselves who, by splitting, have become in part strangers to themselves, subjected, alienated to these other beings who are nonetheless part of themselves" (1999:169–70). Beyond simply serving as a means of crass cultural commodification, performances allow people to objectify their own self-consciousness in a manner that has deep affective results. Through such self-replicating, signifying action, they generate a reflective awareness of these processes of subjectification and alienation in a manner that allows "duplicate selves" to stand without contradiction. In the end, the sacred self is inalienable. The experience of becoming "a living sign" in the process of performance or watching other members of one's community become one—as many Thangmi are now doing—generates a consciousness of the different objectifying tools of practice and performance, and their different but equally important efficacies. In a diverse cross-border community, such consciousness emerges in part from intimate knowledge of the differences in paradigms for cultural objectification in each country and the ability to see such national ethos as frames within which one's own action unfolds.

During a ritual to protect a Darjeeling household from bad luck, Rana Bahadur (no relation to the senior guru Rana Bahadur), a young Thangmi from Nepal who had long lived in India, described this effect: "The politics here are distinct; the politics there are also distinct. In each place, culture must be deployed in different ways." He was a respected shaman's assistant who often played an important role during ritual practices, as well as a cultural performer who wrote and sang many of the lyrics on the popular cassette of Thangmi language songs recorded by the BTWA. Rana Bahadur was one of many Thangmi whose experiences of both India and Nepal as national frames effected a conscious recognition of the differences in technique, efficacy, and audience that defined practice and performance. Another was Sheela, the general secretary of the Sikkim branch of the BTWA, a well-educated woman in her late thirties. She explained the motivation behind the performatization of Thangmi practice I had witnessed in Gangtok: "Thami rituals and traditions are so slow and repetitive. That works back in the *pahar* (N: "the hills," meaning rural Nepal), but here we need something different when we show our culture to others so that the government will notice us." Within this diversity of experience, curiosity about the embodied effects of each form of ritualized action is constant, along with a sense that the relationship between these forms of action enables the ethnic collectivity to synthesize a coherent presence across borders and disparate life experiences.

In one direction, that curiosity manifests in the desire of seasoned Thangmi cultural practitioners from Nepal to watch and, in some cases, participate in stage-managed cultural performances like the one in Sikkim with which this chapter began. In the other direction, many Thangmi in India talk about opportunities to observe cultural practices, such as death or wedding rituals, with the same reverence with which they might discuss an audience with Sai Baba or the Dalai Lama. The increasing exposure of practitioners to performance and performers to practice—through cheaper

and easier cross-border travel and the trend of home-grown VCD production—has generated a debate within the community as a whole about what
constitutes Thangmi culture and what elements of it should be "standardized" for future reproduction.

The fact that this debate is actively taking place within the community
itself, which includes many members for whom practice itself remains
alive and a key component of identity, sets this case apart somewhat from
other discussions of the production of heritage in the global economy.
Kirshenblatt-Gimblett defines heritage as "the transvaluation of the obso-
lete, the mistaken, the outmoded, the dead, and the defunct," and as "a
mode of production that has recourse to the past," to "produce the local
for export" (1995:369). In the Thangmi case, practice remains very much
alive, but it has increasingly come into relationship with performance. The
two coexist. Rather than fetishizing dead practices, emergent desires to
demonstrate heritage through performance for political purposes within
India has in fact encouraged the continuation of practice in Nepal and even
the rerooting of it in India, where it had previously disappeared. For most
Thangmi, heritage has not become entirely detached from living practice
itself, commodified by outside forces and reconstituted for the exclusive
purpose of consumption by others. I suspect that this is not so unusual and
may be the case elsewhere but that the analytical obsession with dichoto-
mizing authentic and inauthentic, practice and theory, has obscured such
dynamics. Instead, although oriented toward external audiences, performance is produced by Thangmi, for Thangmi purposes, in constant conversation with practice itself.

Objectification and commodification are not always synonymous. The
process of self-objectification is one inherent in the human condition, fundamentally expressed through ritual, not one that emerges exclusively in
response to state policies or market forces. While processes of ethnocommodification may be common in the (post)(neo)liberal era,[4] they are not
the only form of ethnic objectification, nor are their resultant objects the
only evidence by which the content of ethnic consciousness should be
understood. Due to the specific properties of ritualized activity, in which
"the celebrant has agent's awareness of his or her action . . . but this is
also preceded and accompanied by a conception of the action as a thing,
encountered and perceived from outside" (Humphrey and Laidlaw 1994:5),
ethnic consciousness produced through ritual action may be "a thing"
without being explicitly commodified within a market context. Moreover,

"it is not the existence of collective ideas about ritual action which constitutes it as a social fact, but common acceptance of rules about ritual action" (267). We can say the same about ethnicity when we view its production as a form of ritualized action: it is not any agreement about what ethnicity *is* that defines it across the collectivity but rather an implicit understanding of the rules of conduct that govern its production. These entail expression through ritualized action, whether those are practices oriented internally toward other diverse members of the collectivity or performances oriented externally toward recognizing agents like the state or the divine world.

These ideas compel further consideration of the relationship between community-internal expressions of ethnic consciousness and external frameworks for recognition—such as states, markets, or global discourses of indigeneity and heritage. The Comaroffs cite a Tswana elder as saying, "If we have nothing of ourselves to sell, does it mean that we *have* no culture?" They interpret this to mean that "if they have nothing distinctive to alienate, many rural black South Africans have come to believe, they face collective extinction; identity . . . resides in recognition from significant others, but the kind of recognition, specifically, expressed in consumer desire" (2009:10). While I agree that identity resides in large part in recognition from significant others, such others may be members of one's own extended community, or members of the divine world, or both—constituencies that are well-addressed through ritualized practices that objectify identity in terms other than that of the commodity. Collapsing all forms of recognition into "consumer desire" flattens the social world into one in which the market is the only meaningful framework for recognition.

Others, including Scott, would have us believe that the state serves as a similarly transcendent source of recognition. The long-standing Thangmi absence from ethnopolitical discourse at the national level reflects the absence of tangible objects of identity recognizable in the terms of the state but not the absence of identity itself. Thangmi performances seek to rectify this disjuncture by objectifying the sacred object of identity through performances—but these occur in tandem with, not instead of, practices that remain oriented toward other recognizing agents.

Both forms of action provoke self-conscious reflection on the frames and contents of ethnicity. The sacred object of identity is not visible on its own but manifests in the process of ritualization. The Comaroffs (2009) assert that ethnicity is experiencing a doubling—both engendering affect and serving as an instrument—and that it is the dialectic between these qualities that defines ethnicity as a whole. Anthropologists have long recognized similar qualities in ritual, and understanding ethnicity as a ritual process works to ameliorate the sense of disjuncture contained in this dual quality of ethnicity. It also moves beyond Scott's assertion of pure intentionality in the process of ethnogenesis by nuancing understandings of how acts of both ethnicity and ritual embody subtle relationships between intention and action.

Historian Sanjay Subrahmanyam offers a trenchant critique of Scott: "It is devilishly difficult to make a case for radical ethnogenesis, on the one hand, and for deep aboriginal rights on the other. Ideas of choice and agency thus come into rude conflict with notions of victimhood and the rights of victims of 'displacement'" (2010:7). He points out that this seems at odd with Scott's long-standing position as a champion of the dispossessed. However, coupling the Comaroffs' proposition that ethnicity emerges from the dialectic between instrument and affect, with an attention to the ritual processes through which ethnic consciousness is produced, takes us beyond the sense of contradiction here. "Radical ethnogenesis"—or a recognition of the constructed nature of ethnicity—need not be at odds with a simultaneous recognition of the affective, deeply real nature of ethnic consciousness that leads to many collective rights claims but also transforms individual senses of self and agency.

Aesthetics, Affect, and Efficacy

The process of performing heritage sometimes has unexpected affective results for the performers. Many Thangmi in India told me that the experience of performance gave them a hint of what practice might be like and encouraged them to seek out practice experiences in the company of Thangmi from Nepal, which in turn gave them a different feel, at the level of the body, for what it meant to be Thangmi. Such interlinkages begin to show how ethnic actors themselves view both practice and performance as integral to their own identity, within a frame of reference that includes individual states, their policies, and the borders between them.

When I asked Laxmi, one of the choreographers of the Sikkim performance, how she and her colleagues conceptualized these dances as Thangmi ones, she shrugged her shoulders and said: "We just choose whichever steps look good. We want to create something that people will want to watch, and will make them remember, 'those Thangmi, they are good dancers.' That will help us." When I pushed further to ask what made these dances particularly Thangmi, she said, "Well, we have Thangmi from Nepal in the group, and they know how to show *sakali* Thangmi culture, so we just trust them." For her, the very presence of the dancers from Nepal—who were stereotyped as having some experience with practice owing to their background in rural villages and their competence in the Thangmi language— was enough to provide an aura of authenticity, although she admitted she did not know what constituted it. She was aware of the aesthetic differences between what she had created as performance and Thangmi practice as such—and their concomitant differences in efficacy. Later, however, she confided that she had been overwhelmed by the experience of the funerary rituals that a Thangmi shaman from Nepal had conducted after the recent death of her brother. This was the first time that Laxmi had participated in a full-blown Thangmi ritual practice because her family had been in the habit of using Hindu priests as officiants, as had been typical for many generations of Thangmi families in India. She was surprised by the positive effect that participating in the ritual as a practitioner, following the shaman's instructions, had on her own fragile emotional state in the wake of her brother's death—a stark contrast to the orchestrating role she was used to playing as choreographer.

That experience motivated her to seek out shamans from Nepal for subsequent rituals, such as her son's haircutting ceremony. She spoke candidly about how participation in these had transformed her experience of what it meant to be Thangmi. She saw these serious, complicated practices as a separate domain from the upbeat performances she choreographed, but it was the former that energized her commitment to the BTWA's political agenda, thereby producing the latter.

In the contemporary cross-border political and cultural economies that shape Thangmi lives, maintaining the pragmatic conditions in which practice can be reproduced necessarily entails mounting performances. Those performances, in turn, must allude to the ongoing life of practice in order to establish their own legitimacy as representations of a culture worthy of recognition. It follows that those with the *sakali* skills of performance cannot advance their own projects without collaboration from those with the *nakali* knowledge of practice, and vice versa. As Surbir would have put it, the beads of the broken necklace must be strung together. The combination of competence in both fields of ritualized action in a single individual is rare, although that is changing, as the examples of relatively young Thang-mi like Rana Bahadur and Laxmi show.

For now, in order to advance their shared goals of reproducing the sacred object of Thangmi identity and securing "existential recognition" from a range of audiences, Thangmi with a diversity of life experiences—in Nepal and India, circular migrants and settled residents of both countries, young and old, gurus and activists, practitioners and performers—continue to work together in a synthetic manner to maintain the rules of conduct governing Thangmi ethnicity. This text is my part of the production, fully costumed in the garb of social scientific authority.

Chapter 3

Origin Myths and Myths of Originality

> In order for a culture to be really itself and to produce something, the culture and its members must be convinced of their originality. (Lévi-Strauss 1979:20)

"I need photos of very 'original' Thangmi," said Paras, as he pushed a stack of photocopied documents across the table toward me, indicating the terms of our exchange. With his signature plaid cap, dark glasses, and Nehru vest stretched over an expanding paunch, the president of the BTWA was the picture of a successful civil servant at the height of his career. Paras had been at the helm of the BTWA since the early 1990s, but due to his posting in the customs office some hours away in urban Siliguri, he was rarely present at BTWA meetings or events. Other members of the organization complained that Paras received credit for successes that he contributed little toward achieving, but his status as a well-educated senior government official lent the organization an air of credibility that even Paras's critics admitted was necessary. In much the same way, albeit on a different symbolic register, Paras now hoped that I could contribute images from my fieldwork across the border in Nepal to lend credibility to the BTWA's application for ST status—the draft materials of which he had just given me on the condition that I contributed to the final version as requested.

"What exactly do you mean by 'original'?" I asked. "You know," he said, raising his eyebrows, as if the fact that I even had to ask diminished his assessment of me, " 'Natural' types of Thangmi, with less teeth than this [he gestured to his own mouth], wide porters' feet with no shoes, clothes woven from colorless natural fibers. But what we really need is more photos of people like that doing *puja* (N: rituals), at *jatra* (N: festivals), you know, *bore* (T: weddings), *mumpra* (T: funerals), all of those things that we can't 'videoalize' so easily here." For Paras, the term "original" conveyed the triple entendre of "authentic" (in the literal sense of "original"), "primitive" (in the sense of "originary"), and "distinctive" (in the sense of possessing "originality"). He located the source of the "original" in the poor economic conditions and ritualized lifestyle that he stereotyped as characteristic of Thangmi in Nepal. For descendants of migrants who left Nepal to settle in India several generations earlier, like Paras, Nepal served as a convenient metonym for an "original" Thangmi culture locked in a static past.

At the level of personal practice, Paras and other relatively elite BTWA leaders distanced themselves from such markers of "originality." It was therefore a relief to them that these characteristics seemed more common among Thangmi in Nepal. However, at the level of political performance, BTWA activists sought to appropriate and package such "primitive traits" and "geographical isolation"—both perceived criteria for a successful ST application—in the service of their own agenda. For this reason, it was frustrating to them that such originality was difficult to document in Darjeeling itself. This is where my photos came in.

At first, I thought that this obsession with locating the "original" in practice and packaging it in discursive terms was exclusive to activists in India like Paras, emerging from a sense of inadequacy that they themselves did not possess such "originality." But I soon realized that in some way or another, the concepts condensed in the root word "origin" played an important role in constituting feelings of Thangminess for almost everyone I worked with. Gurus in both Nepal and India used the terms *shristi* (N: creation) and *utpatti* (N: origin, genesis) to describe the process of ethnic emergence as recounted in their *paloke*, the centerpiece of Thangmi ritual practice that narrates the community's origins. Most Thangmi laypeople were familiar with such stories, which will be recounted later in this chapter, experiencing them as a positive statement of originality that countered feelings of marginalization.

Thangmi ethnic activists in Nepal also used the concepts of "original" and "originality" regularly in their speeches and writings. They typically used the Nepali words *maulik* and *maulikta*, respectively, instead of the English terms as Paras had.[1] For instance, in an argument against misrepresentations of Thangmi as a subgroup of the Tamang, the Jhapa-based activist Megh Raj concluded that "Thami is a complete ethnicity with its own

original identity, existence and pride" (Niko 2003:46).[2] *Maulik*, often translated as "authentic," is to some extent analogous with the term *sakali*, as
introduced in Chapter 2, although the former term gestures toward the
source of ethnic origins in a distant past in a more explicitly historical sense
than the latter.

In this chapter, I show how diverse invocations of shared origins and
originalities indicate a convergence of Thangmi worldviews around what
we might call the sacred originary, recalling Godelier's statement that "the
sacred is a certain kind of relationship with the origin" (1999:169). It is not
shared descent per se but knowledge of a shared myth of it that works as a
universal marker of belonging throughout the transnational Thangmi community by pointing toward the original as that which imbues the sacred
object of identity with its power.

The differences I observed in relationships to and expressions of the
original—which I had initially thought indexed country-specific responses
to the particular politics of recognition encountered in India and Nepal,
respectively—were in fact not determined exclusively by political and economic particularities in each country but rather more by educational and
generational positionalities that entailed different techniques for controlling
and deploying originary power. That a shared narrative of origin constituted the power of Thangminess was so taken for granted it was almost
never stated explicitly. It therefore took me a long time to understand this
fact. Rather, the question up for public debate within the Thangmi community was how to best marshal that sacred power in the service of competing
agendas; so it was these divides that appeared most evident to me.

Orality:Literacy—Myth:Science

Understanding the relationship between oral traditions of shamanism and
literate traditions of Hinduism and Buddhism has been a central concern of
Himalayan anthropology since its inception (Berreman 1964; Fisher 2001;
Holmberg 1989; Mumford 1989; Ramble 1983; Samuel 1993; Ortner 1989,
1995), and relates to broader anthropological debates over the cultural
causes and effects of orality and literacy (Ahearn 2001; Goody 1986, 2000;
Ong 1982; Redfield 1960). The contemporary power struggle between
Thangmi gurus and activists, who respectively wield the power of orality
and textuality within the single ritual system of "Thangmi *dharma*," offers

a new set of insights on this classical theme. The question in the Thangmi case is not whether shamans will disappear or be subsumed by an encroaching literate tradition but whether activists will succeed in appropriating the orally embodied power of their own shamans.

Gurus (and indirectly their adherents) access originary power by propitiating territorial deities through a set of oral recitations that recount origin myths in a ritual register of the Thangmi language. The purposes of these recitations are twofold. First is to secure divine recognition of the special relationship between Thangmi and their territory. Such divine recognition is necessary to ensure a range of positive pragmatic effects, such as good harvests and the continued survival of the community. Second is to reproduce a form of "mythical thought" (Lévi-Strauss 1979:6, [1973] 1987:173, 184) that effects an inseparable link between Thangminess and the oral transmission of cultural knowledge. Such mythical thought is conceptualized by members of the Thangmi community—both guru and activist—to exist in opposition to scientific thought, with its reliance on written transmission. The efficacy of a guru's practice depends upon his power to recite the correct propitiation chants in an embodied manner defined by its orality. In this formulation, lay Thangmi cannot access originary power directly and instead must rely upon their guru to mediate it for them when necessary.

Ethnic activists, however, seek to access originary power directly through "entextualization" (Bauman and Briggs 1990) and "scripturalization" (Gaenszle 2011). They use the technology of writing—primarily in Nepali, not Thangmi and certainly not Thangmi ritual language—to challenge the orally mandated authority embodied in gurus themselves. Bauman and Briggs define "entextualization" as "the process of rendering discourse extractable, of making a stretch of linguistic production into a unit—*a text*—that can be lifted out of its interactional setting" (1990:73). "Scripturalization" adds the sense of "a religious use of the writings, sometimes including the use in ritual" (Gaenszle 2011:282).[3] By writing down myths of origin, as well as the details of the ritual practices that unlock their power, activists attempt to objectify the original for the purposes of political recognition in a manner that bypasses the oral control of gurus.[4] In this formulation, originary power is not fundamentally embedded in the embodied practice of the guru. Rather, originary power can be extracted and redeployed in other contexts (by other agents) in the objectified, entextualized form of the guru's knowledge, as well as in the guru's body as a living sign of itself (Kirshenblatt-Gimblett 1998). For example, an image of several dancing gurus is emblazoned on BTWA certificates issued to recognize outstanding contributions to the Thangmi activist cause.

At the same time, activists seek to mold gurus' mythical thought into the shape of scientific thought. Activist publications suggest that Thangmi must "align our footsteps along with the movement of scientific changes" (Samudaya [2056] 2061:37) in order to remedy the fact that "while the present scientific development has reached a climax, the Thami community is still backward and voiceless" (Niko 2003:10). However, the object of such ostensibly scientific thinking remains Thangmi myth itself; activists do not propose to substitute myth entirely with science at the ontological level. Rather they attempt to refigure it, hoping to achieve improved results by applying what they believe to be a new set of epistemological tools to this age-old object at the core of Thangminess. In this process, they demonstrate that myth remains the object of scientific, as well as mythical thought, and ritual—whether enacted as practice or performance—its expression.

Since activists are almost never gurus themselves (or vice versa), the former's project of entextualization relies upon the latter to provide the raw material by maintaining their embodied, orally transmitted form of practice, which explicitly resists entextualization. This is the paradox that keeps contemporary Thangmi activists interested in the welfare of gurus and that provides gurus with the material conditions to support their continued practice, even in the face of social transformations that might otherwise undercut interest in their power. Just as *sakali* and *nakali* forms of action are mutually constitutive, gurus and activists have come to rely on components of each other's strategies for gaining recognition. Despite their semi-private critiques of each other's agendas and techniques, activists often attend rituals and gurus sometimes participate in political meetings—the respective public forums in which each group demonstrates its power.

Lévi-Strauss suggests that myths function at multiple symbolic levels simultaneously, through geographic, techno-economic, sociological, and cosmological schemas ([1973] 1987:158). These can be variously reinterpreted within a range of enacted contexts—some schemas emphasized, others downplayed at particular historical conjunctures—but the myth endures as a total symbolic system despite contingent shifts in context. Moreover, myths "do not seek to depict what is real, but to justify the shortcomings of reality, since the extreme positions are only *imagined* in order to show that they are *untenable* . . . [and] in abandoning the search for a constantly accurate picture of ethnographic reality in the myth, we gain, on occasions, a means of reaching unconscious categories" (173). This interpretation expands Malinowski's famed reading of myth as "a warrant, a charter, and often even a practical guide to the activities with which it is connected" ([1948] 1974:107–108]), in which mythical texts are wedded to context. It is in the more flexible Lévi-Straussian sense that Thangmi myths can serve as shared objects of identity for both gurus and activists, despite the different contexts—ritual practice and political performance—in which each group primarily enacts and interprets them. Gurus and activists differ not over what myth is, but over how to access and deploy its power to obtain the most effective form of recognition.

It is in this attempt to access originary power that activist strategies of objectification enacted within the frame of political performance (meetings, cultural shows, publications)—often in a specialized linguistic register not easily understood by laypeople—become ritualized activities. Just as gurus' strategies of objectification are enacted within the frame of practice (life-cycle rituals, calendrical festivals, deity propitiations) in ritual language, such political performances assert power by articulating relationships with the sacred originary in ritual forms visible within the social world. In this regard, activist publications that "entextualize" oral traditions are indeed methods of "scripturalization" in the sense that the resulting texts are intended for use in ritual contexts. However, the ritual contexts in which activists imagine their written products will be used are not those orchestrated by gurus for a divine audience but those orchestrated by political actors for a temporal one.

Myth remains a powerful resource for forwarding a range of Thangmi agendas amid shifts in context that rearticulate relationships between individual actors, sacred origins, and modes of expressing the links between them. The actions through which gurus articulate their relationship with myth may be most easily comprehensible under the rubric of "ritual," while those that activists employ may be termed "politics," but the epistemological boundary between these two categories is fuzzy at best because both domains share the ontological referent of the sacred originary. Understanding this shared obsession demands an anthropological approach that recognizes both mythical thinking and scientific thinking, ritual and politics, as mutually dependent components of a totality that encompasses multiple contexts.

The majority of Thangmi are neither gurus nor activists, but most are aware of the different forms of power that each of these groups employ.

Thangmi often express the differences between themselves and people they perceive to be more closely associated with the other form of power in terms of education—whether one is *padhai-lekhai* (N), literally "capable of reading and writing," or not. Gurus and their practice are generally associated with the nonliterate, while activists and their writing are associated with the literate. This is not to suggest that all gurus themselves are illiterate or that all activists are literate. Literacy divides more along generational lines, and to the extent that the majority of gurus belong to senior generations, many of them are only minimally literate. However, this is changing as younger gurus who have been to school begin to climb up the ritual hierarchy. On the activist side, most of those in leadership positions are literate but, again, not all: Shova, for instance, a prominent woman leader in the BTWA, was not literate, and many of the older NTS leaders were self-taught with only basic literacy skills. The issue is not whether one has literary competence but whether one views oral or textual modes of knowledge reproduction as more powerful. These paradigms and their limitations are discussed further below.

For now, let us turn to the figure of the guru as an embodiment of sacred power and to the content of Thangmi origin myths. In the ensuing discussion, I focus on how origin myths and gurus' interpretations of them establish Thangmi identity as sacred within an indigenous classificatory system that valorizes themes of synthesis, producing a sense of "originality" that is at once a source of pride due to its distinctiveness and an embarrassment due to its perceived divergence from criteria for recognition within dominant national discourses.

A Tale of Two Gurus

The anchor of Thangmi ritual practice is undoubtedly the guru. Often referred to as *guru apa*, meaning "guru father," Thangmi gurus play a paternal role within their spheres of influence. Many lay Thangmi look to their guru for guidance when faced with practical decisions of cultural importance: whom to marry, how to conduct a funeral, or when to make offerings to secure a deity's good graces.[5]

In theory, the gurus who officiate at Thangmi rituals should not also act as healers, setting them apart from the popular pan-Nepali image of the *jhankri* (N), or "faith healer" (Hitchcock and Jones 1976; Miller [1979]

1997). There are indeed Thangmi *jhankri* who conduct curative rituals, but they are perceived to be in a separate category of lower status than the gurus who preside over marriage and funerary rites.[6] But the two roles of priest and healer are often conflated in one individual, and apparently, for this reason, the roles are differentiated by unique terms of address in each context. The title for a guru while conducting *mumpra* (T) funerary rituals is *lama bonpo* (T), a term used exclusively for this situation.[7] Similarly, the title *khami* (T) is reserved to address gurus performing *bore* (T) marriage rituals.[8] These terms of address highlight the priestlike function of the gurus when they preside over the life-cycle rituals that are central to producing ethnic identity at the collective level, distinguishing this role from the role of healer, or *jhankri*, adopted when they conduct curative rituals for individuals.

Activist publications make much of these unique titles: for instance, Megh Raj describes the *khami* as one of many "people who organize things at different levels of society," the existence of which serve as evidence of Thangmi "completeness" as an ethnic group (Niko 2003:45). Many activists take the term *lama bonpo* as evidence of the fact that Thangmi were historically adherents of the Bon religion prevalent through much of Tibet and the Himalayas before the advent of Buddhism, and use the terms *bonpo* or *bombo* to connote the practitioners of what they call "ethnic religion" (Niko 2003:40) or "natural religion" (Samudaya [2056] 2061:41).[9]

Both gurus and activists talk about their exclusive reliance on gurus as a marker of identity that sets them apart from other *janajati* groups in Nepal, who in addition to their own shamans, employ ritual specialists from a literate tradition (Buddhist *lama*, Hindu *pandit*, or both) to create a multileveled ritual system (cf. Holmberg 1989; Mumford 1989). Khumbalal, a senior NTS activist, describes how the guru is imagined as a key symbol of Thangmi originality:

> When a child starts hearing and seeing, he first hears the sound of the shamanic drum. He sees the *guru apa* reciting his *mantra*. From that time onwards, he sees nothing except the drum of the *guru apa*; he sees neither the Brahmin priest playing a conch shell and a bell, nor the monk with dark red clothes and a pointed cap who chants, *om mani pame hum*, nor the priest with a cross around his neck, a white shirt and a bible in his hand, nor the Muslim with white clothes and a white cap with two hands on his ears saying *allah ho akbar*. He [the Thangmi child] sees and hears only the sound of the

big drum and the natural world, like the moon, sun, land, gods, goddesses, rivers and streams, hills and mountaintops. He sees only the *guru apa* conducting rituals for the protection and well-being of all the people. (Samudaya [2056] 2061 VS:39)

Although this passage overstates the boundedness of Thangmi communities—most children do in fact see other religious practitioners, even if their families do not employ them—its evocation of the *guru apa* as the central figure in Thangmi ritual life is realistic. Gurus were therefore key interlocutors for me, and I developed particularly close relationships with two such ritual specialists. In Nepal, I worked intensively with Rana Bahadur, as introduced in Chapter 1, in the village of Damarang in Suspa-Kshamawati Village Development Committee (VDC), Dolakha district. In India, I spent many fruitful weeks talking with Man Bahadur, popularly known as Latte Apa, in and around his home in the Tungsung area of Darjeeling municipality in West Bengal.

Rana Bahadur was in his late seventies when I first met him in 1998. Although still respected as the most knowledgeable guru in the area, he had largely withdrawn from public ritual by then and was focused on placating his personal deities to prepare himself for death (Figure 5).[10] I was lucky to spend several months recording his renditions of mythical and ritual schemas, including those detailing Thangmi origins and the funerary cycle, before he passed away in 2003. Latte Apa, who was in his early sixties when we first met in 2000, received his nickname from his long *latte* (N), or matted lock of hair, which he claimed held his power (Figure 6). When not contained by a brightly colored knit hat, which Latte Apa changed daily in an apparent fashion statement, the long lock tumbled down from the crown of his head to brush the floor. An impressive character fully in command of both practice and performance, Latte Apa was the public face of Thangmi life in Darjeeling, both as the chief guru conducting marriages, funerals, and other key rituals, and as the figurehead at the front of many BTWA delegations to cultural programs and political events.

These two senior gurus led parallel lives, with one crucial difference: both were born in Nepal's Dolakha district and migrated to India in their youth, but Rana Bahadur eventually returned to his natal village of Damarang, while Latte Apa chose to settle in Darjeeling. A brief summary of their life stories shows how migration from Nepal to India, and, in Rana Bahadur's case, back again, was central to shaping both of their worldviews, as

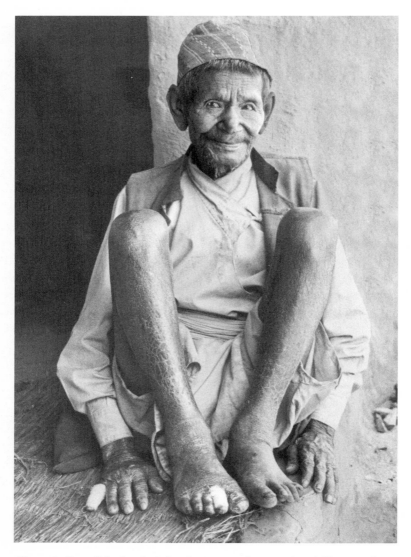

Figure 5. Rana Bahadur, in Balasode, Suspa-Kshamawati, Dolakha, Nepal,
January 2000. Photo by the author.

Figure 6. Latte Apa reciting his *paloke*, in Jawahar Basti, Darjeeling, West Bengal, India, November 2004. Photo by the author.

well as their interpretations of Thangmi origins and the power they held. Introducing them together highlights how national borders do not in themselves produce definitively different forms of practice or performance; we cannot compare these gurus' practices play-by-play, ritual move by ritual move. Rather, the key ritual practitioners in both countries were influenced by similar personal and historical events that took them across borders many times to create repertoires of action framed by political conditions and personal circumstances. This is equally the case for many lay Thangmi, but gurus like Rana Bahadur and Latte Apa had particularly important roles to play in the circulation of ideas about Thangmi identity across borders.

Rana Bahadur

Rana Bahadur was born around 1920 in the village of Suspa, near Dolakha bazaar. His mother died in childbirth with a younger sibling when he was twelve. His father, Bagdole, was a *mizar* (N), a local tax collector who answered to representatives of the central state in Kathmandu. Bagdole's status meant that the family was relatively well off. Nonetheless, they migrated to India during the last decade of British rule, when Rana Bahadur was about twenty years old. He and his father traveled together, picking up menial labor on tea plantations near Siliguri and Jalpaiguri. After they had been in India for about five years, Bagdole died unexpectedly after a sudden illness. Rana Bahadur was left alone far from home with the task of conducting his father's funerary rites. He explained, "This was very difficult. We were so far from home. There were almost no other Thangmi. I looked everywhere to find a guru who could do the *mumpra* correctly. No one knew what I was talking about. I had heard that there was a Thangmi guru from Surkhe [a village in Dolakha] living on another tea plantation nearby. I went to find him, crying all the way. He agreed to come." After this experience, Rana Bahadur resolved to learn more about how the rituals worked. He had not yet been summoned by the deities who later tutored him in shamanic practice, but his interest in learning about ritual practice was piqued by the emotionally and practically challenging experience of conducting his father's last rites far from home.

Rana Bahadur considered returning home after his father's death but had already begun a relationship with the woman who later became his wife and the mother of his six children. Maili was a Thangmi woman from Nepal's Sindhupalchok district who had migrated to India as a child with her parents. In Nepal, marriages and other social alliances between Dolakha and Sindhupalchok Thangmi are rare. But in India, finding a Thangmi wife at all was a windfall. Rana Bahadur first lived with Maili's older sister, but when she left him for someone else, he set his sights on the seventeen-year-old Maili. He was ten years her senior and ready to settle down, and decided to remain in India to court Maili and secure her family's approval.

In 1947, Rana Bahadur and Maili established their own household within the workers' quarters on the tea plantation and soon had a first daughter. Two sons and two more daughters quickly followed, and Rana Bahadur began to think about purchasing his own land and building a house back in Nepal. The 1950 political shifts in Nepal also affected his thinking; the feudal Rana regime had been ousted, and King Tribhuvan was promising a more democratic future (Hoftun, Raeper, and Whelpton 1999; Whelpton 2005). With rumors of major land reform in the air, it seemed like an ideal time to invest savings earned in India back in his home village in Nepal.

At the age of thirty-two, Rana Bahadur began having visions and dreams in which territorial deities from his natal village entreated him to return and become a guru. They directed him toward a forested area called Balasode, southeast of his natal village of Suspa. This location played an important role in the Thangmi origin tale, where the Thangmi foremother Sunari Ama lost a bracelet (N: *bala*) on the journey to Rangathali where she and her husband Ya'apa finally settled (this story is recounted in Chapter 6). When Rana Bahadur and his family arrived in Dolakha, he learned that a large swath of jungle was indeed available for sale around Balasode, and so snapped it up. He and his wife erected a temporary shelter and spent the next year clearing trees, turning the jungle into farmland, and building a house. His youngest son was born soon thereafter—the only one of his six children to be born in Nepal.

Grateful to the deities for guiding him back to Nepal at this fortuitous time, and now finally in a place where he could engage more seriously in Thangmi ritual practice, Rana Bahadur apprenticed himself to a senior guru. He continued to be possessed by deities and said he learned most of what he knew about Thangmi ritual, myth, and origins in these unsolicited encounters. His "formal" shamanic training taught him how to control his trances, but the content of his knowledge was transmitted to him orally by divine beings rather than by a human teacher. This direct connection with the deities was a key element of his power, commanding the respect of many Damarang locals, who were at first somewhat suspicious of this returnee from India. He soon became well-known for his ability to propitiate and placate even the most ornery deities with an impressively detailed style of oral recitation. Once distraught over his inability to conduct his own father's *mumpra* in India, now back in Nepal, he became Suspa's most sought after *mumpra* practitioner.

Latte Apa

Like Rana Bahadur, Latte Apa had an eclectic style. Both men were popularly perceived as powerful gurus for their charismatic personalities rather than their impeccable knowledge or meticulous technique. Thangmi activists in Darjeeling who sought to scripturalize Thangmi ritual practice saw Latte Apa as both a powerful adversary—he was a strong advocate of orality as a definitive component of Thangmi identity—and a powerful asset. With his sonorous voice, unusually tall stature, purposeful stride, and powerful lock of hair, Latte Apa counted much of the Darjeeling lay Thangmi community as members of his unabashed cult of personality. Others, however, found his stranglehold on ritual authority distressing—particularly his emphasis on the power of a ritual language that few could understand—and sought to circumvent it.

Born in 1937 in the Thangmi village of Alampu in the northernmost reaches of Nepal's Dolakha district, Latte Apa was the son of the renowned Kote Guru. Throughout his childhood, Latte Apa followed his father from ritual to ritual, taking on the responsibility of ritual assistant. He lit incense, collected the leaves on which offerings were made, and made the necessary breads and effigies out of rice and wheat flour. When he was eight, his mother died, and his father remarried. Latte Apa's shamanic visions began then:

> I was very upset by my mother's death and started shaking uncontrollably. This was at the time of the new moon, so it was very dark. But two fireflies shone in my eyes, and I walked everywhere like a "zombie," even up on high ridges. I went completely crazy for six months. I crossed the Tamakoshi River in monsoon season, even though everyone said I would drown. But nothing happened—it was like I was sleepwalking. During this time, I started having visions and learning things from the ancestors, just like that. My father died some time after all this began. On the night of my father's death, I sat with the senior gurus all night. I heard a sound like glass breaking, and then everything became clear. From that evening onward, I received "training" every night in my dreams. The deities taught me the ritual chants "line by line." I learned most of what I know now in the first six months of "training" but continued learning every night for three years.

As in Rana Bahadur's experience, Latte Apa's shamanic beginnings were linked to his father's end. For the former, his father's death was a catalyst that compelled him to consider seriously the importance of ritual practice for the first time, while for the latter, it precipitated his direct initiation into his father's lineage of ritual practitioners.

Also like Rana Bahadur, Latte Apa first traveled to India at the age of twenty, having already crossed the mountainous Nepal-Tibet border—no more than ten miles from his village as the crow flies—regularly as a teen-ager to trade grain for salt. The oldest son of two deceased parents, Latte Apa found himself in a situation all too common in Thangmi villages: "I went to India because I had three generations of debt on my shoulders, and there was no way I could pay. I already had to pay high taxes [in kind] on the land I worked, as well as paying for crop seeds out of my own pocket. The situation was unbearable, so I left."

Latte Apa made the journey from Alampu to Darjeeling in 1957 in the company of five friends and, upon arrival, enlisted in the Indian Army as "support staff." After finding himself in several life-threatening circum-stances along the border in Arunachal Pradesh during the 1962 Sino-Indian conflict, he decided to leave the army. He returned to Darjeeling, where he began working as a porter, but his reputation as an accomplished guru spread quickly enough among Darjeeling's migrant Thangmi community that he could soon make his living exclusively from the donations he received in cash and kind for ritual services.

Although only twenty when he first went to India, Latte Apa already had a wife and two small sons in Alampu. The choice to stay in Darjeeling or return to his young family in Nepal was difficult. There were only a small number of knowledgeable Thangmi gurus in Darjeeling at that time, and it was clear to Latte Apa that he could rise to prominence in a manner impossible back in the Thangmi cultural stronghold of Alampu, where there were many gurus already. But his family was waiting for him, and he could have the best of both worlds by joining several of his village friends in the annual circular migrations: spend half the year working in Darjeeling, then return to his family in Nepal with cash in hand to pay off debt and purchase household essentials. After leaving the army and spending several months in Darjeeling, he decided to return to Nepal. He arrived to find that his wife had taken their children and moved in with another man in his absence and that a neighbor had encroached on his land. There was no longer any doubt in his mind that Darjeeling held a rosier future, and after staying in Alampu for two days, he headed east again.

Latte Apa never returned to Nepal before he died in 2009, when a mon-soon landslide swept his house off the Tungsung hillside behind Darjeeling bazaar. However, his reputation was well-known throughout the transna-tional Thangmi community, and he often received visits from aspiring Thangmi gurus who came from Nepal to seek guidance. It was a source of great pride to Latte Apa that despite the abundance of Thangmi gurus in

Nepal, young gurus traveled all the way to Darjeeling to consult him. Latte Apa considered every such visit as a chance to promote his own style of practice, emphasizing to his disciples that the power of Thangmi identity was maintained through the orally transmitted knowledge of its origin. The walls of the small clapboard house that he shared with his second wife, two grown sons, their wives, and an ever-growing number of grandchildren, were a montage of publications, VCDs, and CD covers, certificates, and photos, which demonstrated beyond argument his standing as *the* transnational icon of Thangmi originary power. It was in the person of Latte Apa that strategies for controlling both divine and political recognition most visibly converged.

These brief portraits of Rana Bahadur and Latte Apa show how both gurus' lives—like those of most lay Thangmi—were influenced by experiences of migration and extended residence in multiple locales. Their ritual repertoires were not static structures but rather dynamic processes continually transformed by individual innovation and interaction with broader cultural, political, and scholarly discourses and practices in circulation across the Thangmi world.

Guru Paloke: Origin Myths and Ethnic Classification

The origin myth is chanted at the beginning of almost every ritual event. Although each guru recounts it in a distinctive style, the basic mythic schemas remain consistent. It is the shared recognition of these narrative elements and their relationship to sacred origins that defines belonging in the Thangmi universe. The narrative of the world's creation—and the ensuing genesis of the Thangmi as a people—emphasizes several themes integral to Thangmi identity: their peripheral position vis-à-vis other ethnic groups; the synthetic nature of their ethnic subjectivity; and their simultaneous attachment to specific territories and movement across them. Most Thangmi laypeople—regardless of their background or place of residence—can narrate at least the basic elements of the origin myth and knowledge of it is a key marker of membership in the Thangmi cultural fold.

Origin myths are generally recounted by gurus as part of a broader form of practice known as *paloke* (T). This term refers to the full range of propitiation chants, the ritual contexts within which these recitations occur, and the ritual language in which they are encoded.[11] When I asked gurus directly what *paloke* meant, I received a range of answers, such as "it is everything gurus say," "it is the melody with which we call the deities," "it is the story the deities give us to tell our children about where we came from," and "it is the particular style of Thangmi speech." Activists attempted to pinpoint the concept as "the oral history of the Thami" (Niko 2003:46); "ritual language of the gurus" (Reng 1999:16); "the history of the Thangmi" (Niko 2003:42); and "sayings of the Thangmi guru, our famous oral texts" (Samudaya [2056] 2061:97). I eventually gave up seeking a single, concise definition of the term, but *paloke* seems best explained as an oral tradition encoded in a ritual register of the Thangmi language that establishes the basis for a shared sense of Thangminess by referencing sacred origins.

Given the multiple contexts in which elements of the *paloke* are recited, it is difficult to present a coherent version as recorded in a single practice event. Each guru's *paloke* is distinctive in style, constituting his unique power. I recorded full recitations of the origin myth from six gurus in different locations, as well as many shorter versions offered by gurus, activists, and laypeople. Each of the major Thangmi publications also contains its own take on the story. Rana Bahadur's *paloke* presented the most detailed version of the origin myth itself, as cited below (parts of other gurus' *paloke* are presented elsewhere in the book). Elements of this narrative resonate with a pan-Himalayan myth told by several other groups, including the Tamang (Holmberg 1989) and Mewahang Rai (Gaenszle 2000).[12] An abridged version of the first half of Rana Bahadur's account of the creation of the world and its inhabitants follows. The second half of the story, which details migration into contemporary Thangmi territory, is presented in Chapter 6.

In the beginning, there was only water. The gods held a meeting to decide how to develop this vast expanse. First they created small insects, but these insects couldn't find a place to live since there was only water and no solid land. Consequently, the gods created fish which could live in the water. The insects took to living on the fins of the fish, which stuck far enough out of the water to allow the insects to breathe. The insects collected river grass and mixed it with mud in order to build dwellings on the fins of the fish in each of the four directions: south, west, north, and east.

Then a lotus flower arose spontaneously out of the water, with the god Vishnu seated in the middle. Out of the four directions of the lotus flower came an army of ants. The ants killed all of the fish-dwelling insects and destroyed their houses. The ants took the mud that the insects had used for their dwellings and left, gathering another species of grass as they went. They mixed this with the mud to construct new houses. Then the snake deities arose. It was still dark, so the sun was created.

Eventually, the gods gathered together and decided to create people to populate this vast expanse. Mahadev[13] first tried to make a person out of gold, then one out of silver, then one out of iron, and finally one out of copper. However, none of these metal humans could speak.

Then Vishnu joined Mahadev to try his hand at making people. He made 108 piles of wood and burned each pile down to ash. Then he mixed each pile of ash together with chicken shit, and both gods used this mixture to make a new person. Vishnu built the person from the head down to the waist, and Mahadev built it from the feet up.

The two halves were joined together at the navel. Now the person was ready. The gods called out to it, saying, "Hey, human!" The first people they had made—those of metal—couldn't respond, but this one responded. Then the gods commanded the person to go and die, so it did.

A thousand years passed. During this time, the spirit roamed the earth. Eventually, it ended up near Mt. Kailash, where it entered the womb of a giant sacred cow to be reborn. The cow gestated for seven months, during which time she wandered to a place called Naroban. After another three months, three divine sons were born to the cow: Brahma, Vishnu, and Maheshwor.

The mother cow then instructed her three sons to eat her flesh after she died. She died, and the sons cut her flesh into three portions, one for each son. The youngest son, Maheshwor, went to wash the intestines in the river. As he was washing the entrails, twelve *ved* (N), or sacred texts, fell out of them. Three of the *ved* were washed away by the river, but Maheshwor managed to salvage the other nine.

While Maheshwor was away at the river, the two older brothers buried their pieces of meat in the ground. They did not want to commit the sacrilege of eating their own mother. But when Maheshwor returned, they lied to him, saying that they had already eaten their portions of meat, and urging him to eat his as well. So he ate it. Then the two older brothers revealed their lie and accused Maheshwor of eating their sacred mother. Maheshwor was so angry that he struck the oldest brother, Brahma, with the intestines he was carrying. The intestines wound around his neck and back, becoming the sacred thread of the Bahun [N: Brahmin]. Brahma stole some of Maheshwor's *ved* and went south, carrying the stolen goods. He went to a place called Kasi [the Indian city of Banaras], and his lineage (N: *gotra*) became Kasi *gotra*.

Vishnu ran away to the other side of the ocean and became a king. He had no lineage. Carrying the remaining *ved*, Maheshwor went to the north, chanting *om mani padme hum*. He went all the way to Lhasa [the Tibetan capital], and his lineage became Lhasa *gotra*.

Back in the place where the mother cow's flesh had been hidden, a pond arose. There three groups of people spontaneously emerged: the Barosetu, which included the Bahun, Chhetri, and Lama [ethnically Tibetan peoples, including Sherpa and Tamang], who were under the patronage of Brahma; the Narosetu, which included the Newar, Magar, and Thangmi, who were protected by Maheshwor, and the Karosetu, including the Kami, Sarki, and Damai [occupational castes], whom Vishnu looked after.

Then out of the pond arose a god named Bali Raja, who was responsible for giving caste/ethnicity [N: *jat*] and language to each of these three groups. He said, "Now I will give you *jat*," along with which he gave them languages. To the Barosetu, he gave the *ved*, along with *om bhasa* [N: the language of *om*], and to the Karosetu he gave only an anvil and other tools for working with metal. To the Narosetu, from whom the Thangmi are descended, Bali Raja gave shamanic implements instead of books, language, or tools: they received a golden drum, a golden ritual dagger, a golden plate, a golden water jug, and a golden lamp. These objects arose spontaneously in the hands of the Narosetu.

The Narosetu called on the gods in their three abodes of earth, water, and sky, crying, "Give us knowledge! We will always worship Narobhumi!" The gods of the four directions gave them knowledge and allowed them to stay in each of the four places. The gods also demanded that the Narosetu make offerings to them on Buddha Jayanti.[14]

Up until this time, none of the people could speak. Bali Raja said, "I will divide you into eighteen *jat*, and after I do this, I will give you food and language, too." So they sat in prayer to Bali Raja.

He gave the Barosetu and Karosetu their *jat*. Then it was the Narosetu's turn. There were three Narosetu brothers. The oldest brother then had five sons, who were named and associated with different *jat* as follows: the oldest brother, Ya'apa, became the Thangmi forefather; the next brother, Ma'apa, became the Limbu forefather; then Sa'apa became the Chepang forefather; Ka'apa became the Dhami forefather and Kanchapa became the Rai forefather.

Then Bali Raja gave language to the eighteen *jat*. He first gave language to the other seventeen groups, and by the time he got to the Thangmi forefather Ya'apa, there was nothing left. So Ya'apa had to pick up the leftover bits and pieces of all of the languages that the other groups had already received.

No one had any suffering or pain then. Everyone was happy. Then Bali Raja decided to give seeds to all of the eighteen groups. Each group brought different kinds of containers to collect the seeds. The Sherpa came with a leather bag, the Bahun came with a cloth bag, and the Thangmi came last with a bamboo basket, but there was almost nothing left for them. This is how divisions were made between the receiving and non-receiving jat. The Thangmi fell in the nonreceiving category.[15]

Eventually, Narosetu came to Thimi.[16] There he worshipped Bhume. Until then, Bichi Raj (an incarnation of Vishnu) had been King of Thimi. There were kings in all of the directions, but Bichi Raj was in the middle. One night, Bichi Raj's queen had a dream. She dreamt that Bichi Raj cut down seven banana trees at the base. Bichi Raj interpreted her dream to mean that he would win over seven kingdoms. So he tied the queen up so she couldn't sleep again and possibly have a conflicting dream. Bichi Raj did indeed win seven kingdoms, one of which was Thimi. In the process, he fought with Narosetu as well, and Narosetu was killed. Narosetu's five sons ran away. Ma'apa, Ka'apa, and Sa'apa fled to the West, while Ya'apa and Kanchapa fled together to the East.

*   *   *

Although the first sections of the myth necessarily describe the beginning of the world and the origins of human beings as a general category, the characters quickly become ethnicized. The narrative does not take for granted that the Thangmi are at the center of the world; to the contrary, it assumes that the Thangmi are peripheral, at the edge of every system of ethnic classification with which they are associated. Gurus such as Rana Bahadur and Latte Apa were acutely aware that their myth was not one of primeval emergence from a blank slate as "the people" but rather a tale of fissure from existing groups, reconstitution as a coherent entity, and self-definition in relation to others. With an origin myth that articulates such a relational view of ethnicity (Barth 1969), it is hardly surprising that Thangmi are concerned with seeking recognition—whether divine or political—of their claims to a marginal and ill-defined niche. The tale is largely preoccupied with asserting a Thangmi view of the Himalayan ethnic field, which recognizes the importance of the two major cultural blocs that define it—often schematically termed the Indic and the Tibetan—yet stakes out an alternative position affiliated with neither.

Several elements of Rana Bahadur's narrative and a Tamang myth of origin that Holmberg describes (1989:34–36) are similar: a set of brothers who represent different ethnic groups eat the meat of their divine bovine mother; one brother throws the bovine entrails at the Bahun brother to create his sacred thread; sacred texts emerge from the mother cow's stomach; and the Bahun brother steals his texts from the Kami brother. These aspects of the story give voice to a widespread distaste for the behavior of high-caste Hindus among many of Nepal's *janajati* communities, who have historically felt oppressed by the rigid strictures of Hindu caste hierarchy. Holmberg suggests that "although this Tamang mythic account of caste origins plays on Hindu constructions of order, . . . Tamang translate this material into a different idiom. . . . Tamang not only form a religious society that is their own but one that is . . . governed by a symbology that runs counter to rationalized theories of much of the Hindu-Buddhist world" (1989:37). Much the same may be said of the Thangmi myth, which is clearly recounted as a demotic parody of trickery and exploitation at the hands of Bahuns. The Thangmi slang term for Bahun is *dong* (T)—"intestines"—a word often invoked to comic effect by Thangmi in front of Bahuns who do not understand what is being said.

Yet there is one crucial difference between the Tamang and Thangmi myths: the two narratives classify the ethnic affiliation of the brothers and their descendants differently. In the Tamang myth that Holmberg recounts, "When the sacred texts are divided, the Lama/Tamang receive an equal and separate corpus" (1989:37), and the Tamang constitute an entirely distinct group, structurally separate from the Bahun or Kami. In the Thangmi narrative, however, the Tamang are classed in the same category as the Bahun, Chhetri, and other peoples of Tibetan origin because they all receive written religious texts, while the Thangmi are in an entirely separate category because they receive only shamanic implements and have no textual tradition.

A three-line mythic joke, often told by both gurus and laypeople as a self-deprecating variation on the theme of origins, offers an additional commentary on the Thangmi lack of a literary tradition: "The Kami received their *ved* written on iron tools. The Bahun and Chhetri had no *ved*, but stole them from the unwitting Kami. The Thangmi ate their *ved*, so now we have only oral traditions!" In this saying, which never fails to provoke a laugh when told in Thangmi company, the Thangmi do indeed receive *ved* from the deities in addition to their shamanic implements, but because they are too late to get food from the gods, they eat these religious texts to satisfy their hunger. Having ingested the *ved*, the Thangmi internalize all of their religious knowledge and are bound to maintaining it through oral transmission.

From the Thangmi perspective, the Buddhist Tamang are in an entirely different category, closer in affinity to the high-caste Hindu Bahun and Chhetri than to themselves. Thangmi often invoke this part of the myth as evidence that they are ethnically unrelated to the Tamang in the face of common misconceptions that the Thangmi are a Tamang subgroup. As Latte Apa once described the position of the Thangmi in this ethnic family tree, in which groups are distinguished by their allegiance to textual versus oral authority, "We are the descendants of shamans." This sense of belonging to a lineage that derives its authority exclusively from the power of orally transmitted practices rather than from a textual canon has constituted an essential component of Thangmi identity over time.

The theme of ingesting or otherwise losing one's texts is a common trope in origin myths across the Himalayas and into Burma, Cambodia, Tibet, and southwestern China (Deliege 1993; Gaenszle 2002, 2011; Karmay 1998:123; Mueggler 2001:126; Oppitz 2006). Gaenszle surmises that "there are various reasons why the script and the scriptures got lost: in some cases they were burnt, in others accidentally eaten, or they were lost in a gamble."

He continues, "this myth seems to point at a widespread feeling of embarrassment among oral cultures about not having a scriptural tradition" (2011:8). Some Thangmi also describe their oral traditions as *thutur ved* (N), literally "oral texts" (Niko 2003:41), using a term Gaenszle also notes as prevalent among the Mewahang Rai. However, in Gaenszle's formulation, "the *thutur bed* [= *ved*] of the Rai has only one weakness: being an oral tradition, it is more vulnerable than the others, more susceptible to loss of memory. . . . The apparent superiority of the Great Traditions' literacy makes these increasingly attractive" (2002:34).

But do such myths indicate only embarrassment or weakness? Although this is certainly part of the picture, such analyses tend to overlook the ways that agency may arise out of ambivalent circumstances, as I argue in Chapter 8. In the Thangmi case, a heightened awareness of exclusion from the so-called great traditions is transformed into a positive assertion of identity (see also Scott 2009: chapter 6½), the power of which is only questioned by those within the community whose own claim to orally transmitted knowledge is tenuous. Thangmi have historically viewed orality as a sign of originality and therefore as a strength rather than a weakness. While the Thangmi activists who now seek to scripturalize oral practices may share the desire for literacy that Gaenszle notes among the Mewahang, such activists face the paradox that scripturalization undermines the very basis from which their traditions derive their power as originally Thangmi.

The figure of the guru therefore remains important, even within activist representations seeking to appropriate his power. The singular reliance on gurus for all ritual purposes, without deference to additional ritual specialists who represent the textual traditions of Hinduism or Buddhism (both of whom would be readily available in most of the places that Thangmi live), set the Thangmi apart from other Himalayan ethnic groups—such as the Tamang—with whom they otherwise share a great deal. Holmberg suggests that "multiple specialists are an integral part of all the religious systems of Tibeto-Burman speaking groups in the Himalayas" (1989:4, n.3), providing a long list of ethnographic works that document the role of multiple specialists in the religious systems of such groups. The Thangmi are an exception to this rule, and they evoke this difference to assert their uniqueness. This is not to say that Thangmi ritual practice makes no reference to Hindu and Buddhist traditions. Such references are in fact integral to the synthetic nature of Thangmi religion, but these elements are appropriated by Thangmi gurus, who act as the agents of synthesis on their own oral terms. As "authorized religious personalities" (Niko 2003:42), they create Thangmi *dharma* (N: religion) as a distinct entity that stands apart from either of the two literate traditions that dominate both lay and academic conceptions of religion in the Himalayas.

Oral and Textual Modes of Practice as Classifying Markers

The segment of the origin myth presented above introduces an indigenous classificatory system in which people are categorized according to whether or not they maintain a textual tradition. This offers a provocative variation on the common rubrics for classifying Himalayan groups. The narrative also provides some clues as to why the Thangmi have had trouble conforming to such classificatory regimes, ultimately evading description and remaining largely absent from scholarly and political discourses.

Both states and scholars have struggled to develop terminology at once clear and complex enough to cope with the vast cultural diversity of the Himalayan region. As described in Chapter 1, the 1854 Nepali legal code, or Muluki Ain, codified the position of many of the country's groups, incorporating them within the Hindu caste framework. By contrast, Indian colonial classification projects set up a clear dichotomy between caste and tribe. Early scholarly works promised to move beyond such distinctions, but that task has proven difficult. The 1978 edited volume *Himalayan Anthropology: The Indo-Tibetan Interface*, which contained a collection of essays by Western social scientists working in the region, proposed what became a remarkably enduring model for defining the Himalayan region as an "interface" between the two "great civilizations" of India and Tibet. Christoph von Fürer-Haimendorf summarized this model in the foreword to the volume:

> In the Valleys of this great mountain range Indo-Aryan and Tibeto-Burman languages dovetail and overlap, populations of Caucasian racial features characteristic of North India met and merged with Mongoloid ethnic groups, and the two great Asian religions Hinduism and Buddhism coexist there and interact. . . . Very little is known about the history of the many preliterate tribal societies which for long filled the interstices between the domains of more advanced cultures. . . . For centuries [this area] has been a meeting

point of distinct races and two of the great civilizations of Asia.
(1978:ix-xii)

This model posits two ideal types: the Indic, characterized as linguistically
Indo-Aryan, racially Caucasian, and religiously Hindu; and the Tibetan,
characterized as linguistically Tibeto-Burman, racially Mongoloid, and religiously Buddhist. The problem is how to classify people who fit into neither
category, inhabiting the "interstices" between them, which James Fisher
describes with several colorful metaphors in his introduction to the same
volume: "fringe region," "neither fish-nor-fowl contact zone" (1978:1),
and a "zipper which stitches together these two densely textured cultural
fabrics" (2). We are left to wonder whether there is room left for those
caught between the zipper's teeth to forge their own sense of cultural distinctiveness using the "preliterate" tools at their disposal. In particular, it
remains unclear how blended paradigms for belonging might be defined in
relation to the Indic and the Tibetan types, without aspiring to assimilate
to either one.[17]

Despite the shortcomings of these classificatory rubrics, both activist
and state discourses have appropriated such scholarly descriptions, often
drawing sharper oppositions between the Indic and Tibetan than scholars
originally did. In most cases, religion is taken as the key symbol in the set
of oppositions, with *janajati* groups in Nepal and tribal groups in India
defined foremost by their ostensibly non-Hindu character. NEFIN stipulates one of the criteria for recognition as a *janajati* group as "not included
in the Hindu caste system."[18]

In India, although the nation's secular constitution discourages defini-
tions of difference on a religious basis, a tribal identity is presumed to be a
non-Hindu one (Middleton and Shneiderman 2008; Middleton 2011).
Some activists in Nepal, such as the members of the Mongoloid National
Organization, seek to accord race primary symbolic value over religion
(Hangen 2005a, 2010). This approach has the benefit of acknowledging that
while some groups may have altered their religious practices in response to
Sanskritization (Srinivas 1989) or Hinduization (Fisher 2001), their racial
characteristics continue to mark difference in a normative manner that religious practice no longer does. Despite their divergence on this issue, both
activist approaches to classification link the three characteristics of Tibeto-
Burman language, Mongoloid race, and non-Hindu religion to define subaltern identities in a static manner vis-à-vis the supposedly dominant and

oppressive Indo-Aryan linguistic, Caucasian racial, and Hindu religious identity.

Such categories are problematic for several reasons. At the linguistic level, the terms "Indo-Aryan" and "Tibeto-Burman" reference language families rather than contemporary spoken languages. Although most of Nepal's over one hundred languages are members of these two language families, one cannot be said to speak Indo-Aryan or Tibeto-Burman (Turin 2006). In addition, speaking a language belonging to one or the other of these families does not on its own define racial, religious, or ethnic identity: for example, many Buddhists are mother-tongue Nepali speakers. Moreover, racial mixture has occurred across the Himalayas over many generations. This is the case even among elite families fixated on purity, as historian John Whelpton has argued in regard to Nepal's now-deposed Shah kings (2005). Interethnic marriage is the norm among groups of Nepali heritage in Darjeeling, as described further in Chapter 7. Religious boundaries between Hindu and Buddhist practice are rarely clear-cut. While most Himalayan people can identify with some of the linguistic, racial, and religious characteristics enshrined in the putative Indic and Tibetan paradigms, those characteristics do not always line up neatly in one column.

Such mixture is certainly part of the Thangmi story. In the portion of the myth recounted above, the Thangmi forefather eventually receives language from Bali Raja, but it is not "pure," being instead a mixture of the other seventeen languages. Linguistic research tells us that the Thangmi tongue does indeed link the Newar language and a group of Kiranti languages. Like Newar, Thangmi is a Tibeto-Burman language with long-standing Indo-Aryan influences (Turin 2004a, 2006). People who identify themselves as Thangmi possess a wide range of physical features ranging from stereotypically "Mongoloid" to stereotypically "Aryan" and everything in between. The origin myth alludes to this racial diversity with its mention of Lhasa and Kasi *gotra*, two superclans linked to these important cities to the north and the south, respectively, which are perceived as the source of Mongoloid and Aryan features.[19] (I have often heard Thangmi friends joke with each other about who belongs to Lhasa *gotra* and who belongs to Kasi *gotra* based on the shape of their nose.) These cities also metonymize the Hindu and Buddhist complexes from which many aspects of Thangmi dharma are appropriated: Brahma steals the *ved*, a Hindu text, and goes south to Kasi, while Maheswor heads north to Lhasa chanting *om mani padme hum*, a mantra of Buddhist origin.

The Thangmi myth offers an alternative to the hackneyed categories for classifying Himalayan groups described above: why not instead classify groups according to whether they emphasize an oral or textual mode of religious authority? Such a classificatory schema shifts attention away from essentialized notions of linguistic, racial, or religious content, refocusing instead on what people actually *do*—identity expressed in action. From this perspective, the Thangmi reliance on an orally transmitted shamanic tradition sets them apart from groups who adhere to either Hindu or Buddhist textually legitimated traditions, and aligns them with others for whom oral tradition remains primary, such as the Limbu, Chepang, and Rai, who are identified as the closest ethnic "brothers" of the Thangmi in the myth.[20] Of course, there are aspects of both Hindu and Buddhist tradition that emphasize oral transmission as well as or, in some cases, instead of textual authority, and a nuanced application of the classificatory schema outlined in the origin tale would have to locate practitioners of Hindu and Buddhist oral traditions in the same category as the Thangmi themselves. Nonetheless, Thangmi gurus and laypeople consistently stated that people must be classified according to what they actually do (N: *gareko anusar*). Such statements are made not only by gurus but also by lay Thangmi. One man from Nepal who had worked extensively in India told me that he was perpetually frustrated when people asked "who [i.e., what other groups) are the Thangmi close to?" rather than "what do Thangmi do?" He continued to tell me that it was impossible to explain Thangmi identity with reference to other groups and that he wished he could instead "show" his interlocutors what Thangmi ritual practice looked like. Indeed, Thangmi living and working in multiethnic contexts increasingly use digital media to "show" others what Thangmi life is like. These discussions highlight the importance of action in defining identity from a Thangmi perspective.

Synthetic Subjectivities and Inferior Complexities

How can the origin tale assert Thangmi as somehow fundamentally different from those who identify as Hindu or Buddhist, when Thangmi practice incorporates elements of both Hindu and Buddhist practice? The emphasis on practice and the resultant flexibility regarding ethnic and religious boundaries described above helps solve this riddle. Thangmi self-definitions that openly acknowledge mixture—at linguistic, racial, and religious levels—advance a critique of the received Indic and Tibetan categories. Gopilal, a prominent Thangmi from Dolakha now in his seventies, who had been both a political activist with the Nepali Congress and an important ritual lineage holder, once commented with a wry laugh before launching into an informal rendition of the origin myth, "We are a hybrid (N: *thimbar*) group, from the moment of creation onward; that is how we became Thangmi." The Nepali term *thimbar* is derived from *thimaha*, which connotes hybridity in the biological sense and is used in agricultural contexts to describe the results of plant breeding (Sharma 2057 VS:562). Many Thangmi in Nepal had become familiar with the term through agricultural trainings sponsored by development organizations and had adopted it to describe themselves, often in statements like Gopilal's that demonstrated a self-reflexive sense of humor.

Such self-conscious descriptions of mixture attest to a "synthetic subjectivity": a conscious recognition of the synthesis of diverse linguistic, religious, racial, and cultural elements of which Thangmi identity is comprised. This is not to say that Thangmi are in fact more hybrid or synthetic than any other group—Himalayan or otherwise—in empirical terms, but that they consciously recognize this mixture as part of what makes them who they are rather than subverting it through a narrative of ethnic purity. By vesting ritual authority in their gurus (who do not claim to act as officiants of either pure Hinduism or Buddhism but instead articulate their origins as explicitly synthetic), Thangmi historically located themselves outside the normative line of vision of the Nepali and Indian states, which have relied upon religious identities as definitive markers of ethnicity.

This emphasis on synthesis is one of the reasons why the Thangmi long remained invisible at the political level. Many contemporary Thangmi in both Nepal and India who would like to make ethnic claims on their respective states find the lack of definitional clarity that they encounter in their own myths of origin deeply disconcerting. The problem is not that such activists no longer possess synthetic subjectivity. To the contrary, they have become increasingly aware of it as they have sought to locate themselves within the state's line of vision, often grappling intimately with the disjunctures they feel between their subjective awareness of synthesis as a key feature of Thangmi identity and the perceived political requirements for racial, religious, cultural, and linguistic purity.

For political purposes as well as personal peace of mind, many Thangmi activists would like to find and put on display an "original" Thangmi prototype, clearly categorizable as a "Hindu" or "Buddhist" religious practitioner, an Indo-Aryan or Tibeto-Burman language speaker. But even the most militant must ultimately acknowledge that "after careful study we find that the Thami rites are a combination of Hinduism and Buddhism . . . integrated in the guru system" (Reng 1999:18). Synthetic subjectivity is not always an easy mental state to bear. As Pnina Werbner has suggested, "intentional hybrids create an ironic double consciousness . . . and are internally dialogical, fusing the unfusable" (1997:5) in a manner that can be both productive and debilitating.[21]

Paras, whom we met at the beginning of this chapter, once explained to me in English, "We Thangmi have an inferior complexity." Indeed, this slip of the tongue pinpoints the problem precisely. Paras later explained that he meant "inferiority complex," a term that he and other Thangmi activists used regularly. Paras writes in *Niko Bachinte*, "Our members will have these questions: who are the Thami, where did they come from, and so forth? Those who are smart enough to respond will have an answer for the questioner, but those who aren't will be left without a reply and some of them will even suffer from an inferiority complex" (Niko 2003:9). Rajen similarly explained to me that migrant Thangmi in Darjeeling did not participate in the BTWA's activities because they had an "inferiority complex." Thangmi racial origins and linguistic and cultural practices, along with their resultant synthetic subjective state, are too complex to fit easily within common Himalayan and South Asian rubrics for classifying ethnicity. This sense of not fitting in leads many Thangmi to feel at once inferior and proud of their complexity. The balance between the two depends on the individual's life experiences and ability to negotiate the tensions of double consciousness.

Struggles for Power: Between Orality and Literacy

On a recent trip to Dolakha, I watched a group of children playing in the dirt perk up their ears and listen in rapt attention as Silipitik, a respected village elder in his seventies, recounted the Thangmi origin myth. For individuals like Silipitik, both old and young, who are engaged in Thangmi linguistic and cultural practice on a day-to-day basis, the iterative process of telling and listening to the mythic narrative provides a powerful framework within which to interpret their own lives. In particular, the myth inculcates a sense of pride in the racial, linguistic, and cultural complexity that defines Thangminess by positing it as the basis for Thangmi "originality."

However, the very oral, embodied nature of originary power limits access to it for those who cannot understand the Thangmi language in which the myth is embedded or who are not familiar with the ritual contexts in which it has historically been transmitted. For such Thangmi, the origin myth loses much of its interpretive power unless it can be entextualized in a manner that grants them access to and control over it. Access is achieved by decontextualizing the myth from the embodied ritual practice of the gurus' *paloke*, translating it into Nepali or English, and encoding it in the written word. Control is then asserted by recontextualizing the narrative in a written form that very few gurus have the literacy skills to understand or use. The desire to wield originary power is much of what compels activists like Paras to engage in the political production of identity with what can only be called religious fervor, even if they are not—or especially if they are not—involved in ritual practice in the traditional sense. For such activists, gaining recognition from the states in which they live becomes an existential battle to overcome their own sense of inferior complexity, as Paras and others called it, exacerbated by incompetence in the Thangmi linguistic and ritual domains within which the sacred power of identity has historically been produced.

After recounting the origin myth to his young audience, Silipitik turned to me to complain about the recent proliferation of Thangmi activist publications that he could not read. "From the beginning, our ethnic group has not had writing and reading," he said. His phrasing, echoed by many others of his generation, suggests that writing and reading are tangible items that a group or individual can possess, and as such, are simply not part of the Thangmi cultural inventory. The tension between guru and activist worldviews indicates a broader set of social differences within the Thangmi community indexed by notions of orality and literacy. As Laura Ahearn suggests, "Literacy is not a neutral, unidimensional technology but rather a set of lived experiences that will differ from community to community" (2001:7). Understanding how these dynamics work therefore requires a very brief history of Thangmi educational experiences.

There were no educational institutions in Thangmi areas of Nepal until the late 1940s, when the first primary school was built in what is now Suspa-Kshamawati VDC. Based on oral histories, we can presume that most of the early students were Bahun, Chhetri, and Newar, with very few Thangmi children enrolled. Thangmi children were actively prevented from enrolling by high-caste teachers, whose families acted as moneylenders to Thangmi and saw the prospect of their literacy as a potential challenge (Kharel 2006).

Nonliterate Thangmi were exposed to writing primarily through the loan documents used to appropriate their land and tended to view writing as a technology of exploitation that "belonged" to high castes. Even when underground communist activists arrived in the Thangmi area in the late 1970s and began dismantling some of these barriers to education, many Thangmi remained skeptical about whether literacy would genuinely benefit them (Shneiderman 2010).

Such resistance to formal education eventually dissipated as more schools were built and the potential benefits of education became clearer. Increasing numbers of Thangmi children began attending school in the 1980s. They became part of the broader project of nationalist education in Nepal during the *panchayat* era, during which ethnic difference was cast as backwardness (Pigg 1992; Onta 1996c). By contrast, development was framed in terms of nationalist assimilation to the dominant Nepali-speaking, Hindu path to modernity (Pigg 1992; Ahearn 2001; Tamang 2002). Well into the first decade of Nepal's democracy, only around 56 percent of Thangmi children were ever enrolled in school (HMG/N 1996:23), with high dropout rates (especially among girls), ensuring that only a very small number of Thangmi made it beyond primary school (42).

Formal education levels for Thangmi in Nepal remain low today. The increasing numbers who study at once gain tools to climb the status ladder into mainstream Nepali society and learn to critique Thangmi linguistic and cultural practice from an evolutionary perspective that casts oral traditions—particularly in languages other than Nepali—as "backward" and incommensurable with a literate Nepali modernity. Most Thangmi activists in leadership positions during the period of my research were educated in the 1980s and 1990s. They viewed the very orality of Thangmi practice as problematic since it differed from what they perceived as the standardized nature of the textually based great traditions. Although many of these individuals had grown up in Thangmi-speaking environments where gurus were preeminent community leaders, they felt that advancing educationally and economically within the Nepali national frame required a departure from Thangmi linguistic and ritual practice. As Tek Raj, an NTS youth leader told me, "The fact that we have only oral traditions is very embarrassing to us, and we want to change that for future generations." Another young writer from Dolakha, Ram Kaji, suggested that "to solve all of our problems, we must write a book . . . on the practices of the Thami which will be acceptable to Thamis scattered all over the world so that they can follow the same tradition" (Samudaya [2056] 2061 VS:26).

These ideas converged with those of Darjeeling-based Thangmi activists, educated in the postcolonial secular Indian context in which Nepali itself was a minority language. In Darjeeling, education was far more accessible than in Nepal, and the Thangmi organization even opened its own primary school in 1945, as will be described further in Chapter 5. Unlike their counterparts in Nepal, however, most Thangmi activists in India had little personal experience of the Thangmi language. Although they were eager to collect and understand Thangmi origin myths and ritual knowledge, they were frustrated to find that these existed only in oral forms embedded in the practice of gurus, who resisted scripturalization—a problem that activists in Nepal also encountered.

There were several reasons for this resistance. First, senior gurus belonged to a generation for whom writing signified exploitative power. Second, few were literate themselves and thus felt threatened by this unfamiliar technique of objectification. However, even many younger gurus who did not share the older generation's visceral fear of writing felt strongly that their *paloke* should not be written down. From a guru's perspective— regardless of his age—the oral recitation and transmission of the *paloke* is what generates their originary power as distinctively Thangmi. The essential orality of their practice is viewed as the immutable outcome of the actions of the Thangmi ancestors, who in their hunger swallowed religious texts granted to them by the deities upon creation. As Guru Maila of Suspa explained, "Having swallowed our texts, we must practice our traditions from our *man* (N)." *Man* is an internal, nonintellectual, nondiscursive embodied essence (Desjarlais 2003; Kohrt and Harper 2008; McHugh 2001) in which the stuff of Thangminess resides. Once consumed, the texts became indelibly imprinted on the collective Thangmi *man*, binding Thangmi gurus to the oral, embodied nature of Thangmi practice.

Thangmi gurus are therefore unable to extract what first appeared to me as the discursive aspect of their *paloke* from the embodied expression of it. Early in my research, I would ask gurus to narrate the content of their chants without going into trance, but these requests were met with disdain and the response that the words and the bodily practice—text and context—were inseparable, mutually dependent parts of a whole. Rana Bahadur's assertions that if I wanted to record any of his knowledge, I had to be willing to document *all* of it (as described in Chapter 1), were evidence of the same sort of totalizing thinking. Several gurus with whom I developed close relationships were eventually willing to "stage" their *paloke* for me and my recording devices, but such performances still required all of the usual ritual offerings, and the gurus still went into trance. None of the gurus with whom I worked could recite individual components of the *paloke* without chanting the entire "line," nor could they recite this without going into trance, nor switch back and forth between recitation and explanatory commentary. The *paloke* really were embedded in the consciousness of gurus as a totality and were not meant to be read by others as "texts" in the hermeneutical sense. The content of the *paloke* therefore could not be extracted in easily entextualizable pieces, by me or Thangmi activists.

The total control that this gave gurus over originary power itself was unacceptable to many activists. Their objectives were twofold: to write down elements of myth and practice that could be made easily accessible in written form both to interested Thangmi and to the authorities responsible for political recognition, and, through the techniques of scientific thinking, to standardize diverse gurus' practice into a single canonical text. Their ongoing attempts to meet these goals resulted in a power struggle. Khumbalal writes:

> Our *guru apa* recite spiritual mantras which they make up, but these are not written.[22] The same mantra is passed to his followers in oral, not written form. . . . In order to preserve his power, the guru never teaches his mantra to others. Since the beginning, our community's gurus have taken their mantra with them when they die. Now, how many mantras have these gurus taken with them from ancient times until the present? Since they are not written, the modern generation is forced to suffer to obtain their various practices and mantras. . . . As the practices are done differently by each *guru apa*, it seems that they cannot all be correct. . . . We have no way of knowing if the so-called "guru" in his state of intoxication is pronouncing his mantra correctly or not, or whether he is just making up the sentences, which he has actually forgotten. We don't have written *ved* to prove

it. If we did have them [*ved*] we could correct [the guru], saying, "Here is a mistake, here you have left it unfinished." Not all gurus are like this, but some have hoarded power and tried to dominate our community.

   To solve these problems, the gurus, the intellectuals, and experienced members of the community should sit together and correct our practices. These must be published in a book, with which gurus should train students, and just like other pandits, monks, priests or mullahs, they should try to produce many gurus. (Samudaya [2056] 2061:41–42)

This damning indictment of gurus comes from the same writer whose eulogy of the guru as the symbol of Thangmi originality—the only religious practitioner that Thangmi children should know—was cited earlier in this chapter. Khumbalal considered himself one of the intellectuals invoked at the end of the paragraph. For him the real problem was that despite his high educational and economic status—he held an Indian college degree and ran a successful restaurant franchise in Kathmandu—he still had "no way of knowing" what was really at the root of Thangmi originary power, embedded as it was in the bewildering complexity of oral tradition controlled by gurus. By making such practices legible, Thangmi like him sought to bring their access to ritual power into line with their economic and social power.

   For self-proclaimed "intellectuals" like Khumbalal, this was a highly emotive issue. Despite the promises of a better future through education made in both Nepali and Indian nationalist discourses, in the end, being *padhai-lekhai* (educated, in the sense of being able to read and write) did not in itself grant access to power within the Thangmi community. Education did allow one to attain higher status outside of the Thangmi community, which was one of the necessary tools in campaigns for recognition and a role that individuals like Paras and Khumbalal filled well. But education alone did not establish authority within the Thangmi community, where status was judged not by the quantitative terms of educational and economic success alone but also by the qualitative terms of one's relationship with the sacred originary. Both, in fact, were important, but in many people's eyes, educational and economic success were relatively meaningless in terms of establishing status as Thangmi if one did not also have a strong relationship with the sacred originary.

The concept of *padhai-lekhai* was not so much a literal assessment of one's educational or class status, then, but rather a symbolic statement of which kind of power one chose to prioritize. When Sher Bahadur, a middle-aged man in Dolakha who was literate and extensively involved in community-based development projects said, "Those educated Thangmi don't care about other Thangmi; after they've reached the top, they don't come back here," it was both a way of distancing himself from those whom he accused of taking advantage of others, and discrediting their power by suggesting that once one leaves the village for educational or economic advancement, one is no longer fully Thangmi. Similarly, the Darjeeling activist Nathu's statement that "those who are educated don't respect the 'cultural'" was a way of contrasting the two approaches toward power and situating himself somewhere in the middle. He had no formal education, but nonetheless held a government job and was economically successful— and sided with the gurus in arguing against scripturalization. Speaking from the other side of the fence, as someone who was proud of his education and felt personally affronted by Latte Apa's hold on power, the BTWA general secretary Rajen told me that "there are two 'standards' [of Thangmi]: 'low-level' and the type with 'education.' We've been unable to unify the two." Rajen squarely placed the blame for this divide on the shoulders of those he called "low-level," by which he meant circular migrants from Nepal. These were, however, the very people from whom he solicited cultural information for BTWA publications and performances, as well as linguistic data for the dictionary of the Thangmi language that he compiled.

Even those who proudly called themselves "intellectuals" acknowledged that they could not carry the Thangmi banner alone. Despite his strong critique of gurus, Khumbalal's statement still calls for them to work with "intellectuals" and "experienced members of society" to ensure the community's future. Similarly, Latte Apa visited the BTWA office in Darjeeling bazaar every few days to ask if there was news of the Thangmi ST application or upcoming public events to squeeze into his ritual schedule. The sense of recognition that activists receive in response to the literate power they wield is no less real than that which gurus (and those who employ them) receive in response to the oral power they embody. Both forms of power derive from mutually constitutive processes of objectification— *sakali* and *nakali*—that articulate relationships with the originary for some members of the Thangmi totality.

Radio and VCD as Unifying Forces?

Gaenszle suggests that the emergence of nonliterate technologies, such as cassettes, video, CDs, and VCDs, has among Kiranti communities "led the younger generation . . . to increasingly revalue the oral forms" (2011:17). For Thangmi, too, forms of entextualization that do not rely upon the written word can mediate between oral and literate worldviews. Gurus who resisted having their *paloke* written down not only allowed themselves to be videotaped by me (or "videoalized" by Thangmi activists), but in fact often requested that I document particular ritual events. They were pleased when I returned these recordings to them on VCD, and these discs were regularly viewed on neighborhood decks. Similarly, Latte Apa allowed BTWA activists to sell copies of a four-CD set of his *paloke* as a fundraiser, but he still refused permission to transcribe its contents. Audio and video recordings enabled a compromise between the two groups' agendas: they allowed gurus to maintain their power since there could be no recording without their embodied recitations, but they simultaneously allowed that power to circulate to a broader public—including state agencies—without requiring the gurus to actually be present.

Another medium with similar effects is community radio, which rapidly came to play an important role in Thangmi lives over the last decade, as it did throughout rural Nepal (Onta 2006a). In 2007, NTS received funding from NFDIN for a Thangmi-language radio show called *Thangmi Wakhe* (Thangmi Talk) broadcast on several community radio stations.[23] The host was Tek Raj, the young activist-journalist who had told me that he found the exclusive orality of Thangmi traditions "embarrassing." Guests included activists, gurus, and other Thangmi individuals. I listened to several broadcasts with Thangmi friends and was struck by their emotional response to "hearing the radio speak in our own language," as one of them put it.

I therefore accepted Tek Raj's invitation to interview on the program in 2008. After our brief on-air conversation, we had a cup of tea in the studio's back room. He had a long list of questions for me, which were much more contentious than those posed during the formal interview. He wanted to know what I thought about the relative value of what he called *maukhik* (N) and *likhit* (N)—oral and textual—forms of knowledge production. He was personally troubled by the tensions he felt between these competing forms of power within the community. This was hardly surprising since he was an ambitious man in his mid-twenties, who had grown up speaking Thangmi fluently in a Dolakha village within a popular guru's sphere of influence; but held a B.A. in journalism and was now employed by a mainstream media house in Kathmandu. *Thangmi Wakhe*, which he produced in his free time, was obviously his passion, but still he was concerned that somehow the oral form it took was worth less than the printed articles he wrote in Nepali for his day job. "It's not 'long-lasting,'" he said to me of the radio broadcasts. "I put so much time into it and then it's gone." I suggested that this ephemeral quality might be part of what gave a live broadcast its power, just as a guru's power was embodied in his practice.

A lightbulb seemed to go off in Tek Raj's head as he jumped out of his chair. "Are you saying that my radio show is like a guru's *paloke*, powerful precisely because it is oral?" I nodded. He continued, talking a mile a minute, "And that in fact this orality is our Thangmi originality?"

"I think so," I said, "but that doesn't mean it's true." In that moment, Tek Raj seemed to grasp the contours of the totality that bound him—a well-educated and proudly modern young Thangmi—together with the nonliterate gurus whose practices he had once termed embarrassing, along with every other Thangmi individual.

Chapter 4

Circular Economies of Migration, Belonging, and Citizenship

Kumaiko ghumai, Chhetriko jal, Newarko lekhai, Thangmiko kal.
The Kumai's treachery, the Chhetri's trap, the Newar's forgery, the Thangmi's scalp.
　　　　　　　　　　　—Proverb in Nepali from Thangmi areas of Nepal

Chiyako botma sun phulchha.
Gold blooms on the tea bush.
　　　　　　　　　　　—Proverb in Nepali describing Darjeeling

The Missing Bampa

"I think you are ready to visit Khaldo Hotel," the young Rana Bahadur said to me conspiratorially one day in 2004 at the very end of my first extended stay in Darjeeling. Over the past several months, my eye had often rested on the hotel signboards that dotted the bazaar's steep lanes. There were the colonial curlicues of the Windamere at the top of Observatory Hill, the fruity-colored hues of the Amba Palace down in the center of town, and the Lunar Hotel's long, narrow sign atop a high Clubside building, pointing skyward toward its namesake (Figure 7). But Khaldo Hotel did not sound familiar. "Where's that?" I asked. "You know, you keep asking where the Thangmi laborers who come every year from Nepal stay. I'm trying to tell you that they stay at Khaldo Hotel." This revelation provoked both curiosity and frustration in me. In spite of the congenial roadside acquaintances

Figure 7. Darjeeling Bazaar, Darjeeling, West Bengal, India, January 2005. Photo by the author.

I had struck up with many of the Thangmi porters who spent their days outside looking for work, I had not yet been invited to their homes. This experience diverged sharply from what I had come to expect from my experiences with other groups of Thangmi in both Nepal and India, and I had been unable to solve the mystery of where they all went at night. So I swallowed my irritation and followed Rana Bahadur down the hill.

As we came to a busy intersection I had walked through many times before, he crossed the road and ducked under a low metal archway that appeared to lead into an unremarkable concrete building. But instead of heading up the stairs straight ahead of us, he ducked again into an opening so low I had trouble getting through it with my large backpack. We entered a tunnel-like passageway of the same height. As my eyes adjusted to the darkness, I shivered—it was several degrees colder in here, and very moist—and focused on the point of light coming from Rana Bahadur's cigarette lighter. After turning a few corners, I started to hear voices, and soon we came upon a family of four sitting in front of a wood-burning fireplace etched into the concrete floor. The woman was making tea and nursing a baby, while the man arranged some bags stuffed into a corner. An older child darted back and forth between his two parents. I was relieved when Rana Bahadur sat down by the fire and indicated to me to do the same, since the ceiling was not more than four feet above the floor and I was uncomfortably hunched over. "Welcome to Khaldo Hotel," Rana Bahadur said with a smile, and introduced me to the couple. "They are the proprietors here, you see. They rent this whole place every year"—he gestured further into the darkness—"and rent out rooms to the rest of them for fifty rupees a month." With the smile fading into a wry grin, he continued, "It's a 'full-service hotel,' you see, with meals, laundry, and any other facilities you need included."

I quickly realized that *khaldo* (N) meant "hole in the ground" and that the appropriately named "hotel" was in fact a subterranean warren of rooms in a defunct portion of Darjeeling's colonial sewer system. A corrupt government official managed to collect rent on the whole place from the Thangmi couple with whom we now sat. They were, in turn, somewhere in the middle of the pyramid scheme, collecting rent from approximately 150 Thangmi of all ages who spent the cold winter months living underground in this windowless cave where they could hardly stand up. Nonetheless, upon their return to Nepal, these tenants talked up the joys of Khaldo Hotel to would-be migrants back home. This year's residents were promised a free meal next year for every new renter they brought in.

Could the meager take-home earnings really be worth the privations of half a year, every year, spent in the Khaldo Hotel? Why did so many migrants continue to stay here every year rather than finding more pleasant, permanent places to settle in Darjeeling, as small but significant numbers of Thangmi had done since the late nineteenth century? Was there a more complex dynamic of exploitation and aspiration, social exclusion and belonging, attachment to territory and desire to leave it at play? I recalled the images of sweatshop labor and social mobility that characterized Ellis Island-era America and other well-trodden migrant routes all over the world, and my image of Darjeeling as a land of opportunity where Thangmi came from Nepal for easy economic benefit took a turn toward the more complicated.

The Khaldo Hotel's dingy concrete walls could not be more different from the Thangmi houses of stone, mud, wood, thatch, and occasional corrugated aluminum dotted across the rugged green hills of Nepal's Dolakha and Sindhupalchok districts (Figure 8). As one of Nepal's poorest and most socially excluded groups,[1] most Thangmi survive on small pieces of property that yield barely enough grain to feed families for half the year. Despite their limited resources, Thangmi villagers tend to take pride in their houses, seeing them as the embodiment of their attachment to the territory on which they live. Houses are the physical manifestation of their inhabitants' clan lineages; clan identification is often defined in terms of household rather than individual membership. In this sense, houses are an essential anchor of identity, demarcating the exclusively Thangmi domestic space of human action that determines both the quality of everyday life and the tenor of Thangmi relationships with the divine world.

In Nepal's oldest Thangmi houses—some of whose residents can trace their lineages back over a century to the era when regular migrations to Darjeeling began—the hearth is marked by the *bampa*, a large piece of flat rock rammed vertically into the floor (Figure 9). The *bampa*'s primary present-day function is as a windbreak to protect against the drafts that blow through rough-hewn doors left open in even the most inclement weather, but conjecturing about the *bampa*'s erstwhile ritual purpose is a favorite pastime while seated around the fire. Many Thangmi are eager to recover (or reimagine) the long-forgotten significance of this distinctive feature of Thangmi domestic design, from which one of the female clan

Figure 8. Thangmi houses in Suspa-Kshamawati, Dolakha, Nepal, October 2004. Photo by the author.

Figure 9. *Bampa* in a Thangmi household, Lapilang, Dolakha, Nepal. Photo by Tek Bahadur Thami.

names also derives. One popular explanation in contemporary Thangmi activist circles is that the solid, heavy stone is a symbol of both Thangmi resilience in the face of oppression and of their attachment to the land on which their houses stand. As we sat on the cold floor around the Khaldo Hotel fire, Rana Bahadur invoked these multiple meanings with a terse but revealing statement: "It's just like a Thangmi house, isn't it? Only the *bampa* is missing."

His words helped me understand the complex mixture of motivations that every year compel so many Thangmi to leave their homes in Nepal, where "the air and water are clean"—a stock phrase offered immediately by many Thangmi migrants when asked what they like most about their home village—to travel for days; cross the border into India; live for several months in the airless, waterless, underground urban squalor of a place like the Khaldo Hotel; and carry backbreaking loads up and down the bazaar's sloping roads. At the end of the season, these migrants return to Nepal for several months, often punctuated with short trips across Nepal's northern border to China's TAR, before starting the process over again. As a symbol of the twin experiences of oppression and attachment to territory that characterize Thangmi identities in Nepal, the *bampa*'s absence in migrant abodes like the Khaldo Hotel highlights the "push" and "pull" factors that contribute to Thangmi desires both to travel away from and then return to their home villages.

The Pragmatics of Cross-Border Migration

This chapter explores the pragmatics of Thangmi cross-border circular migration, locating its historical roots in the twin experiences of economic exploitation and social exclusion. In Europe, the phrase "the politics of belonging" (Yuval-Davis, Kannabiran, and Vieten 2006) has largely been used to describe the forms of exclusion and inclusion that permanent immigrants experience in the multicultural states that are their adopted homes. Applied to the Himalayan and South Asian contexts in which Thangmi migration takes place, the concept can usefully encapsulate the forms of inclusion and exclusion that people experience in their home countries and the migrations that such experiences may compel them to undertake. The Thangmi case also illuminates both the importance of single nation-states as frameworks within which belonging is defined and the forceful ways in which such frameworks are unsettled for those who regularly move across national borders (Basch, Glick-Schiller, and Szanton-Blanc 1994; Guarnizo and Smith 1998; Levitt 2001).

The history and ongoing circumstances of Thangmi circular migration provide a window into the transnational aspects of belonging in the Himalayas over time (Pfaff-Czarnecka and Toffin 2011; Toffin and Pfaff-Czarnecka 2014). Contemporary routes of migration from Nepal to Indian city centers, the Middle East, the United States, and beyond have received significant academic attention (Seddon, Adhikari, and Gurung 2001, 2002; Graner and Gurung 2003; Thieme 2006; Bruslé 2010), but the causes and effects of these more recent routes of migration can be better understood in relation to the long history of trans-Himalayan migration between Nepal and adjoining border regions of India and China that Thangmi experiences exemplify. The history and literature of the Nepali "diasporic" experience in northeastern India is also well-documented (Onta 1996a, 1996b, 1999; Hutt 1997, 1998; Chalmers 2003; Sinha and Subba 2003; Subba et al. 2009), but the same cannot be said of the contemporary cross-border connections between people of Nepali heritage in India and Nepal. This chapter takes an initial step toward filling these gaps by tracing the history of what we might call the "translocal" (Guarnizo and Smith 1998; Anthias 2006), "periphery-to-periphery" migration that results in Thangmi "transnational social formations" (Guarnizo and Smith 1998:27) built in corners of Nepal, India, and China, far from any of those countries' political or economic centers. Scholarship seeking to understand the full complexity of contemporary "transnational social spaces" (Pries 2001) must look beyond the global cities that serve as the focal point for transnationalism literature, exploring the full range of geographical and social scales on which such spaces may be embedded in villages, towns, and regional centers, and historicize contemporary formations in relation to long-term patterns of mobility.

I conceptualize "belonging" as the affirmation of the social self—in terms of both its existential presence and its potential for transformative action—that derives from a subjective experience of recognition from a range of agents. These might include the divine world, the state, members of one's own diverse collectivity, or broader constellations of collectivities functioning on local, national, regional, and transnational scales. Rather than seeking to evade the state (Scott 2009), Thangmi have over time sought to control the terms of recognition that govern their relationships with multiple states in order to craft a transnational sense of belonging. This relies upon an experiential understanding of citizenship as a multiple category, in which each country is understood to offer different and complementary aspects of the whole.

Conceptualizing belonging in this manner expands analytical frameworks emerging from the anthropology of migration. Focusing primarily on the economic implications of migration, Michael Kearney's concept of the "articulatory migrant network" (1986:353) builds upon Claude Meillasoux's writings (1981) to suggest that "households may reproduce themselves by participating in two spheres of production" (Kearney 1986:342), with the result that "two generically distinct economies become articulated in large part by circular migrant labor" (344). Kearney highlights the need for studies "of such complex articulation for an entire community . . . that deals with the corresponding articulation—in the second sense—of these variable socioeconomic activities and the corresponding changes in culture and consciousness" (355). In the two decades since Kearney wrote, the literature in this field has burgeoned, but the turn toward diaspora, transnationalism, and deterritorialization as framing concepts for such analyses has moved away from the careful consideration of how multiple modes of reproduction—both economic and social—come to articulate with each other through the experiences of circular migrants. Here I suggest that we might productively return to Kearney's framework to consider more closely not only the articulatory nature of the economic dimensions of circular migration but also of the social and cultural transformations that such circular movements, particularly those across national borders, effect. From this perspective, we can understand belonging as a process of articulation, which unfolds in the "spaces of cultural assertion" (Gidwani and Sivaramakrishnan 2003) that, for people like the Thangmi, emerge through the experience of circular migration.

To emphasize the intertwined political economies and kinship networks that characterize Thangmi experiences of cross-border circular migration, I borrow the term "transnational village" from Peggy Levitt (2001). The Thangmi situation is not an exclusively "diasporic" one, in which migrants leave home to permanently settle elsewhere. Rather, it is one in which the social and economic parameters of home villages are simultaneously augmented and maintained by the experience of migration. Although Thangmi migration initially began in response to economic and social pressures, in the present, circular migration is often a lifestyle choice, suggesting that Thangminess has become grounded in a transnational economy of belonging in which experiences of or, at the very least, knowledge of the particularities of multiple locations makes one's identity complete.

Put simply (and of course there is a great diversity of individual experiences), Thangmi are "richer" in Nepal than in India in terms of property ownership and cultural resources but "poorer" in terms of social inclusion and political resources, to which Thangmi in India have far greater access. Time spent in the TAR adds another dimension, which although typically short (for most not more than one month at a time owing to Chinese regulations), provides a reflective vantage point from which many Thangmi consider their long-term options in the other two countries. Acknowledging the contingent national histories that have led to different experiences in each location illuminates how both social and economic imperatives influence the pragmatics of cross-border migration, pushing and pulling in different directions to create the circular lives that many Thangmi choose. By continuing to move between Nepal, India, and the TAR, circular migrants make the best of three different but equally challenging worlds.

The experience of moving between multiple nation-states, and the multiple sociopolitical frameworks that such movement entails, becomes in itself a paradigmatic feature of Thangmi identity in action, both for those who move and those who stay put in one country or another. Migration strategies are often determined at the household level, with some members migrating regularly, while others stay in place. Kinship and community networks bring settled and migrant Thangmi into regular contact. In the bazaars of Darjeeling and Dram (the TAR border town that adjoins Nepal, also known as Khasa), "Thangmi" is often used as a generic term to refer to migrant porters, just as the term "Sherpa" has come to mean "mountaineer." For instance, a 1997 short story in Nepali entitled "Thamini Kanchi" (Adhikari 1997) uses the term "Thamini"—a feminized form of "Thami"—to describe a downtrodden woman working as a porter in Darjeeling bazaar. To their distress, relatively well-educated Thangmi born in Darjeeling who have never carried a heavy load find they are often assumed to be unskilled wage laborers from Nepal simply because of their name. In this way, the fact of circular wage migration impinges on the self-identifications of all Thangmi regardless of their individual economic or social positions.

In the transnational Thangmi village, notions of belonging as a whole are premised upon the simultaneously occurring experiences of property ownership within a caste-based agrarian system in Nepal, and the social mobility made possible by the comparative impossibility of private property and the concomitant absence of rigid land-based social hierarchies in Darjeeling. In other words, important aspects of Thangmi belonging are produced on both sides of the border, but neither set of experiences is complete without the other. Not all Thangmi individuals experience both worlds equally; rather, "Thangminess" is produced in a synthetic process through which diverse individuals, with as many life experiences in as many places, enact different pieces of the transnational puzzle to create an overarching framework of belonging that allows each individual to make sense of their particular piece.

Belonging in a Translocational World

Attempting to understand Thangmi circular migration and its resultant effects on identity with reference to either economic or social factors alone would miss the complexity of the situation. So would an approach that assumes that migrants primarily seek upward social mobility in a unidirectional manner, as would one that assumes that transnational migration to another country inherently entails a dislocation from one's place of origin or an erasure of national boundaries.

Rather, using the rubric of "belonging," with its focus on the "intersectionality" of different interests in a "translocational" world (Anthias 2006; Yuval-Davis, Kannabiran, and Vieten 2006), clarifies the interplay of forces at work in the Thangmi context. Moving beyond what they see as the fundamentally static nature of concepts like "diasporic identity" and "hybridity"—which despite recognizing multiple identities, compartmentalizes those identities into separate, building block-like components—theorists have used the notion of "belonging" to emphasize instead the processual intersectionality of people's experiences in different locations at different times. Belonging adds an emotive and experiential component to the rights-based notion of citizenship and an individual aspect to the group-based notion of ethnicity.

Furthermore, "belonging and social inclusion. . . . are closely connected. . . . It is through practices and experiences of social inclusion that a sense of a stake and acceptance in a society is created and maintained" (Anthias 2006:21). "Social inclusion" (or *samavesikaran* in Nepali) has become a buzzword within development discourses in South Asia, which tend to conflate the noble goal of such inclusion with the process of realizing it. As Hilary Silver explains, the concept of social inclusion originated in a European policy context, and its applications elsewhere do not always take full account of local histories and dynamics of inequality. Furthermore, "with all the attention to the participation of the excluded," she writes, "it is easy to elide these processes of policy-making with the policies themselves" (2010:200). In development-driven "social inclusion" discourse in South Asia, the importance of measurable indicators at the national level is frequently overemphasized, while the continued prevalence of deeply ingrained, localized practices of exclusion are glossed over. By adding an experiential, emotive aspect to the indicator-driven discussion of inclusion, adapting the concept of "belonging" to the South Asian setting encourages a necessary critical engagement with such discourses.

Thangmi live along a continuum of mobility—ranging from those who have never left Nepal or India to those who are constantly on the move, and everything in between. These experiences are shaped by specific histories of exploitation and exclusion, territorial attachment and movement, at individual, familial, and communal levels. Each Thangmi life is framed both by nation-state boundaries and the ever available prospect of moving across them. Discussions of belonging must therefore be carefully calibrated to the wide range of not only geographical but social locations that frame Thangmi experiences at different moments: the village, the hamlet, the city, the bazaar, the tea plantation, the ethnic organization office, the district magistrate's office, and so on. If belonging is understood to be only the practice and experience of social inclusion at the political level of the nation-state, then many Thangmi have historically not felt that they "belong" in Nepal. Despite the fact that most own property and hold the paper trappings of Nepali citizenship, historically few Thangmi believed they had the capacity to transform the political landscape of Nepal in ways that might grant them a greater sense of belonging. It was this sense of rigidity, and the lack of potential for change at the national level—no prospect of belonging—that compelled many older Thangmi to first make the journey to India. Yet recalling the figure of the *bampa* as a symbol of both resilience and rootedness, these same people felt very strongly that they belonged in their territory, in their villages, in places where they had long defined their own terms of belonging in relationship and resistance to local interethnic status hierarchies, such as those described further in Chapter 8.

Upon arrival in India, Thangmi have not always immediately experienced a greater sense of inclusion at the national level. In fact, their identification as foreigners with low economic status marked them strongly as outsiders. Nonetheless, the lack of rigid status hierarchies in Darjeeling has long afforded them an opportunity to craft their own sense of belonging through community organizations and political action, creating the potential to secure recognition at the national level. As will be described further in Chapter 5, the first Thangmi ethnic association in Darjeeling was registered in 1943, while the first such organization in Nepal was founded only forty-five years later. In comparison with Nepal, "within India . . . there was more potential for the founding of associations with implicit or explicit political aims, or at least social/religious reformist intentions" (Chalmers 2003:207). It was in large part this potential for future belonging, the hope that their children would not have to fight so hard for social inclusion, that kept and continues to keep Thangmi coming back to India. This sense of potential political belonging at the national level in India (which was lacking in Nepal until after 1990), paired with the strong sense of security in local, territorially based belonging in Nepal (which continues to be weak in India), creates a powerful recipe for a "transnational social formation" of belonging. The reproduction of this formation, this transnational village, with all of its social, economic, and cultural prerogatives, depends upon the continuation of circular migration. Indeed, as Creighton Peet noted in 1978, "Migration has in part served as a mechanism for culture maintenance for the Thamis" (1978:461).

Situated Histories of Exploitation and Exclusion in Nepal

The epigraph with which this chapter opened paints a bleak picture of the exploitation that many Thangmi feel characterizes their historical position within Nepal's interethnic socioeconomic order. What does it actually mean, and how does it relate to available historical and contemporary information about Thangmi property ownership, incomes, and inclusion, in other words, the empirical indicators of belonging?

Written records for the Thangmi in particular and the Dolakha region in general are sparse before 1950, but works by Mahesh Chandra Regmi (1980, 1981), Dhanavajra Vajracharya and Tek Bahadur Shrestha (2031 VS), and Mary Shepherd Slusser (1982) provide the basic historical contours regarding settlement patterns, landholding, and Thangmi relationships with other ethnic groups and the emergent Nepali state. Drawing primarily on these written sources, as well as oral histories, this section sketches early Thangmi economic history in Nepal. The following section links this information to census data from India and oral histories about early experiences of cross-border migration.

Kumaiko ghumai, Chhetriko jal . . . The term Kumai designates a Brahmin subcaste. Members of this group were some of the earliest high-caste settlers in historically Thangmi-populated areas of what are now Nepal's Dolakha and Sindhupalchok districts. Along with several Chhetri families, the Kumai began to arrive in the nineteenth century as the Shah dynasty expanded its eminent domain into previously independent parts of hill Nepal.[2] In the proverb, Kumai and Chhetri are both caricatured as slippery characters who exploit their Thangmi tenant farmers by giving them the runaround (*ghumai*) or entrapping them in a net (*jal*).

Newarko lekhai . . . The Newar community of Dolakha bazaar has historically occupied a position of economic and social dominance in the area.

As an important entrepôt on the Kathmandu-to-Lhasa trade route, Slusser suggests that the town of Dolakha was first developed as a Licchavi settlement (1982:85), and then became an independent principality ruled by the ancestors of today's Dolakha Newar population.[3] An inscription located inside the Bhimeshwor temple complex in Dolakha dated 688 in the Newar calendar of Nepal Sambat (AD 1568) includes a list of three social groups: *praja, saja,* and *thami.* Vajracharya and Shrestha suggest that *praja* refers to the Newar population; *saja* describes the inhabitants of the higher villages of Dolakha, such as the Sherpa and Tamang; and *thami* refers to the Thangmi (2031 VS:98). This inscription singles out the Thangmi as the only group that must pay taxes to the Newar rulers on demand, suggesting that a Thangmi community has resided in the villages surrounding the market town of Dolakha since at least the sixteenth century. These Thangmi were apparently compelled to pay taxes to Dolakha's Newar rulers. This potentially exploitative relationship was codified in writing (*lekhai*).

Thangmiko kal. . . . Thangmi narratives suggest that before they became subject to Bahun, Chhetri, and Newar domination, they held large swaths of *kipat* (N), ancestral property recognized by the Nepali state as the exclusive domain of single ethnic communities (Regmi 1976). The concept of *kipat* and its implications for contemporary identity politics are discussed further in Chapter 6. Here I explain how this land was appropriated by high-caste families originating from regions further west, who began to migrate to Dolakha in the mid-1800s. The Thangmi, in turn, moved east to Darjeeling and beyond. Buddha Laxmi of Dolakha's Suspa-Kshamawati VDC, who was in her late eighties at the time of my fieldwork, explained: "When I was a small child there were only ten houses in total between Pashelung and Ramedanda [two hamlets about one mile apart], and now there are ninety-six. There were three houses in Gumphung [another hamlet]; now there are nineteen. There was only one Budathoki [Chhetri] house then; now there are six. . . . Those people came later. They started to come in my grandfather's time; more came to give us trouble during my father's time. He had to go to court to defend his land. There were no positive relations between the Bahun-Chhetri and Thangmi, only fights."[4] This increase in population density and shift in land ownership was in part the result of the changing relationships between Dolakha and the central Nepali state. By the middle of the eighteenth century, although Dolakha remained nominally independent, the area's villagers came under the jurisdiction of King Jagajjaya Malla's tax collectors. Documents show that several villagers

registered complaints of harassment against his tax-collecting officials
(Regmi 1981:12–13). During the same period, the tradition of awarding
military officials and civil servants land tracts as *jagir* (N) in lieu of cash
payment began. After Prithvi Narayan Shah annexed Dolakha, this practice
became commonplace, with army officials receiving payments in land that
had previously been farmed by Thangmi. The redistribution of land accelerated under the rule of prime minister Bhimsen Thapa, who in 1862 VS
(1805–1806 AD) confiscated 82 *khet* (N), or 8,200 *muri* (N), of rice land in
Dolakha as *jagir* for the army (Regmi 1981:15).[5]

After first settling in the area on such *jagir* tracts, many of the less
scrupulous new migrants began appropriating further lands by acting as
moneylenders to their Thangmi neighbors. High interest rates of up to 60
percent per annum made it difficult for Thangmi to pay back their loans.
When a borrower defaulted, the lender would foreclose on his land. Furthermore, in a trend prevalent throughout eastern Nepal during that
period, newcomers enclosed *kipat* land by taking advantage of the Nepali
state's emerging regulation of landholding through the *raikar* (N) system
of tenure, which recognized the transferable and taxable nature of private
property for the first time (Caplan [1970] 2000; K. Pradhan 1991; Regmi
1976:ch. 10).

Man Bahadur, a village elder in Chokati, Sindhupalcok, described the
situation of diminishing trust as follows:

> Originally there were only Thangmi in this area. Eventually, the
> Bahun-Chhetri came and stole our land. In the old days, Thangmi
> would count their days of work by making marks on a piece of
> wood or making knots in a string. This habit was based on trust of
> each other, and trust between employers and employed. This trust
> was destroyed by the Bahuns. . . . What used to cost Rs. 2 (for land)
> now costs Rs. 20,000, so even a debt that sounds small of a few
> rupees was actually big. People had to work off their debt to the
> Bahuns by working on their land, and if they couldn't pay their
> debts in cash, they had to give up their land.

In this way, many Thangmi either fell deeply into debt or became tenant
sharecroppers on land they had previously controlled. However, most families were able to keep enough arable land to feed themselves for several

months of the year. With insufficient land to survive but too much to abandon, the economic scenario in Nepal's Thangmi villages at the end of the nineteenth century encouraged circular migration as a means of maintaining property ownership, while augmenting low agrarian yields with cash income.

The Beginnings of Migration to Darjeeling and Beyond

Chiyako botma sun phulcha. . . . At roughly the same historical moment that the appropriation of Thangmi land accelerated in the mid-nineteenth century, new income-generating opportunities were emerging in Darjeeling. In 1835, the British took control of this virtually uninhabited tract of forested land, which had earlier changed hands several times between the ruling powers of Nepal, Bhutan, and Sikkim. Darjeeling's strategically situated ridgeline, which overlooked the plains of Bengal to the south and the mountains of Sikkim to the north, was to become a bustling hill station for holidaying colonial administrators and the center of colonial tea production (Kennedy 1996; Q. Pradhan 2007). When the British first surveyed the area in 1835, they recorded a total population of only a hundred (Samanta 2000:21). Building infrastructure required workers, and the tea industry founded in the mid-1850s called for especially vast human resources. This is where the Thangmi and other migrants from Nepal came in.[6]

Many of the earliest Thangmi migrants worked on tea estates. First one or two men from a single village would establish themselves as trusted workers, eventually gaining promotion to overseer and recruiter.[7] Traveling back to Nepal every few years, they would return to the plantations with fresh new labor procured through their kinship networks. The tea plantation of Tumsong (often pronounced Tamsang) is a case in point, where the first Thangmi overseer arrived from Dolakha's Lapilang village in the late 1800s. Many Darjeeling Thangmi trace their ancestry to him. The Tumsong tea plantation maintains a majority Thangmi labor force to this day due to the rules of tenure and inheritance governing tea plantation jobs and accommodations since the colonial era.

Another important feature of Darjeeling's colonial tea economy was that almost all large tracts of land were owned by either government or private tea companies, with small allotments granted to plantation workers with temporary rights but no prospect for ownership (Subba 1989). Here

Thangmi migrants encountered for the first time a mode of economic production different from the subsistence economy they knew in Nepal. As the protagonist in Lainsing Bangdel's Nepali-language novel *Muluk Bahira* (Outside the Country) describes the situation he encountered in India upon emigrating from Nepal, "Although there was no land or *kipat* [ancestral land exempt from taxes] in Mugalan [India], one could earn enough to feed one's stomach" (as cited in Hutt 1998:203).

Besides tea, Darjeeling's other major attraction was the British army recruitment center, which opened in Darjeeling in 1857. Enlistment in the Gurkhas became a prize objective for many young men from Nepal's so-called "martial races," a group from which the Thangmi were excluded, as described in Chapter 1. But this did not stop some Thangmi from joining up under assumed names and living a double life as Rai, Gurung, or Magar.

The British preference for certain "races" did not apply to nonenlisted men responsible for road building and other support services, and many Thangmi were contracted by the army on a daily wage basis to work in Darjeeling, Sikkim, Assam, and as far afield as Bhutan and Arunachal Pradesh on road-building gangs. When I asked where they had worked, many older Thangmi said simply, "We went to the 'road.'" Often, they did not know the specific places in which they had worked, and the English term "road" denoted the transient road-building sites that defined their experience.

The rapid development of Darjeeling and its environs, through the powerful combination of tea, resorts, roads, and a strategic border to defend, led to "the most rapid rate of growth on record for nineteenth-century Bengal" (Kennedy 1996:184). By 1881, 88,000 residents of Darjeeling had been born in the district, making up over 60 percent of the total district population (Samanta 2000:22). It is hard to know how many of these were Thangmi. The 1872 Census of India lists 13 Thangmi speakers in Darjeeling, a number that had risen to 319 by 1901 (Grierson 1909:280). However, these numbers are just the beginning of the contentious politics of the census for Thangmi in both India and Nepal. Due to self-misrepresentation of themselves as members of other groups (largely for army recruitment purposes) and the preference for the Nepali language as a lingua franca in Darjeeling's multiethnic context, it is likely that these census figures, which are based on language rather than ethnicity, substantially underrepresent the real numbers of Thangmi. "We spoke Thangmi secretly," explained a senior Thangmi resident of Darjeeling about language use there during the early part of the century. Thangmi were as eager as the rest to be included in the emergent pan-Nepali identity, with the Nepali language as its cornerstone; so speaking Thangmi in public was not a popular practice.

Pre-1950 Narratives of Migration:
Seeking Employment and Inclusion

The narratives presented in this section from Thangmi who migrated from Nepal to Darjeeling before 1950 emphasize different motivations for migration but share a desire to leave behind the land pressure, debt, and social exclusion of rural Nepal. They highlight the relatively unstructured, unhierarchical nature of Darjeeling society at the time, at least in comparison to Nepal. Since everyone in Darjeeling was a migrant, the opportunities for caste-based exploitation through land appropriation, a dynamic endemic to Nepal's agrarian setting, were reduced in Darjeeling's emerging cash economy. This representation of Darjeeling's tea economy as relatively egalitarian stands in contrast to much literature representing the tea industry as a highly classed domain rife with exploitation (Besky 2013; Bhowmik 1981; Chatterjee 2001). Recall that here the contrast is between Darjeeling and Nepal, and although class-based exploitation may be a central feature of tea production in India, such dynamics were not tied to group identity and territory in the same way that they were in Nepal. Tea plantation workers in India therefore possessed a modicum of mobility that far exceeded that available in Nepal, where people felt fixed in both geographical and social place.

Bir Bahadur (no relation to my research assistant by the same name), who was born in Dolakha's Lapilang village and engaged in circular migration for many years before finally settling in Darjeeling, explained, "My father had a loan. I came back here [to Darjeeling] after paying it off. In one month, it accrued Rs. 10 interest on Rs. 100. It was a loan from Lapilang's *maila* [N: middle brother] headman. In those days, they really oppressed us. Because they were rich and we were poor, they had us harnessed to the plow like oxen. It's not like that here [in Darjeeling]." Bir Bahadur's pride at being able to pay back his father's loan after a few seasons of work in Darjeeling was evident and demonstrates one of the economic imperatives that initially made circular migration an attractive strategy for many Thangmi from Nepal. By earning cash in Darjeeling, where migrants could keep costs low by staying in cheap accommodations like the Khaldo Hotel and then using it to pay off debts back in Nepal, Thangmi could ensure that their ancestral property was not appropriated by creditors. As another migrant who paid off debts with Darjeeling-earned cash put it, "We were able to keep our *bampa*." However, most earned just enough to pay off their debts and maintain the status quo but not enough to actually transform the socioeconomic order. As Peet observed, "For the majority of Thamis . . . circular migration has brought just enough income to pay off debts and regain some economic independence from the moneylenders and large landowners. Much of their earnings go, in fact, into the hands of their wealthy Bahun-Chhetri patrons and thus help to support this latter group's dominant position in the community" (1978:461). This assessment matches Kearney's more general observation that rather than leading to improvement as one might expect, "remittances perpetuate status quo underdevelopment" (1986:47). To understand why circular migration continues, we need to look more closely at the impact of what Peggy Levitt calls "social remittances" (2001), and the transformative potential of the new forms of "body politics" that Vinay Gidwani and Kalyanakrishnan Sivaramakrishnan (2003) identify as emergent in the process of circular migration itself.

The late Harka Bahadur, an elderly stalwart of the Thangmi community in Darjeeling, who became known as "Amrikan" because he had worked with American soldiers in Burma during World War II in an army support role, described a different scenario. His parents' relatively substantial property holding in Nepal became inadequate because of a surfeit of sons, leading him to test the greener pastures of Darjeeling's cash economy. As the youngest of six brothers, Amrikan knew that he would have little chance of inheriting an adequate piece of ancestral property. Contrary to Peet's conclusion that birth order and family size were not in themselves predictive of who might migrate (1978:386), men like Amrikan were very conscious of their unique constellation of family size, sibling order, and land inheritance as they made choices for ongoing circular migration or permanent settlement in Darjeeling. Amrikan's position at the bottom of a big family's age-status order did not inevitably lead him to migrate to Darjeeling and ultimately settle there; for many other migrants, superficially similar backgrounds led to different choices, as for the man who decided to settle in Darjeeling because, as he explained, "my youngest brother 'ate' all of our land." Rather, each individual's family situation strongly conditioned the range of options they might choose.

Amrikan described his first impressions of Darjeeling like this:

When I first came here, while I was looking for work, I could tell Thangmi from their faces, and I would also ask, "Are you Thangmi?" And when they said, "We are Thangmi," I would ask, "Where are you from?" And when they said, "We are from Dolakha Dui Number," then we knew each other.[8] That was a good time. Ethnicity was not that important, it was only much later that there was any competition. At that time, you could earn one or two *anna* [N: coin = 1/16 of a rupee] a day; putting it all together in a week you'd have 10 or 15 *anna*. In this place full of money, we were all equal.

Amrikan's description, although perhaps nostalgically utopian, suggests that in Darjeeling, social exclusion was not the insurmountable problem for Thangmi that it had been in Nepal. The fixed agrarian hierarchies that Thangmi migrants had known in their village homes came unmoored in this "place of money," where everyone had an "equal" chance.

Silipitik, a senior figure in Dolakha's Pashelung village, who engaged in circular migration for most of his life but eventually settled in Nepal, described his contrasting experiences in the two countries as follows:

Over there [Darjeeling], no one talked about ethnicity or status unless you were in the army. Here [Nepal], everyone is always harping on about it, who is high and who is low, who is big and who is small. There everyone just worked hard. I remember a speech I heard once in Judge Bazaar [one of Darjeeling's central public squares], where a man said, "Here, there is no caste and no ethnicity, no high and no low. Here, there are only two categories we need to know about, male and female. There are no other divisions in our society."[9] I liked what he said so much, I never forgot it. There, it really was that way, here it never will be. I only came back because I had no brothers and had to care for my mother and our land when she got old; otherwise I would have stayed in that place where people could make speeches like that.

Silipitik's reminiscences of this speech, which he repeated to me on several occasions, encapsulated a powerful moment in the development of his awareness of the different frames that Nepal and India offered for the articulation of belonging. Both in listening to the speech and reflecting on it years later, he became aware of the ways in which his own life was marked by the hierarchies and structures of each location and nation-state he had experienced in his life of circular migration and the choices he had ultimately made between them.

Silipitik, like most Thangmi migrants, had been to Tibet several times before ever traveling to Darjeeling. Although they would travel north from their Himalayan border homes to the towns of Dram/Khasa and Nyalam/Kuti (as the towns were called in Tibetan and Nepali respectively) to trade their grain for salt several times a year, Thangmi never developed trading conglomerates like those well-documented among the Sherpa, Newar, Thakali, and Manangi communities (von Fürer-Haimendorf 1975; J. Fisher 1986; Lewis 1993; Vinding 1998; Watkins 1996; van Spengen 2000). Instead, they traveled alone or in small groups on the rough trail that brought them directly over the mountains to Khasa and Kuti.

Dhanbir, a Thangmi man from Dolakha who had been to Tibet many times in his youth, described his most enduring memories: "The Tibetans called us *rongsha* or *rongba* [Tib: lowlander]. They didn't think we Thangmi were different from other Nepalis. Everyone from this area traveled up there: Thangmi, Newar, Tamang, even Bahun and Chhetri. The Tibetans were friendly and didn't seem to differentiate between ethnic groups, either within their own community or among Nepalis." From an outsider's perspective at least, in Tibet as in Darjeeling, ethnicity did not fix one in place geographically, socially, or economically in the same way it did back in Nepal.[10] Certainly, Thangmi were different from Tibetans, but they were not categorized as low status or exploited as such. Some Thangmi had Tibetan *mit* (N), a fictive kin relation created between trading partners from different ethnic groups. This fact was often recounted to emphasize the relatively egalitarian nature of Thangmi relationships with Tibetans. In these ways, the local status hierarchies that structured Thangmi lives in Nepal were unsettled by contrasting experiences in Tibet as well as India.

The proximity of many Thangmi villages to Khasa and Kuti meant that until the Sino-Nepali border became more difficult to cross after the early 1950s as China occupied the area, most immediate trading needs were met in these Tibetan towns. Between these trading trips to the north and wage labor in Darjeeling, there was little need for Thangmi to travel to Kathmandu. Few Thangmi visited the city until much later, a fact that suggests the Nepali nation-state, with Kathmandu at its political center, was not the most prominent frame of reference for the definition of belonging. Rather, Thangmi had a trans-Himalayan sense of belonging, grounded in the particular localities of Dolakha, Sindhupalchok, Darjeeling, Sikkim, Khasa, Kuti and beyond. Maintaining this translocational formation of belonging—and the economic strategies that supported it—depended upon regular movement across borders rather than upon strong legal or emotional ties to a single nation-state.

Why did so many Thangmi continue to practice circular migration instead of settling permanently in India, as significantly higher numbers of other ethnic groups of Nepali heritage did?[11] Several factors seem to have been at play. First, the Thangmi population in Darjeeling was tiny compared that of other groups. The 1872 ensus that enumerated 13 Thangmi also listed 6,754 Rai 6,567 Tamang and 1,120 Newar. With so many more members, other ethnic groups of Nepali heritage were better situated to recreate their communities in full in a new location. By contrast, Thangmi may have felt uncomfortable settling permanently in a place where they were so few in number and it was difficult to create social networks and maintain cultural practices like funerary rites. Second, although one tea estate did have a majority Thangmi workforce as described above, this was an exception rather than the norm. In general, most Thangmi survived on short-term wage labor and had no rights to settle on tea estate property. Combined with lack of easy access to lucrative army jobs, these factors meant that in comparison other groups, Thangmi long-term prospects in Darjeeling were relatively insecure, although the short-term earnings could be substantial.

Ultimately, although the structures of social exclusion so prevalent in Nepal were substantially softened in Darjeeling, the reality was far from Amrikan or Silipitik's nostalgic descriptions of an egalitarian utopia. While "those entering Darjeeling were free from the Muluki Ain promulgated in Nepal" (K. Pradhan 2004:11)—free from the *structures* of oppression as legislated by the Nepali state—they were not necessarily free from the *practices* of oppression that traveled with migrant Nepalis to Darjeeling. Such hierarchies did not disappear overnight, and despite the potential for economic mobility, Thangmi continued to be treated as inferior by other Nepali migrants. As the Nepali community in Darjeeling began to fashion a self-consciously modern ethnic identity within India in the early twentieth century, its scions sought to excise evidence of "backwardness," of which poor migrant laborers from Nepal, like most Thangmi, were constant reminders. Chalmers explains that "an inevitable concomitant of the emergence of a more concrete and precisely defined conception of Nepaliness was the parallel development of new paradigms of exclusion" (2003:172). The historical details of how Thangmi experienced this exclusion and how they set about rectifying it through social and political engagement will be discussed in Chapter 5. In this kind of environment—where Thangmi were not so badly exploited and excluded as they were in Nepal but were not exactly included either—perhaps it made good sense to hedge their bets by maintaining ownership of the small pieces of property in Nepal on which their sense of territorial belonging was premised.

Nation-States on the Rise and the Making of Multiple Citizens

Three historical events around 1950 radically altered the political contexts that framed Thangmi transnational social formations: Indian independence in 1947 and the ensuing Indo-Nepal Friendship Treaty of 1950; Nepal's first period of democracy in 1950–51; and China's occupation of Tibet from 1949 onward. On the one hand, these events mark key moments in state formation for each country, at which ideas of citizenship and national boundaries were newly concretized. On the other hand, they signal the creation of new resources for the production of belonging by trans-Himalayan populations like the Thangmi. The year 1950 is also the magic date after which James Scott claims that his analysis of "ungoverned" peoples in highland Asia "makes no further sense" (2009:11). In the trans-Himalayan context, 1950 was indeed a watershed of sorts, but this date marks not the end of processes of state enclosure but rather the beginning of ever greater self-consciousness and intentionality among border populations in crafting multifaceted strategies for controlling the terms of recognition, and therefore asserting belonging, vis-à-vis multiple states.

The 1950 Indo-Nepali Friendship Treaty for the first time defined the notion of citizenship in a way that mattered for Thangmi circular migrants. The treaty stipulates an open border between Nepal and India, with no documents necessary to transit across it. Article 7 grants reciprocal rights of residence. But the arrangement does not provide any mechanism for people originating in one country to become full citizens of the other. As citizens of India with Nepali heritage experience it today, the problem is that "according to the treaty every Nepali-speaking person in India is a temporary citizen of the country" (Timsina 1992:51), and "those who are Indian nationals cannot easily prove their citizenship when the Treaty makes no distinction between them and Nepalese nationals" (Hutt 1997:124). For people accustomed to moving back and forth between Nepal and India, the treaty introduced new ideas about singular citizenship within a clearly bounded nation-state that accorded citizens "rights" in exchange for exclusive allegiance. Hutt's discussion of early Nepali language literature on migration confirms this point: "There are very few references in these texts to the political entities of Nepal and India: the émigrés move between Pahar and Mugalan" (1998:202).

The late Latte Apa, who was originally from Alampu village in Dolakha, explained: "When we first came, we did not say 'this is Nepal' and 'this is India.' We had to walk for ten or twelve days through the hills, and one day was no different from the next. It was only when we saw the train that we said, 'This must be India.' We knew that there was no train in Nepal. And then there were the *saheb* [the British]. They did not come to Nepal. Only after they left was there trouble. Then people said 'Are you Indian?' and we had to think about it." Many Thangmi described the early 1950s as a challenging time to be in India. Questions of national allegiance were on the table, and those who wanted to stay felt hard-pressed to demonstrate their Indianness. It was at this historical moment that some Darjeeling Thangmi, such as the Tumsong tea plantation family, intentionally attempted to sever their ties with their brethren in Nepal in order to assimilate their linguistic and cultural practices into the Indian mainstream. As Tumsong's patriarch explained to me, "My father said, 'Our family has been here for generations. You are not to talk with those from Nepal. We do not need the Thangmi language or guru; those are for the *pahar*, not for India.'" Other Thangmi took the opposite approach, such as the guru Rana Bahadur. As described in Chapter 3, he decided that this was the moment to return permanently to Nepal, where the promise of democracy and land reform offered the tempting prospect that the social order might soon become more flexible. Such returnees brought back all they had learned in India, in many cases remaining both socially and economically linked to Darjeeling, and sending their children to work there later while slowly expanding their property base in Nepal with the money they had earned.

For the vast majority, however, these changes were only a temporary disturbance until they came to understand the new system and realized that they could procure at least some of the documents of citizenship in both locations. Such documents did not change others' attitudes toward them—in India they would always be stereotyped as Nepali, and in Nepal those born in India would be stereotyped as outsiders—but these trappings of "paper citizenship" (Sadiq 2008) did provide legal instruments with which to maintain property ownership in Nepal while simultaneously working in India.

Neither Nepal nor India grants citizenship automatically at birth. In Nepal it must be "made" (N: *nagarikta banaunu*), while in India, people speak of "registering" themselves as citizens. Although these processes can make it difficult for deserving citizens to obtain papers, from another perspective, the intentionality required accords a certain level of agency to prospective citizens to choose which combination of documents they want. Many Thangmi originally from Nepal alluded to the fact that obtaining some Indian documents—particularly voter registration cards—was not difficult. From the first post-Independence elections onward, local politicians in Darjeeling viewed circular migrants as a secret weapon to boost their voter base and were eager to register them as voters. Although the ration card was supposed to precede the voter card, with the latter issued on the basis of the former, many Thangmi worked the system in reverse, obtaining a ration card by showing their voter card and complaining that they had not received or had lost the former.

In Nepal, the *nagarikta* citizenship document must be applied for after the age of sixteen on the basis of one's father's citizenship in the locality in which the father is, or was, registered. As long as the father holds citizenship, the son is entitled to it in that locality regardless of whether he was born there or has ever lived there.[12] For Darjeeling Thangmi families, keeping the inheritance of *nagarikta* alive became an important strategy for maintaining property in Nepal, since non-Nepali citizens may not own land. Many young Thangmi men born in Darjeeling described their first trip to Nepal as a rite of passage at the age of sixteen or soon thereafter to "make" their citizenship and visit their family's ancestral land holdings. Several of the men who told me such stories had fathers, grandfathers, and great grandfathers born in Darjeeling—but all still held Nepali *nagarikta*. Nepali citizenship has become a much sought-after commodity for Thangmi from India who wish to work abroad in the Middle East or beyond, since popular wisdom holds that it is much easier to get a visa as a Nepali than as an Indian. In all of these ways, holding documentary citizenship from more than one country has become the norm rather than the exception for many Thangmi. Few people I interviewed felt conflicted over their obligations to more than one nation-state. Rather, they stated that given their level of social exclusion at the national level in Nepal and their lack of property ownership in India, both states in a way owed them the opportunity to also belong to the other.

While notions of citizenship and national borders were defined between India and Nepal, the Chinese occupation of Tibet that began in 1949 led to a decade-long tightening of the northern border across which Thangmi had long traveled. The opening of a redefined border in 1960 altered Thangmi notions of belonging at the national level, as this quotation from Dhanbir illustrates:

> In those days, Kuti [Nyalam] was closer and easier to reach than Kathmandu. We did most of our business in Kuti. We did not think of Kuti as a very different country, although it was high up in the mountains and people spoke a different language, like they did in Dolakha and Sailung [parts of Nepal where Newar and Tamang were respectively spoken]. There was no border or "checking." You had to store your *khukuri* [N: large curved knife] with local headmen when you arrived and pay tax to them when you left. But suddenly the border closed and everything changed. We heard that the Chinese had come and now Kuti was theirs. We could not go. From then on we had to go to Kathmandu, before that there was no reason to go there.

Political changes in a neighboring nation-state contributed toward reorienting Thangmi relationships with their own. With Kuti inaccessible, Thangmi began traveling to Kathmandu more regularly to procure basic goods, and concomitantly began to conceptualize themselves as citizens within Nepal's national framework. However, there were no roads from the Thangmi region to Kathmandu until the mid-1960s,[13] and walking to Kathmandu from Thangmi villages took up to a week—not much less than going all the way to Darjeeling. Moreover, there were few immediate opportunities for work in Kathmandu, since the unskilled labor positions that Thangmi would have qualified for were already filled by others, largely low-caste Jyapu Newar and Tamang from villages closer to the city. This meant that although Kathmandu became the desired destination for short-term trading, the Chinese occupation of Tibet did not significantly affect established patterns of circular labor migration to Darjeeling.

The changes in Tibet did, however, create one other option for a small subgroup of Thangmi who lived at the northernmost fringe of the region, right up against what was to become the Sino-Nepali border in the Lapchi area. In 1960, China and Nepal entered into a series of boundary agreements and treaties, which included a strategic trade of two villages previously in Nepal for two villages previously in Tibet (Shneiderman 2013b). Although they were a minority in these predominantly Sherpa villages, several Thangmi families were affected by these events. Along with the rest of the villagers, they were given the option of staying in their homes and becoming Chinese citizens (with no easy option for dual citizenship since China enforced borders and identity documents rigorously), or moving away to remain Nepali citizens. A small number of Thangmi chose to become Chinese, but in doing so, they were assimilated into the dominant Sherpa group in the area, who were listed as a distinctive "border population" (although not one of the fifty-six *minzu*, or ethnic minorities) by the national classification projects of Chinese ethnology in the 1950s (Mullaney 2010). Some Thangmi derided the choices of these individuals at the time, but such critics were forced to reconsider later when China leapt ahead of Nepal economically. During my fieldwork in the TAR in 2005, I encountered several Thangmi from Nepal who were attempting to claim Chinese citizenship in Nyalam and Dram through certification as Chinese Sherpa, usually by marriage to bona-fide Chinese citizens but occasionally through protracted residence on temporary labor permits. Those trying to claim Chinese citizenship were only a very small percentage of the much larger numbers of Thangmi who spent one month at a time in this Sino-Tibetan-Nepali border zone, taking advantage of the Sino-Nepali border treaty that allows so-called "border citizens" to travel up to thirty kilometers into the other country without a passport or visa (Shneiderman 2013b).

The Future of Circular Migration and Thangmi Belonging

Since the 1950s, ideals of national identity have become ever clearer in all three countries. Constitutions have been propagated, national languages promoted, and the symbolic repertoires of national hegemony solidified. While in some circumstances, Thangmi have sought to evade or even subvert such state-promoted paradigms for belonging, the more enduring image that emerges from the narratives here is one of what we might call circular citizens. Over time, Thangmi have cobbled together a complex sense of belonging reliant upon a balance of rights and obligations lived out in the diverse localities of their transnational village. That village is embedded in multiple nation-states on all of which Thangmi make different but complementary claims. Neither complete citizenship nor total belonging is ever attained within the borders of a single state; rather, circular citizenship entails regular movement across nation-state borders in order to piece together the differentiated prospects for belonging that each national framework offers.

Circular migration between Thangmi areas of Nepal and Darjeeling remains alive and well. In fact, both the numbers of Thangmi migrants in India and China and the duration of their stays increased during the Maoist-state conflict in Nepal. (During Darjeeling's Gorkhaland agitation in the late 1980s, the opposite had occurred.) Yet Nepal's civil conflict, along with other local, national, and international dynamics of development and migration, has also brought about a new set of opportunities for Thangmi in Nepal. These dynamics have combined to create a substantial outmigration of Bahun and Chhetri individuals and families from Dolakha and Sindhupalchok. Some have gone to Kathmandu, while others have moved to Charikot (Dolakha's district headquarters) or Bahrabise, both emergent regional centers, to start businesses or to work in government or development. Still others have joined the growing number of international Nepali migrants going to study or work in white-collar jobs in urban India, the Middle East, Southeast Asia, the United States, and Europe. All of these lifestyle transformations require substantial amounts of capital—to buy land in Kathmandu, invest in a business in a regional town, or finance a ticket abroad—so over the last decade, many of the high-caste landowners of the region have divested themselves of substantial portions of their property. In response, in what we might see as an example of what Tania Li has called indigenous "microcapitalism" (2010), Thangmi have formed cooperatives to buy land vacated by those who once used it as a tool of exploitation against them.

Where has the money for such purchases come from? In part from newly emerging sites of wage labor closer to home—a Thangmi-owned slate mine in Alampu (Kharel 2006), chicken farms and furniture factories, hydropower plants, and road construction projects, to name a few—that allow workers to keep more of their hard-earned wages by living and eating at home. Some individuals have also taken out low-interest loans from

microcredit institutions like the Agricultural Development Bank in order
to finance land purchases, which they are then able to pay back over time
with money saved from living off their own land.

As Bir Bahadur, one of the early migrants quoted above, said about the
changed situation in Nepal from his vantage point in Darjeeling, "Now
they can't oppress us; the Thangmi have won and the Chhetri have all gone
to Kathmandu." He had heard about these shifts from his nephews, who
continued to travel back and forth between Nepal and India. Why were
they still doing so if the environment was indeed now more favorable
in Nepal? "It's fun to travel with my friends and see how things are done
in other places. Also I don't have to eat off of my parents' land," said one
young migrant. Another older man added, "It's how we Thangmi enjoy
ourselves."

Recalling that choices for circular migration were historically diversified
across families throughout the entire transnational social formation, a
range of options continues to be available and desirable. Even for families
who have expanded their landholdings in Nepal, an actual increase in grain
yield may take several years to realize, and in the meantime, it is helpful if
young, able-bodied members live away from home and feed themselves for
several months of the year. Moreover, the trends of microcapitalism and
economic development closer to home are new enough that they have yet
to benefit substantial numbers of Thangmi. Finally, although Nepal's civil
conflict created opportunities for some, the uncertainties and pressures that
came along with it made others want, or need, to leave. For all of these
reasons, circular migration has continued to be practiced by many Thangmi
as a way to "enjoy" (N: *ramaunu*) an otherwise difficult life by seeing other
parts of the world, and perhaps most importantly, other parts of one's own
community. As the choice of such expressions indicates, some component
of belonging may be found in the camaraderie of migration itself.[14]

Turning from the economic to the social, prospects for national belonging in Nepal—"social inclusion"—have improved substantially with the
political transformations of the last several years. Many Thangmi have
sought to capitalize on these opportunities by engaging in political activism
within the frameworks of both ethnic and party politics, as will be discussed
in the next chapter. But again, such activities are part of a larger transnational social formation, and many of those Thangmi individuals most
involved in politics in Nepal trace their activist interests to experiences of
social inclusion and political activism in India, where the potential for such

practices of belonging was visible far earlier. As a former general secretary of the Nepal Thami Samaj explained, "It was only when I went to visit my relatives in Darjeeling and Sikkim in the late 1990s that I understood that we had rights we could demand from the state. At first I wanted to stay there, it was so exciting. But then I thought, 'We can do this in Nepal too, slowly such things will become possible.'" He, like an increasing number of travelers in both directions, did not go to India for wage labor but for what we might call "belonging tourism," in which they went to see how the other half lived. In the other direction, Thangmi born and bred in India also began visiting Nepal regularly in the late 1990s as transportation improved and they became interested in documenting cultural heritage for the purposes of their ST application to the Indian state.

One of the things that Thangmi from India are most eager to see on visits to Nepal are old Thangmi houses with the *bampa* intact. In the late 2000s, a group of politically active Thangmi in Dolakha, many of whom are also part of the buy-back-the-land trend, developed a proposal to make one of the oldest houses in Dolakha with its prominent *bampa* a museum and "cultural heritage site" for Thangmi everywhere. Funding was sought and received from local, national, and international organizations. For Thangmi from India, this idea fulfilled their desires for a link to ethnic territory and ancestral property, as well as being a recognizable heritage site. For Thangmi from Nepal, it signified resilience, and their slow but sure progress toward ending land-based exploitation and achieving social inclusion. For those who continue to move back and forth, this particular house and its *bampa* mark just one point of belonging among many.

Chapter 5

Developing Associations of Ethnicity and Class

> These days, the organization is only concerned with making history,
> it doesn't do social welfare.
> —Nathu, former BTWA treasurer

> We Thami people are in the darkness
> Let us now move toward light
> Let us educate our children
> Let us develop the language and the culture of our ethnicity
> Rather than only hunting in the forest and
> Searching for underground fruits
> Let us use Thami hands in development
> Let us Thami come together
> And join efforts in the development of our country
> Even though we are backward today
> We can go forward tomorrow.
> —Excerpt from the Thangmi-language poem
> "We Must Open the Eyes of Our Soul" by Buddhi Maya Thami
> (Kaila and Yonzon 2056 VS:43)

A faded black-and-white photograph, reproduced in various sepia shades, in so many sizes. Sometimes it is a poster affixed to a wall, laminated against thick plyboard. Sometimes it is pulled out of a wallet, paper thin, scrunched up with the detritus of daily life. On still other occasions, it is a smooth, glossy print, carefully filed in a folder tied with string, sharing space with neatly typed photocopies, which like the photograph seem to take on authority simply by virtue of repeated reproduction and respectful storage. The photograph is always presented with pride.

Whose faces can we make out (Figure 10)? Seated on the ascending levels of a terraced field, twenty or so small children are in the front row, girls in pigtails, boys in tailored jackets. Behind them stand four rows of adults, mostly men wearing *topi* (N) and the telltale flower garlands of a formal event.[1] Several women wear heavy nose rings and shawls draped over their heads. Some smile, even laugh—very different from the sober poses that characterize Thangmi portraiture today. In the center, one man holds a *madal* (N), the two-sided oblong drum whose rhythms mark most important events in Thangmi life. In the upper right-hand corner, a man brings his hands together, offering *namaste* to the camera.

It is 1943 in Darjeeling, at the first formal meeting of the Bhai Larke Thami Samaj (BLTS), the Thangmi organization that would evolve into the Bharatiya Thami Welfare Association (BTWA) half a century later. Or so I am told, again and again, by Thangmi men and women in Darjeeling who eagerly show me this photo—whatever form their own copy takes—when I come calling with questions about Thangmi history. Could the man pictured here have imagined that six decades later his *namaste* would greet a researcher like me—or bureaucrats, activists, and curious Thangmi themselves—proffered as black-and-white evidence of a certain kind of Thangmi history? Not just a history of migrant labor, but one of social organization, cultural practice, and associational capacity.

Sometimes this 1943 photo was presented as one among several in a family collection. The earliest photos show a larger group of similarly attired people splayed out across a hillside, with the penciled notation "Mahakal 1936" now affixed as an integral part of the photo itself (Figure 11). Here too, a man in the upper right-hand corner gestures *namaste* toward the camera. Another photo shows a smaller group of subjects against the backdrop of a wood-paneled interior, seated on chairs behind a black signboard with white letters spelling out "Jyoti Thami Pry-School 1945." Both children and adults are more formally dressed than in the other two photos, and the latter are adorned with *katha* (Tib), white offering scarves in the Tibetan style. Bowler hats and knit caps have taken the place of *topi* for most men, while many women have uncovered heads. This time it is a woman, seated near the center, who offers *namaste*.

Figure 10. Believed to be the first formal meeting of the Bhai Larke Thami Samaj, Darjeeling, 1943. Photo provided by the BTWA.

Figure 11. Believed to be the first photographed public Thangmi gathering, Mahakal, Darjeeling, 1936. Photo provided by the BTWA.

The Mahakal 1936 photo, I am told, shows the first public Thangmi gathering in Darjeeling, although several people from other groups were present as well. The group had assembled for Bhadau Purnima, celebrated as an annual festival across the hills of Nepal in August-September, when Thangmi shamans make the pilgrimage to the high peak of Kalinchok. In 1936, Bhadau Purnima marked the inauguration of a new shrine at the Mahakal temple on top of Darjeeling's Observatory Hill. Several community organizations had donated temple bells. One bell was sponsored by the Thangmi in the photo, although their organization did not yet have a name. Now, at the beginning of the twenty-first century, thousands of bells are tangled across the ever-expanding Mahakal temple complex. When I ask to see it, no one can find the bell donated by Thangmi in 1936, not even Latte Apa, who knows the hillside's labyrinth of worship sites well.[2] That the object cannot be located does not seem to matter to Thangmi, for whom oral traditions often stand in for tangible cultural objects. The act of pouring hard-earned wages into a cast bronze bell takes on the status of origin myth for many contemporary Thangmi activists in India.

The 1943 image is complemented by an incontrovertible piece of evidence indicating that a named and registered organization existed by that year: a rubber stamp kept in a lockbox in the BTWA office bears the year 1943, along with the BLTS name and logo. I am told that the 1943 image shows, for the first time, an exclusively Thangmi group, which had just anointed its members with flower garlands to mark their organization's registration as a legal entity. Clearly pleased with their accomplishment, the assembly still looks somewhat ragtag and rustic, squatting on an anonymous hillside. By the time the 1945 photo was taken, they are seated on chairs inside their own school, where Nepali and other standard subjects were taught for several years before it closed due to lack of funds in the early 1960s. The very fact that the Thangmi school existed, however briefly, tells us that there must be more than meets the eye in the historical narrative of a pan-Nepali national identity created through Nepali language literary production in Darjeeling during this era (Onta 1996a, 1996b, 1999; Hutt 1997, 1998; Chalmers 2003).

Taken together, these photos reveal much about the origins of Thangmi ethnic organization. They also serve as an inverted lens through which contemporary Thangmi activists view themselves and their history, refracting the multiple meanings of activism through half a century of Indian and Nepali nation-making. When Nathu, a self-made paragon of the Darjeeling

Thangmi community who served as the BTWA's treasurer for many years, showed me the 1943 and 1945 photos with pride and care, yet derided the present-day BTWA as "only concerned with 'making history,'" what could he mean?

Associational Histories

This chapter examines the historical trajectories of two Thangmi ethnic associations: what is now the BTWA in India and the Nepal Thami Samaj (NTS) in Nepal.[3] Ethnic associations are often considered part of "civil society" (Chatterjee 2004; Fuller and Bénéï 2000; Gellner 2010a; Kaviraj and Khilnani 2001), in that they serve as mediators between states and specific kinds of citizens. As such, ethnic organizations are productive sites within which to observe the relationships between state policy and subjectivity that constitute the dialectic of ethnicization. However, such relationships are not limited by the associational frame. Rather, it is in the disjunctures between organizational diktat and community sentiment that the dynamics of ethnicization often become starkly evident. In keeping with the synthetic theory of ethnicity-in-action outlined in earlier chapters, here I demonstrate how participation in such organizations can be a form of ritual action constitutive of social difference, the patterns of which must be analyzed in relation to other forms of action in which Thangmi engage.

Cross-border Thangmi experiences demonstrate particularly starkly how people may interpret and internalize the imperatives of state policy, since the case of the other country is always available for comparison, distilled in the structures and practices of the other organization. The shifting relationships between the BTWA and the NTS over time, and between diverse Thangmi individuals and each organization—sometimes supportive and mutually productive, at other times fraught with competition and frustration at perceived inequities and biases—demonstrate the complex processes through which ethnicity is synthesized.

Through their cross-border communication with each other, Thangmi activists in both countries become aware of the varying prospects that their counterparts may have for promoting social welfare and moral reform, achieving community progress and economic development, and seeking political recognition. I suggest that these five objectives have shaped the orientations of Thangmi ethnic organizations at different historical and geographical junctures. Furthermore, each of these objectives has entailed different conceptualizations of Thangmi "culture" and "history" and concomitantly varied approaches to harnessing these objects of ethnicity in the service of social transformation.

The five objectives listed above loosely reference the Nepali language discourses of *unnati* (improvement), *utthan* (upliftment), *pragati* (progress), *vikas* (development), *adhikar* (rights), and *samavesikaran* (inclusion). Thangmi organizations have crystallized around each of these aspirational terms at various junctures. Each term signifies a different ideological paradigm for realizing the consistent objective of forward movement toward an ideal society. Ideas about what constitutes forward movement have shifted between time and place, sometimes dramatically, with attitudes toward culture and history repeatedly revised to keep pace. Yet all of these ideas emerged from the matrix of the Nepali-language public sphere. While influenced by international discourses of modernity, communism, development, and indigeneity, here I argue that experiences of ethnicization in both Nepal and Nepali-speaking India are the results of historical trajectories grounded in the broader processes of political consciousness formation specific to each nation-state, yet dependent upon circulation between them in the transnational Nepali public sphere.

Discourses and Practices of a Nepali Public Sphere

Rhoderick Chalmers (2003) has demonstrated the inherently transnational nature of the literary Nepali public sphere in the first half of the twentieth century. Writing in 1934, Parasmani Pradhan eloquently summarized, "As long as other Nepalis do not find out about what is done by Nepalis living in one corner our *unnati* shall not be achieved" (as cited in Chalmers 2003:111). Taking an Andersonian approach that emphasizes the importance of print capitalism, Chalmers shows how crucial ideas about the content of Nepaliness emerged in both Nepal and India during the period from 1914 to 1940. The specific political and social environments of each country conditioned public expression, yet the vehicle of literary journals enabled a transnational public to engage collaboratively in the discursive production of Nepaliness as a cultural entity that transcended the territorial borders of the Nepali nation-state.

Beyond simply recognizing the analogy between the transnational production of Nepaliness that Chalmers describes and the transnational production of Thangminess under consideration here, I suggest that both emerged within the same public sphere and, as such, demonstrate different aspects of a shared historical process. It is in the Nepali public sphere that such notions as welfare, progress, development, and inclusion emerged; accumulated multiple layers of meaning; and circulated across borders over time, influencing individual and collective Thangmi conceptualizations of themselves as agents of change.

We should not assume that ethnic identities often thought of as constituent elements of Nepal's diversity are bounded by political borders (or are defined by a single region or village). Instead, analytically locating the production of such identities within an overarching, transnational Nepali public sphere allows us to see how the vagaries of identity politics and minority legislation in other countries, such as India and China, have come to bear significantly upon groups with populations in Nepal. Several anthropologists mention in passing the influence of experiences in Darjeeling on ethnic and cultural projects in Nepal.[4] However, the influence of forms of public expression anchored in India on historical processes of ethnicization inside Nepal has not been systematically addressed.[5] I suggest that just as Nepali nationalism was initially produced largely in India, so too were ideas about ethnicity and how to use it to make claims on the state. This was not a one-way street, however: in later periods, such ideas were internalized and reimagined inside Nepal, in relation to Nepal state policies, and then recirculated to communities of Nepali heritage in India. Such processes, repeated again and again, constitute the multilayered feedback loop through which contemporary Thangmi ethnicity is produced. The persistence of Thangmi circular migration makes such cross-border communication more pronounced than it is for many other groups, therefore providing a compelling case study of a more general set of dynamics.

At the same time, understanding the ways in which individual *ethnic* identities have been produced over time in India helps complicate the narrative of Nepali *national* identity production there. Understanding the experiences of individual groups of Nepali heritage in India within the broader process of pan-Nepali identity formation requires a conceptual expansion of the public sphere to include not only the discursive production of literary journals but also ritual practices, cultural performances, and other sorts of identity-producing public actions. Critiques of anthropology for neglecting written sources in Nepali are well taken (Chalmers 2003: 295–96; Onta 1992), but the reality remains that in order to understand what the "subaltern counterpublics" (Chalmers 290, citing Fraser 1992) of Darjeeling's literary heyday may have been thinking, we must move beyond the realm of the written word alone to examine what members of groups like the Thangmi, who are rarely represented in writing, were actually doing.

In its early days, the Thangmi corner of the Nepali public sphere was created not through the circulation of publications but rather through the circulation of people and their practices, although these were articulated in relation to ideas advanced through the public speeches of Darjeeling's intelligentsia. The highlights of literary discourse were communicated to those who could not read through the spoken word. Recall, for instance Silipitik's strong reaction to the speech he heard in Darjeeling about social equality, as described in Chapter 4. Ideas of social welfare and moral improvement so communicated prompted slow but steady shifts in practice across the transnational Thangmi world.

It was only in the 1990s that substantial numbers of Thangmi themselves began to engage in literary production, as some began to question their own commitment to orality and discovered the political power of print.[6] Between 1997 and 2004, four book-length collections of writing by Thangmi about themselves were published (three in Nepal and one in India), along with three dictionaries (two in Nepal and one in India). By this time, other technologically mediated forms of discursive representation were also available, and the proliferation of audio (cassettes, CDs, and radio) and video (VCD and DVD) has diversified Thangmi modes of expression. Regardless, all of these discursive products represent the *sakali* in different *nakali* modes with varying effects (see Chapter 2), each of which enable Thangmi to at once align themselves with broader discourses of social transformation while also (re)producing culture and (re)making history in the idiom of the moment.

This chapter focuses on the long but under-studied period between the 1950s—when James Scott (2009) suggests that the last great state enclosures occurred—and the 1990s, when Jean and John Comaroff (2009) claim that the global ethnocommodification of ethnicity began to accelerate in relation to neoliberal policies. Through my reading of the associational archives of the BTWA and NTS, as found in their respective offices (Figure 12), the missing history of the second half of the twentieth century presented in

Figure 12. Bharatiya Thami Welfare Association office, Darjeeling, West Bengal, India, November 2005. Photo by author.

this chapter helps contextualize contemporary claims about the nature of ethnicity, identity, and the state.

The trajectories of Thangmi activism lead us back and forth across borders to consider how Thangmi deployed the "currency of culture" (Cattelino 2008) at different places and times. This concept enables a move beyond the relatively static notion of symbolic capital to consider how the fungibility of culture itself may transform the terms of economic and political value. By the time I entered the Thangmi social field in the late 1990s, culture, history, and language were in the process of being reconceptualized as sacred objects, which came to represent the core object of identity itself. The day-to-day work of activism carried on within the presence of these objects (meetings, fundraising drives, writing applications) often took on the character of ritual action. Yet at key moments, some Thangmi—often those most heavily invested in earlier paradigms for forward progress—resisted the reformulation of relationships between culture, history, and activism that new paradigms of progress entailed. Such voices from different corners of the transnational Thangmi world show how activist renditions of culture and history at any given place and time represent important, but in themselves incomplete, strands of Thangmi identity production, the full meanings of which only become evident when viewed as part of the whole.

Associational Histories in Darjeeling

The history of Thangmi ethnic organizing begins in Darjeeling, where the BLTS was the first and only Thangmi organization anywhere for almost forty years. This fact inverts the logic of Nepal as the originary fount of Thangmi culture, for if we view ethnic organizations themselves as sites of cultural production, it becomes clear that India is indubitably the source of this strand of Thangmi culture. It was this aspect of Thangmi history that Darjeeling Thangmi took pride in as they showed me their photographs; these black-and-white images were their evidence of a long-standing, distinctive cultural reality, much as ritual practice and origin stories were for many Thangmi in Nepal.

Such associational life was not a realistic option in Nepal before 1950. The Rana state did not allow "civil society" activities.[7] The comparative openness to organizational life Thangmi migrants experienced in India encouraged many of them to stay or to spend a large portion of their time in Darjeeling. Forming an organization to pursue their ethnically specific needs created prospects for belonging different from those available in Nepal.

Identity-based organizing in Darjeeling dates to as early as 1907, when an informal organization submitted a memorandum to the Bengal government demanding the creation of a "separate administrative set-up" in Darjeeling. Formalized as the Hillmen's Association between 1917 and 1919, these early activists aimed to advance the social position of the multiple groups beginning to identify themselves as a unified "hill" community (Subba 1992:78–79; Chalmers 2003:208). Distinguishing themselves from the Bengali "plains" community that had previously mediated most of Darjeeling's interactions with the seat of power in colonial Calcutta, this group included Nepali, Bhutia, and Lepcha members, who put aside cultural differences to form an alliance based on their shared concerns.

Their early demands were couched in the rhetoric of social improvement (N: *unnati*) for the pan-Nepali community (N: *jati*). Chalmers accordingly terms the "nascent Nepali public sphere . . . decidedly apolitical" (2003:204), but soon the challenges of ensuring social welfare generated political aspiration. The All India Gorkha League (AIGL) was founded in Dehradun in 1923 and quickly established branches all over India, publishing Nepali-language materials that linked "specifically Nepali political concerns to the Indian freedom movement" (Chalmers 2003:214). But the heyday of the AIGL lasted only a decade, and by 1933, it had stopped publishing and remained defunct until it was revived in Darjeeling in 1943.

The BLTS was also founded in that year. In the intervening decade, Darjeeling citizens had begun to articulate their concerns in increasingly public forums, making the transition from a discourse of improvement (*unnati*) in a moral sense, through the education and gentrification of individuals, to the more political discourse of social transformation through the upliftment (N: *utthan*) of an entire community within the framework of the emerging Indian state. The Hill People's Social Union (HPSU) was founded in 1934 under the leadership of S.W. Laden La "by a large public convention attended by some six hundred representatives of different communities from across the Darjeeling district, including from villages and tea estates" (*Nebula* 1[1]:10 as cited in Chalmers 2003:211). The HPSU lauched the journal *Nebula* (the initials of which stood for Nepali, Bhutia, and Lepcha) in 1935, bringing discussions of identity issues into the public sphere and linking them to broader political concerns over the place of Darjeeling within both the colonial administration and a future independent India.[8]

During the same period, efforts to improve social welfare at the local level culminated in the founding of the Gorkha Duhkha Nivarak Sammelan (GDNS) in 1932. With the explicit intention of linking "cultural promotion to social welfare," GDNS founder Dhanvir Mukhiya built a public hall that "became the undisputed centre for Nepali theatrical productions while pursuing a mission to the poorer members of society by . . . carrying out funeral rites for destitutes" (Chalmers 2003:202). GDNS founder Mukhiya and HPSU founder Laden La did not get along, and competition emerged between these two early civil society organizations and their chosen modes of promoting social transformation (Chalmers 2003:202, 211): the GDNS through "welfare," or what we might now call "livelihood-based" activism, and the HPSU through political, or "rights-based" activism that aimed to make claims on the Indian state in formation.

Bhai Larke Thami Samaj: Social Welfare for the Thangmi "Family"

Despite tensions between the leadership, both organizations were influential in shaping the BLTS. Thangmi descriptions of the organization's founding suggest that it was originally aligned with the GDNS model of social welfare, while subsequent efforts to fundraise for the Jyoti Thami Primary School benefited from HPSU's direct tutelage in approaching the state.

Amrikan, whose narrative was recounted in Chapter 4, explained that the initial objectives of the BLTS were to raise funds and find adequate numbers of participants for birth and death rituals:

At that time, we started the brother's group. . . . Even though we were not educated, we could run it well enough. . . . In someone's house there would be a birth ritual, or some other event, and all of the Thangmi would together contribute fifty rupees for a "rotating" loan, and whoever's turn it was would be called *larke*, in that way it became Bhai Larke Samaj.[9] Man Bahadur Thami from Kusipa, near Khopa [both villages in Dolakha], said, "Let's get the Thangmi organized and start a group." And then there were sixty or seventy of us; then it was not so hard to do our death rituals.

Meeting the financial and social demands of such elaborate ritual practices was a hardship for migrant Thangmi; recall the guru Rana Bahadur's difficulty conducting his father's funerary rites in India, as recounted in Chapter 3. Most migrants to Darjeeling were far from their own families, who would have provided the human and material resources to conduct rituals in Nepal. They either left Darjeeling to return home when momentous personal events took place or simply carried on with their routine of daily labor, failing to conduct rituals at all. One further option was to approach the GDNS to sponsor rituals, but there was no scope for Thangmi ritual per se within the GDNS's walls. Rather, the GDNS prescribed a Hindu ritual format and called its own in-house priest to officiate.

None of these options was satisfactory. There were in fact several Thangmi gurus working as wage laborers in Darjeeling who had the knowledge and skill to conduct funerary and other rites. However, like everyone else, these gurus struggled to make ends meet and were unwilling to lose their daily wages unless the sponsoring family could compensate. Back in Nepal, both gurus and laypeople were part of the same informal economy where labor was compensated in kind, but in Darjeeling the system fell apart. Without the resources of a kinship network to provide both the necessary offerings and clan and out-clan participants, conducting Thangmi rituals seemed impossible.

In this context, drawing upon the GDNS's social welfare model but moving out of its pan-Nepali Hindu ritual sphere, the BLTS established a fictive kin network to meet both the financial and social needs of migrant Thangmi. BLTS members conceptualized their organizational membership through kinship idioms, as the term *bhai*—brothers—in the organization's title attests. However, their preferred family was an exclusively Thangmi one, not the pan-Nepali "family" invoked in the parallel kinship metaphors of the HPSU and various Nepali writers.[10] Basant, the BTWA general secretary from 1997 to 2003, explained that although his father had been raised by the GDNS orphanage, the organization could not replace a Thangmi "family": "My father lost his parents when he was five. GDNS gave him a place to live, and he was the caretaker of the hall until he died. I grew up there too, and my sister and her family still live there. We owe everything to that organization. They would say, 'We are all one family, one *jati*. If any one of our members succeeds, we all succeed.' They taught my father how to be Nepali but not how to be Thangmi. For that we needed the Bhai Samaj." Although this description is filtered through a generation of social and political experience and may not represent verbatim the views of Basant's father, such sentiments were echoed by several older Thangmi in interviews: although *social* welfare could be conceptualized in broad, pan-Nepali terms, *cultural* welfare required an exclusively Thangmi organization. Drawing upon the GDNS model, which functioned within the Nepali *social* sphere, the BLTS brought the notion of welfare to bear at the *cultural* level on which ethnic identities were still created through ritual practice in the company of kin: those bound by shared descent, if not exactly immediate family.

Once supported by the organizational framework of the BLTS, culture quickly became currency as Thangmi considered how to parlay their successful scheme of rotating loans for ritual practice into something more. In his description of the Thangmi encounter with the HPSU, Amrikan alludes to the class dynamics that belied the latter organization's populist image, as well as to the first deployments of cultural performance as a political tool:

> *Nebula* came along later, and the *thulo manche* (N: big people) we knew found out about it. Our secretary went to ask them for help in approaching the government to ask for money since we didn't have enough to run the school. . . . They told us to show our dances and songs, and play *deusi*.[11] We asked the ministers for help; that's how we ran the school. They gave us 500 to 600 rupees a month . . . but for that we had to dance and sing. At that time, the three *jat* [Nepali, Bhutia, Lepcha] would be called, and we were also included. Since the Bhotes could only perform *dangdangdungdung* [a disparaging imitation of Bhutia cultural practice], we were asked to perform the *maruni* dance and play the *madal*, and for that they gave us money to run our organization.

Like many Thangmi, Amrikan referred to the HPSU as *Nebula*, conflating the name of the organization with the name of the journal it published, in what appears to have been fairly common usage (Bagahi and Danda 1982; Subba 1992:83). Amrikan's statement that it was the *thulo manche*—those of higher status and more education—who first learned about the HPSU's existence suggests that the organization may not have been accessible to Thangmi wage laborers. Moreover, the membership of HPSU's executive committee and governing bodies, as well as of the editorial board for *Nebula* (as reproduced in Subba 1992:81–83), shows Bhutia, Lepcha, Gurung,

Brahmin, Chhetri, Rai, Newar, Limbu, and perhaps Magar names,[12] but there are no Thangmi. While this is hardly surprising given the very small Thangmi population, it helps explain why Thangmi may have felt that the HPSU could not fully represent their political aspirations, just as the GDNS could not cater to all of their cultural needs.

As described by Amrikan, the BLTS secretary first approached the HPSU leadership to ask how to request financial help from the government. But the HPSU did not recommend that the Thangmi approach the government with a political agenda. Instead, they were advised to mobilize their cultural resources to secure financial support. Thangmi performance was apparently seen as a particularly marketable brand of pan-Nepali cultural production. Perhaps owing to its lively *madal* drumbeats, Thangmi cultural performance was viewed as a resource for the Darjeeling community as a whole (in contrast to Bhutia cultural forms, which according to Amrikan did not easily appeal to outside audiences).[13] In exchange for cultural performances, Thangmi received funding for their school, first from the HPSU and later through a municipal grant of seventy-four rupees monthly.

At a time when organizations representing individual ethnic groups of Nepali heritage were just emerging,[14] it is difficult to imagine how the Thangmi, with their tiny population numbers and relatively low economic status, could have maintained an active association without the direct support of a more experienced and well-resourced organization. Viewed as a nonpolitical organization that could contribute cultural resources to overall pan-Nepali political goals, the BLTS was perceived as an additional resource for, rather than as a threat to, pan-Nepali hegemony.

Moreover, the flagship school project of the BLTS promoted the ideal of *unnati* by providing education to poor Thangmi children—in Nepali and English, but notably not in Thangmi. In line with pan-Nepali ideologies in ascendance at the time, the organization strove to produce Thangmi children assimilated into the Nepali-speaking mainstream. The school, which had up to eighty students at its height, was founded "with a view towards minimizing the backwardness of the Thami community" (Niko 2003:11). This statement echoes a 1955 letter to T. Wangdi, deputy minister of tribal welfare for the state of West Bengal, signed by Man Bahadur, the BLTS founder and secretary, that appeals for additional funding for the school because "we Thamis are backward in our Nepali community."

It was within this historical context that many contemporary Thangmi claim that their forebears turned down the opportunity to be listed as an ST in the early 1950s, during the first postindependence phase of classification carried out by the Indian state. As Nar Bahadur, an elder involved in BLTS discussions over this issue at the time explained, "When the idea of Scheduled Tribes first arose, the government asked if we wanted to be listed. But the Tamang had refused, saying that they were too important to be seen as a backward group, and we Thangmi followed suit. We wanted to be seen as Indian citizens with Nepali heritage, not some little 'tribe.'" The Thangmi therefore chose to cast their lot with the Nepali community as a whole rather than with the Bhutia and Lepcha, both of whom were indeed classified as STs in 1950 (Galanter 1984:149). Desiring recognition as full-fledged, modern Indian citizens of Nepali heritage, Thangmi sought to distance themselves from the connotations of backwardness that the tribal designation carried at the time.

"Who could have guessed that this would turn out to be a mistake?" continued Nar Bahadur. By the 1990s, classification as an ST had become the primary objective for Thangmi activists in India. With the death of BLTS founder Man Bahadur Thami in the mid-1960s, the first wave of Thangmi ethnic organizing ended. The BLTS fell into disarray and the school closed. The association was only fully resuscitated in the early 1990s as the Bharatiya Thami Welfare Association, which despite its name, was no longer primarily interested in familial and communal "welfare." In the meantime, Thangmi aspirational ideologies had changed, bringing into focus newfound desires for recognition and rights at the national and transnational levels, along with new techniques for making history.

Marxist Notions of Progress in Nepal

Had notions of social transformation and aspirational ideologies changed so radically for all Thangmi during the intervening half century? Answering this question requires a journey back across the border to examine the origins of Thangmi organizing in Nepal.

Until the advent of democracy after the collapse of Rana rule and King Tribhuvan's 1951 return to Nepal's throne, political agendas were crafted in India by expatriate activists before being launched in Nepal. The Nepali Congress (NC) party was established in 1947 in Banaras, while Pushpa Lal Shrestha founded the Communist Party of Nepal (CPN) in Calcutta in 1949. Pushpa Lal and his supporters returned to Nepal in 1951 but were quickly banned for their violent activities. They operated underground from 1952 to 1956, mobilizing around class issues: land redistribution, tenancy rights, and the abolition of compulsory unpaid labor (Hachhethu 2002:34–35). The CPN was legalized in the late 1950s and stood in the 1959 elections, before King Mahendra terminated Nepal's first experiment with democracy in 1960 and introduced the partyless *panchayat* system. All political parties were once again banned, and the CPN and NC alike went underground. Mahendra's *panchayat* ideology emphasized a hegemonic vision of nationalist development, framed in terms of *vikas* (Pigg 1992, 1993), which intersected with the rapidly increasing presence of international development organizations in Nepal. But in the decade that Pushpa Lal's CPN was active before the *panchayat* curtain fell, the communist notion of progress, or *pragati*—in the sense of class struggle within the Marxist framework of historical materialism—had already left its mark on much of rural Nepal.

The first formally constituted Thangmi organization was located not in Dolakha or Sindhupalchok, where the majority of Nepal's Thangmi population resided, but in Jhapa, an eastern Tarai district bordering West Bengal. Niko Pragatisil Thami Samuha (NPTS), or Our Progressive Thami Group, was founded in 1981, although one of its publications claims that members met informally beginning in 1968 (Patuko 2054 VS:87). Shortly thereafter, between 1971 and 1973, Nepal's Jhapeli activists (who were consolidated into the Marxist-Leninist, or ML, branch of the CPN in 1978) began attacking large landlords, taking their cues from the Naxalite movement then in full swing just across the border in West Bengal (Hachhethu 2002). The Jhapa Thangmi community fell within the sphere of Jhapeli-Naxalite influence, and the NPTS was formed with the clear agenda of harnessing Thangmi concerns about basic subsistence to a larger communist agenda (Patuko 2054 VS).[15]

Jhapa was an important intermediate point in the routes of circular migration between Thangmi villages in Nepal and Darjeeling. With Thangmi settlements located close to the international border crossing along the highway at Kankarvitta (in Nepal), or Raniganj (in India), Thangmi moving in both directions often spent a night or two with relatives in Jhapa. The Nepali government's malaria eradication program in the 1950s (funded in part by USAID) included land and cash incentives for settlement in sparsely populated Tarai areas like Jhapa, and several Thangmi families took up this offer. Most of these settlers were from the village of Lapilang in Dolakha and had long participated in circular migration themselves. Even a few families that had been settled in Darjeeling for several generations (including a branch of the Tumsong tea plantation family, who were also originally from Lapilang) were attracted by the offer of free land inside Nepal. They made use of the Nepali citizenship papers they had maintained in order to return to Nepal, albeit to the Tarai rather than to their ancestral hill villages. From its earliest days, therefore, despite its small size, the Jhapa Thangmi community played a key role in the feedback loop of cross-border Thangmi communication through strong kinship links with both Dolakha and Darjeeling.

It should come as no surprise then that in 1981, the same year that the NPTS registered in Jhapa, another organization was established in Dolakha: Lapilang Gaun Ekai Samiti (LGES), or the United Lapilang Village Committee. Although the organization's name does not mark it as explicitly Thangmi, LGES is identified as the first Thangmi organization in Dolakha (NTS Organizational Profile). Unlike in Jhapa, where the Thangmi were a tiny minority, in Lapilang, where the Thangmi were in the majority (ICDM 1999), it may have seemed unnecessary and perhaps overly provocative to include "Thangmi" in the organization's name. Moreover, although the LGES sought to mobilize people who shared a Thangmi identity, their rallying cry was that of class struggle, not ethnic inclusion.

By 1981, in addition to hearing about the Jhapeli activists, the Thangmi of Lapilang had come under the direct influence of underground CPN-ML cadres in their area. The Thangmi village of Piskar—located just west of the present-day boundary between Dolakha and Sindhupalchok—was chosen as a base area by CPN-ML operatives soon after the party's formal establishment in 1978. The prominent CPN-ML leader Amrit Kumar Bohara was originally from Piskar himself and chose it as a model "village of the masses" for his party's activities (Shneiderman 2010). Bohara, along with Asta Laxmi Shakya (who later became his wife) and a third cadre, Madhav Paudel, were based in Piskar but traveled widely to other Thangmi villages.

Their communist rhetoric resonated well with existing Thangmi concerns about exploitation. Thangmi villagers had long felt oppressed at the hands of landowners, compelling many to settle in India or at least spend much of their time there. Many older Thangmi told me how they were involved in small-scale acts of resistance against landlords long before they ever heard of communism. However, their frustrations were not previously linked to an ideological agenda that extended beyond local power structures or provided an organizational framework to conceptualize themselves as agents of large-scale transformation.

The fact that communism was the primary force in shaping Thangmi political consciousness in Nepal had important long-term implications for the group's ability to organize along ethnic lines and attitudes toward culture and history as political categories. The CPN espoused an orthodox communist line that emphasized the evolutionary model of historical materialism, which posits ethnic, gender, and other group identities as artifacts of class differentiation that will disappear through class struggle. In practice, this meant that CPN-ML cadres like Bohara, Shakya, and Paudel—who were Chhetri, Newar, and Bahun, respectively—engaged Thangmi in their projects largely through discourses and practices of domestication. They sought to cultivate loyal rural cadres with direct lived experience of class oppression while subjugating their ethnic identity to meet the demands of an emerging socialist modernity.

In a 2004 interview, Shakya described her early experiences of living in Thangmi households:

> They never took a bath. They did not know that the pot they cooked food in should be cleaned. After they cooked the food, they would keep it just like that with flies all over the pot the whole day. In the evening they would pour water in it, cook, and eat. I would stay inside and clean the pots. They would go to the fields to work and to collect fodder for the animals. When they came home in the evenings, they would see everything clean. . . . That's how they learned. I did not teach only about politics because there was a need to change the economic situation, the social situation, their ideas, and their lifestyle. . . . They ate beef, and we taught them that they should not eat it.

Shakya's social work was well intentioned, arising out of a genuine concern for Thangmi welfare. But there was also a paternalistic element in her view of Thangmi habits as backward. This is most evident in Shakya's pride in teaching Thangmi not to eat beef. While the consumption of beef was and remains an important marker of Thangmi identity, it had no place within a communist national imaginary shaped by Hindu ideals.

Such prejudices led Thangmi in Nepal with political aspirations to feel that cultural practice (as defined in Chapter 2) was incommensurable with effective political participation at the national level. This did not mean that culture should be stamped out entirely: it could in fact be instrumentalized through performance in the service of particular ideological agendas and was therefore worth maintaining as a resource. But practice per se was best bracketed off as a local field of action separate from the national field of politics.

Until the 1990s, Thangmi tended to deemphasize their ethnic affiliation and cultural particularity in the context of party politics. Jagat Man, who was involved in founding Lapilang's LGES, and remained both a CPN-United Marxist-Leninist (UML) and NTS member when I met him in the mid-2000s, explained:

> Through communism we learned that although we Thangmi were poor, we were not poor because we were Thangmi. We were poor because we lived in a feudal system where the rich exploited us to consolidate their wealth. So we had to challenge them on the basis of class. This was the only way during the *panchayat* time, when you could not talk about ethnic cultures or languages. At that point, these were not part of our political agenda. But Thangmi felt ashamed to talk to people from other groups, and could talk more easily to each other, so it was logical for us to form a Thangmi organization, even though our goal was the advancement of the party, not the ethnicity.

Strategic use of Thangmi kinship and community networks helped achieve *pragati*—"progress," in the evolutionary communist sense—but ultimately ethnicity was only an entry point into class struggle.

For many Thangmi, such logic was forever unsettled by the Piskar Massacre of January 1984 (Shneiderman 2009). For others, this event—where two Thangmi villagers were killed by police and many more were injured at a festival—reinforced their commitment to the communist cause. Over three hundred villagers were arrested for alleged participation in subversive activity, with some held in custody for up to three years without trial. The government's rationale for police action was the fact that Thangmi sharecroppers were singing revolutionary songs at the annual Maghe Sangkranti festival at Mahadevsthan, a local temple, demonstrating how a Thangmi cultural event was deployed in the service of a particular political agenda, with devastating effects (Amnesty International 1987; INSEC 1995).

On the one hand, this experiential linkage between cultural performance and political violence led to a hardening of Thangmi ethnic consciousness as an oppressed group vis-à-vis both the state and the CPN-ML party, whom some Thangmi felt used them as scapegoats (Bohara, Shakya, and Paudel were unharmed in the massacre). On the other hand, the Piskar incident compelled a more cautious separation of culture from politics. Many Thangmi came to fear the public events at which much cultural practice unfolded—territorial deity festivals, funerary rites, wedding parties—both because "Thangmi culture" had now been equated with subversive politics in the eyes of the state and because simply gathering in a large group could draw unwanted attention. After the Piskar Massacre, cultural practice became more insular, especially for those who were not deeply invested in communism already. For those already committed, the Piskar Massacre confirmed the Marxist path and provided an entrée onto the national political stage, but only at the cost of downplaying Thangminess. The CPN-ML eulogized Ile and Bir Bahadur as communist rather than Thangmi martyrs, and little was done to compensate their families or ensure the welfare of Thangmi as a group, despite repeated demands for community reparations (Reng 1999:65–68).[16]

The 1984 Piskar Massacre led to the dissolution of the first Thangmi organizations in Nepal and the factionalization of the community into camps with competing views on the relationship between culture, politics, and progress. It would be more than a decade until some Thangmi began to consider seriously the prospect of crossing party lines to organize around ethnicity.

Converging on Culture

The year 1990 marked a watershed for Thangmi organizations in both Nepal and India, albeit for different reasons. In Nepal, the first Jana Andolan (People's Movement) ended absolute monarchy, with King Birendra lifting the ban on political parties and accepting a new constitution. The end of the *panchayat* system permitted social inequalities to be expressed in an explicitly ethnic idiom for the first time.[17] Ethnic activists soon formed what is now known as the Nepal Janajati Adivasi Mahasangh (Nepal

Federation of Indigenous Nationalities, or NEFIN), registered in 1990 as an umbrella organization for ethnic associations.[18] NEFIN advised the framers of the 1990 Constitution, and for the first time, Nepal was explicitly recognized as a multicultural, multilingual state.

Also in 1990, the Indian government announced a plan to extend reservations to Other Backward Classes (OBCs) as recommended by the 1980 Mandal Commission Report (Jenkins 2003:147). Although the concept of "backward classes" had existed in vaguely defined form since the colonial era (Galanter 1984:154–55), the constituent groups had never been clearly listed, nor had the designation previously carried entitlements like those available to STs and Scheduled Castes (SCs) since 1950. Now, up to 52 percent of India's population stood to receive some form of entitlement (Jenkins 2003:145). Moreover, the government was willing to entertain new applications for ST and SC status for the first time in several decades.

The changes of 1990 yielded new preoccupations with ethnic classification, on the part of both governments and citizens seeking recognition. A 1996 task force of His Majesty's Government of Nepal for the "Establishment of the Foundation for the Upliftment of Indigenous Nationalities" defined *janajati* groups with the following characteristics: "a distinct collective identity; own language, tradition, culture and civilisation; own traditional egalitarian social structure; traditional homeland or geographical area; written or oral history; having 'we-feeling'; has had no decisive role in the politics and government of modern Nepal; who are the indigenous or native peoples of Nepal; and who declares itself as 'janajati'" (NFDIN 2003:6–7). The Indian government's definition of OBC emphasized social and cultural, as well as economic attributes: "'Class' means a homogeneous section of the people grouped together because of certain likenesses or common traits, and who are identifiable by some common attributes such as status, rank, occupation, residence in a locality, race, religion and the like" (Supreme Court of India, as cited in Jenkins 2003:145). Although the terminology is different, the OBC definition shared much with the long-standing criteria for ST status: "indication of primitive traits, distinctive culture, geographical isolation, shyness of contact with the community at large, and backwardness" (Galanter 1984:152). The overlap between OBC and ST definitions, particularly their shared emphasis on the amorphous category of "backwardness," significantly influenced how Thangmi conceptualized their political projects in India: their first application to the government for special status in 1992 requested recognition as "Other Backward Class/Scheduled Tribe," as if there were no difference between the two.

The post-1990 political shifts in both countries had the common effect of countering class and nation as primary identities by situating ethnicity as both an essential marker of social difference and a politically salient category through which to make claims on the state. Before 1990, the cross-border Thangmi community had been influenced by various discourses of social change—from *unnati* to *pragati*—that compelled ethnic identity to be conceptualized as secondary to national and class identities. In India, the pan-Nepali identity ascendant when the BLTS emerged in 1943 had reached its height in the late 1980s with the violent movement for the separate state of Gorkhaland. During the agitation, there was no active Thangmi organization, both because public advocacy of any identity other than a "Gorkhali" nationalist one was risky and because the upheaval of the time made other potential movements pragmatically challenging. Similarly in Nepal, the latter half of the 1980s was devoid of Thangmi ethnic organizations. The concerns around which they might have mobilized were cast as those of class-based peasant identity by the communist movement, and the risks of public protest were formidable in the wake of the Piskar Massacre. In both cases, cultural particularities were submerged by dominant discourses of resistance that emphasized other dimensions of marginalization.

Now, in the early 1990s, the objectification of Thangmi "ethnic culture" (N: *jatiya sanskriti*) seemed to hold one of the keys to increased participation in a slowly democratizing Nepali state that was more willing to entertain ethnic agendas than radical communist ones,[19] as well as to new benefits from an Indian welfare state more amenable to entitlements for small ethnic groups than a separate state for a Nepali nationalist bloc. The earlier political movements in which Thangmi participated had promoted versions of history with little room for ethnic particularities. Proponents of both historical materialism in the sense of *pragati*, and *jati* improvement in the sense of *unnati*, saw society in an evolutionary frame within which "backward" traditions required reform, if not obliteration, in order to move forward toward a utopian future. Now developing a cultural narrative recognizable within the terms of either the Nepali or Indian nation required revisiting history to determine how the synthetic matrix of Thangmi cultural practice could be deployed as evidence of "tradition." A distinctive history based on those very practices—a history of cultural particularity that highlighted the *differences* between groups rather than their common-alities within a grand historical narrative—was perceived as necessary for recognition as *janajati*, OBC, or ST.

Seeking Unitary Histories, Finding Fractured Politics

Thangmi activists in India were the first to realize the necessity of a coher-ent, standardized history as they began compiling their application for OBC status to the state of West Bengal in 1990. Intriguingly, the 1980 Mandal Commission report had listed an OBC group called "Thami" as living in the central state of Madhya Pradesh. This prompted the Darjeeling-based organization to rename itself the All India Thami Association in an effort to link themselves to the group with the same name elsewhere in India. A delegation traveled to Madhya Pradesh to find their long-lost brethren and ask how they had attained OBC status in their state. But as Nathu explained, "We did not know where to start; we had no 'contact.' Maybe the Thami there were entirely different from us, but they had the same name. We tried, but we could not find them."

Their next strategy was to visit Nepal, in 1992, where they hoped to collect information about Thangmi history, culture, and language—all required subject headings on the OBC application form—which they felt inadequately equipped to address on their own. The relatively well-educated, middle-class male BTWA leaders were all from families that had been settled in Darjeeling for at least two generations. Several held govern-ment jobs, and many had been involved in pan-Nepali political projects. None spoke Thangmi or had much experience of Thangmi ritual practice. They were quintessential postcolonial Indian citizens of Nepali heritage, with little sense of Thangmi identity apart from their name (and the persis-tent sense of "backwardness" that it carried) and contact with seasonal migrant laborers from Nepal—some of whom were their kin.

It was these laborers to whom they now turned for "contact" to ensure that their first trip to Nepal would not be like the journey to Madhya Pradesh. For the most part, relationships between Thangmi from Nepal and Thangmi from India were structured in patron-client rather than kin-ship terms, with economically marginal migrant laborers requesting places to sleep or donations of food from established Darjeeling families. The latter generally acquiesced but more out of a sense of pity and obligation than out of familial warmth. According to one circular migrant who had spent part of every year in Darjeeling since the early 1980s, "Before all of this OBC talk, they never wanted to recognize us. Maybe they threw us scraps or employed us instead of others when they needed a load carried, but otherwise they didn't want to be reminded that we were also Thangmi." Joining together to create a coherent ethnic identity with a shared historical narrative across borders, class, and educational experience was not an easy or un-self-conscious process. Rather, it entailed a conscious set of decisions, initiated by Thangmi in India, and later reframed by Thangmi in Nepal for their own purposes, to collude in producing a shared set of historical and cultural objects.

When the BTWA Thangmi leadership arrived in Kathmandu on their first official trip, they used the contacts provided by circular migrants to seek what they imagined as a centralized Thangmi organization. They were overwhelmed by the proliferation of politically factionalized entities that they instead encountered. By 1991, there were five Thangmi organizations registered in four districts of Nepal. None of these were official wings of the various mainstream parties they were close to, but the political fault lines between them were clear. Dolakha had one UML-leaning organization and one Congress-leaning organization. Udayapur's single organization was staunchly communist, in fact much farther left than the UML party line, while Jhapa's organization was Congress affiliated, and Ramechap's again aligned with the UML. Three out of five were leftist organizations espousing various communisms, while two leaned toward the right. None of the leaders deigned to speak with one another. The prospects for creating a unified Thangmi *ethnic* movement that could overcome political differences in which potential activists were already deeply invested were challenging at best.

Most BTWA leaders of the 1990s had steered clear of explicit political affiliation during the Gorkhaland agitation, instead focusing on their government jobs and informal social welfare activities. For Thangmi from India, the passionate maintenance of political boundaries between Thangmi in Nepal was bewildering. So was the geographical dispersion of Thangmi organizations in Nepal since all of the organizations were registered at the district rather than national level. Their priorities, as reflected in the organizations' names, varied from *seva* (social service), to *bhume* (earth; here a reference to the Thangmi territorial deity), to *utthan* (upliftment) and *pragati* (progress). Each claimed authority to speak for all Thangmi, but none of them had mobilized that voice at the national level.

Niko Thami Seva Samiti (NTSS), the organization most closely aligned with the first incarnation of the Nepal Federation of Nationalities (NEFEN), put out a two-page "appeal" in September 1990, which appears to be the first publication by a Thangmi organization after the 1990 People's Movement. I found copies of the thin paper document filed in the BTWA archives, along with other draft materials that eventually made their way into the West Bengal OBC application—handwritten notes for a Thangmi glossary, descriptions of a "birth ceremony" and "Bhumee puja"—suggesting that the BTWA activists picked it up in Nepal. The document was also on file at the NTS office in Kathmandu. It invokes the discourses of *vikas* (development) and *adhikar* (rights) to suggest that "it is important that we Thamis unite in order to access our rights, to preserve our culture, language, social values and good traditions and to develop in every sector, including the political, financial, religious and cultural." However, the pamphlet blames the fragmented nature of the Thangmi world on "feudalists," vesting hopes for future Thangmi unity in class solidarity: "We should clearly understand the feudal practice that creates various illusions about us Thami people. If we don't uproot the feudal system, which has been involved in the practice of injustice and atrocities against us, it will once again succeed in creating various illusions and keeping us under its control. . . . As soon as they hear that we are organised, feudalists will become restless. . . . Then they will panic and try to fragment our organization." The appeal then picks up the discourse of domestication introduced by communist cadres like Bohara and Shakya, suggesting that Thangmi must shed the "wild" (N: *jangali*) image that the nation holds of them in order to become modern citizens of Nepal. This is to be achieved by giving up wild crafts, clothing, and foods, a theme echoed in the poem that serves as this chapter's second epigraph, in which "hunting in the forests for underground fruits" is dualistically opposed to "using Thami hands for development."

The appeal concludes with thirteen demands, the final and most substantive of which is a call for reservations, Indian style: "Depending on their eligibility, unconditional places should be reserved for the backward Thamis in civil service, army, police, teaching and in any other government institution." The Indian government had indicated its intention to implement the recommendations of the Mandal Commission report only a month before the NTSS appeal was issued; but as Nathu explained, he and several other Thangmi had been putting up posters in the Darjeeling bazaar with an appeal for OBC status since 1987 (against the wishes of several

Thangmi involved with the Gorkhaland movement at the time). Such posters made this issue visible for several years preceding 1990, and apparently news traveled fast through the cross-border Thangmi community once the prospect for OBC recognition became more realistic. Gopal, the primary author of the NTSS appeal, explained, "We heard what was going on in India, and we thought it was also time to demand the same facilities here. After all, we are all Thangmi; why should they get something different from us?" The BTWA leadership did not make its first visit to Nepal until several months later, and it would be years until Thangmi activists in Nepal put aside their differences to create a united organization that recognized culture as a political resource to be cultivated rather than a hindrance to development best discarded.

OBC: *na jat, na bhat*

In the meantime, "Thami" were officially listed as an OBC group in West Bengal in 1995. The process was exhausting. Basant, at that time the BTWA secretary, engaged in extended correspondence with both state and central governments, and made several trips to Calcutta and Delhi to ensure that the application had reached the correct offices. The BTWA was then called to defend its application before a commission that visited Darjeeling in early 1995. This caused the leadership some consternation. In the application they had made several normative statements ("it is well-established fact with positive proof that . . .") about the nature of Thangmi culture, history, and society. But the BTWA leadership themselves could not substantiate these. They had described Thangmi as "poor and illiterate" and "daily wage labourers," while they themselves were all relatively well-off, well-educated civil servants. Under "religion," Thangmi were said to "worship Bhume, who is the personification of the land," with their own "primitive shaman culture," but most of the BTWA leadership participated in a predominantly Hindu ritual sphere. Thangmi were said to have "their own tribal language or dialect," which none of the BTWA leadership spoke. Instead of describing themselves, the authors of the application had described Thangmi from Nepal whom they knew as wage laborers in Darjeeling.

As the hearing approached, the BTWA leadership looked both to upper echelons of the Thangmi community for individuals who spoke the best

English and Bengali in order to communicate with state officials, and to its lower rungs to find fluent Thangmi speakers (the BTWA officers themselves were most comfortable in Nepali). "We had to go all together, with both the most educated and the porters," explained Nathu. Paras, the BTWA president, represented the "educated," while several porters were paid day wages to answer questions about culture and language. By virtue of their incomplete citizenship, these individuals were not included in the population statistics submitted with the OBC application (which claimed 4,288 Thangmi throughout West Bengal) and would not benefit directly from any special status attained.[20]

At the same time that they asserted "positive proof" of a distinctive culture, in other parts of the application its authors betrayed their ambivalence about the entire undertaking by stating repeatedly that they had none (or perhaps they were just echoing the refusal to objectify cultural practice that they, like me, had received when they first posed the question "What is Thangmi culture?" to Thangmi gurus in Nepal). The application included the statements: "'THAMI' community have no distinct religion of their own," and "THAMI has got no particular festival of their own," as well as two paragraphs explaining why many Thangmi could no longer speak their own language. At least the authors of the application were honest when they described their "dress" as "nothing special"; stated that their forebears had migrated from Tibet, Burma, and Nepal (although they fixed the dates of migration between 1815 and 1835);[21] and acknowledged that they observed Hindu festivals in addition to their own shamanic ones. It was these statements, which in fact described Thangmi in India most accurately, that BTWA leaders later felt they needed to jettison in order to climb the ST ladder.

By the time I first visited Darjeeling in 2000, the phrase *OBC bhaneko na jat na bhat* (N: "OBC means neither ethnicity nor rice"; with "rice" as a metaphor for the resources that Thangmi had hoped would be forthcoming after they became OBC) was a popular complaint. The OBC designation was perceived to carry neither the social status nor the economic benefits of SC or ST status. No one had understood the differences between OBC and ST when they first applied. It seemed that any recognition from the state would be an achievement. But after becoming an OBC group, they learned that this status only qualified a group for reservations in the civil service and education, but not for the direct economic subsidies and provisions for territorial self-governance that ST status could afford. Moreover, so many other groups had received OBC recognition at around the same time as the Thangmi that the value of the category was diminished.[22]

Another problem was the administrative complexity of attaining an individual OBC certificate. First one had to submit a personal application to the district magistrate's office, including a recommendation letter from the registered association representing the group, and letters from two paternal relatives within the community. The first requirement was challenging for those who were not involved with the BTWA already or who were at odds with its leadership for personal or political reasons (including many of the more recently migrated, less well-off families). The second requirement proved challenging for those who might trace their membership in the group through their mother and therefore could not provide the necessary letters. Then each applicant had to appear in person at a hearing and answer many invasive questions. The upshot was that by 2004, when Thangmi had held OBC status for almost a decade, only 160 individuals had actually obtained certificates within the Darjeeling municipality.[23]

These administrative hurdles were the same for members of ST groups, yet somehow the grass seemed greener on the other side. In addition, two of the most prominent groups, the Tamang and Limbu, were already demanding ST status, and Thangmi feared that if groups with such comparatively large populations received that designation, Thangmi would no longer have any hope of competing for civil service and educational positions. The OBC designation began to seem like a stepping-stone to ST status.

The primary differences between OBC and ST criteria are in the requirements of "primitive traits" and "geographical isolation" for the latter. In Darjeeling layman's terms, these were interpreted to mean "non-Hindu" and "indigenous," respectively. Whether the government of India actually intended them to be read in this way is a subject of great debate (Middleton 2011, 2013), but many Thangmi believed that any Hindu-inflected aspect of religious or cultural practice, or mention of migration from outside of India, might disqualify them. If they were to be legitimate aspirants to the ST title, a much more rigorously bounded notion of Thangmi culture and history would be necessary than that contained in either the OBC application's paradoxical statements or the state-supported developmentalist discourse of 1990s Nepal that sought to mold "primitive" practices into a Hinduized modernity.

A Unified Association: The Nepal Thami Samaj

In 1999, the NTS was established to unify the existing Thangmi organizations in Nepal under a central, nonpartisan aegis. The organization's first objective, as stated in its constitution, was to overcome the factionalized past: "NTS shall not be operated through directive principles of any political party, but it shall be a common social organisation for all the Thamis across the nation" (NTS 2000 constitution, article 2.5.a). Although the organization was registered in Nepal, the constitution articulates an explicitly transnational vision of membership: " 'Thami Society' refers to all the Thamis attached to the cultural, social and religious norms and values of the Thamis from inside or outside of Nepal, who can or cannot speak the Thami language" (NTS 2000 constitution, article 1.2.b).

The careful statement that even those from "outside Nepal" who might not speak the language could belong was clearly designed to include Thangmi from India. Despite the fact that the limited linguistic competence and cultural differences of Thangmi in India prompted many Thangmi in Nepal to dismiss the claims of the former that they belonged to "Thangmi society,"[24] the NTS leadership was impressed by their organizational abilities and success in gaining OBC status and thought the BTWA leadership might be a useful resource as the NTS sought political recognition in Nepal. Thangmi in India were certainly "attached" to cultural, social, and religious norms, albeit in different ways than most Thangmi in Nepal were. Yet despite the inclusive statement of membership in "Thangmi society," membership of the organization itself was restricted to "any Nepali Thami citizen who has completed 16 years of age" (NTS 2000 constitution 3.9.a). As one member of the constitution-drafting committee explained, "We wanted to learn from them [Thangmi from India] but we did not want them to 'dominate' us as the educated have for so long done to villagers."[25] So a compromise was struck: Thangmi from India could be involved in an advisory capacity, but only Nepali citizens could be voting members. This created a substantial loophole, since as described in Chapter 4, many Thangmi who were Indian citizens held Nepali paper citizenship as well. This fact would soon come to have substantial implications for the organization's direction.

Thangmi from Jhapa were central in envisioning this new Thangmi organization, just as they had been during the first wave of Thangmi associational life in the 1970s and 1980s. Megh Raj, a young Jhapa Thangmi, had initiated the call for unification. Since the mid-1990s, he had run a Jhapa-based organization called the Thami Bhasa Tatha Sanskriti Utthan Kendra (TBTSUK)—the Thami Language and Cultural Upliftment Center.[26] Its goal was *utthan*, but here the concept of upliftment was deployed in a novel way, referring to the objects of Thangmi language and culture themselves.

In Megh Raj's view, as articulated throughout the 1999 publication *Dolakha Reng* (Dolakha Flowers), Thangmi villagers had allowed their vast cultural resources to degenerate because they were uneducated, and it was the responsibility of educated Thangmi, ideally with the support of the Nepali state, to retrieve these valuable objects. "No one can deny the fact that the historical facts kept so far in the possession of this ethnic group might be lost forever unless serious concern is shown" (Reng 1999:4), he wrote. In reaching these conclusions, Megh Raj was heavily influenced by the BTWA campaigns for OBC and ST status. His parents had settled in Jhapa after growing up in Darjeeling, and for him, Darjeeling was the clos-est urban center, not Kathmandu. Having completed his BA degree, he was also educationally and economically closer to the BTWA leadership than most NTS activists from Dolakha and Sindhupalchok, who possessed little secondary education. Megh Raj used his mediating position as a Jhapa Thangmi to bring the two groups closer together.

Megh Raj acknowledged that the inability to instrumentalize culture for productive political purposes until now was not the fault of Thangmi themselves, for

> there may be many reasons for their backwardness, including: lack of education, poverty, wild attitude, orthodox traditions, following die-hard conservatism, outdated mentality, lack of self-motivation, disorganised society, decentralisation on the basis of profession, impenetrable geographic condition, lack of contact with outsiders, unawareness, unscientific method of performance, internal strife, prodigal custom, local exploitation, oppression, torture and lack of government policy to ameliorate the condition of people. Such dete-rioration may not only destroy the ethnic identity of Thamis but also their physical existence. It has become imperative for all con-scious people of the country to do their best for the overall develop-ment of this ethnic group and for Thamis themselves to be self-motivated towards it. (Reng 1999:23)

Figure 13. The logo of the Nepal Thami Samaj. Image provided by the NTS.

There was no time to waste in working toward economic development to bring these "backward" yet "original" Thangmi to consciousness and forward the political goals that Megh Raj envisioned. It was the responsibility of already "conscious" Thangmi like himself to rescue their shared cultural history as the basis for an ethnic movement within Nepal. Megh Raj imagined doing this through the creation of "culture heroes" in the form of the Thangmi ancestors Ya'apa and Sunari Ama, creating a Thangmi alphabet, and standardizing ritual practice in textual form. His vision of Thangmi culture, history, and language as objects to be valorized for their very primitiveness and reappropriated by an educated ethnic leadership was quite different from the desire for modernity through developmentalist transformation and eradication of the past expressed in the 1990 NTSS appeal. Megh Raj's ideas owed more to the Indian discourse of upliftment through reservations on the basis of distinctive sociocultural features than to the discourses of progress through communism and development in Nepal on which Thangmi activists from Dolakha and Sindhupalchok had cut their teeth.

Megh Raj worked to bring the leadership of the five extant Thangmi organizations together for a national convention in 1999, the result of which was the NTS, whose constitution was finalized in 2000. The new organization's logo was adapted from one already in use by Megh Raj's TBTSUK, which appeared on the cover of *Dolakha Reng* (Figure 13). It combined several elements referencing Thangmi ritual and cultural practice: framed within the shape of a guru's drum were trumpet flowers, wormwood leaves, and a *madal* drum. Their claim to autochthony was represented by the Gaurishankar massif that dominates Dolakha's skyline. For the first time, a Thangmi association in Nepal was representing itself with ritual objects, such as the drums and leaves central to every practice event. True to form, it was only the constellation as a whole that might be seen as particularly Thangmi. All of the logo's elements were also used by other ethnic groups in Nepal, as well as other groups of Nepali heritage in India.

Class and Social Welfare Die Hard

The NTS launched in the late 1990s, just as Nepal's Maoist movement was gaining ground. The prospects for the NTS to emerge as a genuinely inclusive, unified political front were already weak, given the factionalized histories and economic and educational disparities within the community. The emergence of a violent far-left movement proved yet another obstacle. The Maoist ideology of class struggle was more attractive to many Thangmi who remained subsistence farmers in rural villages than the culturally based vision of ethnic politics promoted by Megh Raj and his supporters in the NTS. A small but influential number of Thangmi cast their lot with the Maoist People's Liberation Army, and the first Thangmi elected to national government ever in 2008 was a Maoist Constituent Assembly member, Chun Bahadur. Some rural Thangmi who held communist visions of progress criticized the NTS leadership as bourgeois intellectuals who appropriated the cultural possessions of impoverished Thangmi to gain stature for themselves: "They're seeking to make themselves big on the basis of our name, language and traditions, but they don't care about our poverty," was a common complaint heard throughout Dolakha and Sindhupalchok in the early 2000s.

As described in Chapters 2 and 3, it was rare to find gurus or others deeply involved in ritual practice who supported the activist appropriation of practice for political purposes. This was made clear during a 2001 NTS conference held at Bhume Jatra in Suspa, Dolakha, when activists invited gurus from across the Thangmi world to recite their *paloke*. The NTS leadership were intent on recording and transcribing each guru's version for their standardization project, but they met with two forms of resistance.

First, the gurus did not see the point of textualization, preferring to maintain power through orality itself. Second, they were wary of efforts to represent a standardized Thangmi religion as part of a broader "Kirant *dharma*." This agenda was motivated by the then ongoing 2001 census, which listed "Kirant *dharma*" as a potential category of identification for the first time,[27] as well as the desires of Thangmi in India to disassociate themselves from Hindu-inflected ritual practices because of the perceived prerogatives of ST classification. As one young guru's assistant who was critical of NTS's strategies recounted, "At the Suspa conference, those from Jhapa made an appeal to follow the Kirant *dharma*. . . . The senior gurus rejected this, saying, 'Why do we have to join with them, we have our own religion: Bhume *dharma*. We should continue to practice this.'" This sense of disjuncture between culture and religion as practiced in Thangmi villages, and their objectification as expedient political objects by those based in Kathmandu, Jhapa, and Darjeeling, was exacerbated by the 2002 election of Khumbalal, a relative of Megh Raj's, as NTS chairman. Born and educated in Darjeeling, he had settled in Kathmandu to start a restaurant business, the success of which enabled him to build a large house in the suburbs by 2002. Megh Raj hoped that Khumbalal's seniority—he was in his late fifties—and economic stature would lend authority to the NTS's agenda.

The first project under Khumbalal's tenure was a publication, for which Khumbalal served as editor, funded by the National Foundation for the Development of Indigenous Nationalities (NFDIN). The book, *Thami Samudayako Aitihasik Chinari ra Sanskar Sanskriti* (The Thami Community's Historic Symbols and Ritual Culture), claimed to be an improvement on all previous Thangmi publications since those were based only on "little truth and big imagination" rather than "historical fact" as this publication claimed to be (Samudaya [2056] 2061:3).[28] The primary intended audience appeared to be not the Thangmi public of rural Nepal but rather the Thangmi public of urban Darjeeling and Sikkim, and through them the Indian state, to which the BTWA was preparing to submit its application for tribal status. The book's opening lines addresses the "brothers and sisters who have been living far from their own ancestors and fighting for identity," suggesting that "although we are living apart geographically, we have common thought and blood flowing in our veins" (3).

I first saw the book in Darjeeling, where several hundred copies were sent before being distributed in Kathmandu or Thangmi villages in Nepal.

When news of the publication reached Nepal, district-level members of the NTS could not contain their outrage. One of them told me, "That Khumbalal is just an Indian *chamcha* [N: spoon, idiom meaning 'sycophant']; he is spending all of the money contributed by NFDIN in *our* name to write a big book that spreads lies about us so that his relatives in India can eat sweets [N: *mithai khanna paunchha*, idiom referring to the perceived rewards of ST status]. And here we still don't have even basic facilities. That money should be going to our development instead." The primary motivation of such Thangmi in Nepal for rallying to the NTS's call for ethnic unification was the promise of securing better basic living standards— "welfare" in the most fundamental sense. In their view, such objectives were being hijacked by cultural politics.

This divide between those who wanted Thangmi associations to focus on basic welfare within the community and those who wanted it to engage in cultural politics to make claims on the state(s) did not map neatly onto the national borders of Nepal and India. It had more to do with educational and economic status, age, and individual ideological orientation. Some of the NTS activists working closely with Khumbalal and Megh Raj at the central level were young Thangmi from villages in Dolakha and Sindhupalchok, who were relatively highly educated (having passed their School Leaving Certificate exams and in some cases attained a college degree) and sought to distance themselves from their roots. At the same time, some of the older BTWA activists embarked upon their own transnational welfare projects in order to register their dissent, while simultaneously reconnecting with their roots in rural Nepal.

In the late 1990s, Nathu's family began raising funds from Darjeeling Thangmi to support a primary school in the Dolakha village of Alampu. Participants in this project explained that they wanted to use their comparatively high levels of education and economic status—which they saw as the lucky result of their forebears' decision to settle in India rather than as evidence of their superiority or fundamental difference—to improve the welfare of their Thangmi brethren in Nepal. The welfare focus of their visits to Nepal was very different from the culture-seeking journeys of the BTWA leadership.

Back in Darjeeling, the two groups came into conflict. The tension centered on different attitudes toward their shared history of migration. The former sought to acknowledge and expand existing ties with Thangmi in Nepal. The latter disavowed their direct links with Thangmi in Nepal, while appropriating cultural and linguistic practices from Nepal as sacred objects within their own form of associationally based ritual activity. This dispute eventually led to Nathu's dismissal from BTWA membership. Other BTWA members would soon experience similar exclusion for their unwillingness to give up Hindu-influenced cultural practices or adhere to new versions of Thangmi history that did not acknowledge migration from Nepal. This is what Nathu meant when he contrasted the agenda of "social welfare" with that of "making history."

Militant Mouse Eaters

Two seminal events occurred for the BTWA in 2003. The Tamang and Limbu received ST status in Sikkim and soon thereafter at the national level; and Basant, the general secretary who had shepherded the OBC application through, died suddenly at the age of thirty-eight from an apparent stroke. The first event raised the Thangmi desire for ST status to a feverish pitch, while the second made it much less clear how they would go about achieving it. Basant was a municipal official with intellectual interests. He read widely and had compiled a substantial dossier of published materials about the Thangmi (much of which was reproduced in the 2003 *Niko Bachinte* publication that he edited), and the combination of his knowledge of the Indian administrative system and his insatiable appetite for learning about things Thangmi was a powerful force without which the organization was at a loss.

Into the void stepped Rajen, a young BTWA member previously best known for his seemingly academic interest in compiling a Thangmi dictionary, based on words collected from informants throughout Darjeeling. Behind Rajen's thick glasses and word lists was revealed a militant ethnic activist, whose offer to fill Basant's shoes as the BTWA general secretary stoked the fires of historical revisionism and cultural manipulation to a new intensity. In order to meet the perceived criteria of "primitive traits" for ST status,[29] Rajen initiated several campaigns to transform the everyday lives of Thangmi in India.

One of his most extreme initiatives was a campaign for the consumption of mouse meat. Rajen remembered an apocryphal tale told by his grandparents about Thangmi eating rodents as a staple food. Although Thangmi in Nepal may have occasionally done so, this was due to poverty, not as a marker of Thangmi cultural identity. Any Thangmi family with other food sources stays away from rodents, while many Thangmi in Nepal continue to eat beef, a consumption practice that was undoubtedly an act of resistance in the historically Hindu nation-state of Nepal (Ogura 2007:452, 473). Moreover, Thangmi intentionally refrain from eating pork, while such consumption is an important identity marker for their Kirant neighbors. Nonetheless, Rajen began a crusade to convince Darjeeling Thangmi to "return" to eating mouse as an expression of tribal identity. Thangmi in India did not otherwise have a distinctive food item, in large part because beef-eating is not taboo in Darjeeling, preventing it from being the marker of oppositional identity that it is in Nepal. With mouse meat, argued Rajen, they could demonstrate their "primitive traits" in an annual government-sponsored ethnic food festival.

The directive to eat mouse meat angered many in India, both from settled families and the migrant population from Nepal. The former group could not see the point of doing something they had never done before in the name of "culture," particularly since nowhere did the government of India clearly state that having a distinctive or primitive cuisine was necessary for tribal recognition. The latter group, who might have eaten rodents or other undesirable foods in their home villages during periods of food scarcity, found the idea insulting because it reminded them of the abject poverty they had left behind and undercut their aspirations for upward mobility in Darjeeling.

Rajen also sent a circular to the BTWA membership stating that Hindu practices were to be discontinued and that anyone who did not comply risked expulsion from the organization. The implication was that members of the organization would lose support for their individual ST certificate when the time came since the organization could withhold the required recommendation letter. Several angry letters in response stated that they would happily risk losing their membership in protest, including one from the Tumsong tea plantation family, who were key financial supporters of the BTWA. They now withdrew their support, stating that they had long taken pride in employing a Hindu *pandit* (N: priest) in their household, whose life contract they were not about to terminate now. The BTWA, like the NTS, was now confronted with serious dissent from within its membership. In order to recapture the semblance of ethnic unity necessary to maintain a functioning organization on both sides of the border, new leadership and agendas were necessary.

Turning Toward Development

In 2004, Khumbalal was ousted from the NTS leadership and replaced by Bhaba Bahadur, a young man in his twenties from the village of Suspa who had been a scholarship student at Buddhanilkantha, one of Nepal's premier English medium schools. He combined in a single person the attributes of both a village Thangmi who spoke his own language, maintained Thangmi ritual practices, and was skeptical of earlier NTS agendas, and the attributes of a *buddhijibi*, or highly educated "intellectual." In Darjeeling, Rajen stepped down, and the executive committee decided to work as a group rather than electing a general secretary, in the interest of maintaining diverse viewpoints at the central level.

In part owing to Bhaba's personal priorities, and in part owing to broader trends in Nepal that brought international development dollars to ethnic organizations, the NTS departed from Khumbalal's cultural politics to adopt what they called a "livelihood-based development strategy" as a primary goal.[30] In 2004, NEFIN received a grant of 1.52 million pounds from the Enabling State Program of the British government's Department for International Development (DFID) to establish the new Janajati Empowerment Project (JEP). As the representative body of one of twenty-four member groups that NEFIN had classified as "highly marginalized *janajati*," the NTS received 300,000 rupees through JEP for the Thami Empowerment Project (TEP). The TEP's objectives were to collect baseline information about Thangmi livelihoods and implement district-level projects for their improvement. The project leader of the TEP was none other than Megh Raj, who was later accused of using a bait-and-switch approach to entice rural Thangmi with the promise of economic development, which quickly transformed into the familiar discourse of rights to be achieved through the manipulation of culture. The TEP also provoked jealousy among the BTWA membership, who saw funding from international development donors as something that Thangmi had access to only in Nepal. There were few comparable organizations operating in Darjeeling due to the protectionist policies of the Indian state. As Rajen put it, "In Nepal they can get real money for development from all of those private donors. We have nothing like that; we have to squeeze every last bit out of the state. That is why ST is so important."

The TEP was short-lived, with only a three-month window of actual operation.[31] However, it presaged the type of projects to come (Shneiderman 2013a) and highlighted the necessity of parsing out the differences, as well as potential points of pragmatic collaboration, among Thangmi who believed in "livelihood-based" versus "rights-based" approaches to progress. It also highlighted the very real structural differences between the types of resources available to Thangmi in Nepal and India.

Cross-Border Conventions: Ritualizing Political Practice

In May 2005, such issues and the fault lines they revealed were aired in public for the first time at the Second National Thami Convention in Kathmandu (the first was in 1999, when the NTS was formed). Approximately 250 Thangmi from five districts of Nepal were present, as well as six members of the BTWA executive committee, who joked that the event should have been called the "First *International* Thami Convention." Another important Thangmi event was slated for exactly the same time: the annual Bhume Jatra festival in Suspa.

The national convention was advertised as a milestone in Thangmi efforts to unify and develop shared goals across political, geographical, economic, and educational divides. The fact that the leadership could schedule it to conflict with Bhume Jatra, a ritual event that all of their publications proclaimed central to their ethnic identity, demonstrated that the activists had in fact constructed a parallel universe for the ritual production of ethnicity through political action. In this arena, culture, religion, and history were divorced from their practice contexts and reobjectified as sacred objects through political performance.

The convention took place in Kathmandu without the participation of any gurus since they were all busy at Bhume Jatra in Dolakha. Yet the proceedings constantly referenced them. In public speeches, activists represented themselves as having sacrificed the opportunity to participate in important rituals to work for progress. However, when I asked in private whether the date was chosen intentionally, I received several whispered answers that "everyone" involved in planning the convention felt that their agenda—which included discussing how the NTS could help the BTWA achieve ST status by contributing cultural documentation, as well as mounting a movement to demand similar reservations in Nepal on the basis of their new "highly marginalized" status—would be better advanced without gurus and their followers there. The participation of gurus at previous meetings had only complicated matters for activists. Their goal now was not to discard Thangmi ritual practice but rather to mold it into a new kind of standardized, *nakali* sacred object detached from the bodies of those who practiced its *sakali* forms (see Chapter 2). But such *nakali* objects could not exist without the continued parallel existence of the *sakali*. Throughout the conference, speeches conjured glorious images of gurus engaged in Bhume Jatra festivities, which were given visual substance in a photo montage on the conference hall wall (to which I contributed images). Although in day-to-day life the choices were rarely so clear-cut, on this particular weekend, Thangmi individuals had to make a choice between participating in one or the other domain of ritualized action: practice or performance.

The conference began with a moment of silence in memory of the deceased: Basant from Darjeeling; Dalaman from Alampu, a district-level NTS leader who had been killed in Dolakha just a few days earlier by Maoists; and Ile and Bir Bahadur, the Piskar martyrs of 1984. Several prominent Thangmi gurus had also died since the last convention, but only certain politically active individuals were propitiated as ancestors whose profile suited the transnational Thangmi political cosmos. In between speeches by well-known *janajati* intellectuals and activists in support of the Thangmi association, as well as myself and Mark Turin, a youth group from Suspa performed the "wedding dances" described in Chapter 2.

The initial impetus for such objectifications of culture had come from India, where the state set the stage for such manipulations by attaching entitlements to the demonstration of cultural difference. However, such paradigms were now becoming naturalized inside Nepal as well. This process had been encouraged by the emergence of a Kathmandu-based ethnopolitical nexus, comprising the state, NGOs like NEFIN, and international agencies like DFID, which viewed culture with much the same essentialist worldview that the Indian state did and linked financial support to the capacity to demonstrate "unique" ethnic traits.

But as argued in Chapter 2, the experiences of people who inhabit such categories rarely conform to external expectations. Rather, for people seeking a synthesis of divine and political recognition, transformations of practice may also yield transformations of consciousness, with unexpectedly agentive results. Deploying the currency of culture can refigure not only the structures of ethnic association but the terms of value itself.

Chapter 6

Transcendent Territory, Portable Deities, and the Problem of Indigeneity

Niko nai guru niko nai barmi niko nai bubu kul deva
Niko nai dharma niko nai karma niko nai nemko mul deva . . .
Niko nai riti niko nai thiti harakai niye tortasa?

Our guru and his assistants, our brothers, our clan deity
Our religion, our destiny, the chief deity of our territory . . .
Why should we give up our practices and customs?
—Refrain of "Niko Nai Jati" (Our Ethnicity),
Thangmi-language song written by Maina and Lal Thami

In June 2008, I sat in a Kathmandu conference room watching a set of increasingly detailed maps project on a screen: first Nepal as a whole, then the central Bagmati zone, then Dolakha and Sindhupalchok districts, and finally a set of hand-drawn maps representing the proposed contours of a Thangmi autonomous region within a federally restructured Nepal (Figure 14). Tek Bahadur pointed to the scribbled names of Thangmi villages and spoke passionately about the need for a clearly delineated Thangmi territory, separate from the Tamang autonomous region encompassing the putative Thangmi region on most proposed maps of federal Nepal.[1] This activist from Lapilang in his mid-twenties had been the personal assistant to the general secretary of NEFIN for several years. Now he was the field coordinator for the Janajati Social and Economic Empowerment Project (JANSEEP), which had organized the day's workshop on the role of "highly

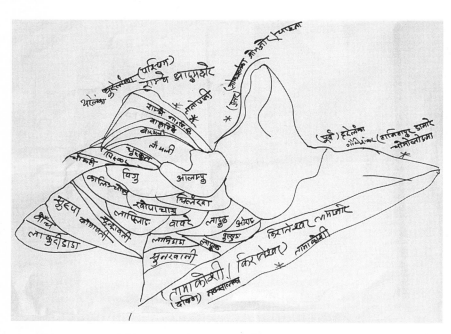

Figure 14. Hand-drawn map of Thangmi villages within the proposed autonomous area, Kathmandu, Nepal, June 2008. Photo by the author.

marginalized" *janajatis* in Nepal's federal restructuring (Shneiderman 2013a).

After Tek Bahadur finished his speech to resounding applause from the audience of ethnic activists and development workers, Jagat Man took the floor. Also from Lapilang, this older man had been a communist cadre, as well as an early ethnic activist. He seconded Tek Bahadur's argument and began to review the evidence supporting Thangmi claims to the territory shown on the maps. He first described the stone inscription at Dolakha Bhimsen temple, which dates Thangmi presence in the area to at least 1568 AD, and mentioned 2001 Nepal census figures to demonstrate the density of the Thangmi population in several VDCs of Dolakha and Sindhupal-chok. Then he began to narrate the Thangmi origin myth, describing how the group came to settle in the areas where they now live. Jagat Man closed his eyes, and his words began to shift from Nepali to Thangmi and take on the cadence of a guru's *paloke*. Someone whispered that Jagat Man had in fact trained as a guru in his youth but had given up that vocation as he became involved in politics. I was impressed by Jagat Man's knowledge but also increasingly aware of the discomfort on the audience's faces. The development workers and activists from other communities shifted restlessly as Jagat Man droned on.

Jagat Man was speaking mostly in Thangmi to address ethnically specific deities, rather than in Nepali, the national language that all in attendance shared. Worse, his recitation did not delineate Thangmi territory in the political terms of maps and borders but invoked the special Thangmi relationship with territorial deities to claim it in ritual terms. When chanted as a guru's *paloke* within the Thangmi-internal frame of practice, the origin myth worked to inculcate a subjective sense of belonging to ethnic territory. But it did not automatically work to transpose this sense of ethnic belonging into the political terms of the nation within the Thangmi-external frame of the workshop.

Effecting this sort of transposition was not impossible and in fact had been accomplished successfully by several other Himalayan groups, such as Gurung (Pettigrew 1999), Mewahang Rai (Gaenszle 2000), and Tamang (Tamang 2009), who had long based political claims to territory on their shamans' ability to propitiate the deities of those places. Indeed, deploying the content of ritual and other cultural practices to legitimize land claims has been an important strategy for indigenous movements the world over. However, the Thangmi activists had not yet fully attended to the work of translation that would make their ritual claims to territory recognizable in the political terms of the state. One of the workshop facilitators, an activist from another ethnic community, interrupted Jagat Man brusquely, asking him to repeat each place name slowly so the facilitator could plot the locations on the map.

Individuals and collectivities can simultaneously possess ritually produced feelings of territorial belonging and politically produced desires for legal rights to territory; however, the two types of relationship to territory do not always interface smoothly. This chapter explores how diverse Thangmi produce the idea of "Thangmi territory" as a transcendent ethnic object that is not limited by the pragmatic realities of the national borders within which it is geographically located. This transcendent territory is produced through a repertoire of ritualized practices and performances that at once ground people in specific locales and engender what James Clifford calls "a portable sense of the indigenous" (2007:206). The sites of Thangmi territory are marked by recognizable geographical features and historical contingencies of place, yet Thangmi "territorial consciousness" (Tamang 2009) is not circumscribed by the geopolitical reality of the national borders within which they sit. Human imaginings of Thangmi territory as a transcendent, translocal, yet unmistakably ethnic space are enabled by the essentially mobile nature of the Thangmi divine world. In this cosmology, although deities may be temporarily emplaced, their essence is portable and in fact resists permanent territorialization.

Exploring the lives of these portable deities, with their deep yet ultimately circumstantial links to territory, provides a way into understanding Thangmi senses of the indigenous. My engagement with this contested concept emerges from ethnographic encounters with Thangmi experiences and deployments of it, in all of their diversity across time and place. There are members of the community who experience indigeneity as a highly problematic category, others who identify strongly with it and believe that it indexes accurately their relationship with the state(s) in which they live, and a range of opinions in between. Here I do not attempt to evaluate whether or not indigeneity is an appropriate framework for scholarly analysis (Beteille 1998; Kuper 2003). Rather, I explore in detail why and how it becomes a functional—if sometimes vexing—logic for those who inhabit it. This is a particularly intriguing puzzle for a highly mobile, cross-border community, where movement itself, not only geographical fixity, is accorded cultural value. I neither accept the category of "the indigenous" as normatively real nor reject it entirely as a mode of false consciousness promoted through global discourses of neoliberalism or market logics, or localized through the instrumental rhetoric of political activists from outside the community (Shah 2010).

Instead, my objective is to describe how Thangmi themselves understand and express the link—or lack thereof—between ethnic bodies and ethnic territory that lies at the heart of the indigeneity concept, and how they articulate these understandings in relation to broader local, national, and international framings of indigeneity (Li 2000; Tsing 2009; Merlan 2009). From multiple Thangmi vantage points, which emphasize the simultaneous emplacement and mobility of both Thangmi people and their deities, we can begin to understand how a community that recognizes itself as a singular ethnic whole may "include people sustaining different spatial and social relations with ancestral places, a range of distances from 'land'" (Clifford 2007:205). In the Thangmi case, these people may be gurus, activists, or laypeople, in urban or rural environments, in Nepal, India, or China's TAR. By taking seriously their varied viewpoints and seeing them as mutually entangled producers of meaning in a shared social field, we can begin to understand how ideas of indigeneity in fact take shape in the "interactional space" (Goffman 1982) among such diverse groups of actors. This, in turn, suggests possible ways of reformulating, or "loosening" (Clifford 2007:200), the indigeneity concept itself to allow for more flexible understandings of the relationships among body, identity, territory, and mobility—on both scholarly and political registers, as well as that of lived experience.

I argue that Thangmi attitudes toward place contain both an element of primordial attachment and an emphasis on the importance of mobility as an identity marker. Using tropes of both territorial belonging and mobility as identity-defining paradigms is not unique to the Thangmi, nor does the combination present a paradox until groups encounter state-mandated classificatory schemes that are perceived to put indigeneity, understood as an embodied link to a specific place of origin, and migration—movement of the body away from that place of origin—at odds. This is the difficult juncture at which Thangmi in India in particular find themselves, with the complexities of their situation as Indian citizens of Nepali heritage making it impossible to construct the "homeland" as a sacred object of identity in the manner that diasporic populations are widely understood to do (Anderson 1991; Axel 2001). This is why I do not use "diaspora" as a primary analytical framework; if "the common denominator exemplifying a diaspora is its vital relation to a place of origin that is *elsewhere*" (Axel 2001:8), Thangmi in India must subvert that relationship in order to establish their claim to indigeneity in India. This displacement leads to fraught relationships with Thangmi in and from Nepal, which ritual techniques that enable participants to at once embody and transcend Thangmi territory help resolve.

The Legacy of Kipat: Ethnic Bodies, Territory, and Indigeneity in Nepal

I turn now to an episode of the Thangmi origin myth from the *paloke*, which follows the genesis episode presented in Chapter 3. We find Ya'apa and Sunari Ama, the Thangmi forefather and foremother, living an itinerant lifestyle deep in the forest. Traveling from the Tarai principality of Simraungadh on the border of Nepal and India,[2] they follow a riverine network along the Indrawati Khola and the Bhote Kosi to reach the village of Suspa in Nepal's contemporary Dolakha district. They have seven sons and seven daughters who marry each other, establishing the unusual Thangmi system of parallel descent. Along the way, the ancestral couple establishes the Thangmi claim to a broad swath of territory across central-eastern Nepal through their clever resistance of a Newar king's attempts at domination. Ya'apa is first punished for encroaching on the Newar king's territory, but then just as he is about to be executed, his wife Sunari produces several gold objects from her hair that she gifts to the king. The king's mind is turned and, instead of executing Ya'apa, grants him a wish. Ya'apa and Sunari request land, and when the Dolakha king asks how much land they would like, they reply, "No more than the size of a buffalo skin." The skin is brought, and the couple cleverly cut it into thin strips that they use to stake out a vast territory. Rather conveniently, the domain that Ya'apa and Sunari claim for the Thangmi in myth more or less maps on to the reality of contemporary Thangmi settlement in Nepal.

When the king grants the couple rights to the territory they have staked out, he says, in the myth, "This will be your *kipat*." This term is most concisely glossed as a "customary system of land tenure" (Forbes 1999:115). However, its full meaning in Nepal's contemporary political context is more complex. It has become shorthand for "indigenous territory" through a series of ideological and symbolic moves. The quest for historical evidence of territorial rights under the system of customary land tenure known as *kipat* occupies a central place in contemporary Thangmi activist projects in Nepal, as it does for many other ethnic communities currently involved in political agitations for self-determination (Limbu n.d.). The economic historian Mahesh Chandra Regmi explains that "rights under *Kipat* tenure emerged not because of a royal grant, but because the owner, as a member of a particular ethnic community, was in customary occupation of lands situated in a particular geographical area" (1976:87). Beginning in 1774, a series of royal decrees issued by Nepal's Shah kings formalized these rights for several groups who now identify as *janajati*, including Thangmi. With this move, the fledgling Nepali state reified in legal terms what was until then a circumstantial link between ethnicity and ancestral territory. Over time, however, as the state sought to exploit both the natural resources embedded in *kipat* lands and the labor of its inhabitants, *kipat* rights were gradually undermined through a series of localized land confiscations. By 1968, all legal distinctions between *kipat* and *raikar*

(N), the generic form of state land ownership, had disappeared (Regmi 1976:16). However, *kipat* was only legally abolished through the cadastral survey of 1994 (Forbes 1999:116)—the year I first visited Nepal.

The term "indigenous" was rapidly adopted by ethnic activists in Nepal in the wake of the U.N. Declaration of the Year of Indigenous Peoples in 1993 and the ensuing 1994 Declaration of the Decade of Indigenous Peoples (Gellner 2007; Hangen 2007; Onta 2006b). This temporal convergence with the abolition of *kipat* highlights how the diminishing recognition of a legal relationship between ethnic individuals and territory, as defined by the Nepali state through the concept of *kipat*, was paralleled by an increasing recognition of an embodied relationship between ethnic individuals and their territory, as defined by the international discourse of indigeneity. Indeed, the documents of global discourse—most notably the U.N. Declaration on the Rights of Indigenous Peoples and the ILO Convention 169 on Indigenous and Tribal Peoples—conceptualize indigeneity as an essential quality that inheres in indigenous bodies (Ghosh 2006; Kuper 2003; Niezen 2003). Possession of this quality in contemporary Nepal is expressed in essentialized, embodied terms—"we are indigenous"—rather than in the territorial terms that might have characterized such assertions of distinctiveness in the past—"we have *kipat*." The now widespread use of the term "indigenous" in political discourse, as well as in legislation like the 2002 NFDIN Act, has inscribed the relationship between ethnicity and territory in the bodies of "indigenous" people themselves. This puts the onus on such individuals to develop a new set of techniques to objectify that relationship and make it recognizable to others, in the absence of state policies that objectify the relationship between ethnicity and territory in the legal terms that *kipat* once did.

This is why many Thangmi activists, along with their counterparts from other ethnic groups in Nepal (Tamang 2009), focused on finding "proof" of their indigeneity. Evidence of their former status as *kipat* holders was perceived to be a powerful form of proof, since legal legitimation of ethnic territory in the past could be conceptualized as historical precedent for new policies. Thangmi activists in Nepal therefore emphasized the tenuous evidence for their historical rights to *kipat*, while downplaying the aspects of their origin myth that suggest their ancestors were migrants.[3] As the Thangmi activist Megh Raj writes in his article, "At the Crossroads of Proof and Conjecture," "It is common belief among Thami that in the past, Newar kings ruled Dolakha and that the primogenitors of Thami were awarded *kipat* land by the Newar kings. . . . We can safely assume that there must have been some proof and witness when a portion of the kingdom changed hands. . . . The bestower of *kipat* as well as the beneficiary must have in their possession written documents or stone inscriptions signifying the exchange. . . . Some such documents are still in the possession of some Dolakha Newars" (Reng 1999:16). In the age of indigeneity, the concept of *kipat* has become refigured as shorthand for evidence of ancestral rights to territory. Although that legal system no longer exists, use of the term *kipat* now expresses the historical consciousness of having once held such territorial rights, as in the simple Nepali phrase, *yo hamro kipat ho* (this is our *kipat*), which I heard often from Thangmi in Nepal in reference to the area where they lived.

Both the sparse historical records and the more fulsome mythical narratives that Thangmi can draw upon in their claims to indigeneity are complicated by their constant references to the Dolakha Newar. The ancestors of the contemporary Newar were clearly already in the area when Thangmi began to settle there, and it was these Newar rulers who first granted Thangmi territorial rights. This history complicates the reified *janajati* narrative of land lost to Indo-Aryan invaders, which Regmi recounts: "The *Kipat* system may have been a relic of the customary form of land control which communities of Mongoloid or autochthonous tribal origin established in areas occupied by them before the immigration of racial groups of Indo-Aryan origin" (1976:87–88). This racialized portrayal of two opposed groups does not account for the more complex history of Thangmi settlement or that of most other groups in Nepal. The problem with all this for Thangmi activists is that the scanty evidence they have of their own indigeneity implicates the Newar as at least equally, if not more, indigenous, owing to their earlier settlement.[4] The Thangmi settlers were in fact granted land rights by a local Newar king, not by the central Nepali state. Later, from the state's perspective, Thangmi *kipat* was incorporated into the national framework, but from the Thangmi perspective, the Newar rulers of Dolakha remained the primary sociopolitical authority in relation to whom they defined themselves.

Although this close relationship with the Newar is seen as a liability by contemporary Thangmi activists in Nepal, who project themselves as the sole indigenous inhabitants of the area claimed as Thangmi territory, it is in fact this in-depth, interethnic historical relationship with the Newar at the local level that creates the conditions for Thangmi in India to conceptualize

Thangmi territory as a translocal ethnic possession that transcends the confines of the Nepali nation-state. When Thangmi began migrating to India in the mid-1800s, they likely did not envision their right to territory in relation to the sociopolitical order of the fledgling Nepali state but rather as a set of localized power relations, with the Dolakha Newar at the top. It was first the Thangmi deities who granted dominion over territory, and second the Dolakha Newar who tacitly allowed Thangmi to maintain this special relationship with the territorial deities. The ritual relationships enacted every year at Dasain between the Thangmi and the Dolakha Newar (see Chapter 8) cemented Thangmi territorial claims vis-à-vis the local Newar authority, who in turn provided a buffer of sorts between the Thangmi and the emergent Nepali state. The fact that Thangmi were not listed in the 1854 Muluki Ain suggests that they were not fully incorporated into the Nepali state at that seminal moment of consolidation.[5] Early migrants to India, then, carried with them a sense of ethnicity produced in practice but not fully articulated in relation to any nation-state.

In 1994, anthropologist Rajendra Pradhan posed the problem of indigeneity for Nepal as follows in one of the first widely circulated popular articles on this topic:

> Do we want to deny the history and tradition of a Nepal where all communities are descended from migrants from outside during different periods of history? Specially when these different waves of migrants have either intermingled or broken up to form the numerous ethnic/linguistic communities which today constitute the peoples of Nepal. . . .
>
> In other words, this whole question of indigenous peoples is a false problem because indigenous peoples do not exist in Nepal; or if they do, the majority of the Nepalis are indigenous, including many of the Bahuns and Chhetris. (1994:45)

I often heard similar arguments throughout the late 1990s and 2000s, primarily from individuals who did not consider themselves *janajati*. Such logic has since become the common currency of various post-2008 political movements in Nepal organized around erstwhile dominant identities (Bahun/Chhetri, *pahadi*), all of which oppose the notion of "identity-based federalism."

Pradhan may represent migratory histories more or less accurately, but such arguments fail to account for the strong feelings of emplacement and territoriality that shape ethnic consciousness, as enacted through ritualized action by community members living both inside and outside the territories in question. Indigenous activists have been equally unnuanced in their rhetoric by positing a one-to-one correlation between each piece of territory and a single group, despite the obvious fact of high mobility that characterizes many contemporary *janajati* lives today, whether to other parts of Nepal, to adjacent countries like India and China, or further afield to the Middle East and beyond.

Nepal's 2007 ratification of the ILO Convention on the rights of indigenous peoples demonstrated that activists had won this debate at the public policy level in the medium term. However, the first Constituent Assembly's inability to promulgate a new constitution after 2008—still awaited at the time of this writing in early 2014—derived in large part from the lack of consensus over how to define the relationship between ethnicity and territory for the purposes of federal restructuring. Exploring the varied possibilities for imagining this relationship that emerge from the experiences of groups like the Thangmi therefore remains crucial within the ongoing process of state restructuring.

The Problem of Indigeneity in India

Rajendra Pradhan's argument against the concept of indigeneity is in fact similar to the legal stance of the Indian state: that there are no indigenous peoples in India. Unlike the "settler states" of Australia, Canada, or the United States, the government of India asserts, historical patterns of migration make it impossible to determine who came first. However, many groups officially recognized as STs by the government of India have increasingly alluded to indigeneity as part of their self-identification over the last two decades. Members of such groups have pressured the Indian government to adopt indigeneity as a legal category since at least 1985, when they began participating in the U.N. Working Group on Indigenous Peoples (Ghosh 2006). Accession to the global category of "indigenous" is by no means a fait accompli for Indian tribal groups, however, both because the state continues to resist that move and because the global juggernaut of indigeneity can undermine locally specific forms of community reproduction and self-governance (Ghosh 2006; Shah 2010). Such arguments build upon a history of scholarly and political debate in India over the colonial construction of the category "tribe" in opposition to "caste." At stake is the validity and ownership of the term *adivasi*, which literally translates as "original inhabitants," and is often used by groups recognized as STs to describe themselves.

Indian citizens of Nepali heritage in Darjeeling were not particularly interested in claiming membership in this category until after 1990, when several factors encouraged them to explore the possibilities of becoming *adivasi* (Rycroft and Dasgupta 2011). Once this became the objective, Thangmi were compelled to think carefully about what tribal status would mean for their relationships to a range of territories, both in India and Nepal, and their public representations of these relationships. Ironically, although India does not recognize the concept of indigeneity, the term *adivasi* within Indian national discourse is popularly perceived to index a link between ethnicity and territory for those recognized as STs, in much the same way as the term "indigeneity" does within global discourse (Karlsson 2013). Through print and visual media that described prominent *adivasi* struggles in other parts of the country—Assam, Meghalaya, Jharkhand—throughout the 1980s and 1990s, Thangmi activists in Darjeeling became aware of the perceived indigeneity requirement of the tribal category to which they aspired, despite the fact that official criteria included only the opaque statement that STs should exhibit "geographical isolation." Thangmi in India thus began considering how to represent themselves as autochthonous, often using "indigenous" in English in conversations with me to explain this part of their project.

The problem with demonstrating such indigeneity was twofold. First, it was common knowledge that the ancestors of contemporary Indian citizens of Nepali heritage had at some point migrated from Nepal. Second, the ethnic heterogeneity of the pan-Nepali community and the mixed residential patterns throughout both urban and rural areas of Darjeeling meant that there was no specific territory to which the Thangmi (or any other group of Nepali heritage) could claim exclusive indigeneity: except, of course, if they wanted to piggyback upon the claims to indigeneity that Thangmi activists in Nepal were already making through the idiom of *kipat*. Although many Thangmi in India were familiar with the idea of Thangmi territory articulated through territorial deity propitiation, claiming territory in Nepal as a marker of indigeneity in India was not only illogical but potentially dangerous since it could mark them as "foreigners." For Indians of Nepali heritage in Mizoram and Meghalaya, such characterizations as "foreign" had resulted in mass expulsions in the 1980s, as they had in the early 1990s for people of Nepali heritage who considered themselves citizens of Bhutan (Hutt 2003).

It was such insecurities—wrought by the paradox of the 1950 Indo-Nepal treaty that ruled out dual citizenship, while making the border permeable—that made it inconceivable for Thangmi in India to produce a diasporic identity through a simple affirmation of a "vital relation with the place of origin" (Axel 2001:8) located in a "homeland" in another country. That geographical place of origin was too close to be a safe source of identity, too unbounded in its potential to claim them rather than allowing them to maintain the agency to claim it. Instead, Thangmi in India felt that they needed to constantly disavow links to Nepal in order to claim their rights as Indian citizens, including the right to demand special treatment via ST status. Nonetheless, the entire complex of ritual practice that Thangmi activists in India sought to deploy as evidence of their tribal nature took for granted the existence of a Thangmi territory in Nepal, the place names and territorial deities of which were recited at every ritual instance in an entirely embodied manner that defied erasure.

Encountering the Originary Other

The puzzle of how to use ideas of Thangmi territory to strengthen their claim to indigeneity in India, while simultaneously disassociating such territory from a physical location within Nepal's national borders, was a burning concern for Thangmi activists in India. One attempt to resolve this conundrum involved the assertion that Thangmi had in fact originally lived in India but then migrated to Nepal, from whence they eventually returned to their point of origin in India. Inverting the emphasis that Thangmi activists in Nepal placed on the origin story's trope of settlement in Dolakha, Thangmi activists in India focused instead on the trope of migration from Simraungadh, now an archaeological site on the Nepal-India border. A document compiled by the Sikkim branch of the BTWA entitled *Thami Community and Their Rituals*, submitted to the Union Minister for Tribal Affairs in 2005, claimed (in English) that "from the books written by some eminent historian the THAMI might have migrated from Asia Minor and settled down in Simroungad (the capital of TIRHUTDOYA 1097–1326 A.D., map is enclosed herewith), bordering present India and Nepal in Western Indian frontiers. . . . This ethnic Thami community is an aboriginal race residing as indigenous inhabitants in North-East region of India from the hoary past." If Simraungadh had indeed been in India, then Thangmi could claim indigeneity on that basis, even though they had spent several generations living in Nepal before returning to their "homeland" in India.

In interviews with me, Rajen, then the BTWA general secretary, refused to talk about his family history, which would contradict his public statements about Thangmi indigeneity in India. During one video interview in early 2005, Rajen accidentally alluded to his father's experiences in Darjeeling as a migrant from Nepal in the 1940s. Some minutes later, he requested that I erase the tape. I complied, but I already knew the details of his family history from interviews with other less militant community members.[6] Rajen's claim was wishful thinking, which even other Thangmi who initially supported it eventually came to question: the Tamang and Limbu attained ST status in 2003, and they too were known to have migrated from Nepal; so why bother claiming indigeneity on such specious grounds?

I first became aware of how much tension these issues could create between Thangmi activists in India and circular migrants from Nepal in 2004 during a *deusi* "cultural program" organized by the BTWA on the Hindu holiday of Tihar (Diwali). BTWA officers had requested a group of Thangmi from Nepal to perform dances and songs in the Thangmi language to raise money for the BTWA, since the leadership did not themselves possess the cultural knowledge to put on such a performance. I traveled by jeep with the BTWA leadership to the site of the program in Jorebunglow, some kilometers outside of Darjeeling bazaar. When we arrived at the appointed time, the performers were not yet there. We waited for over an hour, which the BTWA officers spent complaining about how unreliable, uncultured, and unsavory Thangmi from Nepal were, giving all Thangmi a bad reputation. When the performers arrived, all grown men, Rajen scolded them, calling them "boys" and asking them how they expected Thangmi culture to develop if they could not even be on time for a performance. The Thangmi from Nepal shrugged off this critique, asking how Rajen expected Thangmi culture to develop if their stomachs were not full, and requested drinks and snacks as they prepared to perform.

While we waited for the audience to gather—a multigenerational, multiethnic group from the surrounding area—I spoke with the performers.

They typically spent six months of the year in Darjeeling, although most of them had wives and children back in the Dolakha village of Lapilang, they said. When I asked which place they considered home, one of them said, "This is our village, but that is also our village. Really, they are the same village." Overhearing this conversation, Rajen approached just as I was writing the label for the videocassette I had cued to record their performance, and said, "Well, since it's all one village anyway, please don't write on the cassette that they are from Nepal. Just write that this performance occurred in Darjeeling." It is in this sense of being "all one village" that Thangmi territory can be envisioned as a translocal ethnic territory, which transcends the national borders that appear to circumscribe it. I compromised with Rajen's request by writing "Lapilang dancers in Jorebunglow" on the cassette, using local rather than national descriptors.

This experience demonstrated how circular migrants from Nepal often became foils for the struggles of Thangmi in India to express the complex territorialities that shaped their own sense of Thangminess. On the one hand, the cultural knowledge and performative skill of Thangmi from Nepal were valued as links to the originary content of indigeneity, which could work on both affective and pragmatic levels to articulate Thangmi identity in a productive manner. On the other hand, circular migrants embodied the national other that Thangmi in India worked hard to define themselves in contrast to, making appropriation of their knowledge to shore up claims of indigeneity in India a political gamble. Psychologically speaking, for BTWA activists deeply enmeshed in the pragmatism of tribal politics but insecure about their own lack of cultural knowledge, listening to the songs about territorial deities and Thangmi villages that the Lapilang group performed—with lyrics similar to those cited in the epigraph to this chapter—boosted morale by reminding them how divine recognition worked. "See," Rajen said to me, as we watched the program finally get under way, "How can the government deny us? All of those deities the boys are singing about, aren't they our deities too? They should help us in our 'campaign.'"

The Ritual Solution

That these deities, and the territory they marked as Thangmi, could transcend the physicality of geographical and political borders was further clarified to me some weeks later at an all-night ritual conducted by Latte Apa to banish malevolent spirits from a Darjeeling Thangmi household that had recently experienced a spell of bad luck. I was offered cheap whiskey, which here replaced the home-brewed beer of such events in Nepal. Smoke from the fresh wormwood leaf incense permeated the wood-paneled room as Latte Apa chanted his *paloke*.

Ajay, a teenager born and raised in Darjeeling, took me aside to ask in English, "Do you understand what he is saying?" "A little bit," I responded. "So then you know that he is taking us back to the original birthplace of all Thangmi in order to get the blessings of the deities there?" "Yes," I said. "But you see," said Ajay, "he tries to make it interesting to us too by talking about places that we know—Siliguri, Chowrasta, Tungsung—not just those strange village names somewhere out there in the *pahar* [N: hills] where we've never been." I realized that I needed to listen more carefully. The seemingly familiar cadence of the *paloke* had distracted me from the content of Latte Apa's chant. In fact, he was entering new territory, expanding the origin story to encompass the Darjeeling migrations. Instead of leaving off in Dolakha, where Rana Bahadur's rendition ended, Latte Apa's *paloke* incorporated place names that Thangmi migrants from Nepal to India encountered on their long journey. As Latte Apa brought the narrative right up to the doorstep of the house in which we were sitting, I began to understand how he was ritualizing the process of migration and turning it into an integral part of the origin myth itself.

Latte Apa's *paloke* in practice shows how origin myths do more than describe "creation" at a fixed moment in the mythic past; they are themselves creative forms that incorporate ongoing collective experiences as part of their narrative. Latte Apa's extension of the ritual chants to include migration to Darjeeling worked to make young Thangmi in India, like Ajay, feel included in the practice by ritually transforming familiar local places into Thangmi territory rather than simply limiting it to an area of rural Nepal that was alien to young Thangmi in India. In this process, deities were ritually "deterritorialized" from their abodes in Nepal and "reterritorialized" not just in India but in a transcendent conception of Thangmi territory. I use these terms from Deleuze and Guattari (1977) not to suggest "a weakening of the link between culture and place" (Inda and Rosaldo 2002:14) but rather an expansion of such links to new locations.

A Landscape of Deities and Ancestors

At first, Latte Apa's capacity to do this seemed novel and specific to the Darjeeling context. On further analysis of my ethnographic materials from

Nepal, however, I realized that Thangmi there also conceptualized divine territory as at once immanent and transcendent. The divine Thangmi world seemed to mirror the tension between fixed residence and movement that characterized the human Thangmi world. Or was it the other way around?

In a paradigm widely attested across the Tibetan cultural zone extending into the Himalayas, group identity is embedded in particular territories, which are personified by deities (Blondeau 1998; Blondeau and Steinkellner 1996; Buffetrille and Diemberger 2002; Huber 1999a, 1999b; Ramble 1997; Tautscher 2007). These deities and their whims control the agricultural productivity of the land, as well as the fates of the people who work it. In many cases, such deities are linked to sacred mountains. Himalayan Hinduism manifests a similar paradigm in the cults of *kul devata* (N), lineage deities identified with individual clans (Chalier-Visuvalingam 2003; Gaborieau 1968; Michaels 2004).

Such territorial and lineage deity traditions are conflated in the worship of the single Thangmi deity of Bhume.[7] As in the song that serves as the epigraph to this chapter, Bhume is commonly referred to both as *mul deva* (T; N-*devata*)—the chief territorial deity—and *kul deva* (T)—a lineage deity. Bhume is a pan-Himalayan earth deity, whose worship is a cornerstone of shamanic practice for many ethnic groups (Gaborieau 1968; Lecomte-Tilouine 1993). However, Thangmi conceptualize the ritual practices through which they propitiate Bhume as evidence of their special relationship with the deity in its unique instantiation within Thangmi territory.

Marie Lecomte-Tilouine (1993) suggests that in the Gulmi district of western Nepal, Bhume unites in a single divine entity what she calls the "tribal" notion of territoriality and the Hindu "Indo-Nepalese" notion of lineage as key markers of group cohesion and power. She attributes this mixture to the history of cohabitation between Magar and caste Hindu settlers in the area. Bhume, she argues, affirms both groups' claims to territory and power at once: the Magar exclusively propitiate Bhume's territorial aspects, while caste Hindus propitiate its lineage aspects. Bhume is similarly multivalent for Thangmi, but they control both the territorial and lineage aspects of Bhume's worship. Non-Thangmi do not participate directly in the deity's worship at all, except to receive consecrated offerings from a Thangmi officiant. Propitiating Bhume at once enables Thangmi to assert ritual control over their territory and to assert the power of Thangmi identity—in the sense of lineage—itself. This fusion of Bhume's territorial and lineage aspects demonstrates the synthetic nature of Thangmi subjectivity and illustrates how Bhume instantiates Thangmi conceptions of ethnicity as the intersection between territorial belonging and shared descent.

Have Bhume, Will Travel

"As they walked and walked from Simraungadh, Ya'apa and Sunari Ama brought Bhume with them," explained Guru Maila of Suspa, emphasizing this most important divinity's peripatetic tendencies. Bhume is both integrally attached to territory wherever Thangmi settle and eminently transportable when they move. Having made the journey from Simraungadh with the ancestral Thangmi couple, "Bhume stayed here in our village of Suspa, here in Rangathali where our ancestors settled," as proudly broadcast in a song written by a youth group based near Rangathali, in present-day Suspa-Kshamawati VDC, Dolakha. But this site's importance stretches far beyond the residents of Suspa; the largest communal Thangmi propitiation ritual in Nepal is Bhume Jatra, held on the full moon of Buddha Jayanti. The festival draws thousands annually to the Suspa Bhumethan temple near Rangathali.

Bhume resides in a black rock that embodies the essence of both the earth and Thangmi identity. However, the Suspa rock is not unique. Instead, it is infinitely replicable wherever Thangmi go. Dolakha and Sindhupalchok districts have long been peppered with minor Bhumethan, where the deity can be worshipped by those who cannot travel to Suspa. Bhumethan have also been established in Jhapa and Darjeeling. As one man who had relocated from Lapilang to Jhapa explained, "After we built our Bhume temple, we thought, 'We can really stay here permanently.'" Suspa remains the Thangmi Bhume's chief abode, and propitiation rituals conducted elsewhere must always refer to it. But as an all-pervasive earth deity present in every natural site, there is in fact nowhere that is *not* Bhume's abode. Therefore, the deity can be propitiated anywhere Thangmi reside.

This divine flexibility—the capacity to simultaneously sacralize a particular piece of earth and to be present everywhere—and the transcendentalization of territory that it enables account in part for the resilience of Thangmi identity within a context of high mobility. Bhume's enduring presence in Suspa creates a focal point around which the concept of Thangmi territory can be produced as a source of a distinct identity. Yet the very divine entity that gives this territory its symbolic power is infinitely expandable, manifesting in multiple sites wherever the people who believe in it recognize its presence. The territory claimed by contemporary activists in Nepal as Thangmi *kipat* in political terms (with Bhume's chief temple in Suspa at its center) is in ritual terms only a temporary holding pen for practices that can go anywhere that Thangmi go. Bhume itself came from somewhere else with Ya'apa and Sunari Ama, and although installed in Suspa for at least five hundred years—adequate time for the surrounding communities to develop an attachment and accord interpretive importance to its current location—the deity's continued residence there is a matter of tradition, not primordial necessity. For Thangmi in India, this reading of Bhume's territoriality is key: its current location in Suspa is seen as a chance resting place for both deity and people, a location determined by the contingencies of history, not by an essential, unshakable link between territory-divinity-identity. Like Bhume, Thangmi identity is everywhere and nowhere at once, linked to a notion of sacred territory that transcends the geographical physicality of its location.

A Captive God

The evening before the annual Bhume Jatra in Suspa in May 2000, several gurus went into trance, channeling the deities and preparing to receive their *jokhana* (N), or spiritual forecast, for the year. At the house of the *pujari* (N: priest) everyone crowded around closely to hear whatever pronouncements might be made. The senior shaman Junkiri's breathing was punctuated by sharp cries as his eyes rolled back in his head. He shook with the force of possession as the deity entered him. Slowly the guru's unintelligible grunts and cries gave way to words, and a single phrase emerged, repeated over and over: "I have been tied."

The *pujari* and the gurus' assistants looked perplexed. People pushed and shoved to get closer to Junkiri so they could hear the divine words for themselves. "I've been tied, I've been tied," the guru moaned, his voice rising to an eerie wail. Everyone looked at each other, seeking some insight to make sense of this utterance. Eventually the *pujari* raised his eyebrows. "Eh heh . . ." he said with the rising intonation of a question. "Bhume must be upset that we have built walls around its place of worship in Suspa. The god feels tied down; it cannot move."

The previous year, Gopal, a Thangmi schoolteacher in upper Suspa, and an active member of the NTS, had launched a fundraising campaign to build a temple around the Bhumethan rock near Rangathali. The 2000 Bhume Jatra was the building's inaugural year, the first time the deity was surrounded by stone walls. With wooden rafters, a yellow aluminum roof topped with a monasterylike steeple, and an elaborately carved wooden door, the new structure looked appropriately synthetic, alluding to both Hindu and Buddhist Himalayan temple architecture. Despite the temple's hefty price tag of over 500,000 Nepali rupees (over $7000 at the time) and 742 days of villager manpower, Bhume apparently remained unimpressed.

Junkiri's *jokhana* gave voice—the voice of the deity itself—to an existing sense of frustration among many villagers about what had happened to the Bhumethan. Although some agreed with Gopal's logic that spending money and time on such a structure showed their devotion to the deity and would also help make Thangmi practices more recognizable to outsiders, many felt that to enclose Bhume was to challenge the very source of the deity's power. After all, Thangmi came to make offerings to the rock itself, embedded in the earth, not icons or statues installed in a temple (Figure 15). My hostess in Balasode expressed her opinion on the matter: "For us Thangmi, Bhume is part of the earth. We are different from Hindus and Buddhists because we do not need temples to know that Bhume is with us. Now the temple that they have built makes our Bhume seem small and like any other Hindu deity. The walls separate us from Bhume. I do not want to go inside there now. That temple belongs to Gopal, not to Bhume or common Thangmi people like us."

For her, building walls around Bhume set up a stark division between sacred and profane, which was at odds with the way many Thangmi conceptualized Bhume as at once part of the earth and part of themselves. To people who shared this view, the temple building seemed to aspire to Hindu mores, not to encourage Thangmi practice. Indeed, Gopal, the temple building coordinator, had also authored the 1990 pamphlet cited in Chapter 5, which advocated a path to progress that disavowed "wild" Thangmi practices in favor of a Hinduized modernity. When I asked him about the rationale behind the temple, he told me that the walls served to keep non-Thangmi out. They needed to act fast, he said, to protect Bhume against encroaching Hinduization. In his desire to preserve an exclusively Thangmi space, his logic appealed to the very exclusivity of Hinduism itself.

Figure 15. *Pujari* making offerings at Suspa Bhume in 1999, shortly before its enclosure, Suspa-Kshamawati, Dolakha, Nepal. Photo by the author.

Clearly, Bhume was not happy and expressed those sentiments through Junkiri's *jokhana*. As the guru's trance subsided and Junkiri stopped shaking, whispers echoed across the room. People were discussing how to placate the angry deity. Some were upset that Bhume did not receive the community's investment in the new temple as a sign of devotion. Others felt vindicated by the deity's protest and proposed a special propitiation ritual to apologize and ask the deity how to make good. Still others suggested that they needed to explain more effectively to Bhume that the temple building was a form of development, which would strengthen the position of the Thangmi community vis-à-vis local caste Hindu families, ultimately ensuring Bhume's position as the chief territorial deity of the region.

These deliberations soon gave way to the desire to conclude the ritual at hand. It was after 4:00 a.m., and a chicken was brought in for sacrifice. Junkiri deftly ripped off its head, spraying blood across the ritual altar. Then it was time for participants to make their own offerings to the deities.

A long line of people clutching chickens stretched out through the door into the courtyard. Once all of the chickens were dispatched, the guru's assistant removed the bamboo tray of *puchuk* (T: grain effigies) from the room. Walking away from the house, he crossed the nearest small stream and broke the *puchuk* into small pieces. He returned one piece to the *pujari*, who ate the consecrated offering. The guru's assistant then found a child to take another piece of the *puchuk* across the river: the customary offering to non-Thangmi families there. Finally, he distributed additional *puchuk* pieces to the assembled audience in the immediate area of the *pujari*'s house. The preliminaries to Bhume Jatra conducted at the *pujari*'s house were now finished, and everyone returned home to sleep before arriving at the Bhumethan itself for the main event later.

Bhume as Cultural Performance

While the gurus slept, villagers of all ages gathered at the Bhumethan for an afternoon "cultural performance" (N: *sanskritik karyakram*) in honor of Bhume Jatra. While waiting for the gurus to arrive at the *pujari*'s house the night before, I ventured next door to watch a village youth group rehearsing songs for this event. The leader was Gopi, the *pujari*'s teenaged son, who had written several songs in the Thangmi language. One was entitled "Yapati Chuku and Sunari Aji"—alternate and equally common names for Ya'apa and Sunari Ama—which set the portion of the origin myth about the ancestral couple to music.[8] The performance group's inspiration came in large part from Darjeeling, in the form of *Amako Ashis* (N: "Mother's Blessings"), billed in the liner notes as "the first Thangmi language cassette" and received with great enthusiasm in Dolakha. When I asked whether they were ready for their upcoming performance, Gopi laughed nervously and confided that it was going to be the group's debut, in fact the first time anything of the sort had been performed at Bhume Jatra.

While the *pujari* enacted Bhume's ritual in practice inside the Bhumethan, his son was at the forefront of the performance tradition developing outside the temple. As the *pujari*'s oldest son, Gopi was next in line to take on the responsibilities of Bhume's annual propitiation. Gopi was crafting performances that objectified his father's practice and translated it into catchy musical refrains more accessible to a broad range of listeners. The *pujari* himself was not displeased, taking great pride in Gopi's performance and leadership abilities, but the difference between father's and son's relationship with Bhume indicated the diversification of Thangmi cultural production.

The new enclosure around the Bhumethan was also part of this transformation. The building introduced a stark separation between the space for ritual practice—which would by necessity be conducted inside now, in a clearly delimited Thangmi-only space in close proximity to Bhume itself, as embodied in the black rock—and the space for cultural performance, which would take place outside in a public, interethnic environment. Perhaps effecting this separation between practice and performance was part of the intended objective of the temple-building project in the minds of activists like Gopal. By shifting practice—the actual propitiation of the deity by the gurus—to a behind-the-scenes space inside the temple, hidden from public view, the activists could reorient public attention to the realm of cultural performance, over which they themselves maintained control. Khumbalal, the senior activist whose diatribe about gurus' control of Thangmi culture was cited in Chapter 3, had traveled from Kathmandu to attend this inaugural Bhume Jatra at the new temple.

Now, at around 3:00 P.M. on the afternoon of Bhume Jatra, Gopal began the cultural program with an amplified welcome to the nearly one thousand villagers gathered under a bright-red welcome banner. Gopi's group performed several song-and-dance numbers in the Thangmi language on a wooden stage, with the aid of an erratically functioning microphone. Then several students from the local high school performed another dance to a Nepali pop tune and read poetry they had composed for the occasion. Between each item, Gopal asked for donations to cover the remaining costs of the new building. Several NGOs working in the district made announcements about their current projects, and then political leaders from the main parties took their turns, along with Maoist guerrillas, who were present in civilian dress.

Finally, the program began to wind down as dusk fell. Just as people were beginning to disperse, the sound of the gurus' drums began to echo across the hills, getting closer and closer. The gurus were working their way up the hill from the *pujari*'s house, preparing to make an entrance that would remind festivalgoers that ritual power could not be expressed fully through performance alone.

Marking Ethnic Territory: Bhume as Identity
Icon and Pilgrimage Site

The debate over the new temple building had subsided by the time Bhume Jatra rolled around again. Those who had opposed the building began to accept its reality as part of their local landscape, and the deity appeared placated by an additional set of propitiation rituals organized some months later. Gopal decided to capitalize on the temple's apparent success by proposing it as the site for a four-day-long "national Thangmi conference" on the occasion of Bhume Jatra in 2001. With financial support from a Japanese NGO, Thangmi from all over Nepal and India were invited to gather in Suspa for Bhume Jatra. At least twenty gurus participated, along with around two thousand laypeople.

This was the first opportunity for many Thangmi from India, as well as the most far-flung Thangmi settlements in eastern Nepal, to actually see the site where the Bhume they had heard so much about stood. Some of the participants from India took photos of the new Suspa Bhumethan building home, and by 2003, the image graced the cover of *Niko Bachinte*, the first substantial publication of the BTWA (Figure 16).

After appearing on the publication cover, the image began to pop up everywhere in Darjeeling: on poster-sized photo prints adorning household walls, on invitations to BTWA events, and on certificates presented to participants in BTWA-organized cultural events. Despite the distaste with which many Thangmi in Nepal had originally viewed the temple building, its image quickly became iconic in India. It then circulated throughout the transnational Thangmi public sphere, returning to Nepal in 2007 on the cover of *Reng Patangko*, a Thangmi-language music cassette produced in Kathmandu.

The Bhumethan shown on the cover of *Niko Bachinte* appeared to float in space, a freestanding architectural icon unmoored from its physical setting. There were no people or other contextualizing details to indicate the building's location in a rural hill village in Nepal. The caption for the photo, which is reproduced on the title page of the publication, read, "The Bhumethani in Suspa—the auspicious pilgrimage site of the Thami community. The 'Bhumeshwor' was set up there in unknown times by a historic couple from the Thami community, Yapati and Sunari, from Simraungadh. This temple is situated on an exciting hill in Suspa, to the northeast of Charikot, the district headquarters of Dolakha, from where it can be reached on foot

भारतीय थामी वेलफियर ऐसौसिएशनद्वारा
प्रथम प्रस्तुति
(स्मारिका)

निको बचिन्टे

Figure 16. Suspa Bhume temple enclosure as it appears on the cover of *Niko Bachinte* (2003).

in three hours" (Niko 2003:1). This paragraph captured several characteristics of the concept of Thangmi territory emerging in India. First, it valorized the locality in which the temple was situated without mentioning Nepal at all. Second, it emphasized the migration of the ancestors to this location from Simraungadh. Third, it presented the Suspa Bhumethan as a pilgrimage site to which one traveled from afar rather than as the abode of a local deity intimately involved in everyday life.

Reconceptualizing the Suspa Bhumethan as a pilgrimage site was part of an effort to mark the contours of Thangmi ethnic territory by establishing symbolic links between a set of Bhume temples. This territory was imagined in translocal rather than transnational terms. It was the links between each locale that mattered—Suspa, Jhapa, Darjeeling—not the nation-states in which they were nested.

Making the Suspa Bhumethan a pilgrimage site opened new possibilities for asserting Thangmi claims to ethnic territory. Emerging out of activist agendas in India, the idea of Suspa Bhumethan as a pilgrimage site was initially articulated in a translocal idiom that downplayed the temple's situatedness within the nation-state of Nepal. Yet it was the very fact that Thangmi who resided outside the geopolitical borders of Thangmi ethnic territory wanted to visit the Bhumethan that brought the Suspa temple, as well as the people who lived around it, into relationship with ideas of an exclusive ethnic territory articulated in relation to national and transnational regimes for recognizing indigeneity. Indeed, for activists who lived outside the bounds of ethnic territory, the Suspa Bhumethan had become sacralized as an easily recognizable symbol of that territory's existence, and the journey to the temple—rather than simply the events that took place once one was there—began to take on the ritualized qualities of pilgrimage. For most participants in the festival, however, the temple was still right next door.

Some Himalayan territorial deities—usually identified with sacred mountains—can be transferred from one physical abode to another as people themselves move from place to place (Buffetrille 1996). In Darjeeling, some Thangmi had taken the initiative to do this themselves, building small shrines outside their homes, where they propitiated Bhume in the private-lineage deity sense. The families who had done this said that only after they procured a metal trident originally consecrated at the Suspa Bhumethan did they feel that their own shrines were efficacious. The deity was eminently portable, yet without that physical link to the Suspa Bhumethan, the deity would not recognize the new shrine as its abode.

Despite the long-standing existence of these private shrines to lineage deities, Bhume's presence in its communal territorial deity aspect was not yet fully realized in Darjeeling during my fieldwork. Instead, Bhume propitiations were conducted at the large Mahakal temple above Darjeeling bazaar. Like Kalinchok in Nepal, this large complex was an interethnic ritual site, with both Hindu and Buddhist shrines, as well as shrines dedicated by individual community and ethnic organizations for the special use of their members. In the earlier phase of pan-Nepali identity construction in Darjeeling, Mahakal had been a key site for the demonstration of ethnic unity. In the absence of separate ritual spaces, every group of Nepali heritage conducted its rituals there; indeed, this is where the 1936 photo described in Chapter 5 was taken. By the early 2000s, however, the interethnic ritual space of Mahakal no longer felt adequate. Along with initiating pilgrimages to the Suspa Bhumethan, Thangmi activists in India sought to establish a similarly exclusive marker of Thangmi ethnic territory in Darjeeling. In 2005, Darjeeling municipality approved the BTWA's proposal to build the temple on a piece of land where a defunct Thangmi-owned jam factory stood.

At the groundbreaking ceremony, Latte Apa planted in the earth a small metal trident from the Suspa Bhumethan, which he had commissioned a circular migrant from Nepal to deliver. Some BTWA members questioned the need for this link to Suspa, but Latte Apa insisted that without this physical connection, the deity might not recognize its new abode. Many speakers at the program declared that having their own Bhume temple would signify that the Thangmi community had finally "arrived" in India, both as citizens in general and as a community deserving of ST recognition. Having their own Bhumethan meant they would no longer need to reference the Suspa Bhumethan in Nepal as the source of their immediate territorial power, thereby once and for all confirming their status as full Indian citizens. They could point to Bhume's physical presence in the temple building as incontrovertible evidence of the link between ethnicity and territory not just in Nepal but in India too—providing the foundation of a new indigenous identity.

Even before the temple building was completed, the Bhumethan construction site became an important communal location at which Thangmi from both India and Nepal gathered. The very idea of a Bhumethan in Darjeeling seemed to create parity between Thangmi from Nepal and their counterparts in India by emphasizing their shared identity as inhabitants of

Bhume's domain. Through the processes of reconceptualizing the Suspa Bhumethan as a pilgrimage site and building a new Bhumethan in Darjeeling, Thangmi ritual productions of a transcendent ethnic territory had converged across national borders. Each Bhumethan simultaneously served as an anchor for a shared set of propitiation practices through which identity was produced at the local level, as well as serving as a pilgrimage site to those from far away, together marking the translocal whole of Thangmi ethnic territory. The political deployments of this territory would differ within each nation-state framework: in Nepal, it would be used to claim an autonomous territory within the restructuring federal state, while in India it would be used to claim an ethnically specific tribal identity, in contrast to the pan-Nepali territorial autonomy sought by those who demanded the separate state of Gorkhaland—but the mechanisms through which such territory was produced in each location were converging. For people who moved back and forth between Nepal and India for labor rather than pilgrimage, encountering evidence of Bhume's presence everywhere they went just confirmed what they already knew: that it was all one village, in which Bhume was everywhere and nowhere at once.

Chapter 7

The Work of Life-Cycle Rituals and the Power of Parallel Descent

Yo parampara hoina, kam ho.
This is not tradition, it's work.
—Ram Bahadur, Dumkot guru, of a funerary ritual in Dolakha, 2004

This chapter explores how life-cycle rituals effect the "work" of social reproduction across the Thangmi community. The marriage (T: *bore*) and funerary (T: *mumpra*; *mampra* in Sindhupalchok dialect) cycles posit a specific quality of Thangminess as a prerequisite for their success, while providing a means of recognizing that quality in one's self by articulating clan affiliation. This quality is not based on an essential notion of purity embodied in idioms of blood (Clarke 1995) or bone (Levine 1981) as elsewhere in the Himalayas, but rather in a processual concept of how one becomes Thangmi—or, more accurately, how one "does Thangminess"—by participating in a set of synthetic rituals.

As argued in Chapter 3, Thangmi modes of self-recognition emphasize action ("what Thangmi do") rather than essence ("what Thangmi are"). Life-cycle rituals show how Thangminess is not only constructed through the discursive imperatives of political recognition but is produced through the affective imperatives of spiritual recognition, even for those Thangmi whose desire to participate in the latter is prompted by the former. Such individuals still have children, marry, and part with their dead. They too come to recognize themselves as Thangmi by asserting clan identities through life-cycle rituals. The affective experience of such practices both counter and condition political agendas. My analysis of life-cycle rituals illuminates the relationship between structure and sentiment—in the long-debated terms of ritual theory (Metcalf and Huntington 1991:51), or the relationship between instrumentality and affect in the terms of classical ethnicity theory—in producing and reproducing ethnicity through ritualized action.

The Habise *Chant*

In 1999, I attended my first of many *mumpra* in Suspa. As I entered the kerosene lamp-lit house for the all-night *habise* (T) ritual that prefaced the following day's major funerary rite (T: *jekha mumpra*), I was surprised to hear several voices chanting *om mani padme hum*. I recognized this as the mantra of the Buddhist deity Avalokiteshvara (Skt) or Chen Rezig (Tib). I did not expect to find it in this Thangmi ritual presided over by Guru Maila. In previous conversations with me, this guru had ardently advocated "Thangmi *dharma*" as a distinctive religion that could not be adequately understood through Buddhist, Hindu, or Kirant categories. When he finally took a break for a sip of beer, I asked Guru Maila why he was using a Tibetan Buddhist mantra. "What are you saying?" he responded gruffly. "It's not Tibetan or Buddhist; it's Thangmi ritual language." Surely he was aware of the mantra's Tibetan origin, I countered. "Well of course, Tibetan and Tamang lamas use this too," he said. "But when we chant it, the language becomes Thangmi; otherwise the *sidumi* [T: spirit of the dead person] wouldn't understand. Isn't that obvious?"

I felt embarrassed. I was trying to relate everything I encountered to one of the great traditions, just as earlier ethnographers must have done when they concluded that the Thangmi "do not have any exclusive ritual worth mentioning" (Subba 1993:185) because most ritual elements seemed familiar from Hindu and Buddhist contexts. The fact that the *habise* had a clearly identifiable Tibetan cognate did not mean that it was "Tibetan" in any essential sense, just as the fact that Guru Maila was addressed as *lama bonpo* in his role as funerary priest did not mean that he was a lama in the Tibetan sense. The *habise* had its own meanings and effects within this Thangmi ritual complex. Guru Maila explained that the soothing repetition of the *habise* prepared the spirit for the transformations of the *mumpra* the following day, reassuring the spirit that it would be well cared for during the process.

For a moment, Guru Maila's statement that the *habise* had to be Thangmi so the spirit could understand made perfect sense: indeed, how could a Thangmi spirit be expected to understand a language not its own? In the harsh light of the next morning, however, Guru Maila's logic appeared utterly tautological. If this chant, which even the guru acknowledged had non-Thangmi antecedents, became Thangmi in the ritual context simply because the spirit already was, what actually constituted the spirit's Thangminess? How did we know that the spirit was not something else, or that other rituals or languages would not work equally well to effect its transition to the realm of the ancestors?

Clan Identities, Marriage, and Death

Over time, I came to understand that the prerequisite for becoming a Thangmi ancestor in death was the possession of a Thangmi clan identity in life, which was explicitly affirmed at the time of marriage. An individual's Thangminess therefore had to be publically asserted through the affirmation of clan identity during the marriage ritual cycle, which often took several years to complete. By the time of death, possibilities for alternative identities were foreclosed. To be efficacious—to accomplish its "work," to use the metaphor that Thangmi regularly invoked—the *mumpra* had to take place within a bounded Thangmi frame of reference. These parameters took shape between the nodal points of the guru himself, the clan members and out-clan affinal relatives required for certain ritual tasks, the household in which the ritual took place, and the ritual language used to invoke the spirit's presence, all of which had to be Thangmi. The objective of *bore* marriage rituals, then, was to socially validate couples as legitimate reproducers of Thangminess at the individual level (often after the biological fact of reproduction since marriage rituals were commonly completed long after children were born), while the *mumpra*'s objective as funerary rite was to create ancestors attached to Thangmi territory, thereby guaranteeing the persistence of Thangminess at the communal level. Throughout these processes, clan affiliations facilitated the relationship between individual and communal levels of identity.

Unlike funerary rituals, marriage rituals varied substantially across time and place, and were more influenced by normative ideologies of gender and sexual propriety in both Nepal and India. Still, the ritual objectives of both marriages and funerals, and the specific concept of Thangminess they entailed, remained fairly constant. As Robert Hertz famously noted, the similarity between marriage and death rites "expresses a basic analogy" ([1907] 2004:209): both bring about a fundamental change of status. Indeed, the Thangmi *bore* includes a fictive *mumpra* for the girl, whose departure from her natal family is treated as a symbolic death. Taken together, these two life-cycle rituals provide the signposts for a Thangmi soul's journey through life and beyond.

What Makes a Thangmi Soul?

Thangminess was understood as an embodied quality but one whose existence could only be fully validated through participation in the life-cycle rituals that prompted its self-recognition. This quality of Thangminess was not necessarily present from birth, since in many cases it was never ritually affirmed until marriage, at which time a clan identity could be assigned by a guru if it had not been inherited from one's father or mother—if one was not Thangmi by descent. Once an individual's clan affiliation was affirmed through the rituals of marriage, it could not be easily rejected.[1] All of this held true even for people assimilated to pan-Nepali practices in Darjeeling: even the Tumsong tea plantation family, for example, had passed on knowledge of their clan name through otherwise increasingly Hinduized generations. The very ability to state their clan affiliation marked them as Thangmi (to themselves and others), even though they did not maintain the associated ritual practices that might have engendered a greater sense of self-recognition.

Antonius Robben suggests that personal experiences of death may deeply influence anthropologists' ethnographic approach to the topic (2004:13). My ninety-six-year-old grandmother died in 2004 while I was conducting fieldwork, transforming my understanding of the ritual production of Thangminess. It was logistically impossible for me to reach her funeral in time, but I wanted to mark her passing in some way and so I asked Latte Apa if he could conduct her *mumpra*.

Latte Apa listened to my request carefully. "You must be suffering now that your grandmother has died; we all suffer when one of our own goes," he said. "But I need to think about it further. Can you come back tomorrow?"

The next day I slipped back down the muddy path to his one-room house. He was sitting cross-legged on the bed. "Ah hah, here you are," he said. "Your request kept me from sleeping last night since I did not know the answer right away. No one has ever asked me to do a *mumpra* outside the Thangmi community before." I was surprised to hear this authoritative figure admit the limits of his knowledge and flattered by the attention he had devoted to the issue. "Here is the problem," he said: "I could do the *mumpra*, which might give you a feeling of satisfaction. But that is because you have been living with Thangmi people for a long time and you understand what it means. But your grandmother—now I am sure she was a respectable member of her own society in life—but she was not a Thangmi. She was not born a Thangmi, and I do not think she married a Thangmi." He looked to me for confirmation. "True," I said. He continued,

> This means she did not belong to a Thangmi clan, and so, speaking truthfully, nothing about her was Thangmi. So her spirit, which has not yet left the world of the living, would not respond when I call it to come into the grains [with which the body is reconstructed during the *mumpra*]. She would not know that I was talking to her. Since she never saw a *mumpra* in life, how would she know what it was in death? Anyway, her soul must be hanging around her own house, or maybe the house of her oldest son; that is why *mumpra* are always conducted near the house of the chief mourner. We are too far away for her soul to travel. No, I am sorry; it will not work, and it could even be dangerous. It could confuse her if she heard you calling her since she would not understand how to become an ancestor in the Thangmi way. I do not know what would happen to her soul if that happened, but I don't think you should wish for it. What does your *jat* do after death anyway? I think that is what you should do, and I cannot do that.

My request had compelled Latte Apa to consider his ritual logic carefully. His answer helped me understand that Thangmi practice, although synthetic, could not encompass the souls of those who were not already Thangmi. Unlike the universalizing tradition of Buddhism, which incorporates new devotees without regard to their background, the Thangmi world-view—like my natal Judaism—limits access to those who possess an internal quality that defines them as already part of that system. However, both allow "conversion" in the context of marriage, at which point Thangminess can be conferred through the assignment of clan identity. I shared with Latte Apa my rudimentary knowledge of Jewish funerary practices and agreed that these would be more suitable for my grandmother.

Thangmi Clans: Parallel Descent in Theory and Practice

> In Rangathali Ya'apa and Sunari Ama had seven sons and seven daughters. But there was no one for these sons and daughters to marry, except each other, which was impossible since they were brother and sister. So Ya'apa and Sunari . . . decided to assign each of the children separate clans, after which they could marry each other. They gave arrows to their sons and held an archery contest. Wherever each son's arrow landed, that place or thing would become his clan name. Then they went to see what kind of work each daughter was doing, and that became her clan name.

This mythic episode is part of the *paloke*. As one of the most widely discussed portions of the origin myth among Thangmi everywhere, it functions as a sociological schema in the Lévi-Straussian sense ([1973] 1987:163). The raison d'être of the clan system appears to be removing the stigma of incest from the inevitable marriage of brother to sister. However, this problem does not become evident until the children have reached marriageable age. In contemporary practice, children born to Thangmi parents possess an incipient clan affiliation based on descent from their mother or father, but these memberships are only made socially explicit at marriage.

The myth also crucially outlines a system of parallel descent, in which men and women have separate clan affiliations, which they pass on to their same-sex children.[2] Opposite sex siblings with the same biological parents can never be of the same clan because they inherit their clan identity from their same-sex parents. This makes clan exogamy in choosing marriage partners sound easy since all men and women are already members of different clans. To the contrary, it becomes more complicated because the clan affiliations of *both* the potential marriage partner and his or her sisters or brothers are considered. Ideally, there should not be any shared clan affiliations through either the male or female line for seven generations.[3]

In theory, women should inherit and use their mother's clan name exclusively, but in reality, women often identify themselves by their father's and, in some cases, husband's clan name as well. Already in 1978, Peet stated that "clearly all informants agree that there were originally named female kin groups, but their exact form and function could not be remembered" (229). I found that knowledge of female clans in particular but male clans as well was rapidly disappearing or transforming in both Nepal and India. I explore these transformations at the end of this section, after describing the range of male and female clan names, their meanings, and their geographical distribution:

> "Ya'apa then told his seven sons and daughters [who were now married to each other] to migrate to different areas. To decide where to go, the seven brothers climbed to the top of Kiji Topar ['Black Summit,' the Thangmi name for Kalinchok], where they held a second archery contest. Each brother followed his arrow and went to live with his wife wherever it landed. The places were Surkhe, Suspa, Dumkot, Lapilang, Kusati, Alampu, and Kuthisyang."

Just as every guru has his own *paloke*, every Thangmi village has its own clans, the complexity and inconsistency of which can be frustrating to those who desire standardization. If the mythical migrations described in the origin story are grounded in historical reality, these regional differences may be explained by the fact that inhabitants of each area are descended from the clan that settled there, especially if early Thangmi practiced patrilocal marriage, as they do today. Over time, the population might have expanded through group-exogamous marriage, with new clans emerging in response to inheritance disputes and other social fissures.

Such transformations are also common in India, where Thangmi from different parts of Nepal have met and married over several generations. One finds the most eclectic range of clan names in Darjeeling, where Thangmi who trace their heritage to different villages in Nepal intermingle. However, membership is concentrated in a few clans since early migrants often came to Darjeeling through kinship networks, making certain clans overrepresented.

It is impossible to provide an exhaustive list of all clan names attested in different locations.[4] Instead, I present the clan names found in the

Damarang and Pashelung areas of Suspa-Kshamawati VDC, Dolakha, as an example.

According to Rana Bahadur and Guru Maila, the original clans, seven each, male and female, were as follows (in no particular order):

Male	Female
akal akyangmi	*budati*
kyangpole akyangmi	*yante siri*
areng akyangmi	*khatu siri*
dumla akyangmi	*calta siri*
danguri akyangmi	*alta siri*
mosanthali akyangmi	*khasa siri*
jaidhane akyangmi	*bampa siri*

All of these have commonly known etymologies in the Thangmi language, with the exception of *jaidhane*, which remains a subject of conjecture. Several male clans are traceable to specific plant names, in which the arrows of the original Thangmi brothers are said to have lodged, while many of the female clan names allude to design features of Thangmi houses. Other male clans found in this area, but not considered to be among the "original" seven, are *budapere*, *dungsupere*, and *saiba akyangmi*. Two further clans, *roimirati* (male) and *apan siri* (female), will be discussed below.

Akyangmi, which appears in all of the male clan names, means "people of the needle wood tree" (N: *chilaune*; Latin: *Schima wallichii*).[5] *Akal* refers to a flowering tree (N: *chiplo kaulo*; Latin: *Machilus odoratissima*). *Kyang-pole* means "trunk of the needle wood tree." *Areng* denotes an oak tree (N: *arkhaulo*; Latin: *Lithocarpus elegans*), while *dumla* refers to the common fig (N: *nebharo*; Latin: *Ficus carica*).

Danguri means "the searcher." According to the myth, one of the sons collected the arrows after the contest. When he returned them to his parents, they dubbed him, "the one who searches." In one version of the story, the son never finds his own arrow. He returns bearing only six arrows and is fated to spend the rest of his life wandering. Some Thangmi speculate that the first migrants to India must have come from this clan. *Mosanthali*, which means "place of the spirits," or "cremation ground," is the single clan name derived from Nepali.[6] This brother's arrow is said to have landed in a cremation ground, an intriguing allusion to the central role of funerary rites in constituting Thangminess. However, contemporary members of this clan have no special role in death rituals. If there were any clan-specific

statuses or occupations in the past, they are now defunct. In the contemporary Thangmi world, it is not the identity conferred by membership in any
particular clan that is important but rather the larger identity as Thangmi
that the possession of a Thangmi clan name affirms—regardless of which
one.[7]

The seven daughters received their clan names while their brothers were
busy shooting their arrows. While the clan names of their brothers
were determined by the plants their arrows hit, the women's clan names
were derived from whatever task they were doing. *Siri*, suffixed to the end
of each clan name, is derived from the Indo-European term *sri*, which is
prefixed as a form of respectful address for men across South Asia. The
question of how this became attached to Thangmi female clan names as a
suffix, and why the *budati* clan alone does not have it, remain puzzling.

Budati is a Thangmi ritual language term for a leaf plate for ritual offerings. Two other female clan names derive from plants: *calta siri* from *calta*
"edible fern shoot" (N: *unyu*; Latin: *Dryopteris cochleata*), and *alta siri* from
altak, or rhododendron (Latin: *Rhododendron arboreum*). The remaining
female clan names allude to features of the Thangmi household. *Yante siri*
refers to the quern: the *yante* (N: *jato*) is a two-layered circular hand-driven
millstone with a wooden handle. This remains a prominent feature of
Thangmi houses in Nepal. *Khatu siri* refers to the backstrap handloom,
khatu (T), once commonly used to weave clothes out of nettle and hemp
fibers. This is now a rare occupation, but many households still possess
looms. *Khasa siri* derives from *khasa* (T), "ladder, wooden steps or stairs,"
which this daughter was making from a tree trunk when the clan names
were assigned. *Bampa siri* refers to the large, flat black stone placed upright
between the hearth and the door. As described in Chapter 4, this is a distinctive feature of Thangmi homes and a potent symbol for contemporary
activists.

Thangmi Egalitarianism?

These clan names highlight the de facto differences between "men's work"
and "women's work." Most of the male clans reference the natural world,
or specialized activities such as migration and funerary ritual. Female clans
are associated with everyday modes of domestic production, such as grind-
ing grain, collecting fodder, weaving, and cooking. However, there are

equal numbers of male and female clans, and the names themselves are not inherently gendered. None of the female clan names refer to gendered activities, such as childbearing, nor do the clan names subordinate women and women's activities to men and men's activities. The clan system, therefore, in theory instantiates an "egalitarian" model of social organization, one of the features of Thangmi society noted consistently by all researchers (von Fürer-Haimendorf in 1974 field notes, as cited in Shneiderman and Turin 2006; Miller [1979] 1997; Peet 1978; Genevieve Stein, personal communication). Thangmi do not maintain social divisions based on purity and pollution like caste Hindu communities or in more subtle ways within other *janajati* communities.[8] Both in household conversations and political representations, egalitarianism is cited as a distinctive feature of Thangminess. "We can differentiate our ethnic group from others by the fact that we say, 'men and women are equal,' " my hostess in Suspa explained.

Thangmi gender relations in practice are more complex. In Nepal, Thangmi women lag far behind men in terms of development indicators like literacy and political participation. Few women had ever held office in the NTS, although there have been several female general members. In the household, however, women are often engaged in decision-making processes and do not feel that they experience marginalization in the ways that they observe among their caste Hindu neighbors. Binita, a Dolakha woman who was born a Chhetri, explained that she wanted to marry a Thangmi to escape the oppressive gender hierarchy of her natal community. She was not disappointed in the relative gender equality she experienced in her post-marriage identity as a Thangmi woman.

In India, by contrast, Thangmi women are more involved in associational life and politics, with several women holding leadership positions in the BTWA. But within the discourses of *unnati* and pan-Nepali nationalism that prevailed in Darjeeling for most of the twentieth century, the notion of parallel descent and the egalitarianism derived from it were seen as anti-modern idiosyncrasies to be jettisoned. In India, even old women usually did not know their mother's clan name, while in Nepal, most women over thirty still identified themselves by it. However, younger women in Nepal also did not use their mother's clan names. Rather, they had begun to identify themselves with their fathers' or husbands' clan names. As Kamala, a Suspa woman in her mid-twenties, responded with frustration when I queried why she stated her father's clan rather than her mother's when asked about her affiliation, "How would I know her clan? I never asked and my mother never talked about it." In contrast, she was well aware of her father's clan identity, which was often stated publically in marriage and death rituals.

Kamala's experience shows how normative Hindu-influenced gender ideologies have begun to impinge upon Thangmi practices over the last several decades. Related transformations include increasing stigmatization of marriage after childbirth and previously liberal attitudes toward multiple sexual partners. Marriage was historically not expected until a relationship resulted in children—as the guru Rana Bahadur's proud tales of his seven partners (only the last of whom bore children) attested. Rather than bringing about greater equality, increased exposure to national and global discourses of gender and empowerment may have eroded existing egalitarian systems (Leve 2007; Pettigrew and Shneiderman 2004; S. Tamang 2002).

The Politics of Clan Affiliation and Parallel Descent

As female clan identities were diminishing in importance, male clan identities were taking on new meanings. In the 1990s, many activists in Nepal began to use clan names as a surname in place of "Thami." This was a label slapped upon them by the state, they argued, not their own ethnonym, which was "Thangmi." In India, by contrast, since the group had sought support and recognition from the state since the 1940s on the basis of its name, using obscure clan names in public seemed counterproductive. Some Thangmi in India who began using clan names after hearing of this movement in Nepal were actively reprimanded by the BTWA leadership for damaging ethnic unity. By the late 2000s, the use of clan names in public documents and speeches was decreasing in Nepal, apparently for reasons similar to those that kept it from becoming popular in India. The prospect of recognition within some sort of affirmative action system loomed on the horizon of state restructuring in Nepal, and Thangmi feared they might lose their hard-won but still minimal political visibility by shifting to clan names even less recognizable than "Thami."

As Thangmi in both Nepal and India sought to objectify distinctive ethnic features for political purposes, they faced the challenge of how to valorize parallel descent as unique, without affirming the historicity of the incest that generated it. Many activists found this part of their origin myth morally repugnant, even if it served well to demonstrate their "primitive-ness," as required for ST recognition in India. Such concerns might be dismissed with the argument that myth is just myth and therefore not indicative of the sexual behavior of "real" Thangmi. But activists had invested so much in "proving" the "truth" of other aspects of the origin myth, especially in relation to claims of indigeneity, that it would be diffi-cult for them to regard the incest as myth while treating other parts of the myth as "truth." Instead, they discounted the incestuous versions of the myth and worked to craft a new history. In a version of the origin story first appearing in the 1999 *Dolakha Reng* and repeated in the 2002 *Thami Samudaya* and 2003 *Niko Bachinte* publications, there are in fact *two* ances-tral Thangmi couples whose children marry each other, thereby avoiding the problem of incest. The first couple remains Ya'apa (Yapati Chuku) and Sunari Ama (Sunari Aji), as in the oral renditions of the myth that I recorded, while the second couple is called Uke Chuku and Beti Aji.[9] Khumbalal strongly advocates this version: "It is said that as there was no one else from the same ethnic group for the children of Yapati Chuku and Sunari Aji, so the seven daughters and seven sons were married to each other. This saying obviously can't be true. Those who tell these stories, whether scientists, old people from the Thami community, or foreigners, must be telling these stories on the basis of what they hear from elders, not by doing research. . . . It is 100% mistaken that the sons and daughters of Yapati Chuku and Sunari Aji were married with each other" (Samudaya [2056] 2061:17). This critique of the origin myth—or at least of the way it is told by "old people"—is not perceived to undermine the contemporary presence of parallel descent or its power as an ethnic marker. Megh Raj argues against the incestuous version of the origin myth but elsewhere in the same publication claims that "the female subcastes are unusual and proof of the originality of our identity" (Reng 1999:27). Rather than acknowledging that myth is about social impossibility in the Lévi-Straussian sense, as gurus do, activists seek to rewrite the myth as the Malinowskian charter they desire.

Becoming Thangmi at Birth

Birth is the least important aspect of the life cycle for establishing an indi-vidual's Thangminess. Many families call a guru to conduct a *nwaran*, a

Nepali term for "naming ceremony" (Turner [1931] 1997:354). Unlike marriage or death rituals, where a senior guru is required, lower-status *jhankri* may also officiate at *nwaran*. Some gurus refused to conduct this ritual even though families requested it. Rana Bahadur stated that this was because it was an invented tradition derived from caste Hindu practices. The *nwaran* was not common in Dolakha when he left for India around 1940, Rana Bahadur claimed. He only saw it after he returned to Nepal in the late 1950s, with its popularity increasing steadily throughout the ensuing decades. For Rana Bahadur, the *nwaran* was not a Thangmi ritual but one that some families favored as they aspired to Hinduization, of which he was critical. In an illuminating commentary on the nature of synthetic subjectivity and its ritual expression, he differentiated in kind between the wholesale appropriation of a Hindu ritual like the *nwaran* and the integration of individual Hindu or Buddhist elements (such as head shaving or the *habise* chant within the *mumpra*) into rituals that established their own synthetic Thangmi frame.

The *nwaran* in fact seemed most important to Thangmi in urban Kathmandu and Darjeeling. There were three reasons for this. First, it was a very brief ritual with simple offerings, much easier to organize than the multistage wedding or funerary rites with their esoteric offerings of natural and agricultural products often unavailable in urban contexts. Second, since it could be conducted by minor *jhankri* as well as gurus, there was a much greater prospect of finding an appropriate officiant.[10] Finally, since it was similar to Hindu naming rituals, it did not provoke embarrassment for Thangmi living in multiethnic environments, as the more "unusual" wedding and funeral rituals could.

Performed on the third or fifth day after birth, the *nwaran* disperses the ritual pollution of birth. This permeates the house, affecting all of the child's immediate family. All of these relatives must attend the ritual, during which the officiant consecrates the household with a mixture of cow urine, turmeric, wormwood leaves, and *kuruk* (N: "an edible tip of *Asparagus plumosus*" (Turner [1931] 1997:100), and ties a string soaked in this mixture around the baby's wrist. This protects the child as it ventures outside the house; until receiving this consecrated bracelet, the baby must be kept inside. The officiant then pronounces the child's full name for the first time, invoking his or her clan name based on the same-sex parent's affiliation. Finally, a chicken is sacrificed to the household's tutelary deity to ensure the child's future success, and the guru or *jhankri* is offered the meat, along with alcohol and unhusked rice.

If the *nwaran* is done at all in village households in Nepal, it takes less than half an hour and occasions minimal publicity. Extended family members and neighbors may not even know it is occurring. This understated approach results in part from the fact that infant mortality rates remain high, so parents do not want to ritually mark the birth of a child. Many Thangmi in rural Nepal said that the most important feature of the *nwaran* was the audible pronunciation of the child's clan name but that they prefer this to be done discreetly, without full ritual articulation.

By contrast, in Darjeeling, and to some degree in urban Kathmandu and Jhapa, the *nwaran* has become an important expression of ethnic identity. BTWA activists eagerly sought opportunities to publicly state their clan names, even if the ritual form within which they did so was not distinctively Thangmi. Adapting to such desires, Latte Apa did not critique the *nwaran* as Rana Bahadur did. Instead, the senior Darjeeling guru made the pronunciation of the child's name a more elaborate affair, taking as his model a part of the wedding ritual. There, the guru inserts brief histories of the bride's and groom's lives into the *paloke*, mentioning the places they have lived and their accomplishments in the same recitative style in which the locations along the ancestors' migratory routes are enunciated. In the *nwaran*, Latte Apa described the parents' accomplishments and stated their clan names several times as he built up to pronouncing the child's clan name: "And now this child, the son of Radha of the Alta Siri clan and Dipesh of the Akyangmi clan, this child of an Alta Siri mother and an Akyangmi father, he is now Akyangmi; let us welcome this new Akyangmi to the world."

At home, Latte Apa used "Akyangmi" as a pet name for his grandson: "Eh, Akyangmi, come here and eat your rice!" Latte Apa's deceptively simple habit served two purposes. First, it made his grandson aware of his Thangminess on an everyday basis, which Latte Apa felt was especially necessary since the child's mother—the guru's daughter-in-law—was by birth a caste Hindu who had received her Thangmi clan name at marriage. Second, without apparent political pretense, it communicated the distinctiveness of Thangmi identity to Latte Apa's neverending stream of Thangmi and non-Thangmi visitors. "Akyangmi, that's an unusual name," someone would invariably say, giving Latte Apa the opportunity to explain the term's significance and launch into a brief recitation of the origin myth if he felt so inspired.

Such rhetorical strategies were both necessary and effective given Darjeeling's ethnically heterogeneous residence patterns, in which neighbors—who were usually from varied ethnic backgrounds—sought inclusion in each other's lives. Most settlements had an interethnic neighborhood organization, which sponsored life-cycle rituals for all residents. Unlike in Nepal, where Thangmi generally lived in ethnically homogenous areas and outsiders were rarely present at such occasions, in Darjeeling a large proportion of attendees at any life-cycle ritual were non-Thangmi. Such diversity had once compelled participants to deemphasize the ethnically specific aspects of their practices in favor of a generic pan-Nepali Hinduism (Chalmers 2003:273), but in the post-1990 reorientation toward tribal recognition, both gurus and activists used such occasions to convey to others how unique they and their rituals were. Even the *nwaran*, which had very little distinctively Thangmi content, could be refashioned as an opportunity to objectify the rules of Thangmi ethnicity for all to see.

Initiation Rites Under Construction

It was in this sense that the *chewar* ritual was also "under construction" as part of the Thangmi life-cycle in Darjeeling. This haircutting ceremony for boys between the ages of three and five was an initiation rite, well documented across the Himalayas in various forms for the Tamang (Fricke 1990; Holmberg 1989), Newar (Gellner 2010b), and caste Hindu groups (Michaels 2004). Such rituals were not common among Thangmi in Nepal, and I first heard the term *chewar* in Darjeeling in 2004. There, several members of the BTWA who had experienced this ritual as a generic, pan-Nepali practice (either having their own hair cut or participating in the ceremony for neighborhood friends) sought to fashion a Thangmi version of it. The BTWA activists substituted the mantras chanted by a Hindu pandit or Buddhist lama with a written portion of the *paloke*. Most gurus refused to participate in this ritual neologism, compelling families to recite the *paloke* themselves without a guru's guidance, which necessitated the scripturalization of the *paloke*. The *chewar* therefore became an arena for activists to publicly demonstrate their successful appropriation of originary power through the twin processes of scripturalization and ritual invention. This ritual reframing had occurred over the course of more than a decade: the 1992 OBC application did not mention the *chewar* at all, while the draft ST application of 2005 highlighted it as a distinctively Thangmi ritual. These assertions were backed up by the "videoalized" documentation of the ritual conducted for the son of Laxmi, the choreographer introduced in Chapter 2. As Laxmi proudly screened the VCD for me, she explained, "The *chewar* is so important to us now; it is the one practice that people like me can understand and do ourselves." The ritual also made its way back to Nepal in the 2002 *Thami Samudaya* publication, which contains a set of stage direction-like instructions for the *chewar* (Samudaya [2056] 2061:68).

There was only one problem with promoting the *chewar*: its similarity to Hindu practices, as well as to the *chewar* of other groups. Unlike the OBC category, for which religion was not perceived to be diagnostic, there was a growing sense that eligibility for ST status was conditional on a group's ability to demonstrate their unique, non-Hindu nature through performance (Middleton 2011, 2013). Shova, a BTWA activist, told me that during the 2006 Cultural Research Institute review of ST aspirant groups, one of the researchers critiqued the Thangmi demonstration with the comment, "You must not 'touch' anything which has to do with the Hindu religion." Moreover, videoalized rituals turned out to be insufficient; Shova reported with indignation that the researchers said, "Only 'live' will do." Latte Apa was thus called in at the last minute to demonstrate Thangmi ritual in practice before the review board—with the explicit instructions that all Hindu allusions be removed—and the *chewar* VCD quietly slipped out of the Thangmi application package.

Despite their feelings of empowerment at accessing originary power without a guru's mediation through the *chewar*, activist attempts to package this power for the state failed as a consequence of bureaucratic biases about what "tribal" culture should be. Contrary to the activists' expectations, the state itself privileged practice over outright objectifications of it in text or video, and also privileged the figure of the guru over that of lay practitioners, thereby reifying precisely the form of power that activists hoped state recognition might ultimately help subvert. The policies of a democratic, secular state that in theory were designed to "uplift the marginalized," regardless of culture or religion, were stymieing activist attempts to democratize ritual power and perpetuating the Hindu-tribe dichotomy.

Becoming Thangmi at Marriage

"Marriage is about bringing our community together. It's about the bride and the groom and their families recognizing each other. The details don't matter so much, it's the way people feel that's important," said Bir Bahadur, as we reviewed notes from a Dolakha wedding in early 2005. In his role as research assistant, Bir Bahadur was frustrated with my persistent questions about the meanings of the Thangmi language terms for each phase of the *bore* (T) ritual cycle: *sauti, ayu, cardam, seneva*. I was also fascinated by the symbolic meaning of each item placed on a wicker winnowing tray and suspended from the rafters of the groom's house as his family's lineage deities were propitiated, like the *rapeng* (T*), a dead frog. But Bir Bahadur urged me to look at the big picture, to consider the purpose that marriage rituals served at the communal level rather than fixating on the details of an idealized ritual form, which, as he reminded me, hardly existed. Unlike funerary rites, which followed a remarkably similar sequence everywhere, marriage rituals varied immensely according to location and historical juncture. I therefore consider the marriage rituals in a more general social sense without describing any ritual schema in full, while I do the opposite in the subsequent discussion of funerary rituals.

Bir Bahadur continued to explain that the wedding we had just observed in Dolakha was part of a post-1990 trend. With encouragement from NTS and BTWA activists, gurus had agreed to return to a more "traditional" Thangmi ritual form, largely defunct for several decades as Hinduized ritual frameworks were adopted. The central acts of exchange through which the two families recognized each other and affirmed the couple's clan identities, along with the wedding songs performed to the beat of a *madal* drum and the requisite consumption of alcohol, had remained fairly constant over time. However, the celebratory idiom within which these actions were carried out had shifted, with symbolic items like dress, gifts, and food brought into line with pan-Nepali Hindu norms over the latter half of the twentieth century (Figure 17).

The immediate impetus behind the appropriation of Hindu styling for Thangmi weddings was the fact that one of the primary offerings had been the hindquarters of a cow. The bride's family had to slaughter the animal to indicate their acceptance of the groom's offer, and then cure the meat for consumption in the *sauti* (T; N: *koseli*) "engagement" ritual. The hind leg, however, was saved and displayed above the hearth until the marriage

Figure 17. Groom and bride at the center of their wedding procession, both dressed in styles common across Nepal, Chokati, Sindhupalchok, Nepal, February 2008. Photo by the author.

rituals were actually completed. This could take months or, in some cases, years. Around 2005 VS (1948 AD), in the waning days of Rana rule, a Thangmi headman from Suspa named Sure, who served as a liaison between the local community and the central government, was berated by an official from Kathmandu after the latter caught sight of a bovine leg in the rafters of a Thangmi house. The official threatened to immediately arrest anyone who so brazenly displayed evidence of illegal activity—to kill a cow was a felony in the Hindu state of Nepal until 2006—and Sure sent a message out across the region that any such evidence should be immediately destroyed. He then began a campaign to convince state representatives that Thangmi marriage practices had transformed completely so that cow slaughter was no longer necessary. In its most extreme form, this entailed inviting Hindu pandits rather than Thangmi gurus to conduct wedding rituals.

This reformist agenda (which might be conceptualized as an early instance of activism, although there was no formal organization to support it) drove a wedge between two community factions. Some supported Sure's plan on the grounds that it would protect them from persecution and improve their standing in the eyes of the Hindu state. Others decried it because they felt marriage rituals to be an essential expression of Thangmi-ness and beef eating an act of resistance against the Hindu state. Although Sure's faction eventually won out and marriage practices were largely trans-formed, the contours of this social divide remained evident in Dolakha half a century later. Many characterized Sure and his descendants as slippery social climbers who had assumed the unpleasant brahmanical features of their oppressors, while others valorized Sure as a savior, who alerted Thang-mi to the error of their ways. The former group was in the majority and soon returned to using Thangmi gurus as the primary wedding officiants.

But it became more difficult to reverse the Hinduization that had already occurred as *panchayat*-era policies further promoted such transfor-mations in the service of nationalist modernity. Bir Bahadur jokingly described the common sight of Thangmi gurus chanting their *paloke* at otherwise Hindu-style weddings as *khacchar biha* (N): "mongrel wed-dings." Awareness of the historical process through which this mix had become normalized as specifically Thangmi demonstrated another facet of synthetic subjectivity at work.

The situation only began to change in the mid-2000s, as activists emboldened by a decade of *janajati* politics began urging gurus and families to "return" to their earlier forms of practice. Still, opinion was divided, and even those who were in favor were unsure exactly how to implement this change. Every wedding I witnessed had a different balance of "old" and "new," and it was often unclear which was which, or for whom. These inconsistencies troubled many activists, as well as young people and their families when it came time to plan a wedding. When I asked laypeople about Thangmi marriage practices (or asked them to describe their own wedding), they almost always began by telling me that standardization of marriage rituals should be a priority for the NTS.

These concerns were also high on the BTWA agenda. Thangmi who migrated to India before Sure's intervention in the late 1940s may have brought knowledge of earlier marriage practices with them, but these were quickly subsumed by the pan-Nepali forms that developed in Darjeeling's multiethnic environment. BTWA leaders pinned their hopes of videoalizing a Thangmi wedding on circular migrants but were disappointed when the wedding of two migrants from Nepal in Darjeeling contained a messy array of largely Hinduized practices instead of evidence of a coherent, "original" ritual. Later, members of the BTWA were pleased to discover that a group of circular migrants regularly gathered to play the *madal* and sing old Thangmi language wedding songs from Nepal. These provided the inspiration for the musical style of the *Amako Ashis* cassette, which in turn served as the soundtrack for the performance billed as a "wedding dance" described in Chapter 2. While the *chewar* hair-cutting ceremony was a suitable site for the exercise of a new kind of ritual power precisely because it had no history as a Thangmi practice, the long history of ritual mixture surrounding the "Thangmi wedding" allowed multiple forms of power to stand.

Most gurus seemed surprisingly unconcerned with the debate over the ideal form of a Thangmi wedding. At first I thought they had lost control over this particular domain so long ago that it was no longer a battle worth fighting. Later, I came to understand that despite their temporary displacement from the ritual process, they had never really ceded control of the underlying social power inherent in this ritual cycle. Even at the height of Hinduized marriage practice, gurus were still called upon to investigate clan histories, pronounce partners marriageable, and oversee the *sauti*, the preliminary set of exchanges of alcohol and rice flour breads (substituted for the erstwhile cow leg), at which time the clan identities of the bride and groom were affirmed. Hindu priests from outside the community simply could not possess this ethnically specific knowledge. Whatever other purposes weddings might come to serve, their fundamental social function was to affirm the Thangminess of their protagonists by pronouncing their clan affiliation in public for the first time since birth and, in some cases, for the first time ever.

"Conversion" to Thangminess

During the *sauti*, marriage partners without a Thangmi clan name were assigned one by the guru. This seed of Thangminess could be brought to fruition through participation in future rituals, and ultimately in transformation as an ancestor after death. This category of "converts" comprised both women and men from other ethnic backgrounds who married Thangmi partners.[11]

Intergroup marriage was common for Thangmi in Darjeeling, as it was for most other groups of Nepali heritage. If the Thangmi population was indeed initially thirteen, as listed in the 1872 census, it is hardly surprising that they married outside the group. Genealogical work I conducted with three Thangmi families that had settled in Darjeeling for three, four, and seven generations revealed that approximately 75 percent of marriages over time were with non-Thangmi.[12] Partners were from other groups of Nepali heritage, including Rai, Limbu, Tamang, Magar, Gurung, Newar, Bahun, and Chhetri, and from other Indian communities, including Bengali, Bihari, Marwari, Muslim, and various *dalit* groups. Although some Thangmi expressed unease about marrying a *dalit* in theory, many prominent Darjeeling Thangmi had done so and did not appear to experience any stigmatization. In this way at least, the ideal of Thangmi egalitarianism was realized through a lack of concern about caste-based status. Thangmi women who married men from other groups generally assimilated to their husband's ethnicity, but many also retained a strong sense of Thangminess. This suggests that although one could gain Thangminess at marriage, one did not necessarily lose it by marrying outside the group. Sheela, the Gangtok BTWA secretary, explained why she was so involved with the Thangmi organization, even though she had married a Bahun: "Naturally I am interested since the first name I had in my life was Thami." The fact that she used the hyphenated Thami-Dahal as a surname drove the point home.

Intergroup marriage rates were much lower in Nepal, where most Thangmi lived in ethnically homogenous areas. Comparable genealogical work in Nepal turned up only one instance of intergroup marriage before the present generation,[13] in which I was familiar with four cases. In one, a Newar man lived with his wife's Thangmi family; in the other three, Chhetri (Binita, the schoolteacher described above), Tamang, and Gurung women lived with their husbands' families as Thangmi. As Binita explained, "Before our marriage Guru Maila gave me my Thangmi clan name. In the community I came from, women do not have their own names. It felt very special, and still I think about that name every day."

Indeed, women who had become Thangmi by marriage in both Nepal and India were often hyperaware of their clan names, talking about them openly in public. This habit had the opposite effect of that intended, since it diverged sharply from the mannerism of other Thangmi women, who would almost never mention their clan names except in ritual contexts. For instance, BTWA secretary Rajen's wife, who identified as Chhetri by birth (although her mother was Rai), greeted every participant who came through the door at a BTWA-sponsored event by introducing herself by her clan name and asking each newcomer theirs. Many Thangmi from Nepal who attended this event were clearly uncomfortable with her behavior, since although not secret, in their experience, clan names were not pronounced casually. This recent convert's novel use of clan names highlighted her simultaneous Thangminess and non-Thangminess.

Although disconcerting to some at a visceral level, the fact that this woman possessed both qualities at once could not be construed as contradictory within the ideological framework of an ethnicity, which, as we may recall from Chapter 3, defines itself through multiple forms of mixture. In Darjeeling, most people who called themselves Thangmi—and were involved in seeking recognition from the state on that basis—in fact had mothers, grandmothers, and great-grandmothers who were something else. This mixed reality—which was similar for most Darjeeling inhabitants, regardless of what ethnic name they held and which organization they joined—was living proof that pan-Nepali nationalist ideology had worked and should have provided a powerful challenge to legal classificatory rubrics that emphasized ethnic boundedness. But unlike gurus, who had long used the mixture invoked in their *paloke* to challenge hegemonic ideas about ethnic purity in village Nepal, activists were not yet emboldened enough to use their cultural resources to challenge state-supported notions of tribal distinctiveness in India.

In crafting an alternative platform for recognition, activists might have started with a portion of the origin myth that shows how people from hybrid backgrounds may be integrated into the Thangmi social world. As recounted by Rana Bahadur,

> When the brothers went to reclaim their arrows, they found a female child in the woods. She was the daughter of a forest spirit (T: *apan*; N: *ban manche*). They took her back with them and she joined the family, becoming the eighth sister. . . .
>
> There was no one for her to marry, so she went to meditate in retreat in a cave. The Dolakha king heard from his hunters that there was a woman sitting alone in the jungle, and he requested that they bring this woman to him. He liked her, so he moved his previous wife to a different house and married this Thangmi woman. After some time, the Thangmi brothers went to check on their sister in the cave, but to their surprise she was gone. They suspected the king, so they went to look for their sister in Dolakha. They danced

with costumes and instruments to attract her attention, wherever she might be. She saw them out of the palace window, but told them not to touch her because she was pregnant with the king's child. Eventually they convinced her to leave, and she came back to live with them in Suspa. Later she gave birth to twin boys, who became the first of the *roimirati* clan.

This eighth daughter, who appears only in some versions of the myth, is given the clan name *apan siri*—"respected forest spirit." In this way, she is brought into the Thangmi fold, only to leave again to marry a Newar king. However, she does not "become" Newar as we might expect, nor do her children; instead they all return to live as Thangmi, with the two sons becoming the primogenitors of the *roimirati* clan. *Roimi* means "Newar," and *rati* is used interchangeably in Thangmi with *jati*; so *roimirati* means simply "the Newar group."[14] This part of the myth provides a script for dealing with hybrid members—whether daughters of forest spirits or sons of Newar kings—by incorporating them through the attribution of new clan names that underscore rather than conceal their hybrid origins.

Becoming an Ancestor

There is little between marriage and death in one's own life cycle to mark it as particularly Thangmi. There are no rituals surrounding pregnancy, for instance, or the attainment of a certain age (like the Newar *bura janko*, Hindu *chaurasi puja*, or Tibetan Buddhist *thar chang*). But this does not mean that life is ritually empty. Rather, participating in other people's life-cycle rituals affords ample opportunities to fully realize one's own Thangminess.

Funeral rituals are key, largely because they are not contested as all the other rituals described in this chapter have been. The ritual sequence has a built-in provision for flexibility in the form of a myth recited at the conclusion of every *mumpra*, which details the ritual's own transformation over time. This flexibility is part of what has allowed it to endure across time and place. Recall that the first ever Thangmi association, the Bhai Larke Thami Samaj (BLTS), was founded in 1943 for the express purpose of organizing *mumpra* (see Chapter 5), which suggests that there is a high degree of historical continuity in this ritual's importance as a site of identity production.

Participation in the funerary rites of one's family and friends was generally recognized as a diagnostic feature of Thangminess. The exceptions proved the rule: one family in a rural area of the Darjeeling district was infamous for using lamas to part with their dead in Buddhist style, while the Tumsong tea plantation family employed Hindu pandits, and some recent converts to Christianity in Nepal expressed an oppositional identity by boycotting the *mumpra* of their own immediate relatives. The guru Rana Bahadur's youngest son, for instance, refused to participate in his father's *mumpra* after converting to Christianity, although he had previously trained as a guru like his father. These choices for alternative death rituals were routinely invoked by others as evidence that the individuals involved had lost their Thangminess. In Nepal, such doubt was generally expressed in the idiom of breaking kinship bonds: "If his faith does not allow him to come to our father's *mumpra*, he cannot be our brother any longer." In Darjeeling, such choices were seen as a break in political ranks: BTWA officers refused to issue a recommendation letter for an OBC certificate to a member of a family who had not employed a guru for a recent funeral.

Perhaps the *mumpra* prompted these powerful reactions because "the issue of death throws into relief the most important cultural values by which people live their lives and evaluate their experiences" (Metcalf and Huntington 1991:25) or because "the community in its enduring aspect is constructed by reference to the dead" (Bloch and Parry 1982:36). For the Thangmi, this was quite literally so. The underground world of the ancestors to which spirits were dispatched through the *mumpra* anchored the soil upon which living Thangmi walked. To question the efficacy of the Thangmi *mumpra* was to question the very potential for Thangmi social reproduction by negating the process through which Thangmi territory was produced through the bodies of the ancestors. As described in Chapters 4 and 6, this territory and its stone symbols—the household *bampa* and the Suspa Bhumethan—held different valences within the ideological constructions of Thangminess in India and Nepal, but ultimately Thangmi territory was a sacred object for one and all. By embedding ancestral bodies in the land, the *mumpra* was the process through which individual souls became part of the collective sacred and thereby the best link the living had to originary power.

As a synthetic ritual that integrated elements associated with both Buddhist and Hindu practice within a distinctively Thangmi framework, legitimated as such by the guru as officiant and the clan affiliations of the participants, it expressed the ideology of synthesis underlying Thangmi subjectivity at multiple levels. Here gurus most visibly demonstrated their powers, and even militant activists did not meddle with gurus' mastery over ritual form during the actual practice of a *mumpra*—although they might seek to scripturalize its components for later use.[15]

The following description sketches the *mumpra* ritual cycle, drawing upon observations of ten events between 1999 and 2005 in various parts of Nepal and India, as well as further explanations elicited from guru and laypeople. I describe a sequence that is repeated three times: at death, at the *ocyana* (T: minor) *mumpra* three days after death, and at the *jekha* (T: major) *mumpra*, conducted a minimum of thirteen days after death but often several months later.[16]

Ritual Actors

There are four primary sets of ritual actors. First are the *kiryaputri* (N), sons and brothers of the deceased.[17] Thangmi *kiryaputri* must observe several ritual taboos shared with their caste Hindu counterparts: consuming meat and salt is prohibited during the period of pollution, as is dancing and singing. Another set of ritual prohibitions emphasizes the ethnic boundaries of the funerary rites and their integral role in defining Thangminess. During the period between death and *mumpra*, the senior *kiryaputri* (often the oldest son) cannot cross a river, sleep anywhere but in his own house, or speak with people from any other ethnic group. The integrity of the ritual process as a Thangmi-only affair embedded in Thangmi territory is established from the outset through these imperatives to maintain the boundaries of both geographical and ethnic space. In Darjeeling, the first two taboos are upheld, but the last one must be interpreted flexibly. Since interethnic residence and marriage is common, neighbors and kin by marriage who want to be involved in the event often belong to other ethnic groups. Latte Apa reinterpreted the ethnic taboo in geographical terms by instructing mourners not to speak with anyone who did not live within the immediate vicinity of the deceased's house, but he also reminded the participants that this adaptation was necessitated by the pragmatic reality of Darjeeling life.

The second actor is the *kutumba* (N), who must be a male member of one of the six clan groups other than that of the deceased.[18] Often this role is played by a *damari* (T; N: *juwai*; son-in-law or husband of a younger sister) or *jarphu* (N: *bhinaju*; husband of an elder sister), but any other out-clan member is acceptable.[19] The *celibeti* (N), or immediate female relatives of the deceased, also play a prominent role. Throughout the ritual cycle, they organize elaborate food offerings, or *syandang* (T).

Last but not least are the gurus. Often, a senior guru is accompanied by several younger gurus in training, who help gather the materials for ritual offerings and make these while the senior guru chants his *paloke*. Together, they engineer a series of transformations: the body is disposed of, reconstructed, and ultimately attached to Thangmi territory as an ancestor.

The Funeral Procession

After a tiger's bone horn (T: *mirkang*) or conch shell (N: *sankha*) is blown by the acting *kutumba* to announce the death, the family and ritual actors gather at the home of the deceased. A bier (T: *marangseng*) is made out of two bamboo or wooden sticks, and three supports of bamboo or wood are attached at the level of the corpse's feet, chest, and forehead. Historically, the corpse was fixed to the bier with a rope of Himalayan nettle (T: *nangai*; N: *allo*; *Girardinia diversifolia*). In contemporary practice, it is usually tied with *babiyo* (N; *Ischaemum angustifolium*) or strips of fabric torn from a white cummerbund. Gurus stress the importance of securing the corpse with natural materials rather than plastic twine. Man-made material would interfere with the body's reintegration with the land, a prerequisite for the spirit's timely departure.

Before the funeral procession begins, husked and unhusked rice are offered on leaf plates, which are placed in a small hand-hewn wooden bowl (T: *toke*). A tool is placed on top of the rice—a knife for a man or a sickle for a woman—and the entire offering bowl placed on a bamboo tray (T: *lembe*). Men usually carry knives, whereas women carry sickles for their field work, and the associated tool travels with them in death. The corpse bearers (T: *guthimi*) carry this tray as they walk, along with a hoe, altered so that the blade faces opposite its normal placement,[20] and an axe to cut firewood for the pyre. Two small, white cloth flags are attached to bamboo poles and carried ahead of the corpse. These will mark the head and foot of the body after its cremation and absorption into the land.

The procession prepares to set off from the house to the cremation ground, called the *mosandanda* (N), or "ridge of the spirits." Each Thangmi settlement in Nepal has its own *mosandanda*, usually located in the forest at an uninhabited high point above the village. This is a practical choice: the only uninhabited areas are above villages, and since the ritual must be conducted in a place where the land can be deeded to the deceased, it cannot be land belonging to anyone else. The Nepali state has recognized some *mosandanda* as *dharmik ban* (N: religious forests), protecting them from encroachment. Each of the seven male Thangmi clans has its own designated site on the *mosandanda*. Women are now cremated in the space designated for their husband's clan, although they may once have had separate cremation sites.

In the more densely populated, multiethnic urban setting of Darjeeling, such exclusive cremation grounds are impossible. Thangmi cremate their dead at government-built concrete shelters on the outskirts of each settlement. Gurus must conduct an additional set of preliminaries to sanctify this public place first as Thangmi and then as the clan-appropriate cremation site. In so doing, gurus invoke the attributes of *mosandanda* found in Thangmi villages in Nepal, just as they make reference to the Suspa Bhume when consecrating new Bhume shrines in Darjeeling. Despite geographical distances, the ancestral territory in which Thangmi bodies are embedded is ritually continuous.

The wail of a conch shell announces the procession to the cremation site. As the mourners walk up the hill, the corpse bearers throw roasted, unhusked rice (T: *layo*; N: *laya*) at each crossroads. The corpse's head must face forward. At the base of the *mosandanda*, or just in front of the concrete shelter, the corpse bearers dig three times in the ground with the inverted hoe and offer *layo* over the hole. The corpse is paraded around this hole three times counterclockwise and then turned as it completes its final circumambulation so that the feet face forward. This journey to the top of the hill finds parallels in Magar, Gurung, and Rai processions to cremation or interment places (Forbes 1998; Oppitz 1982; Pettigrew 1999).

Cremation: Attaching the Body to the Land

The procession now reaches the cremation site, where a funeral pyre is built. Six wooden nails (T: *thurmi*; N: *kila*; Tib.: *phurba*) are planted in two parallel lines to define the area where the corpse will be burned. The finely carved image of a guru's *thurmi* will be familiar from Chapter 3, where it came to serve as a symbol of Thangmi identity for the BTWA. Here, the nails are rough-hewn pieces of wood burned in a pyre, which themselves have little symbolic value; it is the work they effect—pinning the body to the land—that is important. On top of these stakes, a wooden platform of seven layers is built with thin strips of overlapping wood. The corpse is paraded around the structure three times, and the tiger's bone horn or conch shell is blown. A small fire (T*: *rojeme*) is made some distance from the corpse, and three torches are lit. Two *kiryaputri* place torches at the corpse's head and feet. The *kutumba* places the last torch at the corpse's chest. An entire *chyatamarang* (T*) tree is burned on top of the corpse.

The act of "pinning down" the body at once suggests both a "body-based" spatiality that invokes the "Indic" concept of the mandala to establish links between the body and the cardinal directions,[21] and a "tribal" version of this, which "is based on territorial notions (e.g., sacred mountains) that are largely absent in the traditional Indic conception" (Bickel and Gaenszle 1999:19). Janet Gyatso (1987) outlines the archetypal Tibetan myth of a demoness's subjugation by "horizontal crucifixion"—attachment to the land by a series of nails—through which her body parts become embodied in local geographical features. Versions of this story are found throughout the Tibetan and Himalayan world (Ramble 2008); a Thangmi myth in which the body of the demon Madhukaite (also known as Markep-apa) becomes embedded in local territory is part of the *paloke*. Wherever a variation of this story is told, corporeality orients notions of direction and location, with the landscape perceived as pieces of the demonic body.

The Thangmi practice of "pinning down" a corpse before cremation occurs on a more localized, human scale, but the effect is similar. The piece of ground to which the corpse is attached adopts the features of the body itself at the same time as the physical body becomes part of this territory. Although each corpse lays claim to only one small piece of land demarcated by the six wooden stakes, the concept of embodied land is abstracted and the physical earth conceptualized not only as the realm of the ancestors but as physically produced through their bodies.

Thangmi sometimes use the Hindu idiom of *swarga* (N)—"heaven"—to describe the final destination of the spirit after death, but the ritual chants that dispose of the body and dispatch the spirit instead focus on the underworld. This is not a Judeo-Christian hell, but a subterranean spirit world where Thangmi marginalization in the aboveground human world is reversed. As Latte Apa once explained, "The deities hid all of our sacred objects underground. That is why the ancestors must go there, so that they can finally use them. It is their territory, our real Thangmi territory. This is why Thangmi history is so unknown, because nothing is visible aboveground."

Reconstructing the Body

The next part of the *mumpra* invokes "a recurrent theme in Hindu religious thought . . . the homology which is held to exist between the body and the cosmos." This inverts the Tibetan concept in which the body is embedded in territory by suggesting that "all the gods and the whole of space are present within the human body" (Parry 1994: 30).[22] Before the corpse is reduced to ashes, one piece of flesh is removed and offered to the spirit as it leaves its body, along with the leftover unhusked and cooked rice, the knife or sickle, and the wooden handle of the backwards hoe. The *sikitip* (T), or last bit of flesh, represents the body of the deceased and forms the focal point of the next part of the ritual cycle back at the house. When the cremation is finished, a flag is placed at the head and another at the foot of the funeral pyre.

The participants trickle down the hill following the same route they used to climb it and bathe in the nearest river or water tap. The officiating guru brings up the rear. As he bathes, he chants, "The deceased's spirit is under the earth, the spirits of the living are above the earth," a phrase that recurs throughout the entire ritual cycle. After washing, the group returns to the base of the *mosandanda* or the cremation shelter, where a hole was dug earlier with the inverted hoe. The hole is filled with branches of thorny plants. This prevents the spirit from returning to the world of the living and encourages it to accept the transformations its body has undergone.

The entire group returns to the deceased's house, where the gurus conduct the *sikitipko bhakha* (T). In the next ritual phase, the spirit of the deceased will be transferred from the *sikitip* to an assemblage of foodstuffs from which its body is reconstructed. Until the body is properly honored and integrated with the earth, the spirit of the deceased remains awkwardly in the land of the living. The spirit cannot depart until the body is ritually transformed into a feature of the local landscape. It hangs around in domestic space, and in the days between death and the final funeral rite, rice must be offered at several places within the house to feed the spirit. In

Figure 18. Latte Apa and his colleagues chant their *paloke* during a *mumpra*, with offerings laid out on leaves atop bamboo mats, in Rangbull, Darjeeling, January 2005. Photo by the author.

later phases, the spirit is embodied in different objects, ultimately a chicken, in which form it finally departs from the land of the living. These successive embodiments each emphasize a different part of the soul, all of which are simultaneously present in the living but must be dispatched separately in death.

The body is reconstructed with food items that double as offerings to the deceased.[23] Two long pieces of wood (T*: *ulangseng*) are paralleled on the ground. A bamboo mat (T: *cheti*; T*: *elebethere*) is built, always eight-by-eight strips square. A large, flat *mumpra aja* (T: "funeral leaf") is placed upside down on the bamboo mat. Ground millet flour is sprinkled on the leaves. The other items are placed on top (Figure 18). The chicken that will eventually embody the spirit is shown to the assembled guests at this time and then put away until the final funeral rite some days or months later.

The gurus begin to chant, first recounting what occurred at the ridge-top cremation ground. The entire ritual is described, and the relationship between body and land made explicit. The spirit is reminded that it has been granted a piece of land, the very same piece of land that it has become, as in Rana Bahadur's chant:

> This offering has now been given.
> Now that piece of land has been put aside for you. Isn't that so?
> On this small piece of land, a flag has also been planted where your
>   forehead was. Isn't that so?
> And at your feet another flag has been planted. Yes now,
> And on this piece of land a seed has also been planted.
> And cooked rice and vegetables have been placed on your pillow.
>   Isn't that so?
> The spirits of the dead are under the ground, the spirits of the living
>   are exposed above the ground but are contemptible in
>   comparison. Isn't that so?
>
> Now we have arrived at the house of the funeral rites, so listen to
>   this melody of the *sikitip*.
> Through this melody of the sikitip now your body has become one
>   with the mud of the earth.
> Your body has become one with the rocks. Isn't that so?
>
> From above you have become one with the trees and seedlings, now
>   you have become one with the weeds and bushes of the jungle.
>   Isn't that so? The spirit of death that killed you, don't send it
>   to us.

Once the body has been disposed of and integrated into the land, the focus shifts to reconstructing it with food items, each identified with a specific part of the body.[24] These are all products of the fertile soil into which the deceased's body has been integrated and therefore can be used to generate a new "body" inseparable from the land itself. This body provides the conduit through which the spirit is escorted away from the land of the living. The food items are offered on a large funeral leaf, and the chant continues:

> The pieces of wood below are your shinbones, so come. Having said
>   that these are your shinbones, come. Yes now.
>
> From the bamboo mat all of your ribs have been made, so come.
>   Yes now.

Having made these funeral leaves your skin, come. Yes now.
From the flour is made all of your fat, so come. Yes now.
From the soybeans are made your eyes, so come. Yes now.
From the upside down breads are made your two ears, so come. Yes
  now.
From the corn is made all of your teeth, so come. Yes now.
Now having made these ritual offerings, from the yams are made
  your brain, so come. Yes now.
Having made your kidneys in the name of the grain balls, come. Yes
  now.
From one of the upside down breads is made your spleen, so come.
  Yes now.
From the rice ball is also made your heart, so come. Yes now.
Don't say this isn't enough, don't get angry. Yes now.
Since we have made these offerings to you, spirit, don't send us
  other death spirits. Yes now.

After reconstructing the body, the gurus call the spirits of the dead to feast. Inviting the spirits respectfully as guests protects the living from their wrath.

As the ritual comes to a close, the spirit is expected to have understood and accepted the transformations its body has endured: cremation, absorption in the earth and dominion over it as an ancestor, and finally reconstruction with products of the earth. By now, the spirit should be placated and honored with its new position as an ancestor embodied in the land beneath its descendants' feet.

Finalizing Death

The ritual is now over for the day. The next part of the cycle is the *habise*, as described at the beginning of this chapter, which occurs the night before both the minor and the major *mumpra*. While the mourners chant *om mani padme hum*, the gurus propitiate territorial deities to whom the mourners present cooked rice as offerings. These are then disposed of outside, and the spirit continues its journey through the *itil isako bhakha* (T), a ritual episode which takes place on the same night as the *habise*. The spirit is transferred into an offering of rice contained in a small open-weave bamboo basket, the *itil isa* (T*). Each mourner adds a handful of cooked rice to the basket after it is hung on a wooden stake outside. Then each male relative sprinkles a few drops of purified water on the rice. Sitting outside, the entire party drinks grain beer, which on this occasion only is called *rem* (T*). The *habise* chanting continues all night, and when it becomes light, the *itil isa* is thrown out of the basket as an offering to the spirit of the deceased. The *kutumba* must carry the rice across a river in order to dispose of it. In Darjeeling, some families also light 108 small butter lamps during the *habise* as offerings to the deceased, but this Buddhist-inspired addition is contentious.

In the morning, after the *itil isa* has been disposed of, the main portion of the *mumpra* begins. The mourners shave their heads and don white clothes, wearing only one of their shirtsleeves like Hindu mourners. Another ritual basket is arranged, called *solo* (T*), which looks similar to the one used the night before, with layers of leaves and rice, this time topped with three walnuts. The *solo* is placed in front of the gurus at the beginning of the ritual. Later in the day, the spirit of the deceased will be transferred to this container.

The gurus sit outside under the temporary shelter constructed especially for the *mumpra*. Their assistants make two large rice balls (T: *phorokko isa*; N: *pinda*). These must be molded carefully so that they do not break as other offerings are placed on top of them; this would bring bad luck upon the family of the deceased. These are placed on an upside down funeral leaf in front of the gurus. This leaf and its contents are placed on one of the bamboo mats, while the other offerings for reconstructing the body are placed on the second mat. One mat is for offerings from those whose parents are still alive, while the other is for those whose parents are deceased: the latter group must make an additional offering to their own parents' ancestral spirits.

As the gurus chant, the female relatives place offerings on the bamboo mats, including millet flour, cooked rice, milk, and bottles of beer or spirits. These are offered to the deceased. The women also bring plain breads and alcohol for the mourners, who throw cooked rice on the funeral leaves to demonstrate that they are no longer ritually polluted. The taboo on eating salt is now lifted. Then the guru collects offerings of rice from the mourners and gives them to the *kutumba*, who consolidates them in his hand and waves it three times around the large rice balls. Then offerings must be made to the each of the seven male and female Thangmi clans. In theory, a representative of each clan should be present, but this is difficult given the variation in clan distribution. Instead, members of as many clans as possible are invited, and each individual receives a portion of the offering, even if this means that it must be divided into more than seven pieces. It is for this moment of the *mumpra* that people make the most effort to be present; the opportunity to represent one's clan is not to be missed, and people often vie with each other to receive the offering if more than one member of their clan is present. The rice balls are left outside, and when the gurus' chants are finished, they call the spirit to eat. Then the rice ball is placed on an upside-down bamboo tray. The *kutumba* picks it up and walks far enough to cross a river (or even a small stream or drainage pipe) and disposes of it. This section of the ritual is known as *daciko bhakha* (T), since these offerings are called *daci* (T*).

The reconstruction of the body that was performed on the day of death is now repeated by the gurus in exactly the same manner (but called *sereringko bhakha* [T] rather than *sikitipko bhakha*). When the chants and offerings are completed, everyone eats. Now a bawdy skit about going hunting is enacted, providing welcome comic relief. This is called *ahare thesa* (T*; N: *shikar khelne*) and must be performed by two *kutumba*. They procure a long piece of wood to which they tie a small piece of red meat called *ahare* (T*).[25] The two *kutumba* carry the long stick on their shoulders, shouting "let's go hunting!" They walk a short distance above the shelter and shout down lewd comments about the participants to embarrass the spirit and make it want to leave. Then they return, as if from a hunt, and approach the gurus, who question them about the hunt. "Where did you go?" "What did you kill?" "To which deities did you make offerings for good luck?" The gurus then instruct the hunters to remove their "kill" (the small piece of meat) and roast it. They return the meat to the gurus, who place it on the full bamboo mat, saying, "Look, spirit, we've brought you a fine kill from the big forest! Spirit, come and eat!" In Darjeeling, this component of the ritual was felt to be so obscene that women were asked to leave (including me), while in Nepal, women as well as men eagerly looked forward to a good laugh.

The spirit now begins its final journey. In the next three sections of the ritual, it is called and controlled by the gurus, transferred from the bamboo mat—where it has resided since it was called to eat the piece of meat—to the *solo* basket which has been waiting since the morning, and ultimately dispatched to the realm of the ancestors through the chicken that was put aside for this purpose at the time of death. Unlike the earlier phases of the ritual, when the gurus' attitude toward the spirit was one of cajoling appeasement, they now take a stricter approach, scolding and threatening the spirit with consequences if it does not depart. The senior guru holds the chicken tightly and directs his voice toward it. After calling the spirit into the body of the chicken several times in an increasingly threatening tone, the guru tips the chicken down to eat rice from the *solo* basket. If the chicken eats, the spirit is happy and has entered into the chicken, but if the bird does not eat, the spirit remains unconvinced. Usually it takes some time until the bird eats. The gurus repeat the chants to call the spirit into the body of the chicken, with different family members taking turns holding the bird. Whoever is holding the chicken when it eats is revealed as the favorite family member of the deceased. When the spirit enters the chicken's body, it becomes known as the *gongor pandu* (T*). When this happens, the temporary shelter is immediately broken down.

Holding the chicken, the gurus go into trance to accompany the spirit on its final journey to the realm of the ancestors. Shaking hard, the chief guru throws the chicken over a ridge and falls backward, fainting into the arms of someone waiting behind to catch him. This is the *mumpra*'s climactic moment. Everyone watches intently, out of both a voyeuristic desire to see the powerful guru faint and a practical desire to receive affirmation that the soul has finally departed from the land of the living and will not cause further trouble. Fainting is both a demonstration of the guru's power—in his capacity to access the ancestral world—and a public admission of the limits of it, since he loses consciousness entirely, unlike in any other ritual. Several laypeople commented that the gurus' loss of consciousness demonstrated that their power was not absolute and could perhaps be refashioned in other forms. Once the chicken is thrown, its name changes again to *thang* (T*). After returning to consciousness but still in trance, the guru confirms that the deceased has reached the underworld, and he can also see whether anyone else's soul has been mistakenly taken along. If this has indeed happened, an additional ritual component called the *ayu* (T/N) is conducted to recall this person's soul to the world of the living.[26] The *kutumba* collects the chicken and may keep or eat it as he chooses.

Everyone begins to disperse, but the ritual still must conclude with a recitation of the *gardul puran* (T),[27] a myth about how Thangmi conducted their death rituals long ago. Rana Bahadur narrated it as follows:

Long ago, one child went missing from each Thangmi house. No one knew where their children had gone. One clever man finally devised a series of traps to catch the child-stealer: he hid an egg in the fireplace, he dropped an ant in the oil, and put a snake in the water jug. Finally, he set a mousetrap on the threshold of his house and fashioned an arrow out of bamboo, which he left on the veranda. He left one child inside the house, while he hid to watch what happened.

Lo and behold, a woman came to eat the child. First she stoked the fire, but the egg hidden inside the fireplace burst and burnt her eyes. Then she tried to wash her face with the water, but the snake bit her. Then she tried to rub oil on the wound to soothe it, but the ant in the oil bit her. She was in so much pain that she tried to run away, but she got caught in the mousetrap, and then finally tripped on the line attached to the arrow, which shot out and pierced her skin. She still tried to escape, but dripped blood along the path as she ran. The man who set the traps followed her. Finally, she reached a cave, where she fell down and started wailing from the pain, "Aya! Aya!" She was about to die when the man confronted her, saying, "Aha! You haven't learned anything through your escapades. And now you're about to die. But I won't kill you. I will bring you whatever you need to die peacefully. What do you need?"

She said, "I need 360 bundles of wood, 360 funeral bearers, 360 axes, 360 sickles, 360 wooden nails, 360 fire tongs, 360 piles of wood, 360 dead oxen, and 360 buckets of grain beer." So the man collected all of these things, and the woman died. The 360 funeral bearers took her body to the cremation site. They had to wash 360 times after cremating her.

In the old days, this is what was needed to conduct a *mumpra*. If all of these things weren't collected, the spirit would not depart the world of the living. These were the traditions for a long time.

Many years later, an orphan came along. He was a funeral bearer at a mumpra along with 359 other people. Each person was supposed to bring one of each of the necessary items to make up the required 360. But the orphan went to the funeral empty-handed. Everything was counted at the cremation ground, and the orphan was exposed. The others said, "Well, you go sit by the corpse, and we'll go collect the extra things you neglected to bring." While he was sitting there waiting, the corpse came back to life and started a fight. The corpse said, "Why have you tied me up in three places?" As the corpse and the orphan argued, they kept changing places.

The corpse would jump out of his shroud, and the orphan would jump in. Suddenly, they saw the other funeral bearers returning. At that moment, the corpse was outside and the orphan was inside the shroud. The corpse called out, "Eh! The funeral bearers are coming! Come out and I'll go in!" But the orphan just scolded the corpse. The corpse was afraid that the funeral bearers would hit him if they found him out of the shroud. Finally, the orphan agreed to come out, saying, "But you, corpse, must promise to do whatever I say." The corpse agreed.

The orphan began: "From now on, corpses should not be wrapped in such elaborate shrouds. From now on, only three funeral bearers should be necessary." And he reduced all of the numbers to three. Instead of the 360 oxen, he asked that only one small bird be offered. He continued, "If I can be burned quickly with just one small flame, rather than with all the pomp and ceremony of 360 piles of wood, I will come out of your shroud." The corpse agreed, and they changed places, just as the funeral bearers were returning. They were so upset that they had had to collect the extra wood and waste time, so they ordered the orphan to make the funeral pyre on his own. They all left and went to bathe 360 times. The orphan set the fire, and the corpse was burned easily in just a minute. And the orphan bathed just three times. While the others were still bathing 360 times, the orphan went to the deceased's house. He was already there when the other funeral bearers arrived. Confused, they asked him how he had finished the work so quickly, and got angry with him, not believing that he had cremated the corpse properly. But when the guru and the mourners had to prepare rice to feed the spirit three days and three nights after the cremation [in the minor *mumpra*], they saw that indeed the body had been fully burned. They believed the orphan, and when they returned, he explained the new system to them and said, "From now on we won't go to such extravagant expenses. We don't need 360 of everything."

And that is the end of the story.

With this narration at the end of each *mumpra*, gurus recognize the possibilities for and periodic necessity of ritual change. Many have experienced such contingencies in their own lifetimes and have molded the ritual accordingly. Just as the ritual holds within its form diverse elements, as well as multiple orientations toward embodied territoriality, it also provides a framework for pragmatic adaptation. All of these factors contribute to its resilience, and campaigns for reform like the one outlined in the *gardul puran* have in fact been successful—such as one led by Jhapa-based activists in the early 2000s to reduce alcohol consumption during *mumpra*. Like the protagonist of the *gardul puran*, these activists did not attempt to ban the ritual use of alcohol entirely, since alcohol is a crucial part of the offerings, but rather sought to minimize its use.[28] Although some gurus were initially reluctant to accept the proposed changes, they eventually assented in the face of overwhelming popular support for the proposal that all could benefit if every *mumpra*-holding family agreed to contribute roughly the amount saved from alcohol purchases to a rotating village credit fund for community projects. During the course of my research, the actual amount of alcohol expected in ritual offerings decreased dramatically everywhere, and such rotating credit funds were set up in many locales.

Ultimately, this adaptation did not directly challenge the *mumpra*'s structure or contravene its ritual power. Gurus who actively took up the cause (like Latte Apa and Guru Maila, both of whom incorporated references to the alcohol reform movement into their *paloke*) found that it contributed to their popularity because it showed that despite their power struggle with activists for control over originary power, they could compromise in order to adapt to "modern" expectations. This was just one of the many ways that the competing ideologies of Thangminess converged in practice through the *mumpra* ritual. Whatever their personal commitments, participation in a *mumpra* left each participant feeling that they, too, belonged and therefore had a vested interest in maintaining the structure of the ritual, even if some sought to revise particular details. Structure and sentiment, instrumentality and affect were all part of the ritual whole.

Memorializing Bodies

The *mumpra* ritual cycle concludes with the construction of a *chautara* (N), or memorial resting place, in honor of the deceased. This memorial is not built on the actual site where the spirit was attached to the land at the point of cremation but elsewhere, usually on a busy village path. The *chautara* is therefore a metaphorical memorial rather than a direct marker of an ancestor residing beneath it. Peter Metcalf and Richard Huntington propose that "memorialization amplifies the equation . . . between the fate of the body and the fate of the soul. The corpse, by association with its container, is made enduring and larger than life in order that its owner's name be the same" (1991:151). However, the Thangmi emphasis is not on making the specific individual "larger than life" but rather on endowing the community as a whole with a lasting, recognizable, territorially grounded presence. *Chautara* building is a communal affair, with members of each clan required to participate, just as they did during the *mumpra*.

The inscriptions on these rough stone memorials often read only "Thangmi," or "Thami," without a personal name or other individual details. The lines of *chautara* so inscribed, encountered along paths leading into Thangmi areas in Nepal, explicitly identify the terrain as Thangmi territory by reminding all who pass that the surrounding hillsides are full of Thangmi ancestors. Ultimately, it is the Thangmi social body that is made lasting and larger than life, fortifying the communal edifice from within which individual projects of recognition and acts of resistance are launched.

As we walked along a village path bounded by rows of weather-worn *chautara*, Bir Bahadur's mother once told me, "The exploiters know they cannot fully own the land they have extracted as payment for unfair debts from us because we don't let them forget that their crops grow out of the bodies of our ancestors." Soon after our conversation, she herself became an ancestor after a sudden illness. Her voice rang poignantly in my ears as I watched members of every clan work to build her *chautara* with Bir Bahadur, who could not stop the tears streaming down his face.

Resisting the End of a Ritual

In October 2006, on Dasami, the tenth day of the Hindu festival of Dasain, a buffalo calf bled to death in the courtyard of Devikot. This temple complex dedicated to the tantric goddess Tripura-Sundari is perched on a hillside below the Dolakha bazaar. For the first time in remembered history, there were no nearly naked Thangmi men waiting, in trance, to drink warm blood directly from a buffalo's vein as it was severed by a Newar butcher.

Called *nari* in Thangmi, or *hipathami* in Newar, every year these two Thangmi men (Figure 19) and their entourage walked the four hours from their village of Dumkot to Dolakha on the appointed day to commit this dramatic act. Their blood drinking was the visual and visceral climax of a much larger ritual cycle, comprising both Devikot Jatra and Khadga Jatra ("Sword Festival"). These events were localized Dolakha versions of the Dasain (Dussera) rituals that take place throughout Hindu South Asia during the harvest season (Krauskopff and Lecomte-Tilouine 1996).

For the *naris*, the ritual process had begun two weeks earlier on the new moon, when they began going into trance for periods every morning and evening. Two days before walking to the Dolakha bazaar, they began fasting and remained in trance for progressively longer periods each day, while gurus propitiated the full congregation of Thangmi territorial and lineage deities, requesting divine protection for the high-profile ritual act that the *naris* would perform. The *naris* themselves were not shamans or ritual practitioners in any other context, but common Thangmi men who had inherited this annual responsibility through their father's clan lineage.

Devikot-Khadga Jatra (as I will hereafter call the combined ritual cycle) is a classic instantiation of ritual multivocality (Ohnuki-Tierney 1987).

Figure 19. *Naris* anointed with red powder to mark them as demons, shortly before drinking blood at Devikot Jatra, Dolakha bazaar, Dolakha, Nepal, October 2004. Photo by the author.

This chapter explores how such flexible ritual forms work to produce ethnic consciousness and its concomitant agency in affective terms, while also reproducing the material conditions that enable the relational frameworks of ethnicity writ large. At the outset, let me state simply that from the *naris'* perspective, they are chosen by the goddess Maharani to drink sacrificial blood as a sign of their special relationship to the divine source of ritual power; whereas Newar officiants say that the sacrificed buffalo embodies a demon, whose pollution the *nari* must absorb in order to protect the purity of the Newar *dharmaraja*, or religious king, who leads the divine army forward to vanquish the demon Mahisasura.

Newar kings ruled the region until it was brought under the control of Shah kings in the late 1700s. As detailed in Chapter 4, the first written evidence of Thangmi residence in the Dolakha area dates to the 1500s and is a statement of Thangmi tax obligations to Dolakha's Newar rulers. Thangmi participation in the ritual was historically funded by a piece of land managed under the *guthi* (N) land tenure system. Thangmi were entitled to work this land deeded to a Newar communal ritual association yet from the annual yield were required to provide all of the ritual provisions necessary for Devikot-Khadga Jatra. Within the political economy of this historical relationship between Thangmi and Newar, Thangmi ritual participation may be understood as fulfilling the conditions of their continued peaceful residence within a Newar-dominated polity. But the differing ritual interpretations I have sketched out here, and the relations of power they encode, are at the crux of both the ethnographic and political dynamics of the ritual's end in 2006.

When I first began working with the Thangmi in the late 1990s, Devikot-Khadga Jatra was an annual highlight for people throughout the region, both as participants and observers. When I asked what the most important Thangmi ritual was, many people mentioned Devikot-Khadga Jatra. People from various Thangmi villages who had no personal connection to the ritual itself made these statements as often as those from Dumkot who were related to the *naris* or otherwise involved with the ritual. Devikot-Khadga Jatra was also the focus of auto-ethnographic articles by Thangmi writers in all four of the major Thangmi-authored publications available by 2006.

I was puzzled by the fact that participation in a ritual that appeared to take Thangmi to the nadir of impurity was so prominent in their schemes of self-recognition. I read Casper Miller's careful description of Devikot Jatra, in the 1979 *Faith Healers in the Himalayas*. He suggested that the ritual demonstrated a "double view" of the world and reality ([1979] 1997:77), in which the Thangmi believed one thing to be happening while the Newar saw something else. This analysis made sense yet did not seem to account fully for the ritual's prominence in Thangmi identity statements. I wanted to understand more and also to know if the ritual process itself, as well as the meanings people attached to it, had changed in the quarter century that had elapsed between Miller's work and my own. I therefore made Devikot-Khadga Jatra a focal point of my early research in Dolakha in 1999 and 2000, and returned to observe it again in 2004 and 2005 after spending much of the intervening time in Darjeeling.

Thangmi Being "Really Tribal"

When my Thangmi interlocutors in India discovered I had spent time in the Thangmi villages of Nepal, one of the first questions they routinely asked was whether I had witnessed Devikot-Khadga Jatra. When they learned I had not only seen the festival but had recorded it on video, executive committee members of the BTWA asked me to show the video so they could see Thangmi being "really tribal," as they enthusiastically described the event. Such requests became so frequent that I decided to organize a few formal screenings of the Devikot-Khadga Jatra footage. At first unintentionally, these events became public forums for diverse members of the Thangmi community in Darjeeling to express their views about Devikot-Khadga Jatra.

It turned out that Thangmi from Nepal were generally consistent in feeling that participation in the ritual was a positive statement of identity, which showcased their special command of originary power before a multi-ethnic public. "We may look like demons, but if we don't go, the Newar can't have their ritual, and that is our power," stated a migrant worker from Nepal in one of the public forums in Darjeeling, echoing the rhetoric I had heard often in Nepal. Thangmi in India, however, were tensely divided over the question of whether Devikot-Khadga Jatra was a positive identity statement that should be continued or a negative sign of Thangmi impurity and domination at the hands of others that should be stopped as soon as possible.

It was clear that the debate over Devikot-Khadga Jatra was ongoing within the Thangmi community long before I arrived. My contribution of visual images, which few Thangmi in India had previously seen, except in a few blurry photos from Miller's book, only served to sharpen the debate. Those who agreed with Thangmi from Nepal that Devikot-Khadga Jatra was a positive expression of Thangmi identity argued that not only was it a long-standing "tradition," which Thangmi clearly wanted to continue (otherwise why would they keep doing it?) but that it was incontrovertible evidence of their "tribal" nature.

Many young Thangmi in India were aligned on this side of the debate. Older members of the BTWA did not necessarily agree. One such man stood up to speak passionately at several video screenings about how the footage of Thangmi drinking blood caused him deep personal pain, even making him feel physically sick, since the images showed his Thangmi brethren forced into a disgusting act by the Dolakha Newar who dominated them. He argued that Thangmi participation in Devikot-Khadga Jatra should be banned immediately and even requested the BTWA to organize a "mission" to go and "convince" the Dumkot Thangmi to end this tradition. Much of the senior BTWA leadership shared this opinion, although most were not so eager to assume responsibility for ending the ritual. Any intentional action in this direction would clearly alienate a large portion of the Thangmi community in Nepal, as well as the BTWA's own younger members.

This generational divide showed starkly how "tribalness" was a new kind of aspirational identity for Thangmi in India, the political desire for which did not always match its affective contents. For older BTWA members who had grown up striving to be modern Indian citizens within a pan-Nepali, Hindu idiom, watching Thangmi consume buffalo blood produced visceral feelings of aversion. Yet the same people were passionate advocates for ST status at the political level, and these were indeed the types of actions that symbolized tribal identity within popular and governmental imaginations. By contrast, for younger activists becoming involved with the BTWA during the 1990s, the images of Thangmi drinking blood produced visceral feelings of pride and excitement at their tribal heritage. The fact that such positive feelings were based on the fetishization of Thangmi in Nepal doing things that Indian activists themselves were not eager to do is beside the point here, which is rather that younger activists were more than willing to identify themselves with such behaviors in a way that older individuals were not. The terms of recognition in India had shifted so substantially after the implementation of the Mandal Commission Report in 1990—or at least had been perceived to shift in this manner—that the younger generation had actually come to *feel* very differently than the older generation about what it might mean to refigure Thangminess as a tribal identity. Such transformations demonstrate well how processes of ethnicization within a set of national or transnational frames may be not only instrumental—compelling people to objectify or performatize certain practices for their political value—but affective, changing at the subjective level the way people feel about their own participation in such actions.

As the stakes in the ST game increased with the 2003 attainment of that status by two other groups of Nepali heritage in Darjeeling—the Tamang and Limbu—and senior BTWA members receded further into the background through illness and death, the younger faction who sought to valorize Devikot-Khadga Jatra as a site of Thangmi identity production won out. Toward the end of my first long fieldwork stay in Darjeeling in 2004, I was summoned to a special meeting of the BTWA executive committee, where I was asked to contribute to the organization's activities in several ways. Their highest priority was that I write an article about Devikot-Khadga Jatra, illustrated with photos, that they could include in their ST application.

Complicit Agendas

This request was not out of line with my own agenda at the time. I had already considered writing an article about Devikot-Khadga Jatra. I worried that my observations from the 1999 and 2000 events were becoming dated and felt that Devikot-Khadga Jatra would be a suitable topic for an early academic publication. I also felt increasing pressure to make my ethnographic material available to the *naris* and their communities in Dolakha, as well as to the NTS. Although there was at the time no explicit system of reservations or benefits attached to *janajati* recognition in Nepal, nor even the contentious public debate about such possibilities that emerged after 2006, many Thangmi there were becoming increasingly aware of the national and international indigenous people's movement and, like their counterparts in India, felt that documentation of the ritual could be useful to them.

On a trip to Dumkot, I asked the *naris* and gurus involved in Devikot-Khadga Jatra whether I could write about the ritual and use their photos in an academic publication. I worried that such textualization might challenge or diminish the *naris'* power or make them feel that I was taking advantage of them. But these issues did not seem to concern the *naris*. In answer to my question, Sukhbir, the senior *nari* in whose house I sat, rummaged in the rafters to pull out a dog-eared, termite-eaten copy of the original 1979 edition of Miller's book, which fell open immediately to the spread of photos depicting the *nari* in trance. He said, "Yes, you must write a new book. We can't even see ourselves in this one anymore, it is so old. If your purpose was not to write a book, why did you come?" Everyone nodded in agreement.

This was a very different kind of accusation from those I had occasionally had to defend myself against from other Thangmi, who suspected that I might be personally profiting from the sale of photos I had taken of them. The *naris* seemed to be saying that I had a responsibility to write about what I had seen at Devikot-Khadga Jatra in order to validate their efforts over the course of several years to welcome me into their homes, include me in their entourage as they walked from Dumkot to Dolakha, and explain the complexities of their ritual role. In this context, my writing could provide a sense of existential recognition, augmenting rather than challenging the *naris'* power.

All of these issues weighed on my mind as I watched the debate over Devikot-Khadga Jatra unfold in Darjeeling. I often had to bite my tongue to avoid expressing too strongly my own opinion: since the *naris* themselves felt proud of their ritual role and not only wanted to continue it but wanted it recognized in writing, a BTWA mission to terminate the tradition would prove counterproductive both for their organization and for the Thangmi as a whole. I was therefore pleased when such proposals began to weaken and popular opinion backed the younger leaders who advocated the continuation of the ritual. In this context, the 2004 request that I write an article about Devikot-Khadga Jatra felt like a vindication of sorts, foremost for the *naris* and their status within the Thangmi community at large, but also for me and my assessment that the ritual was indeed a key arena of Thangmi identity production.

I set about writing the article in early 2005, and by the end of the year, it was published in the *European Bulletin of Himalayan Research*, just in time to take copies to Darjeeling on my next field trip there (Shneiderman 2005). The BTWA leaders were pleased I had taken their request so seriously. For me, their desire for the article provided the impetus to move forward with my own long-standing idea of writing it. As my academic career progressed, I stood to benefit from the publication as much, if not more, than the BTWA, the NTS, or the *naris* themselves. My relationships with these varied groups of Thangmi were cemented through the publication, demonstrating well the complicity that George Marcus describes as characteristic of contemporary multisited research projects (1999:103).

In that 2005 article, I suggested that the Dasain ritual complex, of which Devikot-Khadga Jatra in Dolakha was part, served to ritually reaffirm the sociopolitical order and establish a nested set of relations between ethnic communities, local rulers, and the central Nepali state (Burghart 1984; Holmberg 2000; Krauskopff and Lecomte-Tilouine 1996; Pfaff-Czarnecka 1996). On a phenomenological level, I argued, the ritual served as a source of embodied social and religious power for Thangmi participants within the web of local hierarchical relationships. For Newar participants, it provided a means of asserting political power at the national level by deploying central symbols in a show of domination over local populations, such as the Thangmi. I borrowed Judith Butler's (1997b) terms to suggest that Thangmi participation in Devikot-Khadga Jatra resulted in an "ambivalent agency," which appropriated power from the source of domination but, in the process of its reformulation on Thangmi terms, effected a shift in consciousness from that of subordination to that of generative identity production.

Devikot-Khadga Jatra, I proposed, was a clear ethnographic example of a situation in which the power "which the subject is compelled to reiterate turns against itself in the course of that reiteration" (Butler 1997b:12). As a calendrical ritual, Devikot-Khadga Jatra is annually reiterated, containing within itself the constant promise of resistance. The ritual framework is indeed structured by the dominant Newar need for socioreligious scapegoats, but the power accrued by individual Thangmi *nari* through the ritual performance takes on a life beyond the ritual, becoming a foundation for identity production within the realm of Thangmi social relations. Yet this appropriation of ritual power is not detached from an awareness of the source of that power, as Miller's "double view" formulation would suggest. Instead, by self-consciously acknowledging that ritual power is an important source of Thangmi agency, Thangmi identity at once reiterates and resists that power itself.

The final turn of my argument in the 2005 article suggested that for Thangmi to refuse participation in Devikot-Khadga Jatra would undermine the very basis of their identity on a psychological level. Rather than situating themselves in opposition to the ritual by boycotting Dasain—a strategy adopted by other *janajati* groups in Nepal to highlight the history of political domination embedded in this national holiday (Hangen 2005b)—Thangmi were committed to reiterating it in order to continue appropriating the ritual's power for their own purposes, thereby transforming its terms in the process.

At the same time, there were symbolic plays on the theme of refusal. The Newar festival could not proceed without the involvement of the Thangmi, so at a fundamental level the Thangmi participants maintained control over the ritual's efficacy. Threatening refusal allowed Thangmi to refigure the ritual on their terms. For this reason, the threat of refusal itself had become embedded as part of the performance. For instance, Casper Miller recounts a story about a year in which the Thangmi refused to come to Dolakha because of a land dispute that affected their compensation for ritual duties ([1979] 1997:89–91). When the Thangmi failed to appear, the goddess possessed the entire Dolakha Newar population instead and drove them all the way to Dumkot. There they found the *nari* shaking wildly under the goddess's influence. Although their families urged them to stay away from Dolakha, the *nari* could not refuse the goddess, and so followed the Newar contingent back to Dolakha of their own accord.

Every year I observed the ritual, some conflict or another caused the *naris* to threaten that they would not return the following year. The Newar always gave in to Thangmi demands. In 1999, the lunar calendar inserted an extra day between Navami (ninth day of Dasain) and Dasami (tenth day of Dasain), of which the Thangmi were not aware. So the Thangmi group arrived in Dolakha one day early, and the Devikot priests asked them to wait an additional day to perform the ritual. The *nari* refused since they must fast from the moment they leave their homes and did not want to go hungry. They repeatedly threatened to leave, and several times began walking back up the path toward Dumkot. The Newar priests called them back each time, eventually agreeing to hold the entire ritual a day ahead of schedule.

In 2004, a dispute took place inside the Devikot temple, shortly before the sacrifice was to be made. The Devikot priests must anoint the *nari* with red *sindur* powder all over their bodies to mark them as demons. The priests had forgotten to purchase a new stock of *sindur*. With only a bit of red powder at their disposal, they painted a few barely visible marks on the *nari* and pushed them outside. The *naris*' attendants became incensed, shouting that this was unfair to the *naris*; if they went through the ritual without first being transformed they would be tainted with impurity in their daily lives rather than simply within the clearly demarcated ritual context. The Thangmi threatened to leave without completing the ritual. The priests shoved the *naris* roughly, shouting that they did not understand the problem, but the *naris* held their ground. Several minutes later a new packet of *sindur* was delivered and the ritual continued.

These examples demonstrate how the annual threat of refusal asserted Thangmi power, unsettling the Newar assumption of dominance that otherwise remained unquestioned. However, I wrote, the Thangmi had never followed through on the threat. In the end, they always participated, for the threat of refusal was not nearly as powerful as enacting the ritual itself. These acts constituted Thangmi agency, while the threat of refusal that always preceded it laid bare, as Butler puts it, "the ambivalent scene of agency, constrained by no teleological necessity" (1997b:15).

A Sign of the Times

In October 2006, one year after my article was published, the Thangmi called their own ritual bluff. My assertion that the threat of refusal was not nearly as powerful as the reiterative action of the ritual itself was off the mark. Or to be more generous, it described an earlier paradigm that no longer applied by 2006 and had probably already begun to weaken several years earlier. I was too close to notice and also too invested in the "teleological necessity" of interpretive certainty that scholarly analysis entailed, thereby curtailing its real potential for agency. Could I have seen it coming? Perhaps, if I had read the tension between Newar and Thangmi that seemed to increase year by year as a sign of these particular times instead of as a timeless structural feature of the ritual itself.

After subduing my initial disbelief, I had to come to terms with the fact that most Thangmi seemed unconcerned by this turn of events, including the same people who just a few years earlier had told me how important the ritual was to them. Conditioned as much by my interactions with the *naris* in Dolakha as with activists in Darjeeling, each seeking recognition in their own way, I had wanted to believe that I understood their desires and could even help fulfill them. The sudden disappearance of what had seemed to me an important ritual felt like a personal betrayal and rattled my confidence as an ethnographer. I wanted to resist the end of the ritual, but instead it seemed to resist my analysis.

What actually happened in 2006 to finally transform the threat of refusal into a real refusal? Captioning a photo of the Newar dancers at Khadga Jatra, the *Kathmandu Post* suggested that "due to a protest from the Maoists, the tradition of drinking a water buffalo's blood and carrying its head was cancelled this year."[1]

I knew that the Maoists had in fact been calling for the cancellation of Devikot-Khadga Jatra for several years. They had been active in the area since the late 1990s (Shneiderman and Turin 2004; Shneiderman 2009) and did not like ostentatious displays of power put on by anyone but themselves. Since the April 2006 second People's Movement, the Maoists had emerged aboveground as public figures. By October 2006, when Devikot-Khadga Jatra was due to take place, the Comprehensive Peace Agreement—which would be signed the following month in November 2006 to officially end the conflict—was already in sight. It therefore seemed odd that the Maoists would choose this particular moment to call for the cancellation of the ritual. Furthermore, their earlier demands to end the ritual had been oriented toward the public festival as a whole and applied to all participants, not just Thangmi, and to all ritual elements, not just the act of blood drinking. In any case, the Newar organizers of the event had always refused to comply. Many Dolakha Newar were middle-class members of civil society—teachers, hospital administrators, shopkeepers—whose goodwill the Maoists in large part depended upon, and perhaps this emboldened them to ignore the Maoist calls to cancel their public Dasain rituals. In any case, it seemed unlikely that a Maoist threat that had gone unheeded for several years would suddenly bring about such a dramatic change of heart.

As I arrived in Dolakha some weeks after the ritual would have taken place, I ran into Ram Bahadur on the road. He was the youngest of the Dumkot gurus at thirty. I asked him whether the *naris* and the rest of the Dumkot community were upset about the Maoist decree. "You believed that too?" he laughed. I was confused, and asked him to explain further.

> We held a meeting in Dumkot and decided that it was finally time to stop going. See, the *guthi* doesn't provide enough for us, I think you know that, and it was getting harder and harder to go. The *naris* said they could go into trance at home. Sukhbir [the senior *nari*], he is so old now that he can barely walk to Dolakha, why should he suffer? Before, we always thought about not going, but we were worried that the Newar would make our lives difficult; we needed them. Now, we don't need them so much anymore; it's only they who need us. They were so embarrassed and angry when we didn't come that they told everyone it was because of the Maoists. It's true that the Maoists had been asking us not to do it for a long time, but that is not why we stopped.

Ram Bahadur explained the end of the ritual in a very matter-of-fact manner, which put my own initial dismay in perspective. But could it really be true that just like that, the *naris* had decided they did not need to go anymore? If so, it was a tremendously agentive act but one that canceled out the power they had previously garnered through participation in the ritual. What was qualitatively different about this new form of agency, and did other Thangmi relate to it as representative of their own identity in the same way they had related to the ritual act itself?

Gopilal, a senior figure of Thangmi society in his sixties who was required to participate in the annual ritual due to his *roimirati* clan lineage, as well as being a long-standing Nepali Congress activist, helped me understand further. I asked him why they felt that they did not "need the Newar so much anymore," as Ram Bahadur had put it. Gopilal replied, "After the People's Movement last spring [April 2006], everyone felt different. We saw that the King could no longer stop what the people wanted. It's time for the old rulers to go and for people's democracy to take their place. For us, the Newar were like the King is for the whole country, and just like that their rule is also finished." Gopilal's statement pointed back to Dasain's history as a ritual of state power, which, as I have described, worked to legitimate nested levels of ruling power from the Shah kings at the top down to the rulers of individual principalities at the local level, like the Newar of Dolakha. Gopilal seemed to be saying that the old frameworks within which power was asserted had dissolved in the wake of the 2006 People's Movement, as the fate of Nepal's ruling Shah dynasty became clear.[2] At an ideological level, the loss of royal power also deeply unsettled the Dolakha Newar position in national hierarchies of rule, even if nothing had changed overnight in their local economic or social status. With the 2006 People's Movement and the ensuing moves toward elections, a constituent assembly, and the restructuring of Nepal as a secular federal democratic republic, the sociopolitical order of Hindu divine kingship within which Dasain had served as a power ritual at the national level had fallen away, along with the local instantiation of it in Devikot-Khadga Jatra. The country's political transformation meant that the Dolakha Newar were no longer the local proxy for royal rule and therefore no longer in control of the ritual power out of which the Thangmi had learned to craft their own.

Upon reflection, I came to see that the end of Thangmi participation in Devikot-Khadga Jatra demonstrated forcefully that the sacred object of Thangmi identity transcended any single set of historically embedded practices or performances that at one time produced it. The agency to produce this object was diffuse, located in the multiple actions of all those who identified as Thangmi, not in any single piece of writing—academic, activist, or otherwise—which limited that agency by promoting any one of the many possible interpretations of it as singularly enduring beyond the active frame of its own production. For some Thangmi, writing itself was one such form of agentive action: this was certainly the case for the activists who worked hard to produce *Dolakha Reng* or *Niko Bachinte*, formulating their own positions as Thangmi as they wrote. But the resultant texts did not, as they hoped, encapsulate the totality of Thangminess in all of its variations, nor did the *paloke* of the guru, which could not fully incorporate the experiences of young, educated Thangmi, for whom writing had become an embodied necessity just as orality was for the gurus.

I myself had become complicit in constructing Devikot-Khadga Jatra as a timeless structure that was somehow essential to the production of Thangmi identity rather than recognizing it as a contingent practice that articulated aspects of Thangmi identity in a manner recognizable to a specific audience at a specific time and place. Unable to anticipate what was just around the corner, the text of my own 2005 article was similarly incomplete, just as this book is.

As far as I know, the Indian government has not been informed about the ritual's end, and my article stands as the primary description of it in the 2005 Thangmi application for ST status, which remains pending at the time of writing, along with approximately seven hundred others from across India. Perhaps its presence in the file had no effect anyway, or even the opposite effect of that desired by the activists who had solicited it. "Why is there an article about a ritual in Nepal here anyway?" I can imagine the bureaucrat saying, as he tosses the file to the bottom of the stack. I may never know exactly how it was received; some details are probably best left beyond the limits of ethnographic knowledge.

Uncertainty in the New Order

The end of Devikot-Khadga Jatra was probably one of many signs across the country that the ritual idiom of state power that had defined Nepal as a nation since the eighteenth century (Burghart 1984) was in its dying days. But what was to replace it, and how would Thangmi agency be articulated within whatever framework emerged?

Let me return to the young guru Ram Bahadur's assertion that the *naris* could still go into trance at home. Indeed, this is apparently what has happened every year since 2006: the *naris* still begin shaking and go into trance on the same day they used to; the gurus still come to sit with them and guide them through their journey to the divine world; and the *naris* still experience the goddess riding them. The aspects of Devikot Jatra oriented toward the Thangmi divine world continue and have in fact been reframed within an exclusively Thangmi practice context that looks much like the propitiation rituals for Thangmi territorial or lineage deities.

Returning to the definitions of practice and performance advanced in Chapter 2, we may recall that performance is a form of ritualized action conducted in the public domain for non-Thangmi publics that objectifies certain aspects of the sacred object of Thangmi identity for the purposes of political recognition. This is precisely what the Thangmi participation within the public event of Devikot-Khadga Jatra did within the historical context of the Newar polity of Dolakha.

On another level, however, the *naris* engaged in an internally focused practice, in which they communed with the goddess Maharani. In this sense, the *naris'* act was at once both practice and performance, which converged in the particular frame of Devikot-Khadga Jatra in Dolakha for a substantial period. As of 2006, however, these two elements have been delinked: the performance is no longer conducted, but the practice has been reframed within an exclusively Thangmi context in Dumkot. The fundamental characteristics of Thangmi ritual power as articulated in practice have not changed, but the ways that this power is performatized for presentation to broader public audiences have.

The composition of those audiences, or, in other words, the agents from whom Thangmi seek recognition of their power, have changed along with the scale on which that power is conceptualized and the idiom in which it is expressed. Rather than seeing the regional, Newar-dominated public sphere of Dolakha as the outer limit of their agency as expressed through the ritual idiom of Devikot-Khadga Jatra, Thangmi have now begun to conceptualize the national Nepali public sphere as a primary arena within which agentive power must be demonstrated through the idiom of ethnic activism in order to secure recognition.

Perhaps contrary to expectations, active participation in the Nepali national public sphere is much newer for most Thangmi than participation in the transnational public sphere created through circular migration between Nepal and India. As demonstrated in Chapters 4 and 5, the sense that one could "belong" in India in political terms from very early on, in a way that one could not belong in Nepal, was one of the factors motivating Thangmi to settle in India or at least spend much of their time there. The *naris* themselves had all engaged in circular migration at some time in their lives. Unlike other Thangmi, however, they did not feel that they had the option to settle permanently in India since they felt compelled to return to

Nepal every year in order to carry out their ritual duties. One might think they would settle in India precisely to avoid these obligations; however, they feared the consequences that lack of participation might wreak on their extended families remaining behind in Dolakha. Most Thangmi villages had some sort of ritual obligation to the Dolakha Newar during other calendrical rituals throughout the year, although none were so dramatic as the blood drinking of the Dumkot *naris*. For instance, Thangmi from Lapilang had to provide materials for and pull the chariot at the Machendranath festival in the spring. These responsibilities may be one explanation for why substantial numbers of Thangmi engaged in circular migration rather than settling in India permanently. Their localized ritual obligations to the Dolakha Newar tied them to their home territory but did not preclude participation in the political life of another country. They did not until much later consider themselves citizens of Nepal with political obligations— or desires for recognition—at the central level in that national public sphere.

These histories illuminate how the Thangmi communities of Nepal and India began to develop along different trajectories over time. For those who remained based in Nepal, identity was produced primarily through the power of ritual within the framework of a Hindu state, while for those who settled in India, identity was produced primarily through associational politics, or what we might call the power of association, within the framework of a secular state. Ongoing circular migration, however, bound the two groups together. As I have argued throughout this book, knowledge of both places has long been a hallmark of Thangminess, and here we might extend this assertion to encompass knowledge of and appreciation for both ritual and political forms of power. Thangmi from Nepal marveled at the power of political speeches they witnessed in India as early as the 1940s and 1950s; much later, Thangmi from India came to Devikot to marvel at the *naris'* bold act. However, as Silipitik, the elderly Dolakha resident who had spent much of his life in Darjeeling explained, the form of civic power that he witnessed in political speeches in Darjeeling during and soon after the Indian independence movement had little place within the ritually legitimated sociopolitical order of the Nepali state. Circular migrants like him were aware of how such power worked in India, indeed were fascinated by it, but they were also all too conscious that until the order changed at the highest level in Nepal, there was little point in expressing power in those terms back home.

Multiple Agencies

The 2006 People's Movement in Nepal did not emerge overnight. Rather, it was the culmination of decades of political activism dating back at least to 1950, with the civil conflict between the Maoists and state forces that began in 1996 only the most recent turn in an ongoing process of state restructuring. Throughout these decades, while young activists from Nepal (Thangmi and otherwise) traveled to India to learn about the techniques of politics, in Nepal the sociopolitical order and its power rituals stood fast. Thangmi became involved in party politics, largely via communism, and then ethnic activism, and slowly political power and ritual power began to articulate with each other. Activists set out to write about the Thangmi role in Devikot-Khadga Jatra and the *naris* threatened refusal. But still, every year, they continued to drink blood, and Thangmi everywhere continued to tell me how important this act was in constituting their identity. The agency generated through the *naris'* performance was not erased by emergent forms of democratic political agency; rather, the former provided the foundation for the latter's existence. Both forms of agency were fundamentally ambivalent in the sense that they remained subject to the conditions of larger sets of power relations. Just as Nepal's king coexisted with an elected parliament for fifteen years, the two strategies for articulating ethnic agency coexisted for several decades, as personified in the figure of Gopilal, who was one of the rare individuals with command of both party politics and ritual action. For most Thangmi, however, it would be a long time before the agency produced through political action became evident in a recognizable manner—before they recognized themselves in it, or it in themselves—in the same way that they recognized the agency produced through the *naris'* ritual performance.

This was one of the monumental challenges with which Thangmi had to contend at the turn of the twenty-first century: how to present the sacred object of their own identity in a manner powerful enough to simultaneously occasion recognition from Thangmi laypeople from a range of backgrounds *and* from the national (Nepali and Indian) and transnational publics (such as development organizations and the international indigenous rights movement) in relation to which they now oriented themselves. The *naris'* ritual act, with its double meaning, its binding of practice and performance, had accomplished this perfectly within the frame of the old sociopolitical order. The uncertainties and democratic messiness of the new order meant that no single ritual act was likely to fit the bill. Rather, gurus, activists, and laypeople were experimenting with a range of ritualized practices and performances at different times and places, complemented by other strategies of self-objectification, such as writing about themselves and videoalizing their life-cycle rituals. The concatenation of all these actions, ordered within the framework of multiple modern states and the transnational public sphere that linked them, were becoming the new rituals through which Thangmi engaged with the states in which they lived.

The end of Devikot-Khadga Jatra therefore did not signify the end of a fundamental, if ambivalent, aspect of Thangmi agency as I had presumed when I first heard the reports that the Maoists had forced the *naris'* hand. Instead, it signified the diffusion of Thangmi agency across multiple geographical, political, and ritual frames, enacted in a range of practices by as many individuals, who at times only ambivalently recognized the others' role in their shared project. The challenge for Thangmi now is synthesizing these forms of action in a manner that will enable them to control the terms of their own recognition, transforming the ambivalent agency of the past into decisive forms for the future.

Thami ke ho?—What Is Thami?

"Hello, hello," Rajen's voice rang out across the cavernous Gorkha Duhkha Nivarak Sammelan (GDNS) auditorium in the center of Darjeeling Bazaar. He was testing the sound system for the public program at which my husband and I were to speak about our research with the Thangmi and show video footage from our fieldwork in Nepal. Invitations for this December 2004 event had been circulated to the entire BTWA membership, and a poster hung outside the GDNS building to advertise the event to the broader public: "First Time in Darjeeling: Thami Documentary Film Show ON BIG SCREEN." The GDNS hall had not been renovated since its construction in the 1930s, and rigging up a functional projection system was challenging. As people began to trickle through the doors—circular migrants with their load-carrying head straps slung over their shoulders, civil servants taking a lunch break, children sprung from school for this special occasion—I noticed a large, cloth-draped box blocking the screen we had painstakingly erected. "What's that?" I asked nervously.

"That? It's a gift for you from the Thangmi people, to express our appreciation for all you have done," said Rajen, "Don't worry; we plan to present it to you in the first part of the program, before you show the video. It won't cause you any trouble."

My curiosity was piqued. While the sound check continued, I could not help but sneak a quick look under the cloth, which upon closer inspection appeared to be layers of *katha*—white offering scarves in the Tibetan style, printed with the BTWA *thurmi* logo and the words "Bharatiya Thami Welfare Association, established 1943, Thangmi *raksha*" (T: guru's necklace). The *kathas* covered a glass box. Inside sat a model of what I immediately recognized as a Thangmi house. Made of wood, bamboo, and clay, each

Figure 20. Model Thangmi house presented to Sara Shneiderman and Mark Turin by members of the Bharatiya Thami Welfare Association, Darjeeling, West Bengal, India, December 2004. Photo by Bir Bahadur Thami.

tiny detail had been crafted precisely, from the thick, thatched roof to the hinged doors to the small hand mill that actually turned. A *madal* drum sat just outside the door, accompanied by a bamboo flute on which was etched the word "THAMI." Next to the box sat two certificates, recognizing our "service" to the community and wishing for our good health through the process of publishing the results of our work (Figure 20).

I was overwhelmed by the care and expense that had gone into producing this unusual gift and wanted to understand more about its provenance. Several hours later, after we had formally received the glass-boxed Thangmi house to a standing ovation, showed our videos, and engaged in a lively public discussion with the over two hundred Thangmi audience members, I finally had a chance to ask about the gift as we sat down at a restaurant with several BTWA officers and members.

Rajen explained that they had commissioned a young Thangmi man named Saroj to make the Thangmi house. Saroj had completed a course in woodworking and made his living doing commercial artwork, but had never crafted anything for the Thangmi community before. Rajen had approached Saroj about modeling a Thangmi house after a tense meeting of the BTWA central committee, in which the officers had determined that since there was no obviously Thangmi object to gift us, they had to create one. They had first considered offering us a *thurmi*, or possibly a guru's drum, but these items would make problematic gifts. Both were passed down through the guru's lineage, becoming efficacious only in the guru's hands, and even if such an item could be secured, treating it as a mundane gift would be a surefire way to raise the ire of the gurus. Instead, they needed a sacred object with secular content, so to speak—something event organizers could imbue with the originary power of Thangmi identity, yet maintain control of without requiring a guru's mediation.

A Thangmi house in a box was the perfect solution. A house was something that everyone had—not particularly the domain of gurus, activists, or any other particular interest group—and was at once a symbol of clan affiliation, community, and territory. Most Thangmi in India did not actually live in houses that looked like the one in the box; rather, this was clearly a representation of an imagined ideal Thangmi house in rural Nepal. But this fact did not seem to alienate anyone as I imagined it might. Instead, the house appeared to be a multivalent symbol that everyone could relate to, either as a literal representation of a lived experience of "home" or as a figurative representation of a desire for such a "home"—a metaphor for a clear and recognizable identity. Thangmi from Nepal who attended the program at which the house was presented to us oohed and aahed at the glass box just as Thangmi from India did, many of whom told me proudly in the ensuing days that making the model and gifting it to us was an important achievement for the BTWA.

We took the house back to Kathmandu (minus the glass box, which we apologetically left behind in Darjeeling out of fear it would break in transit). It became a fixture of our living room and a source of endless fascination for Thangmi from rural Dolakha and Sindhupalchok who visited us in the city. Ram Bahadur, the young guru from Dumkot, was particularly intrigued. "*Eh heh*, it's a 'real' Thangmi house, isn't it?" he said, when he visited in early 2005. He fingered each part of the model carefully and asked where it came from. Upon hearing that it was a gift from Darjeeling, he laughed and said, "Well, if they can make this over there, they must be 'real' Thangmi too. I wasn't sure about that."

I was taken aback by this statement. What was it about the capacity to build a model of a house that one had never lived in—Saroj, the craftsman, said that he had in fact only seen photos of such houses—that made someone a "real" Thangmi? Apparently, it was the capacity to objectify something that other Thangmi could recognize as "real"—whether that be a house, a ritual practice, or, in the most abstract sense, Thangminess itself.

For Thangmi seeking recognition, whether in spiritual, political, or scholarly domains, possession of a clan affiliation combined with the capacity to objectify one's relationship with the Thangmi sacred originary—in other words, the capacity for ritualized action that articulates Thangminess as a recognizable object—is what made one a "real" Thangmi. That such ritualized action had multiple recognizable forms, from deity propitiations to political conferences, was taken for granted as part of the synthetic, collectively produced nature of Thangminess itself.

Throughout this book, I have sought to demonstrate that ethnicity is produced neither exclusively within the boundaries of single nation-states nor in a flat and undifferentiated world of global discourse or flow. Rather, ethnicity is produced within multiple nation-state frames, as well as in the feedback loops that connect them. Policies of recognition, the schemes of classification on which they are based, and the benefits that they enable are legally implemented within individual countries, but the effects of such legislation on ethnic consciousness often transcends borders. Ethnicity, therefore, as the broader sets of social relations within which identities are sacralized, takes shape at the intersections of locality and transnationality, nation-state and border, village, town, and city, with belonging embedded in the diverse particularities of all these places.

The circular migration that characterizes Thangmi lives is just one of many types of mobility today, just as the particular constellation of historical, ritual, political, economic, linguistic, and other elements that shape Thangmi synthetic subjectivity is only one of many possible articulations. All of the arguments presented in this book are therefore partial, based on ethnographic work with a limited group of individuals who recognized themselves as Thangmi. I undertook the task of writing an ethnography of the Thangmi as a distinct group in part because Thangmi themselves desired this, but along the way I came to understand that many of the experiences that shaped Thangmi lives were shared with others. In this sense, my ethnography of the Thangmi may be read as a particular set of stories about a more general set of ongoing historical processes in the Himalayas and South Asia over the last half century.

The conclusion of my fieldwork in 2008 was by no means the end of an era in any objective sense, and it remains to be seen how the Thangmi community will be transformed by current dynamics and their unknown futures. These include Nepal's political transformation from a Hindu monarchy to a secular federal democratic republic; the renewed movement for a separate state of Gorkhaland in India; the revision of citizenship and affirmative action legislation in both countries; and the ongoing deployment of the transnational categories of indigeneity, marginality, and social exclusion to make localized claims for rights and funds from states, as well as multilateral organizations and NGOs. Within these contexts, it will be important to watch new modes of Thangmi expression in radio, print, and digital media. So too should we watch new sites of identity production, such as development and advocacy projects like JANSEEP (Shneiderman 2013a), and broader political forums, such as Nepal's Constituent Assembly and Darjeeling's Gorkhaland Territorial Administration.

For the vast majority of Thangmi, life will go on in the action of the everyday, hand mills perhaps giving way to electric mills, thatched roofs to aluminum, rickety jeeps to air-conditioned buses. If the last ten years are any indication of what is to come, new roads will be carved out of hillsides, schools built alongside them, and loans taken to buy land elsewhere. Territorial deities will continue to gather in response to the *paloke* of young gurus like Ram Bahadur, and new temples will be built in their honor, where Thangmi will come on pilgrimages of self-recognition. Thangmi will be born, marry, and die, affirming their individual and communal Thang-miness in the process. Houses will remain starting points for journeys across borders, as well as anchors to territory, cultural heritage sites, and a symbol in a box of all of these things. Gurus, activists, and laypeople will continue to debate the nature of originary power.

In the future, I hope that when Thangmi hear the question *Thami ke ho?* some will point to this book: my modest contribution to their quest for sacred objects. Even if they have not seen or read it, I hope that they will know that this "book about Thangmi culture and history" (as the anticipated result of my research was often referred to) now exists. Its contents may not please everyone equally, but I hope that its symbolic form will be of use to all.

Glossary

adhikar (Nepali), rights
adhunik (Nepali), modern
adivasi (Nepali), indigenous
adivasi janajati (Nepali), indigenous nationalities
anautho chalan (Nepali), unusual traditions
ayu (Thangmi < Nepali), soul, life essence
bampa (Thangmi), hearthstone
bhai (Nepali), younger brother
bhakha (Nepali), melody
bharat (Nepali/Hindi), India
bharatiya (Nepali/Hindi), Indian
bhat (Nepali), cooked rice, food
bhinaju (Nepali), elder sister's husband
bhume/bhumi (Thangmi/Nepali), earth, soil, ground, territorial deity
bore (Thangmi), wedding
buddhijibi (Nepali) intellectual, educated person
celibeti (Nepali), immediate female relatives
chamcha (Nepali), spoon (sycophant)
chautara (Nepali), memorial resting place
cheti (Thangmi), woven bamboo mat
chewar (Nepali/Thangmi), haircutting ceremony for boys
dalit (Nepali), formerly "untouchable" caste
danguri (Thangmi), the searcher
dasain (Nepali), major Hindu festival held in the autumn (September-October)
deusi (Nepali), festival on the fifth day of *tiwar* or *diwali*
deva (Thangmi); *devata* (Nepali), deity
dharma (Nepali), religion

dong (Thangmi), intestines

gardul puran (Thangmi), myth recited at end of *mumpra* funerary rites

gotra (Nepali), lineage

guru (Thangmi < Nepali), shaman, ritual practitioner (derived from the Sanskrit *guru*, meaning any religious teacher, in Thangmi the term refers specifically to shamans)

guru apa (Thangmi), guru father

guthimi (Thangmi), corpse bearers (derived from the Newar *guthi*, referring to an incorporated religious association)

habise (Thangmi), part of *mumpra* funerary rite; recited on the night of death

hamro (Nepali), our

hipathami (Newar); *nari* (Thangmi), lineage of Thangmi men who drink blood during Devikot-Khadga Jatra

jagir (Nepali), land gifted for military service

jana andolan (Nepali), people's movement

janajati (Nepali), nationalities

jangali (Nepali), wild

jarphu (Thangmi), elder sister's husband

jat/jati (Nepali), caste/ethnicity

jatiya sanskriti (Nepali), ethnic culture

jato (Nepali), two-layered, circular, hand-driven millstone

jatra (Nepali), festival

jekha mumpra (Thangmi), major funerary rite

jhankri (Nepali), faith healer

jokhana (Thangmi/Nepali), fortune

juwai (Nepali), son-in-law or younger sister's husband

katha (Nepali), story

katha (Tibetan), white offering scarves

khaldo (Nepali), hole in the ground

khami (Thangmi), title for guru while he is officiating a wedding

khet (Nepali), wet cultivated field

khukuri (Nepali), large, curved knife

kila (Nepali), wooden nail

kipat (Nepali), ancestral land exempt from taxes

kirant/kiranti (used in several regional languages), umbrella term referring to several ethnic groups of eastern Nepal and the language family associated with them, including Rai and Limbu groups

kiryaputri (Nepali), sons and brothers of the deceased

koseli (Nepali), engagement ritual

kul deva (Thangmi)/*kul devata* (Nepali), lineage deity

kutumba (Nepali), son-in-law or husband of younger sister

lama (Nepali/Tibetan), Buddhist priest, ritual specialist

lama bonpo (Thangmi), title for guru while he is officiating death ritual

latte (Nepali), matted lock of hair that contains guru's power

layo (Thangmi)/*laya* (Nepali), roasted unhusked rice

likhit (Nepali), written, textual

madal (Nepali), two-sided, oblong drum

maila (Nepali), middle brother

man (Nepali), internal, nonintellectual, nondiscursive, embodied essence

masan (Nepali), burning ground, burial ground, cemetery, ghost

maukhik (Nepali), oral

maulik/maulikta (Nepali), original/originality

mirkhang (Thangmi), tiger's bone horn

mit (Nepali), fictive kin relation between trading partners of different ethnic groups

mizar (Nepali), local tax collector

mosan (Thangmi < Nepali), spirit of a dead person

mosandanda (Thangmi < Nepali), ridge of the spirits

mosanthali (Thangmi < Nepali), place of the spirits, cremation ground

mtha' mi (Tibetan), people of the border

mugalan (Nepali—archaic), India

mul deva (Thangmi), chief territorial deity

mumpra (Thangmi), funerary rites

mumpra aja (Thangmi), funeral leaf

muri (Nepali), measure of a field's yield (160 pounds of grain)

nagarikta (Nepali), citizenship

nagarkoti (Thangmi), children of Newar-Thangmi unions

nakal parnu parchha (Nepali), get carefully dressed/made up

nakali (Nepali), copy, imitation

namaste (Nepali), greeting

nari (Thangmi); *hipathami* (Newar), lineage of Thangmi men who drink blood during Devikot-Khadga Jatra

niko (Thangmi), our

nwaran (Nepali/Thangmi), naming ceremony

ocyana mumpra (Thangmi), minor funerary rite

padhai-lekhai (Nepali), capable of reading and writing, educated

paloke (Thangmi), oral tradition encoded in ritual register of Thangmi language

panchayat (Nepali), system of partyless democracy from 1960 to 1990

pandit (Nepali), Hindu priest

phorokko isa (Thangmi), rice balls

phurba (Tibetan), wooden nail, dagger

pragati (Nepali), progress

puchuk (Thangmi), grain-flour effigy

puja (Nepali), ritual

pujari (Nepali), priest/temple caretaker

raikar (Nepali), government-regulated system of private land tenure

raksha (Thangmi < Nepali), shaman's necklace

ramaunu (Nepali), to enjoy

roimi (Thangmi), Newar

rongsha/rong (Tibetan), lowlander

sakali (Nepali), real, true, original

samaj (Nepali), society

samavesikaran (Nepali), inclusion

sankha (Nepali), conch shell horn

sanskriti (Nepali), culture

sanskritik karyakram (Nepali), cultural performance

sauti (Thangmi), engagement ritual

seva (Nepali), social service

seva (Thangmi), greeting used instead of Nepali *namaste*

shristi (Nepali), creation

sindur (Nepali), red powder

singo (Nepali), complete, undivided, whole

swarga (Nepali), heaven

syandang (Thangmi), funerary food offerings

take (Thangmi), one-sided drum

thali (Nepali), place, ground, spot

thang mi (Tibetan), people of the steppe

thimaha/thimbar (Nepali), biological hybridity/hybrid

thulo manche (Nepali), big people

thurmi (Thangmi), wooden nail, dagger

thutur ved (Nepali), oral texts

tihar (Nepali), Hindu festival following *dasain*, held in October-November

topi (Nepali), cotton cap worn by men
unnati (Nepali), improvement
utpatti (Nepali), origin, genesis
utthan (Nepali), upliftment
ved (Nepali), sacred text
vikas (Nepali), development
yante (Thangmi), two-layered, circular, hand-driven millstone; quern

Notes

Preface

1. I use "Thangmi" except when citing others who use "Thami." The former is the ethnonym in the Thangmi language, while the Nepali and Indian states and non-Thangmi usually use the latter.

2. The 2011 Nepal census enumerates 28,671 Thangmi. Many Thangmi believe their actual population to be significantly higher.

3. A 2004 Darjeeling municipality survey enumerated 4,500 Thangmi within its jurisdiction. By 2005, an ongoing Bharatiya Thami Welfare Association survey had documented close to 8,000 Thangmi across West Bengal and Sikkim.

4. Borrowed from Nepali, or perhaps even directly from Sanskrit, the term *guru* has been indigenized to mean "shaman," or ritual practitioner, in the Thangmi language. After this first instance, I do not italicize the term.

5. VS indicates the Nepali Vikram Sambat calendar—approximately fifty-seven years ahead of the Gregorian calendar (2061 VS is AD 2004–2005).

6. Michael Hutt argues that both "Nepali" and "Nepalese," as well as "Gorkha" and "Gorkhali," were coined by the British (1997:113), and that there was no equivalent indigenous term that was not caste or ethnic group-specific to denote nationals of Nepal before these were appropriated (116). See also Chalmers (2003:ch. 5).

7. David Gellner's 2003 *Resistance and the State: Nepalese Experiences* is a notable exception. Gellner argues that there is nothing more offensive about "Nepalese" than there is about "Japanese" (personal communication).

8. In Sikkim, these dynamics are different once again, with many people preferring "Sikkimese Nepali" rather than "Gorkhali." Although "Sikkimese Nepalis" share the experiences of migration and participation in the Nepali-language public sphere, many seek to disassociate themselves from the political agenda of Gorkhaland.

9. Tanka Subba (1992) proposes "Nepalese" for citizens of Nepal and "Nepali" for the ethnicity within India, but this is problematic for many citizens of Nepal who reject "Nepalese" for the reasons described above.

10. A 2004 survey I conducted found approximately four hundred Thangmi full-time residents in Kathmandu. The majority were still officially registered as residents

of Dolakha or Sindhupalchok. *Dolakha Reng* estimates that there are approximately three hundred Thangmi in Jhapa (Reng 1999).

Chapter 1. Of Rocks and Rivers—Being Both at Once

1. For ease of reading, and because the term *adivasi*, or "indigenous," is deeply contested in both Nepal and India, I use *janajati* to refer to self-defined noncaste Hindu ethnic communities of Nepal throughout this book. See Gellner (2007), Hangen (2007, 2010), Lawoti and Hangen (2012), and Onta (2006b) for details of the *janajati* movement in Nepal; and Ghosh (2006), Jaffrelot (2006), Kapila (2008), Middleton (2011, 2013), Rycroft and Dasgupta (2011), and Shah (2010) for considerations of *adivasi* and tribal politics in India.

2. Middleton's attempt to anonymize entire ethnic communities campaigning for tribal recognition in Darjeeling (2011) illustrates this tendency.

3. Since the British did not classify the Thangmi as a "martial race" fit for recruitment into the Gurkha regiments, many Thangmi in the colonial era enlisted as "Rai" or "Gurung."

4. On the historical relationship between ethnicity and state formation in Nepal, see Burghart (1984), Caplan ([1970] 2000), Gellner, Pfaff-Czarnecka, and Whelpton (1997), Hangen (2010), Holmberg (1989), Lawoti and Hangen (2012), and Levine (1987).

5. The Thangmi/Thami language has long been mentioned in comparative linguistic classifications (Benedict 1972; van Driem 2001, 2003; Grierson 1909; Shafer 1966, 1974; Stein 1972; Toba 1990), but Turin was the first to conduct extensive field research on the language (1998, 2002, 2003, 2004a, 2004b, 2012).

6. Peet (1978) did not focus on the Thangmi per se but on economics and migration in general in an unnamed village in Dolakha district. However, his thesis contains a wealth of asides about Thangmi life.

7. Father Casper Miller's *Faith Healers in the Himalaya* ([1979] 1997) is a notable exception that has been widely reprinted in Nepal and India. It contains two chapters describing Thangmi ritual practice in the broader multiethnic context of Dolakha district, as discussed in Chapter 8.

8. This assertion has no basis in Thangmi self-representation. The Nepal Thami Samaj submitted a critical letter to the editor refuting Manadhar's claims and protested when he later received a prestigious journalism award.

9. Linguistically speaking, Thangmi share more with Kiranti groups than with Tamang (Turin 1998). When asked whom they feel closest to, most Thangmi will mention Rai and Limbu. However, owing to their primary residence in an area with a substantial Tamang population, they have more often been erroneously recognized as a Tamang subgroup. Chapter 3 details indigenous Thangmi schemes of ethnic classification.

10. Summarizing the probable historical relationships between Himalayan groups, Nick Allen posits that the ethnonym of what he calls "the lowly Thami"

(1978:11, n.2) may be related to Tamang, Thakali, or Gurung ethnonyms, citing footnotes from the work of Alexander Macdonald (1966) and Michael Oppitz (1968) to support this proposition. Such references seem to take on a life of their own, with later scholarly works citing the same supposition without new evidence (Steinmann 1996:180; Pommaret 1999:65–66; W. Fisher 2001:224, n.13). Turin (2002) corrects these misunderstandings.

11. Genevieve Stein (personal communication) describes Thangmi in Alampu village in the late 1960s and early 1970s as "running and hiding" whenever state representatives approached. On land tenure and state-local relations in Nepal, see Caplan ([1970] 2000); Regmi (1976); and Holmberg, March, and Tamang (1999).

12. Letter from the Welfare Department of the Government of Sikkim sent to the president of the All Sikkim Thami Association, 13 October 1999.

13. Sanskritist colleagues have offered the more literal "customs of our caste" as an alternative translation. This is also correct, but does not fully reflect the productive meanings that my interlocutors ascribed to these phrases, or the fact that English-speaking Thangmi routinely translated *jati* as "ethnicity" rather than "caste."

14. Thangmi make their first documentary appearance in George Grierson's 1909 *Linguistic Survey of India*. Grierson presents what he calls "incomplete" data, collected by Sten Konow from a population of 319 Thangmi speakers in India (mostly Darjeeling and Sikkim) in the 1901 colonial census (1909:280–81). Konow also mentions earlier data collected for the 1872 census, in which only 13 Thangmi speakers were enumerated.

15. The first substantive history of modern Nepal published in English by a Euro-American academic press is John Whelpton's 2005 *History of Nepal*.

Chapter 2. Framing, Practicing, and Performing Ethnicity

1. My use of the terms "border people" and "cross-border community" derive from Thomas Wilson and Hastings Donnan's (1998) reframing of what they call the "border concept" in pragmatic ethnographic terms. See also Shneiderman (2013b).

2. Thangmi speakers insert these Nepali terms into otherwise Thangmi discourse, as they do with many other loan words. *Nakali* has other meanings in Nepali that are not implied here: it can refer pejoratively to someone who cares too much about their appearance.

3. Hylton White (2010) uses this term in an online critique of the Comaroffs' *Ethnicity Inc.*

4. Keith Hart (2010) also questions the temporal horizon of the Comaroffs' argument.

Chapter 3. Origin Myths and Myths of Originality

1. The use of English instead of Nepali terms in Darjeeling reflects broader patterns of language usage there and does not directly indicate the educational status of the speaker.

2. The original Nepali is worth citing here: "*Thami euta singo 'jat' ho jasko maulik pahichan, astitwa, ra san chha.*" *Singo* connotes a complete, undivided whole.

3. Building on the terms "literization" and "literarization"—the "initial process of inscription" and the process of "turning into literature," respectively (Pollock 1998:41)—Gaenszle suggests that the term "scripturalization" adds the sense of "formation of a sacred scriptural tradition" (2011:282).

4. Another plank of this agenda has been the search for a "lost" Thangmi script to render the process of entextualization easier and more politically effective. Unlike the Limbu and Lepcha who can claim historical proof of unique scripts as a symbolic resource, Thangmi has never had its own orthography. Devanagari needs only minor modifications to represent Thangmi phonology accurately (Turin and Thami 2004).

5. R. Creighton Peet wrote, "It is the *jhankris* who were and still are important Thami leaders in many non-political activities, but especially religious, ritual and social events" (1978:254). I differ with Peet's definition of "politics" and suggest that gurus are key political actors.

6. Such division of labor has been documented for other Himalayan groups, for example, the Mewahang Rai (Gaenszle 2002:57–66). Peet observed it within the Thangmi community: "among *jhankris* there seem to be two different types, the more respected being also the more knowledgeable, the others acting mainly as shaman-mediums in diagnosing and curing disease" (1978:271).

7. For Tamang, *lama* and *bonpo* refer to two distinct categories of ritual practitioners. *Lama* are Buddhist, while *bonpo* are shamanic practitioners (Holmberg 1989). For Thangmi, in contrast, *lama bonpo* is a compound term referring exclusively to the officiant at a death ritual.

8. To Nepali speakers, the aspirated *khami* is distinct from the unaspirated *kami* (the *dalit* blacksmith caste), but many Thangmi suggest that this is another cause of their misrecognition as a low-caste group.

9. In the Tibetan context, *bonpo* or *bon* refers to a specific lineage that the Dalai Lama recognized as a fifth sect of Buddhism in the 1970s. "The modern Bonpo are to all intents and purposes the followers of a Buddhist religious tradition, with certain differences of vocabulary from the other four major traditions of Tibetan Buddhism, but no major difference in content" (Samuel 1993:326). This definition is substantially different from Thangmi activist definitions of *bonpo* as practitioners of "natural religion."

10. Rana Bahadur's nickname was Pilandare, but he requested that I use his legal name when writing about him. By contrast, Latte Apa asked that I use his nickname rather than his legal name of Man Bahadur.

11. *Paloke* may be compared with the Kirant *muddum*: "a central and highly complex notion whose meanings . . . may be glossed as 'oral tradition,' 'ancestral knowledge,' or—more generally—'traditional way of life'" (Gaenszle 2002:31).

12. I use the term "pan-Himalayan" in the Lévi-Straussian sense of "pan-American myths" (1979:27) to describe mythic schemas shared among multiple neighboring groups.

13. Mahadev and Maheshwor are both names for the Hindu deity Shiva.

14. The festival commemorating Buddha's birth, and the day on which Bhume Jatra is held—the calendrical ritual honoring the earth deity, Bhume, as described in Chapter 6.

15. Here, the Nepali terms *paune* and *napaune* are literally translated as "receiving" and "nonreceiving," but in the contemporary context, "included" and "excluded" might be a more appropriate gloss.

16. A Newar town located in the Kathmandu Valley, on the eastern outskirts of the contemporary city.

17. Further attempts to provide more nuanced terminology include Andras Höfer's "Tibetanid" and "Tibetanoid" to describe, respectively, peoples outside political Tibet whose linguistic and cultural practices are similar to those found inside Tibet, and those with higher levels of "Hinduization" who still speak Tibeto-Burman languages ([1979] 2004:43); Charles Ramble's food-based "tshampa-eater" versus "rice-eater" to describe the Tibetan and Indic cultural paradigms (1993); and Nepali journalist C. K. Lal's (2003) linguistically defined "Hindu Aryan Nepali Speakers" (HANS) to describe the dominant group in contrast to the rest of Nepal's populace. The latter is also analogous to political scientist Mahendra Lawoti's (2005) "Caste Hindu Hill Elites" (CHHE).

18. As cited on the NEFIN website page titled "Definition of Indigenous," http://www.nefin.org.np/list/Definition-of-Indigenous/5/0/4.

19. The Mewahang Rai also use these terms (Gaenszle 2000:356).

20. When asked who they share most commonalities with, Thangmi assert a close connection to Rai and Limbu groups. However, Thangmi do not eat pork or raise pigs, while consumption of pork is an important identity marker for most Rai.

21. Stan Mumford suggests just how psychologically challenging maintaining synthetic subjectivity might be within Himalayan social contexts: "Most Tibetans . . . thought that my dual project of receiving enlightenment from the lamas and also learning from the Gurung shamans would result in confusion or even insanity. The lamas thought me in danger of acquiring a divided mind" (1989:5).

22. Here Khumbalal appears to use "mantra" as a synonym for *paloke*.

23. Soon thereafter, the Communist Party of Nepal (Maoist) also began broadcasting in Thangmi across Dolakha district on another frequency.

Chapter 4. Circular Economies of Migration, Belonging, and Citizenship

Thanks to Tanka Subba for the translation of the Thangmi proverb in the epigraph.

1. The Nepal Multidimensional Exclusion Index (Bennett and Parajuli 2013) identifies Thangmi as "highly excluded," in the most disadvantaged 25 percent of eighty caste and ethnic groupings.

2. In nationalist histories, Prithvi Narayan Shah's 1769 "unification" of Nepal is cited as the modern nation's birth. However, ethnic and regional activist tellings of

Nepali history often replace "unification" with "domination" and the former is debunked as "myth."

3. The earliest written record from the area dates to 1324 AD. Dolakha is mentioned as the refuge destination for a deposed Mithila king who died en route (Slusser 1982:259).

4. Thangmi often use the hyphenated "Bahun-Chhetri," but this fails to recognize the differences in cultural practice and economic status between the two. Indicators show that Chhetris are generally less well-off than Bahuns (Bennett and Parajuli 2013).

5. *Khet* (N) is a wet cultivated field, while one *muri* (N) equals approximately 160 pounds of harvested grain.

6. Many of Nepal's caste and ethnic groups migrated to Darjeeling and other parts of India during this historical period, but ongoing circular migration is less common.

7. Today's plantations employ men and women in a roughly egalitarian manner, but oral histories suggest that colonial managers preferred men for the initial work of clearing forest to plant tea. Only once it was assured that the plantation would be successful and year-round labor was needed were men encouraged to bring their families. Thereafter, women were also employed, constituting a substantial portion of today's workforce. See Chatterjee (2001) and Besky (2013) regarding gender on contemporary tea plantations.

8. *Dui Number*, "Number Two," was the Nepali administrative zone encompassing Dolakha district before the country's reorganization into seventy-five districts in 1961 (Baral 2012:123–24).

9. Silipitik could not identify the speaker or the political context of this event.

10. Tibetan societies have their own social hierarchies, which may not have been evident to Thangmi travelers (Fjeld 2008).

11. Hutt cites a 1974 survey in which 48 percent of ethnically Nepali residents of Darjeeling tea estates had never traveled outside the district, and only 13 percent had ever visited Nepal (1997:123).

12. In 2006, Nepal's citizenship laws were revised to allow women to pass citizenship on to their children.

13. The Arniko Highway from Kathmandu to Lhasa, which runs through Sindhupalchok, was completed in 1966. The linked Jiri road from Khadichaur to Charikot (Dolakha's district headquarters) was completed in 1985.

14. These statements echo similar findings on the "enjoyable" aspects of labor migration in India (cf. Shah 2010: ch. 5).

Chapter 5. Developing Associations of Ethnicity and Class

1. The *topi* is a cotton cap widely recognized as a symbol of Nepali identity.

2. Eighty-three-year-old Nar Bahadur Thami claims that the original bell was stolen (Niko 2003:53).

3. Both organizations have changed name several times. I use the abbreviations BTWA and NTS except when discussing specific historical moments in which alternative names were used.

4. Ortner (1989) describes a Sherpa lama who founded a monastery in Khumbu with Darjeeling-earned cash. Macdonald (1975:129) and Des Chene (1996) describe Tamang and Gurung writings from Darjeeling in discussions that otherwise focus on ethnic identity in Nepal. Guneratne (2002) and Krauskopff (2003) discuss cross-border influences on Tharu movements, while Gaenszle (2011) considers the same for Kirant organizations.

5. Makito Minami is a notable exception, writing, "it seems that ethnic movements in Nepal originated in Darjeeling" (2007:490).

6. Karna Thami, a leading member of the Darjeeling Nepali Sahitya Sammelan (Nepali Literary Council), is an exception to this chronology. Born in the 1940s, he was active on the Darjeeling literary scene beginning in the 1960s. He first explicitly addressed Thangmi identity in the 1999 article "Thami Sanskritiko Kehi Ilak" (Some Foundations of Thami Culture) in the journal *Nirman*.

7. This is not to say that there were no forms of local organization in Nepal; village councils and other community support organizations such as the *dhikur* are well-documented (W. Fisher 2001:90–104). However, these were intended to regulate group internal social affairs, not to mediate relationships between groups and the state in the sense that "civil society" connotes.

8. Despite the pro-independence position of the earlier Dehradun-based AIGL, the Darjeeling community maintained fraught relations with the Indian independence movement. They tried to leverage their ongoing demonstrations of loyalty to the imperial government in exchange for administrative independence from Bengal. This strategy was unsuccessful, leaving Darjeeling citizens with the worst of both worlds: no administrative autonomy, and a constant question mark over their loyalty to independent India owing to both their perceived associations with Nepal and their attempts to curry favor with the British. These are the historical underpinnings of the political turmoil Darjeeling continues to experience today.

9. The origin of the term *larke* is murky. The literal meaning in Nepali is "follower" or "subservient individual" (see Sharma 2057 VS: 1163), although perhaps the BLTS founders intended it to mean "member." It may also derive from the Hindi *ladke*, or "youth."

10. Chalmers (2003:255–56) describes how kinship terminology was pervasive in descriptions of the Nepali community during the phase of identity building from 1914 to 1920. However, such language fell out of common usage by the 1930s (56). This analysis suggests that the Thangmi choice of kinship terminology in naming their organization in 1943 was not just a mimicry of other organizations' terms but a statement that despite the rhetoric of pan-Nepali unity, real kinship was found in the company of ethnic compatriots.

11. *Deusi* is "a festival which begins on the fifth day of the *tiwar* festival (= *diwali*). On this day children and others come round to give blessings and receive alms: the leader says something or other. . . . The others cry in chorus *deusi*" (Turner

[1931] 1997:317). *Deusi* performances are commonly used to raise funds for social welfare organizations.

12. The name "Thapa," held by several members, can designate either Chhetri or Magar.

13. The *madal* was promoted as a national symbol in *panchayat* Nepal after 1962 (Stirr 2013:373). Amrikan's narrative demonstrates that it was already understood as a pan-Nepali symbol more than twenty years earlier in Darjeeling, but one wielded more effectively by certain ethnic groups than others.

14. Minami writes, "Ethnic movements among Nepali migrants to Darjeeling began in the years between 1920 and 1940, when the Kirantis, Newars, Damais, Viswakarmas (Kamis), and Tamangs, all formed their own ethnic/caste associations" (2007:490). Gaenszle also mentions several Rai organizations founded in the 1920s and 1930s (2011).

15. This stands in contrast to other early ethnic associations in Nepal, which were founded on a social-welfare model akin to the BLTS (W. Fisher 2001:139; Hangen 2007:15).

16. In 2012, Amrit Kumar Bohara told me that the CPN-ML had finally rectified this injustice by funding a new school in Piskar.

17. Restrictions had gradually loosened over the course of the 1980s (Hangen 2007:3).

18. Initially the Nepal Janajati Mahasangh, or Nepal Federation of Nationalities (NEFEN), *adivasi* and "indigenous" were added only in the early 2000s, changing the organization's name to the Nepal Federation of Indigenous Nationalities (NEFIN). The group had eight member organizations at its founding, growing to fifty-four by 2007 (Hangen 2007:24). Several additional groups have since sought membership (Shneiderman 2013a).

19. The CPN-UML joined the Nepali Congress in the 1990 fight for democracy. This marked the beginning of their shift toward the center, enabling the Maoists' success as the latter took advantage of disillusioned UML cadres (Shneiderman 2009).

20. The official BTWA census included only those whose forebears were Indian citizens in 1950.

21. A small number of Thangmi families migrated to Burma from Nepal, relocating to India later.

22. Eight other groups of Nepali heritage were granted OBC status in 1995: Bhujel, Newar, Mangar (known as Magar in Nepal), Nembang, Sampang, Bunghheng, Jogi, and Dhimal.

23. This figure was provided by a municipal secretary who collated records since 1995.

24. See Turin (2014) on the complicated relationships between language competence, identity, and belonging.

25. Some informants explained this more bluntly as a tit-for-tat in response to the BTWA's exclusion of those who could not prove citizenship in India before 1950.

26. The organization was formally registered as Niko Thami Utthan Manch Nepal, but Thami Bhasa Tatha Sanskriti Utthan Kendra appears on all of its published materials. Following Megh Raj's preferences, I have used the latter.

27. Some Thangmi argue that acceding to the category of "Kirant *dharma*" would build stronger political standing, without assimilating to one of the "great traditions" of Hinduism or Buddhism. This remained an active debate through the 2011 Nepal census.

28. The book bears a publication date of 2056 VS but was actually only printed and distributed in 2061 VS.

29. Materials produced by the BTWA usually gloss this as *anautho chalan* in Nepali. This translates literally as "unusual" or "extraordinary" "traditions" in the folkloric sense.

30. Around the same time, NFDIN changed its name in Nepali from Adivasi Janajati Utthan Kendra to Adivasi Janajati Vikas Pratisthan, signaling a broader shift from the ideals of "upliftment" (*utthan*) to those of "development" (*vikas*).

31. This was apparently due to administrative complications at NEFIN; funds were disbursed to the NTS three months before the end of the fiscal year during which they had to be spent. This was not well understood at the grassroots level.

Chapter 6. Transcendent Territory, Portable Deities, and the Problem of Indigeneity

Note to epigraph: "Niko Nai Jati" (Our Ethnicity), Thangmi-language song written by Maina and Lal Thami from Alampu, recorded in Darjeeling by the BTWA on the cassette *Amako Ashis* (Mother's Blessings).

1. G. N. Rimal (2007) and Pitamber Sharma (2007) map early proposals for Nepal's federal structure.

2. Thangmi often respond to questions about their origins by invoking Simraungadh, an ancient settlement in the Tarai, of which there are now only archaeological remains (Ballinger 1973). There may have been a link between an early Mithila king, Hari Simha Deva, and the Dolakha region (Miller [1979] 1997; Slusser 1982; Vajracharya and Shrestha 2031 VS). When his kingdom "straddling the Bihar-Tarai border" (Slusser 1982:55) was conquered by Muslim forces in 1324–25 A.D., this king fled toward Dolakha but died en route. His sons and entourage reached their destination but were imprisoned by Dolakha's rulers. It may be Hari Simha Deva's Tarai principality that the Thangmi refer to as Simraungadh. Several Thangmi publications attempt to substantiate this but lack conclusive historical evidence.

3. For groups whose origin stories tell of migration from the north (i.e., Sherpa, Tamang, Gurung), historical links to Buddhist Tibet have been deployed as positive identity markers within the "non-Hindu" *janajati* movement (McHugh 2006). However, since the Thangmi myth locates their origins in Simraungadh, somewhere along the present-day Nepal-India border, no such valorization is possible.

4. Whether Newar should be classified as *janajati* is an ongoing contentious debate, both within the Newar community itself and among broader *janajati* and non-*janajati* Nepali publics. They speak a Tibeto-Burman language and practice Buddhism

in addition to Hinduism, yet are economically and politically "advantaged" compared with other *janajati* groups, and historically held power in the Kathmandu Valley and other important polities like Dolakha.

5. It remains a mystery why Thangmi were listed as rightful holders of *kipat* lands but were not classified in the Muluki Ain.

6. By late 2005, Rajen had softened his position. He apologized for making me erase the tape and said I was free to use the entire interview. By this time, he was no longer general secretary of the BTWA and was reflecting on the positions he had taken while in office.

7. *Bhume* is derived from the Sanskrit *bhumi*, "earth," meaning "soil" or "ground" in contemporary Nepali. The Thangmi Bhume is nongendered, so I use the pronoun "it."

8. *Chuku* (T) and *aji* (T) mean "father-in-law" and "mother-in-law" respectively. These variations make the ancestral couple "in-laws" rather than 'parents' from the perspective of the speaker, and the choice of terminology generally depends upon the speaker's clan affiliation.

Chapter 7. The Work of Life-Cycle Rituals and the Power of Parallel Descent

1. This begs the question of what happens to people who never marry (a very small percentage of the adult Thangmi population). I never observed a *mumpra* for an unmarried individual but was told that it would diverge from the usual ritual form since there would be no affinal relatives or sons to act as the primary mourners.

2. The term *parallel descent* was coined by William Davenport (1959:579). Systems that fit this description are rare anywhere in the world but have been described for the Apinaye of Brazil (Maybury-Lewis 1960); the Quechua of Peru (Isbell 1978); the Ainu of Japan (Sjöberg 1993:68); and the Ömie of Papua New Guinea, although here the author prefers the term "sex-affiliation" (Rohatynskyj 1997). Melvyn Goldstein suggests that in historical Tibet, "all laymen and laywomen in Tibet were serfs (*Mi ser*) bound via ascription by parallel descent to a particular lord (*dPon-po*) through an estate. . . . Sons were ascribed to their father's lord but daughters to their mother's lord" (1971:15).

3. Thangmi kinship terminology is mapped by Mark Turin (2004b, 2012).

4. See the attempt in Reng (1999:26–27).

5. All Nepali and Latin botanical terms are cited from Turin (2003).

6. *Mosan* derives from the Nepali *masan*: "burning ground . . . burial-ground; cemetery; ghost" (Turner [1931] 1997:496); *thali* "place, ground, spot" (294–95).

7. Peet similarly observed, "Thamis behave as if general kindred ties (agnatic, cognatic, affinal) were about as important as any specific patrilineal connections" (1978:230).

8. NEFIN suggests that egalitarianism is common to all *janajati* groups, citing this as criteria for recognition. However, clan-based hierarchies have long featured in the internal cultural politics of many *janajati* groups, as documented for the Gurung by

Alan Macfarlane (1997). *Nan Ni Patuko* asserts that in Lapilang, the three clans of Markebhot, Sansari, and Akyangmi "performed ritual duties for the other Thamis and are dependent on others for a living" (Patuko 2054 VS:4), a statement repeated in *Thami Samudaya* (Samudaya [2056] 2061:20). My data does not affirm this, although it may have been true at some point in the past. Several gurus and laypeople dismissed this as the fantasy of activists who wanted to appear more "modern" (i.e., more "Hindu") by claiming a hierarchical caste system.

9. *Nan Ni Patuko* (2054 VS) posits only one couple and does not appear concerned with the incestuous nature of their children's relationships. However, the couple is named Uke Chuku and Beti Aji. In some oral renditions, these are alternate names for Ya'apa and Sunari Ama. Activists who are otherwise concerned with standardization have exploited this variation to suggest that these were actually two different couples.

10. The fact that the *nwaran* could be conducted by *jhankri* might suggest that there are actually multiple officiants with the Thangmi ritual system, but here the exception proves the rule since many gurus themselves did not consider the *nwaran* a Thangmi ritual at all.

11. Philippe Ramirez (2013) describes comparable ethnic "conversions" elsewhere in the Himalayas.

12. Tanka Subba reports a 32 percent rate of "intercaste marriage" in early 1980s Rangbull, a village on the outskirts of the Darjeeling bazaar (1989:69). This is a higher rate than in two successively more remote villages, in which 27 percent and 13.7 percent, respectively, of marriages were intercaste, leading Subba to suggest that intercaste marriage is higher in urbanized areas. This may account in part for the higher rates of intergroup marriage that I documented since the majority of my interlocutors lived in urban areas. Other relevant factors include the twenty-year time gap between Subba's research and my own, and that Thangmi are relatively unconcerned with status and hierarchy and so are likely to have a higher intergroup marriage rate than the more ethnically diverse subjects with whom Subba worked. Keera Allendorf (2013) discusses marriage in contemporary Darjeeling.

13. People in previous generations who married non-Thangmi may have decided to settle in India for that reason, since despite Thangmi flexibility, in broader social terms Nepal was a more challenging place for interethnic couples. This has changed to some extent since 1990, particularly in urban areas, but intergroup marriage is still not the acceptable norm in Nepal that it is in Darjeeling.

14. In Dolakha, *roimirati* also refers to the offspring of more recent unions between Newar men and Thangmi women. In Sindhupalchok, members of the original *roimirati* clan and present-day children of such liaisons are distinguished. The latter are called *nagarkoti*. David Holmberg (1989:70) describes similar usage of this term among Tamang for children of Newar men and Tamang women.

15. *Nan Ni Patuko* offers an overview of the ritual and the *gardul puran* tale (Patuko 2054 VS:22–23). *Thami Samudaya* provides details in an instructional style.

The last line states that the *cheti* (T), the woven mat on which offerings are placed during the *mumpra*, is "a unique identifier of the Thami community" (Samudaya [2056] 2061 VS:85–92).

16. According to gurus and older lay informants, a generation ago all *jekha mumpra* were conducted in the Nepali month of Pus (January-February), regardless of when the person died. Conducting this rite thirteen days after death is a more recent adaptation to Hindu norms.

17. There is no Thangmi-language term for this or many other ritual concepts. Axel Michaels (1999) offers useful definitions of *kiryaputri* and other Nepali-language funerary terms.

18. The Nepali meaning of *kutumba* is similar, but slightly different in scope: "family, relations, esp. relatives of daughter's husband' (Turner [1931] 1997:96).

19. Thangmi do not fit the pattern that Michael Oppitz (1982) describes for Magar and Gurung in which death rituals cement affinal ties by assigning responsibilities to the deceased's son-in-law. Since Thangmi do not practice matrilateral cross-cousin marriage, which is the prerequisite for Oppitz's model, this is not surprising.

20. Such inversions are a common feature of death rituals throughout the Himalayas. See Nick Allen (1972:86) on the Thulung Rai and Martin Gaenszle on the Mewahang Rai (1999:56).

21. Balthasar Bickel and Martin Gaenszle (1999:17) contrast this body-based notion with the "geomorphic" spatiality common among Kiranti groups. Here space is ordered via directional notions derived from montane geography rather than the human body. The Thangmi language demonstrates evidence of both geomorphic and homomorphic forms of spatial ordering (Mark Turin, personal communication).

22. Jonathan Parry explains that this notion is "explicitly elaborated in the *Garuda Purana* (part 15), to which the Banaras sacred specialists continually refer" (1994:30). The Thangmi *mumpra* concludes with a reference to this text. However, the Thangmi *gardul puran* does not match the content of the Garuda Purana text, while the earlier ritual segment, *sikitipko bhakha*, has some narrative overlap with it.

23. Many other Himalayan groups deploy effigies of the deceased (Ramble 1982; Oppitz 1982). Descriptions of Thakali (Vinding 1982) and Newar (Gellner 1992) funerary rites mention body reconstructions with food items, but as ritual components of minor importance compared with the effigy. For Thangmi, no effigy exists other than this assemblage of foodstuffs, which highlights again the direct correlation between body and land via natural products. In this regard, the Thangmi process of bodily reconstruction appears more like the orthodox Hindu "refinement of the body" in Banaras (Parry 1994: chapter 6).

24. Many of these body-part terms in Thangmi ritual language have cognates in early classical Newar (Kashinath Tamot, personal communication). See also Turin (2004a) on Thangmi/Newar lexical correspondences and Shneiderman (2002) for a list of the Thangmi and Nepali names of each food item used in the *mumpra*.

25. Some gurus claim that in the past a whole animal was used. This suggests that as in the wedding ritual, an unsavory use of bovine flesh may have been jettisoned during the period of Hinduization. But it is unclear why it did not lead to wholesale restructuring of the *mumpra* as it did for the *bore*.

26. *Ayu* means "lifespan" or "life essence" in Nepali; in Thangmi it has come to mean "soul", and also refers to this specific ritual episode during which errant souls are recalled.

27. Some gurus refer to this myth as *alolorungko kura* (T), invoking the reed mat (T: *alolorung*) in which corpses were wrapped before the advent of cotton cloth. The title, *gardul puran,* may be related to the Garuda Purana (Parry 1994:30).

28. The Maoists attempted an unsuccessful comprehensive alcohol ban in Thangmi villages in Nepal from 2001 to 2006.

Chapter 8. Resisting the End of a Ritual

1. Photo appearing in the *Kathmandu Post*, October 5, 2006, p. 1.

2. The People's Movement of April 2006 ended Gyanendra Shah's fourteen months of autocratic direct rule. He was formally deposed in May 2008.

Bibliography

VS indicates the Nepali Vikram Sambat calendar—approximately fifty-seven years ahead of the Gregorian calendar (2061 VS is AD 2004–2005).

Adams, Vincanne. 1996. *Tigers of the Snow and Other Virtual Sherpas*. Princeton: Princeton University Press.

Adhikari, R. L. 1997. *Thamini Kanchi*. Kathmandu: Bhanu Prakashan.

Ahearn, Laura. 2001. "Language and Agency." *Annual Review of Anthropology* 30: 109–37.

Allen, Nick. 1972. "The Vertical Dimension in Thulung Classification." *Journal of the Anthropological Society of Oxford* 3(2): 81–94.

———. 1978. "Fourfold Classifications of Society in the Himalayas." In *Himalayan Anthropology*, edited by James Fisher, 7–26. Paris: Mouton.

Allendorf, Keera. 2013. "Schemas of Marital Change." *Journal of Marriage and Family* 75(2): 453–69.

Amnesty International. 1987. *Nepal*. New York: Amnesty International.

Anderson, Benedict. 1991. *Imagined Communities*. London: Verso.

Anthias, Floya. 2006. "Belongings in a Globalising and Unequal World." In *The Situated Politics of Belonging*, edited by Nira Yuval-Davis, Kalpana Kannabiran, and Ulrike Vieten, 17–31. London: Sage.

Appadurai, Arjun. 1990. "Disjuncture and Difference in the Global Cultural Economy." *Public Culture* 2(2): 1–24.

———. 1998. "Dead Certainty." *Public Culture* (10) 2: 225–47.

———. 2004. "The Capacity to Aspire." In *Culture and Public Action*, edited by Vijayendra Rao and Michael Walton, 59–84. Stanford: Stanford University Press.

Austin, John. 1975. *How to Do Things with Words*. Cambridge, MA: Harvard University Press.

Axel, Brian. 2001. *The Nation's Tortured Body*. Durham, NC: Duke University Press.

Bagahi, S. B., and Ajit K. Danda. 1982. "NE-BU-LA." In *Tribal Movements in India, Volume 1*, edited by K. S. Singh, 339–48. Delhi: Manohar.

Ballinger, Thomas. 1973. "Simraongarh Revisited." *Kailash* 1(3): 180–84.

Banks, Marcus. 1996. *Ethnicity*. London: Routledge.

Baral, L. S. 2012. "The New Order in Nepal Under King Mahendra, 1960–1962." In *Autocratic Monarchy*, edited by Pratyoush Onta and Lokranjan Parajuli, 193–94. Kathmandu: Martin Chautari.

Barth, Frederik. 1969. *Ethnic Groups and Boundaries*. Boston: Little, Brown.

Basch, Linda; Nina Glick Schiller; and Christina Szanton Blanc, eds. 1994. *Nations Unbound*. New York: Gordon and Breach.

Bauman, Richard. 1975. "Verbal Art as Performance." *American Anthropologist* 77(2): 290–311.

Bauman, Richard, and Charles Briggs. 1990. "Poetics and Performance as Critical Perspectives on Language and Social Life." *Annual Review of Anthropology* 19: 59–88.

van Beek, Martijn. 2000. "Beyond Identity Fetishism." *Cultural Anthropology* 15(4): 525–69.

Bell, Catherine. 1992. *Ritual Theory, Ritual Practice*. New York: Oxford University Press.

Benedict, Paul. 1972. *Sino-Tibetan*. Cambridge: Cambridge University Press.

Bennett, Lynn, and Dilip Parajuli. 2013. *The Nepal Multidimensional Exclusion Index*. Kathmandu: Himal Books.

Bentley, G. Carter. 1987. "Ethnicity and Practice." *Comparative Studies in Society and History* 29(1): 24–55.

Berreman, Gerald. 1964. "Shamans and Brahmins in Pahari Religion." *Journal of Asian Studies* 23: 53–69.

Besky, Sarah. 2013. *The Darjeeling Distinction*. Berkeley: University of California Press.

Beteille, André. 1998. "The Idea of Indigenous People." *Current Anthropology* 39(2): 187–91.

Bhowmik, Sharit. 1981. *Class Formation in the Plantation System*. Delhi: People's Publishing.

Bickel, Balthasar, and Martin Gaenszle, eds. 1999. *Himalayan Space*. Zürich: Völkerkundemuseum Zürich.

Bista, Dor Bahadur. 1967. *Peoples of Nepal*. Kathmandu: Ministry of Information and Broadcasting.

Bloch, Maurice, and Jonathan Parry. 1982. "Introduction." In *Death and the Regeneration of Life*, edited by Maurice Bloch and Jonathan Parry, 1–44. Cambridge: Cambridge University Press.

Blondeau, Anne-Marie, ed. 1998. *Tibetan Mountain Deities*. Vienna: Österreichischen Akademie der Wissenschaften.

Blondeau, Anne-Marie, and Ernst Steinkellner, eds. 1996. *Reflections of the Mountain*. Vienna: Österreichischen Akademie der Wissenschaften.

Bourdieu, Pierre. 1977. *Outline of a Theory of Practice*. Cambridge: Cambridge University Press.

———. 1990. *The Logic of Practice*. Stanford: Stanford University Press.

Briggs, Charles. 1996. "The Politics of Discursive Authority in Research on the 'Invention of Tradition.'" *Cultural Anthropology* 11(4): 435–69.

Bruslé, Tristan. 2010. "Introduction" (Special issue: Nepalese Migrations). *European Bulletin of Himalayan Research*, 35–36: 16–23.

Buffetrille, Katia. 1996. "One Day the Mountains Will Go Away—Preliminary Remarks on the Flying Mountains of Tibet". In *Reflections of the Mountain*, edited by Anne-Marie Blondeau and Ernst Steinkellner, 77–90. Vienna: Österreichischen Akademie der Wissenschaften.

Buffetrille, Katia, and Hildegard Diemberger, eds. 2002. *Territory and Identity in Tibet and the Himalayas*. Leiden: Brill.

Burghart, Richard. 1984. "The Formation of the Concept of Nation-State in Nepal." *Journal of Asian Studies* 44(1): 101–25.

Butler, Judith. 1997a. *Excitable Speech*. New York: Routledge.

———. 1997b. *The Psychic Life of Power*. Stanford: Stanford University Press.

de la Cadena, Marisol, and Orin Starn. 2007. "Introduction." In *Indigenous Experience Today*, edited by Marisol de la Cadena and Orin Starn, 1–32. New York: Berg.

Caplan, Lionel. (1970) 2000. *Land and Social Change in East Nepal*. Kathmandu: Himal Books.

Cattelino, Jessica. 2008. *High Stakes*. Durham, NC: Duke University Press.

Chalier-Visuvalingam, Elizabeth. 2003. *Bhairava*. Brussels: Peter Lang.

Chalmers, Rhoderick. 2003. "We Nepalis." Ph.D. diss, School of Oriental and African Studies, University of London.

Chatterjee, Partha. 2004. *The Politics of the Governed*. New York: Columbia University Press.

Chatterjee, Piya. 2001. *A Time for Tea*. Durham, NC: Duke University Press.

Chu, Julie. 2010. *Cosmologies of Credit*. Durham, NC: Duke University Press.

Clarke, Graham. 1995. "Blood and Territory as Idioms of National Identity in Himalayan States." *Kailash* 17(3/4): 89–132.

Clifford, James. 2007. "Varieties of Indigenous Experience." In *Indigenous Experience Today*, edited by Marisol de la Cadena and Orin Starn, 197–224. New York: Berg.

Clifford, James, and George Marcus. 1986. *Writing Culture*. Berkeley: University of California Press.

Cohn, Bernard. 1987. "The Census, Social Structure and Objectification in South Asia." In *An Anthropologist Among the Historians and Other Essays*, 224–54. Delhi: Oxford University Press.

Comaroff, John, and Jean Comaroff. 2009. *Ethnicity, Inc.* Chicago: University of Chicago.

Davenport, William. 1959. "Nonunilinear Descent and Descent Groups." *American Anthropologist* 61(4): 557–72.

Deleuze, Gilles, and Félix Guattari. 1977. *Anti-Oedipus*. New York: Viking.

Deliege, Robert. 1993. "The Myths of Origin of the Indian Untouchables." *Man* 28(3): 533–49.

Des Chene, Mary. 1996. "Ethnography in the *Janajati-yug*." *Studies in Nepali History and Society* 1(1): 97–162.

————. 2007. "Is Nepal in South Asia?" *Studies in Nepali History and Society* 12(2): 207–23.

Desjarlais, Robert. 2003. *Sensory Biographies*. Berkeley: University of California Press.

Dirks, Nicholas. 2001. *Castes of Mind*. Princeton: Princeton University Press.

van Driem, George. 2001. *Languages of the Himalayas*. Leiden: Brill.

————. 2003. "Mahakiranti Revisited." In *Themes in Himalayan Languages and Linguistics*, edited by Tej Ratna Kansakar and Mark Turin, 21–26. Kathmandu: South Asia Institute and Tribhuvan University.

Durkheim, Émile. (1912) 1995. *The Elementary Forms of Religious Life*. New York: Free Press.

Ehrhard, Franz-Karl. 1997. "'The Lands Are Like a Wiped Golden Basin.'" In *Les Habitants du toit du monde*, edited by Samten Karmay and Philippe Sagant, 125–38. Nanterre, France: Société d'Ethnologie.

Fisher, James, ed. 1978. *Himalayan Anthropology: The Indo-Tibetan Interface*. The Hague: Mouton.

————. 1986. *Trans-Himalayan Traders*. Berkeley: University of California Press.

————. 1990. *Sherpas*. Berkeley: University of California Press.

Fisher, William. 2001. *Fluid Boundaries*. New York: Columbia University Press.

Fjeld, Heidi. 2008. "Pollution and Social Networks in Contemporary Rural Tibet." In *Tibetan Modernities*, edited by Robert Barnett and Ronald Schwartz, 113–38. Leiden: Brill.

Forbes, Anne Armbrecht. 1998. "Sacred Geography on the Cultural Borders of Tibet." In *Tibetan Mountain Deities*, edited by Anne-Marie Blondeau, 111–21. Vienna: Verlag der Österreichischen Akademie der Wissenschaften.

————. 1999. "Mapping Power." *American Ethnologist* 26(1): 114–38.

Foucault, Michel. 1977. *Discipline and Punish*. New York: Pantheon.

Fricke, Thomas. 1990. "Elementary Structures in the Nepal Himalaya." *Ethnology* 29: 135–58.

Fuller, Chris, and Véronique Bénéï, eds. 2000. *The Everyday State and Society in Modern India*. New Delhi: Social Science Press.

von Fürer-Haimendorf, Christoph. 1964. *The Sherpas of Nepal*. Berkeley: University of California Press.

————. 1975. *Himalayan Traders*. London: John Murray.

————. 1978. "Foreword." In *Himalayan Anthropology: The Indo-Tibetan Interface*, edited by James F. Fisher, ix-xii. The Hague: Mouton.

Gaborieau, Marc. 1968. "Le partage du pouvoir entre les lignages d'une localité du Népal central." *L'homme* 18 (1–2): 37–67.

————. 1978. *Le Nepal et ses populations*. Brussels: Editions Complexe.

Gaenszle, Martin. 1999. "The Making of Good Ancestors." In *Ways of Dying*, edited by Elisabeth Schömbucher and Claus Peter Zoller, 49–67. New Delhi: Manohar.

————. 2000. *Origins and Migrations*. Kathmandu: Mandala Book Point.

————. 2002. *Ancestral Voices*. Münster: LIT Verlag.

———. 2011. "Scripturalization of Ritual in Eastern Nepal." In *Ritual, Heritage, and Identity*, edited by Christiane Brosius and Karin Polit, 281–97. Delhi: Routledge.

Galanter, Marc. 1984. *Competing Equalities*. Berkeley: University of California Press.

Gautam, Rajesh and Ashoke Thapa-Magar. 1994. *Tribal Ethnography of Nepal*. Delhi: Book Faith India.

Gellner, David. 1992. *Monk, Householder, and Tantric Priest*. Cambridge: Cambridge University Press.

———. 1997. "Introduction." In *Nationalism and Ethnicity in a Hindu Kingdom*, edited by David Gellner, Joanna Pfaff-Czarnecka, and John Whelpton, 3–32. Amsterdam: Harwood.

———, ed. 2003. *Resistance and the State*. New Delhi: Social Science Press.

———. 2007. "Caste, Ethnicity and Inequality in Nepal." *Economic and Political Weekly* 42(20): 1823–28.

———. 2010a. "Introduction." In *Varieties of Activist Experience*, edited by David Gellner, 1–14. Delhi: Sage.

———. 2010b. "Initiation as a Site of Cultural Conflict Among the Newars." In *Hindu and Buddhist Initiations in India and Nepal*, edited by Astrid Zotter and Christof Zotter, 167–81. Wiesbaden: Harrassowitz Verlag.

Gellner, David; Joanna Pfaff-Czarnecka; and John Whelpton, eds. 1997. *Nationalism and Ethnicity in a Hindu Kingdom*. Amsterdam: Harwood.

Ghosh, Kaushik. 2006. "Between Global Flows and Local Dams." *Cultural Anthropology* 21(4): 501–34.

Gidwani, Vinay, and Kalyanakrishnan Sivaramakrishnan. 2003. "Circular Migration and the Spaces of Cultural Assertion." *Annals of the Association of American Geographers* 93(1): 186–213.

Godelier, Maurice. 1999. *The Enigma of the Gift*. Chicago: University of Chicago Press.

Goffman, Erving. 1971. *Relations in Public*. New York: Harper and Row.

———. 1974. *Frame Analysis*. Cambridge, MA: Harvard University Press.

———. 1982. *Interaction Ritual*. New York: Pantheon.

Goldstein, Melvyn. 1971. "Serfdom and Mobility." *Journal of Asian Studies* 30(3): 521–34.

———. 1998. "Introduction." In *Buddhism in Contemporary Tibet*, edited by Melvyn Goldstein and Matthew Kapstein, 1–14. Berkeley: University of California Press.

Goody, Jack. 1986. *The Logic of Writing and the Organization of Society*. Cambridge: Cambridge University Press.

———. 2000. *The Power of the Written Tradition*. Washington, DC: Smithsonian Institution.

Graham, Laura. 2005. "Image and Instrumentality in a Xavante Politics of Existential Recognition." *American Ethnologist* 32(4): 622–41.

Graner, Elvira, and Ganesh Gurung. 2003. "Arabko Lahures." *Contributions to Nepalese Studies* 28: 295–325.

Grierson, George, ed. 1909. *Linguistic Survey of India (Vol. III, Part I, Tibeto-Burman Family)*. Calcutta: Superintendent of Government Printing, India.

Guarnizo, Luis, and Michael Smith. 1998. "The Locations of Transnationalism." In *Transnationalism from Below*, edited by Michael Smith and Luis Guarnizo, 3–34. New Brunswick, NJ: Transaction.

Guneratne, Arjun. 1998. "Modernization, the State, and the Construction of a Tharu Identity in Nepal." *Journal of Asian Studies* 57(3): 749–73.

———. 2002. *Many Tongues, One People*. Ithaca, NY: Cornell University Press.

Gupta, Akhil, and Kalyanakrishnan Sivaramakrishnan, eds. 2011. *The State in India After Liberalization*. London: Routledge.

Gyatso, Janet. 1987. "Down with the Demoness." In *Feminine Ground*, edited by Janice Willis, 33–51. Ithaca, NY: Snow Lion.

Hachhethu, Krishna. 2002. *Party Building in Nepal*. Kathmandu: Mandala Book Point.

Hale, Charles. 2006. "Activist Research v. Cultural Critique." *Cultural Anthropology* 21(1): 96–120.

Handler, Richard. 1984. "On Sociocultural Discontinuity." *Current Anthropology* 25(1): 55–71.

———. 1986. "Authenticity." *Anthropology Today* 2(1), 2–4.

———. 2011. "The 'Ritualization of Ritual' in the Construction of Heritage." In *Ritual, Heritage and Identity*, edited by Christiane Brosius and Karin Polit. Delhi: Routledge.

Hangen, Susan. 2005a. "Race and the Politics of Identity in Nepal." *Ethnology* 44(1): 49–64.

———. 2005b. "Boycotting Dasain." *Studies in Nepali History and Society* 10(1): 105–33.

———. 2007. *Creating a "New Nepal."* Washington, DC: East West Center.

———. 2010. *The Rise of Ethnic Politics in Nepal*. London: Routledge.

Hardman, Charlotte. 2000. *Other Worlds*. Oxford: Berg.

Hart, Keith. 2010. Review of *Ethnicity, Inc.*, *American Anthropologist* 112(3): 480–81.

Hertz, Robert (1907) 2004. "A Contribution to the Study of the Collective Representation of Death." In *Death, Mourning and Burial*, edited by Antonius Robben, 197–212. Malden, MA: Blackwell.

Hitchcock, John. 1966. *The Magars of Banyan Hill*. New York: Holt, Rinehart and Winston.

Hitchcock, John, and Rex Jones, eds. 1976. *Spirit Possession in the Nepal Himalayas*. Warminster, UK: Aris and Phillips.

(HMG/N) His Majesty's Government of Nepal. 1996. *Nepal Multiple Indicator Surveillance*. Kathmandu: UNICEF and National Planning Commission Secretariat.

Höfer, Andras. (1979) 2004. *The Caste Hierarchy and the State in Nepal*. Kathmandu: Himal.

Hoftun, Martin; William Raeper; and John Whelpton, eds. 1999. *People, Politics and Ideology*. Kathmandu: Mandala Book Point.

Holmberg, David. 1989. *Order in Paradox*. Ithaca, NY: Cornell University Press.

———. 2000. "Derision, Exorcism, and the Ritual Production of Power." *American Ethnologist* 27(4): 1–23.

Holmberg, David, and Kathryn March, with Suryaman Tamang. 1999. "Local Production/Local Knowledge." *Studies in Nepali History and Society* 4(1): 5–64.

Huber, Toni. 1999a. *The Cult of Pure Crystal Mountain*. New York: Oxford University Press.

———, ed. 1999b. *Sacred Spaces and Powerful Places in Tibetan Culture*. Dharamsala: Library of Tibetan Works and Archives.

Hughes-Freeland, Felicia, and Mary M. Crain. 1998. "Introduction." In *Recasting Ritual*, edited by Felicia Hughes-Freeland and Mary M. Crain, 1–20. London: Routledge.

Humphrey, Caroline, and James Laidlaw. 1994. *The Archetypal Actions of Ritual*. Oxford: Oxford University Press.

Hutt, Michael. 1997. "Being Nepali Without Nepal." In *Nationalism and Ethnicity in a Hindu Kingdom*, edited by David Gellner, Joanna Pfaff-Czarnecka, and John Whelpton, 101–44. Amsterdam: Harwood.

———. 1998. "Going to Mugalan." *South Asia Research* 18(2): 195–214.

———. 2003. *Unbecoming Citizens*. Delhi: Oxford University Press.

(ICDM) Integrated Community Development Movement. 1999. "Profile of the Village Development Committee of Lapilang." Unpublished manuscript.

Inda, Jonathan Xavier, and Renato Rosaldo. 2002. "Introduction: A World in Motion." In *The Anthropology of Globalization*, edited by Jonathan Xavier Inda and Renato Rosaldo, 1–34. Malden, MA: Blackwell.

INSEC. 1995. "Appendix 3." *Human Rights Yearbook 1995*. Kathmandu: INSEC.

Isbell, Billie Jean. 1978. *To Defend Ourselves*. Austin: University of Texas Press.

Jackson, Jean, with María Clemencia Ramírez. 2009. "Traditional, Transnational and Cosmopolitan." *American Ethnologist* 36(3): 521–44.

Jaffrelot, Christophe. 2006. "The Impact of Affirmative Action in India." *India Review* 5(2): 173–89.

Jenkins, Laura. 2003. *Identity and Identification in India*. London: Routledge Curzon.

Jenkins, Richard. 2002. "Imagined but Not Imaginary." In *Exotic No More*, edited by Jeremy MacClancy, 114–28. Chicago: University of Chicago Press.

Kaila, Bairagi, and Amod Yonzon, eds. 2056 VS. *Rastriya Bhasako Kavita Sangalo* [A Compilation of Poetry in National Languages]. Kathmandu: Rastriya Janajati Vikas Samiti.

Kapila, Kriti. 2008. "The Measure of a Tribe." *Journal of the Royal Anthropological Institute* 14: 117–34.

Karlsson, Bengt. 2013. "The Social Life of Categories." *Focaal* 65: 33–41.

Karmay, Samten. 1998. *The Arrow and the Spindle*. Kathmandu: Mandala Book Point.

Kaviraj, Sudipta, and Sunil Khilnani, eds. 2001. *Civil Society*. Cambridge: Cambridge University Press.

Keane, Webb. 1997. *Signs of Recognition*. Berkeley: University of California Press.
Kearney, Michael. 1986. "From the Invisible Hand to Visible Feet." *Annual Review of Anthropology* 15: 331–61.
Kennedy, Dane. 1996. *The Magic Mountains*. Berkeley: University of California Press.
Kharel, Dipesh. 2006. *Heavy Loads Toward a Better Life*. MA thesis. Tromso, Norway: University of Tromso.
Kirshenblatt-Gimblett, Barbara. 1995. "Theorizing Heritage." *Ethnomusicology* 39(3): 367–80.
———. 1998. *Destination Culture*. Berkeley: University of California Press.
Kohrt, Brandon, and Ian Harper. 2008. "Navigating Diagnoses." *Culture, Medicine, and Psychiatry* 32: 462–91.
Krauskopff, Gisèle. 1989. *Maîtres et possédés*. Paris: Éditions du CNRS.
———. 2003. "An 'Indigenous Minority' in a Border Area." In *Resistance and the State*, edited by David Gellner, 199–243. New Delhi: Social Science Press.
Krauskopff, Gisèle, and Marie Lecomte-Tilouine, eds. 1996. *Célébrer le Pouvoir*. Paris: CNRS Éditions, Éditions de la MSH.
Kuper, Adam. 2003. "The Return of the Native." *Current Anthropology* 44(3): 389–402.
Lal, C. K. 2003. "The Necessary Manufacture of South Asia." *Himal Southasian*. January 2003.
Lall, Kesar. 1966. "The Thami." *The Rising Nepal*. Kathmandu. 3.
Lawoti, Mahendra. 2003. "The Maoists and Minorities." *Studies in Nepali History and Society* 8(1): 67–97.
———. 2005. "Democracy, Domination and Exclusionary Constitutional Engineering Process in Nepal, 1990" In *Contentious Politics and Democratization in Nepal*, edited by Mahendra Lawoti, 48–74. Delhi: Sage.
Lawoti, Mahendra, and Susan Hangen, eds. 2012. *Nationalism and Ethnic Conflict in Nepal*. London: Routledge.
Leach, Edmund. 1964. *Political Systems of Highland Burma*. Boston: Beacon.
Lecomte-Tilouine, Marie. 1993. "About Bhume, a Misunderstanding in the Himalayas." In *Nepal Past and Present*, edited by Gerard Toffin. New Delhi: Sterling.
Leve, Lauren. 2007. " 'Failed Development' and Rural Revolution in Nepal." *Anthropological Quarterly* 80(1): 127–72.
Levine, Nancy. 1981. "The Theory of Rü." In *Asian Highland Societies in Anthropological Perspective*, edited by Christoph von Fürer-Haimendorf. Delhi: Sterling.
———. 1987. "Caste, State, and Ethnic Boundaries in Nepal." *Journal of Asian Studies* 46(1): 71–88.
Lévi-Strauss, Claude. 1979. *Myth and Meaning*. New York: Schocken.
———. (1973) 1987. "The Story of Asdiwal." In *Structural Anthropology*, Volume 2, 146–97. Harmondsworth, UK: Penguin.
Levitt, Peggy. 2001. *The Transnational Villagers*. Berkeley: University of California Press.

Levy, Robert. 1990. *Mesocosm*. Berkeley: University of California Press.

Lewis, Todd. 1993. "Newar-Tibetan Trade and the Domestication of 'Siṃhalasārtha-bāhu Avadāna.'" *History of Religions* 33(2): 135–60.

Li, Tania. 2000. "Articulating Indigenous Identity in Indonesia." *Comparative Studies in Society and History* 42(1): 149–79.

———. 2010. "Indigeneity, Capitalism and the Management of Dispossession." *Current Anthropology* 51(3): 385–414.

Limbu, Pauline. n.d. "From Kipat to Autonomy: Land and Territory in Today's Limbuwan Movement." Unpublished paper.

Linnekin, Jocelyn. 1991. "Cultural Invention and the Dilemma of Authenticity." *American Anthropologist* 93(2): 446–49.

Macdonald, Alexander. 1966. "Les Tamang vus par l'un deux". *L'Homme* 6:27–58.

Macdonald, Alexander. 1975. *Essays on the Ethnology of Nepal and South Asia*. Kathmandu: Ratna Pustak Bhandar.

Macfarlane, Alan. 1976. *Resources and Population*. Cambridge: Cambridge University Press.

———. 1997. "Identity and Change Among the Gurungs (Tamu-Mai) of Central Nepal." In *Nationalism and Identity in a Hindu Kingdom*, edited by David Gellner, Joanna Pfaff-Czarnecka, and John Whelpton, 185–204. Amsterdam: Harwood.

Majupuria, Indra, and Trilok Chandra Majupuria. 1978. *Marriage Customs in Nepal*. Kathmandu: Indra Majupuria.

———. 1980. *Peerless Nepal, Covering Broad Spectrum of the Nepalese Life in Its Right Perspective*. Delhi: Smt. M. Devi.

Malinowski, Bronislaw. (1948) 1974. "Myth in Primitive Psychology." In *Magic, Science and Religion*, 93–148. London: Souvenir.

Manandhar, Rajendra. 2011. "Dolakhako Thamiharu Aphulai 'Yeti' ko Santan Bhanchan" [The Thami of Dolakha Say They Are the Descendants of Yeti]. *Spacetime Daily*, Kathmandu. January 11, 2011.

March, Kathryn. 2002. *If Each Comes Halfway*. Ithaca, NY: Cornell University Press.

Marcus, George. 1999. "The Uses of Complicity in the Changing Mise-en-Scène of Anthropological Fieldwork." In *The Fate of "Culture,"* edited by Sherry Ortner, 86–109. Berkeley: University of California Press.

Marcus, George, and Michael Fischer. 1986. *Anthropology as Cultural Critique*. Chicago: University of Chicago Press.

Maybury-Lewis, David. 1960. "Parallel Descent and the Apinaye Anomaly." *Southwestern Journal of Anthropology* 16(2): 191–216.

McDougal, Charles. 1979. *The Kulunge Rai*. Kathmandu: Ratna Pustak Bhandar.

McHugh, Ernestine. 2001. *Love and Honor in the Himalayas*. Philadelphia: University of Pennsylvania Press.

———. 2006. "From Margin to Center." In *Tibetan Borderlands*, edited by P. Christiaan Klieger, 115–26. Leiden: Brill.

Meillasoux, Claude. 1981. *Maidens, Meal and Money*. London: Cambridge University Press.

Merlan, Francesca. 2009. "Indigeneity: Global and Local." *Current Anthropology* 50(3): 303–33.

Metcalf, Peter, and Richard Huntington. 1991. *Celebrations of Death*. Cambridge: Cambridge University Press.

Michaels, Axel. 1999. "Ancestors, Demons and the Ritual Impossibility of Death in Brahmanical Hinduism." In *Ways of Dying*, edited by Elisabeth Schömbucher and Claus Peter Zoller, 112–34. New Delhi: Manohar.

———. 2004. *Hinduism*. Princeton: Princeton University Press.

Middleton, Townsend. 2011. "Across the Interface of State Ethnography." *American Ethnologist* 38(2): 249–66.

———. 2013. "Scheduling Tribes." *Focaal* 65: 13–22.

Middleton, Townsend, and Sara Shneiderman. 2008. "Reservations, Federalism and the Politics of Recognition in Nepal." *Economic and Political Weekly* 43(19): 39–45.

Miller, Casper. (1979) 1997. *Faith Healers in the Himalaya*. Delhi: Book Faith India.

Minami, Makito. 2007. "From *tika* to *kata*?" In *Social Dynamics in Northern South Asia:* Volume 1, edited by Hiroshi Ishii, David Gellner, and Katsuo Nawa, 477–502. Delhi: Manohar.

Mishra, Chaitanya. 2012. "Ethnic Upsurge in Nepal." In *Ethnicity and Federalisation in Nepal*, edited by Chaitanya Mishra and Om Gurung. Kathmandu: Central Department of Sociology/Anthropology.

Mueggler, Erik. 2001. *The Age of Wild Ghosts*. Berkeley: University of California Press.

Mullaney, Thomas. 2010. *Coming to Terms with the Nation*. Berkeley: University of California Press.

Mumford, Stan. 1989. *Himalayan Dialogue*. Madison: University of Wisconsin Press.

(NEFIN) Nepal Federation of Indigenous Nationalities. "Definition of Indigenous." http://www.nefin.org.np/list/Definition-of-Indigenous/5/0/4.

(NFDIN) National Foundation for the Development of Indigenous Nationalities. 2003. *National Foundation for Development of Indigenous Nationalities*. Kathmandu: NFDIN.

Niezen, Ronald. 2003. *The Origins of Indigenism*. Berkeley: University of California Press.

(Niko) Thami, Basant, and Sheela Thami-Dahal, eds. 2003. *Niko Bachinte* [Our Morning]. Darjeeling: Bharatiya Thami Welfare Association.

Northey, W. B., and C. J. Morris. 1928. *The Gurkhas, Their Manners, Customs and Country*. London: J. Lane.

(NTS) Nepal Thami Samaj. 2000 (2056 VS). *Nepal Thami Samajko Bidhan* [Constitution of the Nepal Thami Samaj]. Kathmandu: NTS. Unpublished manuscript.

———. 2004. *Organizational Profile*. Kathmandu: NTS. Unpublished manuscript.

————. 2005. *Second National Convention Report*. Kathmandu: NTS. Unpublished manuscript.

Ogura, Kiyoko. 2007. "Maoists, People and the State as Seen from Rolpa and Rukum." In *Social Dynamics in Northern South Asia:* Volume 2, edited by Hiroshi Ishii, David Gellner, and Katsuo Nawa, 435–75. Delhi: Manohar.

Ohnuki-Tierney, Emiko. 1987. *The Monkey as Mirror*. Princeton: Princeton University Press.

Ong, Walter. 1982. *Orality and Literacy*. London: Methuen.

Onta, Pratyoush. 1992. "Whatever Happened to the 'Golden Age' [of Nepali History]?" *Himal* 6(4):29–31.

————. 1996a. *The Politics of Bravery*. Ph.D. diss. Philadelphia: University of Pennsylvania.

————. 1996b. "Creating a Brave Nation in British India." *Studies in Nepali History and Society* 1(1): 37–76.

————. 1996c. "Ambivalence Denied." *Contributions to Nepalese Studies* 23(1): 213–54.

————. 1999. "The Career of Bhanubhakta as a History of Nepali National Culture, 1940–1999." *Studies in Nepali History and Society* 4(1): 65–136.

————. 2006a. *Mass Media in Post-1990 Nepal*. Kathmandu: Martin Chautari.

————. 2006b. "The Growth of the *Adivasi Janajati* Movement in Nepal After 1990." *Studies in Nepali History and Society* 11(2): 303–54.

Oppitz, Michael. 1968. *Geschichte und Sozialordnung der Sherpa*. Innsbruck: Universitätsverlag Wagner.

————. 1982. "Death and Kin Amongst the Northern Magar." *Kailash* 9(4): 377–421.

————. 2006. "Die Geschichte der verlorenen Schrift." *Paideuma* 52: 27–50.

Ortner, Sherry. 1978. *Sherpas Through Their Rituals*. Cambridge: Cambridge University Press.

————. 1989. *High Religion*. Princeton: Princeton University Press.

————. 1995. "The Case of the Disappearing Shamans, or No Individualism, No Relationalism." *Ethos* 23(3): 355–90.

————. 1996. *Making Gender*. Boston: Beacon.

————. 1999. "Thick Resistance." In *The Fate of "Culture,"* edited by Sherry Ortner, 135–64. Berkeley: University of California Press.

Parry, Jonathan. 1994. *Death in Banaras*. Cambridge: Cambridge University Press.

(Patuko) Thami, D. B., ed. 2054 VS. *Nan Ni Patuko*. Kathmandu: Niko Pragatisil Thami Samaj.

Peet, R. Creighton. 1978. "Migration, Culture and Community." Ph.D. diss. New York: Columbia University.

Pettigrew, Judith. 1999. "Parallel Landscapes." In *Himalayan Space*, edited by Balthasar Bickel and Martin Gaenszle, 247–70. Zürich: Völkerkundemuseum Zürich.

Pettigrew, Judith; Sara Shneiderman; and Ian Harper. 2004. "Relationships, Complicity and Representation." *Anthropology Today*. 20(1): 20–25.

Pettigrew, Judith, and Sara Shneiderman. 2004. "Women and the Maobadi." *Himal Southasian* 17(1): 19–29.

Pfaff-Czarnecka, Joanna. 1996. "A Battle of Meanings." *Kailash* 18(3/4): 57–92.

Pfaff-Czarnecka, Joanna and Gérard Toffin, eds. 2011. *The Politics of Belonging in the Himalayas*. Delhi: Sage.

Pigg, Stacy. 1992. "Inventing Social Categories Through Place." *Comparative Studies in Society and History* 34(3): 491–513.

———. 1993. "Unintended Consequences." *South Asia Bulletin* 13(1/2): 45–58.

Pignède, Bernard. (1966) 1993. *The Gurungs*. Kathmandu: Ratna Pustak Bhandar.

Pollock, Sheldon. 1998. "India in the Vernacular Millennium." *Daedalus* 127(3): 41–74.

Pommaret, Francoise. 1999. "The Mon-pa Revisited." In *Sacred Spaces and Powerful Places in Tibetan Culture*, edited by Toni Huber, 52–75. Dharamsala: Library of Tibetan Works and Archives.

Povinelli, Elizabeth. 2002. *The Cunning of Recognition*. Durham, NC: Duke University Press.

Pradhan, Kumar. 1991. *The Gorkha Conquests*. Oxford: Oxford University Press.

———. 2004. *New Standpoints of Indigenous People's Identity and Nepali Community in Darjeeling*. Kathmandu: Social Science Baha (Mahesh Chandra Regmi Lecture Series).

Pradhan, Queenie. 2007. "Empire in the Hills." *Studies in History* 23(1): 33–91.

Pradhan, Rajendra. 1994. "A Native by Any Other Name." *Himal* 7(1): 41–45.

Pries, Ludger. 2001. "The Approach of Transnational Social Spaces." In *New Transnational Social Spaces*, edited by Ludger Pries, 3–36. London: Routledge.

Ramble, Charles. 1982. "Status and Death." *Kailash* 9(4): 333–60.

———. 1983. "The Founding of a Tibetan Village." *Kailash* 10(3/4): 267–90.

———. 1993. "Whither, Indeed, the Tsampa Eaters." *Himal* 6: 21–25.

———. 1997. "Tibetan Pride of Place." In *Nationalism and Ethnicity in a Hindu Kingdom*, edited by David Gellner, Joanna Pfaff-Czarnecka, and John Whelpton, 379–413. Amsterdam: Harwood.

———. 2008. *The Navel of the Demoness*. New York: Oxford University Press.

Ramirez, Philippe. 2013. "Ethnic Conversions and Transethnic Descent Groups in the Assam-Meghalaya Borderlands." *Asian Ethnology* 72(2): 279–97.

Redfield, Robert. 1960. *The Little Community and Peasant Society and Culture*. Chicago: University of Chicago Press.

Regmi, Mahesh Chandra. 1976. *Landownership in Nepal*. Berkeley: University of California Press.

———. 1980. *Regmi Research Series Cumulative Index for 1980*. Kathmandu: Regmi Research Series.

———. 1981. *Regmi Research Series Cumulative Index for 1981*. Kathmandu: Regmi Research Series.

(Reng) Thami, Megh Raj, ed. 1999. *Dolakha Reng*. Jhapa: Thami Bhasa Tatha Sanskriti Utthan Kendra.

Riccardi, Ted. 1975. "Sylvain Lévi." *Kailash* 3(3): 5–60.

Rimal, G. N. 2007. *Infused Ethnicities*. Kathmandu: ActionAid Nepal.

Robben, Antonius. 2004. "Death and Anthropology." In *Death, Mourning and Burial*, edited by Antonius Robben, 1–16. Malden, MA: Blackwell.

Rohatynskyj, Marta. 1997. "Culture, Secrets, and Ömie History." *American Ethnologist* 24(2): 438–56.

Rycroft, Daniel, and Sangeeta Dasgupta. 2011. *The Politics of Belonging in India*. London: Routledge.

Sadiq, Kamal. 2008. *Paper Citizens*. New York: Oxford University Press.

Sagant, Philippe. 1996. *The Dozing Shaman*. Delhi: Oxford University Press.

Samanta, A. 2000. *Gorkhaland Movement*. Delhi: A.P.H. Publishing.

(Samudaya) Thami, Khumbalal, and T. B. Thami, eds. (2056) 2061 VS. *Thami Samudayako Aitihasik Chinari ra Sanskar Sanskriti* [The Thami Community's Historic Symbols and Ritual Culture]. Kathmandu: NTS.

Sapkota, Prem Prasad Sharma. 2045 VS. *Dolakhako Thami: Jati Tatha Sanskriti—Ek Adhyayan* [The Thami of Dolakha: A Study of Ethnicity and Culture]. Jhapa.

Samuel, Geoffrey. 1993. *Civilized Shamans*. Washington, DC: Smithsonian Institution Press.

Scott, James C. 2009. *The Art of Not Being Governed*. New Haven: Yale University Press.

Seddon, J. David; Jagannath Adhikari; and Ganesh Gurung. 2001. *The New Lahures*. Kathmandu: Institute of Development Studies.

———. 2002. "Foreign Labour Migration and the Remittance Economy of Nepal." *Critical Asian Studies* 34(1): 19–40.

Shafer, Robert. 1966. *Introduction to Sino-Tibetan, Part I*. Wiesbaden: Otto Harrassowitz.

———. 1974. *Introduction to Sino-Tibetan, Part IV*. Wiesbaden: Otto Harrassowitz.

Shah, Alpa. 2010. *In the Shadows of the State*. Durham, NC: Duke University Press.

Sharma, B. K. 2057 VS. *Nepali Sabdasagar*. Kathmandu: Bhabha Pustak Bhandar.

Sharma, Pitamber. 2007. *Unraveling the Mosaic*. Kathmandu: Himal.

Shneiderman, Sara. 2002. "Embodied Ancestors." In *Territory and Identity in Tibet and the Himalayas*, edited by Katia Buffetrille and Hildegard Diemberger, 233–52. Leiden: Brill.

———. 2005. "Agency and Resistance in the Thangmi-Newar Ritual Relationship." *European Bulletin of Himalayan Research* 28: 5–42.

———. 2009. "The Formation of Political Consciousness in Rural Nepal." *Dialectical Anthropology* 33(3/4): 287–308.

———. 2010. "Creating 'Civilized' Communists." In *Varieties of Activist Experience*, edited by David Gellner, 46–80. Delhi: Sage.

———. 2013a. "Developing a Culture of Marginality." *Focaal* 65: 42–55.

————. 2013b. "Himalayan Border Citizens." *Political Geography* 35: 25–36.

Shneiderman, Sara, and Mark Turin. 2004. "The Path to Jansarkar in Dolakha District." In *Himalayan People's War*, edited by Michael Hutt, 77–109. London: Hurst.

————. 2006. "Revisiting Ethnography, Recognizing a Forgotten People." *Studies in Nepali History and Society* 11(1): 97–181.

Silver, Hilary. 2010. "Social Inclusion Policies." Australian Journal of Social Issues 45(2): 183–211.

Sinha, A. C., and Tanka Subba, eds. 2003. *The Nepalis in Northeast India.* New Delhi: Indus.

Sjöberg, K. 1993. *The Return of the Ainu.* Chur, Switzerland: Harwood Academic.

Slusser, Mary Shepherd. 1982. *Nepal Mandala.* Princeton: Princeton University Press.

van Spengen, Wim. 2000. *Tibetan Border Worlds.* London: Kegan Paul.

Srinivas, M. N. 1989. *The Cohesive Role of Sanskritization and Other Essays.* Delhi: Oxford University Press.

Stein, Genevieve. 1972. "Swadesh 100 Word List for Thami." In *Comparative Vocabularies of Languages of Nepal*, edited by A. Hale, A. M. Hari, and B. Schöttelndreyer, 37–38. Kirtipur: Summer Institute of Linguistics and Tribhuvan University.

Steinmann, Brigitte. 1996. "Mountain Deities, the Invisible Body of Society." In *Reflections of the Mountain*, edited by Anne-Marie Blondeau and Ernst Steinkellner, 179–218. Vienna: Verlag des Österreichischen Akademie der Wissenschaften.

Stirr, Anna. 2013. "Tears for the Revolution." In *Revolution in Nepal*, edited by Marie Lecomte-Tilouine, 367–92. Delhi: Oxford University Press.

Subba, Tanka. 1989. *Dynamics of a Hill Society.* Delhi: Mittal.

————. 1992. *Ethnicity, State, and Development.* Delhi: Har-Anand.

————. 1993. "Thami." In *People of India: Sikkim*, Volume 39, edited by K. S. Singh, 184–88. Calcutta: Seagull.

Subba, Tanka; A. C. Sinha; G. S. Nepal; and D. R. Nepal, eds. 2009. *Indian Nepalis.* Delhi: Concept.

Subrahmanyam, Sanjay. 2010. "The View from the Top" (review of *The Art of Not Being Governed*). *London Review of Books* 32(23): 25–26.

Tamang, Mukta. 2006. "Culture, Caste and Ethnicity in the Maoist Movement." *Studies in Nepali History and Society* 11(2): 271–301.

————. 2009. "Tamang Activism, History, and Territorial Consciousness." In *Ethnic Activism and Civil Society in South Asia*, edited by David Gellner. 269–90. Delhi: Sage.

Tamang, Seira. 2002. "The Politics of 'Developing Nepali Women.'" In *State of Nepal*, edited by Kanak Mani Dixit and S. Ramachandaran, 161–75. Kathmandu: Himal Books.

Tambiah, Stanley. 1996. *Leveling Crowds.* Berkeley: University of California Press.

Tautscher, Gabriele. 2007. *Himalayan Mountain Cults.* Kathmandu: Vajra.

Taylor, Charles. 1992. "Multiculturalism and 'The Politics of Recognition.'" In *Multiculturalism: Examining the Politics of Recognition*, edited by Amy Gutmann. 25–74. Princeton: Princeton University Press.

Thami, Karna. 1999. "Thami Sanskritiko Kehi Ilak" [Some Foundations of Thami Culture]. *Nirman* 19(34): 521–36.

Thieme, Susan. 2006. *Social Networks and Migration*. Münster: Lit Verlag.

Timsina, Suman Raj. 1992. *Nepali Community in India*. Delhi: Manak.

Toba, Sueyoshi. 1990. *Thami-English Dictionary*. Kathmandu.

Toffin, Gérard, and Joanna Pfaff-Czarnecka, eds. 2014. *Facing Globalization in the Himalayas*. Delhi: Sage.

Tsing, Anna. 1993. *In the Realm of the Diamond Queen*. Princeton: Princeton University Press.

———. 2005. *Friction*. Princeton: Princeton University Press.

———. 2009. "*Adat*/Indigenous." In *Words in Motion*, edited by Carol Gluck and Anna Tsing. Durham, NC: Duke University Press.

Turin, Mark. 1998. "The Thangmi Verbal Agreement System and the Kiranti Connection." *Bulletin of the School of Oriental and African Studies* 61(3): 476–91.

———. 2002. "Ethnonyms and Other-nyms." In *Territory and Identity in Tibet and the Himalayas*, edited by Katia Buffetrille and Hildegard Diemberger, 253–70. Leiden: Brill.

———. 2003. "Ethnobotanical Notes on Thangmi Plant Names and Their Medicinal and Ritual Uses." *Contributions to Nepalese Studies* 30(1): 19–52.

———. 2004a. "Newar-Thangmi Lexical Correspondences and the Linguistic Classification of Thangmi." *Journal of Asian and African Studies* 68: 97–120.

———. 2004b. "Thangmi Kinship Terminology in Comparative Perspective." In *Himalayan Languages*, edited by Anju Saxena, 101–39. Berlin: Mouton.

———. 2006. "Rethinking Tibeto-Burman." In *Tibetan Borderlands*, edited by P. Christiaan Klieger, 35–48. Leiden: Brill.

———. 2012. *A Grammar of Thangmi with an Ethnolinguistic Introduction to the Speakers and Their Culture*. Leiden: Brill.

———. 2014. "Mother Tongues and Language Competence." In *Facing Globalization in the Himalayas*, edited by Gérard Toffin and Joanna Pfaff-Czarnecka, 372–396. Delhi: Sage.

Turin, Mark, with Bir Bahadur Thami. 2004. *Nepali–Thami–English Dictionary*. Kathmandu: Martin Chautari.

Turner, Ralph. (1931) 1997. *A Comparative and Etymological Dictionary of the Nepali Language*. New Delhi: Allied.

Vajracharya, Dhanavajra, and Tanka Bahadur Shrestha. 2031 VS. *Dolakhako Aitihasik Ruprekha* [A Historical Review of Dolakha]. Kathmandu: Institute of Nepal and Asian Studies.

Vansittart, Eden. 1918. *Gurkhas*. Calcutta: Office of the Superintendent, Government Printing, India.

Verdery, Katherine. 1994. "Ethnicity, Nationalism, and the State." In *The Anthropology of Ethnicity*, edited by Hans Vermeulen and Cora Govers, 33–59. Amsterdam: Het Spinhuis.

Vinding, Michael. 1982. "The Thakalis as Buddhists." *Kailash* 9(4): 291–318.

———. 1998. *The Thakali*. London: Serindia.

Warren, Kay, and Jean Jackson, eds. 2002. *Indigenous Movements, Self-Representation, and the State in Latin America*. Austin: University of Texas Press.

Watkins, Joanne. 1996. *Spirited Women*. New York: Columbia University Press.

Werbner, Pnina. 1997. "Introduction." In *Debating Cultural Hybridity*, edited by Pnina Werbner and Tariq Modood, 1–28. London: Zed.

Whelpton, John. 2005. *A History of Nepal*. Cambridge: Cambridge University Press.

White, Hylton. 2010. "Identity and Property in Precarious Times." Johannesburg Workshop in Theory and Criticism (blog). http://jhbwtc.blogspot.com/2010/07/john-and-jean-comaroff-with-eric-worby.html.

Willford, Andrew. 2006. *Cage of Freedom*. Ann Arbor: University of Michigan Press.

Williams, Brackette. 1989. "A Class Act." *Annual Review of Anthropology* 18: 401–41.

Wilson, Thomas, and Hastings Donnan. 1998. "Nation, State and Identity at International Borders." In *Border Identities*, edited by Thomas Wilson and Hastings Donnan, 1–30. Cambridge: Cambridge University Press.

Yuval-Davis, Nira; Kalpana Kannabiran; and Ulrike Vieten. 2006. "Introduction." In *The Situated Politics of Belonging*, edited by Nira Yuval-Davis, Kalpana Kannabiran, and Ulrike Vieten, 1–14. London: Sage.

Muluk Bahira (book by Lainsing Bangdel), 114
Muluki Ain legal code, 11, 14, 84, 119, 177
mumpra funerary rituals, 68, 197, 219–220, 225, 227–229, 232–234. *See also* death rituals

nagarikta citizenship document, 122
nakali, 43–44, 95, 168. *See also* performance and practice of Thangmi identity
names, clan, 202–207
naming ceremony (*nwaran*), 207–210
Nan Ni Patuko (Thangmi publication), xii
nari (*hipathami*), 235–236, 240–241, 243, 248–251
National Foundation for the Development of Indigenous Nationalities (NFDIN), 14, 42, 96, 162–163, 175, 271 n. 30
nation-states, 7, 18–19, 36, 39, 41–44, 107, 109, 120–124, 255
Naxalites, 23–24, 145
Nebula (journal), 139–140, 142
Nepal Federation of Indigenous Nationalities (NEFIN), 14, 85, 149–150, 166, 168–169, 267 n. 18, 270 n. 18, 271 n. 31, 272 n. 8
Nepal Federation of Nationalities (NEFEN), 154, 270 n. 18
Nepali Congress (NC), 24, 88, 144, 246
Nepali language, xiii–xiv
Nepal Multidimensional Exclusion Index, 267 n.1
Nepal Thami Samaj (NTS): establishment of, 158, 161; guru involvement in, 161–162; history of, 133, 158–161; livelihood-based development strategy of, 166–167; logo, *160*; performances hosted by, 34; radio show created by, 96; Second National Convention Report, 42; factions of, 162–164
Newar: community, 18, 79, 91, 98, 110–111, 118–119, 123, 210, 241–246, 248–249, 267 n. 16, 270 n. 14, 270 n. 22, 273 n. 14, 23, 271–272 n.4, 273 n. 14, 23; language, 11, 86, 273 n. 24
Niko Bachinte (Thangmi publication), xii, 10, 89, 191, 207, 246–247
Niko Pragatisil Thami Samaj (NPTS), 145
Niko Thami Seva Samiti (NTSS), 154
nongovernmental organizations (NGOs), 13, 30, 37, 168, 190–191, 256
nwaran (naming) ceremony, 207–210

objectification, 50–52, 56, 66
oral traditions, 63–67, 84–87, 89–97
origin myths, 1–2, 61–97; ethnic and religious boundaries in, 87–89; gurus' perspectives on, 67–84; literate traditions of, 63–67, 84–87, 89–95; oral traditions of, 63–67, 84–87, 89–97; significance of, 62
Other Backward Class (OBC) status, 14, 34, 150–159, 164, 211, 219
otherness, 54

padhai-lekhai (educated), 67, 94–95
paloke: in death rituals, 221, 225; defined, 1–2, 76–77; discursive aspect of, 92–93; and haircutting ceremony, 210; and indigeneity, 183; mythology in, 201; and origin myths, 62, 76–84
panchayat (system of partyless democracy in Nepal 1960–1990), 23–24, 91, 145, 148–149, 214
parallel descent, 174, 201–204, 206–207
Parbatiya Hindus, 11
Pashelung (hamlet of Suspa VDC, Dolakha district, Nepal), 111, 117, 202. *See also* Suspa-Kshamawati VDC
Patuko. *See Nan Ni Patuko* (Thangmi publication)
Paudel, Madhav, 146
Peet, R. Creighton, 11, 110, 116, 266 n.5
People's Liberation Army, 161, 250. *See also* Maoists, People's War
People's War, 25. *See also* Maoists, People's Liberation Army
performance and practice of Thangmi identity, 32–60; affective results of, 58–60; Bhume ritual, 189–191; and cross-border subjectivities, 41–44; definitions, 36–39; and ethnicity as synthetic action, 39–41; and ethnocommodification, 36, 53–58; intentions behind, 44–46; recognition of, 50–53; sacred objects involved in, 46–50; and self-consciousness, 36, 50–55, 57–58; Thangmi perspectives on, 34
Piskar Massacre (January 1984), 148–149, 151
Piskar village, (Sindhupalchok district, Nepal), xv, 24, 146–151, 168, 270 n. 16
political contexts, 22–26, 138–155, 161–168
political recognition, 11–12, 16, 28, 64, 76, 81, 93, 133, 158, 168, 196, 248, 255

pork consumption, 165, 267 n.20
Pradhan, Parasmani, 134
Pradhan, Rajendra, 178
pragati (progress), 134, 145, 148, 151, 153

radical ethnogenesis, 58
radio, 96–97, 136, 256
Rai: communities, 10, 18, 77, 80, 83, 97, 114, 119, 143, 171, 216, 222, 264 n.9, 266 n.6, 267 n.20; languages, 11
Ramechap district, Nepal, xi
Rana political regime in Nepal, 14, 22–23, 72
Rangbull (Darjeeling district, West Bengal, India), xvi, 225, 273 n. 12
recognition: divine (*see* divine recognition); of *janajati*, 152; political (*see* political recognition); Thangmi community's desire for, 10–13; and Thangmi self-consciousness, 50–53
Regmi, Mahesh Chandra, 110, 174, 176
religion, 184–186. *See also specific headings*, e.g., Buddhism, Hinduism, Thangmi *dharma*
rituals: Bhume Jatra (*see* Bhume Jatra); Devikot-Khadga Jatra (*see* Devikot-Khadga Jatra); life-cycle (*see* Life-cycle rituals); recitations at, 1; spiritual forecasts, 186–189; territorial/lineage deity propitiations 47, 64, 76, 185
Robben, Antonius, 199

sakali. See also performance and practice of Thangmi identity: defined, 63; objectification with, 95; overview, 43–44, 47, 50; and Thangmi politics, 168
samavesikaran (inclusion), 108, 134. *See also* inclusion, social inclusion
Sanskrit, xiii
Scheduled Caste (SC) status, 150
Scheduled Tribe (ST) status, 14–16, 32–34, 150–151, 156–157, 164–165, 240
Scott, James C., 53, 57, 58
scripturalization, 64. *See also* literate traditions
Second National Thami Convention, 167–168
self-consciousness, 36, 50–55, 57–58
self-objectification, 56
Shah dynasty of Nepal, 14, 86, 110, 112, 174, 236, 246, 267 n.2

Shakya, Asta Laxmi, 146, 147, 149, 154
shamanism, xi–xii, 1, 3, 9, 12, 45, 47, 63–64, 72–74, 79, 82, 87, 155, 171, 184, 186–187. *See also* gurus, *jhankri*
Sherpa community, 18, 79–80, 107, 111, 118, 124, 269 n. 4, 271 n. 3
Shrestha, Pushpa Lal, 144–145
Shrestha, Tek Bahadur, 110
shristi, 62. *See also* origin and originality myths
Sikkim, India, xi, xvi, 32–33, 55, 58, 13–114, 119, 127, 162, 164, 180, 263 n. 8, 265 n. 12
Siliguri (Darjeeling district, West Bengal, India), 61, 72, 183
Silver, Hilary, 108
Simraungadh, 180–181, 185, 191, 193, 271 n. 2
Sindhupalchok district, Nepal, xi, xv, 25, 72, 100, 110, 119, 125, 146, 161, 163, 169–170, 185, 196, 213, 268 n. 13, 273 n. 14
Sivaramakrishnan, Kalyanakrishnan, 116
Slusser, Mary Shepherd, 110, 111
social inclusion, 108, 126. *See also* inclusion; *samavesikaran*
social remittances, 19, 116
social welfare, 140–144
souls, 199–201
spiritual forecasting, 186–189
Starn, Orin, 31
state control, 7, 36
state recognition, 8, 14, 57, 211
Stein, Genevieve, 11, 265 n. 11
Subrahmanyam, Sanjay, 58
Surkhe village, (Dolakha district, Nepal), xv
Suspa Bhumethan. *See* Bhume
Suspa village, (Dolakha district, Nepal), *See* Suspa-Kshamawati VDC
Suspa-Kshamawati VDC, xv, 48, 69, 70–73, 90, 92, *102*, 111, 161–162, 166–168, 174, 185–188, 191–195, 197, 202, 213, 218–219, 222. *See also* Balasode, Pashelung

Tamang: community, 10–11, 18, 62, 77, 79, 81–83, 111, 118–119, 144, 157, 164, 169, 171, 181, 197, 210, 216, 239, 265 n. 10, 266 n. 7, 269 n. 4, 270 n. 14, 271 n. 3, 273 n. 14; language 123, 264 n. 9
tea industry, 113–115
Thakali community, 4, 18, 118, 265 n. 10, 274 n. 23

Thami Bhasa Tatha Sanskriti Utthan Kendra (TBTSUK), 159

Thami Community and Their Rituals (publication), 180–181

Thami Empowerment Project (TEP), 166–167

Thami Samudayako Aitihasik Chinari ra Sanskar Sanskriti (publication), xii, 162–163, 207, 211

Thangmi/Thami individuals (listed by first name): Ajay, 183; Basant, 141–142, 155, 164, 168; Bhaba Bahadur, 166; Bir Bahadur (of Lapilang/Darjeeling), 115, 126; Bir Bahadur (of Piskar), 149, 168; Bir Bahadur (of Suspa, "Lile"), xiii, 27, 121, 212, 214, 234; Buddha Laxmi, 111; Chun Bahadur, 161; Dalaman, 168; Gopal, 155, 187, 190–191; Gopal Singh, 28; Gopilal, 88, 246, 250; Guru Maila (Lalit Bahadur), 48, 92, 185, 197–198, 203, 216, 233; Harka Bahadur ("Amrikan"), 116–117; Ile Bahadur, 149; Jagat Man, 148, 170–171; Junkiri, 186–188; Kamala, 205–206; Khumbalal, 68–69, 93–95, 162, 163, 166, 190, 207; Kote Guru, 74; Latte Apa (Man Bahadur), 12–14, 28, 50, 69, 71, 73–76, 82, 95, 121, 182–183, 194, 199–201, 209, 224–225, *225*; Laxmi, 58–60, 211; Mahendra, 42; Man Bahadur (of Alampu/Darjeeling), *see* Latte Apa; Man Bahadur (of Chokati), 112; Man Bahadur (of Dolakha), 12; Man Bahadur (of Kusipa/Darjeeling), 140, 143–144; Megh Raj, 62–63, 68, 158–163, 166, 175, 207; Nar Bahadur, 144; Nathu, 95, 128, 132, 152, 154, 156, 163–164; Nirmala, 10; Paras, 61–62, 89–90, 94, 156; Ram Bahadur, 196, 245–247, 254–255; Rana Bahadur (senior guru of Balasode), 27–29, 69, *70*, 71–74, 77, 98–99, 217–218, 226; Rana Bahadur (of Dolakha, working in Darjeeling), 55, 60, 203; Sheela, 55, 216; Sher Bahadur, 95; Shova, *49*, 67, 211; Silipitik, 89–90, 117–119, 136, 249; Tek Bahadur, 103, 169–170; Tek Raj, 92, 96–97

Thangmi/Thami ethnicity, 1–31, 168; academic study of, 3–9; and bordering communities, 19–22; and cross-border feedback loop, 17–19; defined, xi; *dharma* (religion), 63, 84, 86, 197; historical contexts of, 22–26, 133–134, 138–140; lack of ethnography on, 9–12; political contexts of, 22–26, 138–155, 161–168; in the public sphere, 134–138; recognition of, 12–17, 31, 155–158; role of researchers studying, 27–31; unified association of, 158–161

Thangmi ethnic organizations. *See specific organizations, e.g.:* Bharatiya Thami Welfare Association, Nepal Thami Samaj

Thangmi in China, 20–21; citizenship issues with, 124; identification as, 3

Thangmi in India: class status in, 14–15; and dual citizenship, xiv, xv; identification as, 3; places of settlement for, xv–xvi; property ownership and resources of, 106

Thangmiko kal, 98, 111–112

Thangmi language, xi, xiii, 11, 15, 59, 64, 77, 90, 95–96, 121, 159, 203, 212

Thangmi ritual language, xiii, 47, 64, 197

Thangmi Wakhe (radio show), 96–97

Thapa-Magar, Ashoke, 11

Tharu community, 18, 38, 51–52, 269 n. 4

Thulung Rai community, 274 n. 20

thurmi (wooden ritual dagger), 47, *48, 49*, 50, 222–223, 252, 254

Tibetan Autonomous Region of China (TAR), xi, 3, 18, 20–22, 103, 106–107, 120, 124, 172

Tin Mile (Darjeeling district, West Bengal, India), xvi

transnational villages, 106, 110, 125

Tumsong tea plantation, (Darjeeling district, West Bengal, India), xvi, 113, 121, 146, 165, 199, 219

Tungsung (Darjeeling district, West Bengal, India), xv, 69, 75, 183

Turin, Mark, xi, 11, 168, *253*, 264 n. 5, 265 n. 10, 270 n. 4, 272 n. 3 and 5, 274 n. 24

Udayapur district, Nepal, xi, xv

UN Working Group on Indigenous Peoples, 178

Unified Communist Party of Nepal-Maoist (UCPN-M), 24. *See also* Maoists

United Lapilang Village Committee (Lapilang Gaun Ekai Samiti), 146

unnati (improvement), 134, 139, 143, 151, 205

utpatti (origin), 62. *See also* origin myths
utthan (upliftment), 134, 139, 157, 159, 271
 n. 30

Vajracharya, Dhanavajra, 110
VCD technology, 96–97, 211
vikas (development), 134, 145, 154. *See also*
 development

Village Development Committee (VDC), 170

Wangdi, T., 143
wedding dances, *33, 34, 35,* 168, 215
Werbner, Pnina, 89
West Bengal, xi, 6, 23, 26, 32, 69, 71,
 131–132, 137, 143, 145, 152, 154–156
Whelpton, John, 86

Acknowledgments

This project has spanned fifteen years and many countries. Recognizing all those who contributed to this book is a fitting challenge with which to conclude it.

I received major research funding from the Fulbright Commission (1999–2000), the National Science Foundation (2001–2006), the Foreign Language and Area Studies Fellowship (2002–2003), the Social Science Research Council (2005–2007), and the American Council of Learned Societies/Mellon Foundation (2008–2009). Small grants came from the Department of Anthropology and the Einaudi Center for International Studies at Cornell University; St. Catharine's College and the Frederick Williamson Fund at the University of Cambridge; and the Firebird Foundation. Final preparation of the manuscript and production of the book was supported by the A. Whitney Griswold and Frederick W. Hilles Funds at Yale University.

Some chapters draw upon earlier publications with permission. Parts of Chapters 1, 2, and 3 appear in *American Anthropologist* 116(2):279–95, "Reframing Ethnicity: Academic Tropes, Politics Beyond Recognition and Ritualized Action Between Nepal and India," and in *Ritual, Heritage and Identity: The Politics of Culture and Performance in a Globalised World* (Christiane Brosius and Karin Polit, eds.), "Synthesising Practice and Performance, Securing Recognition: Thangmi Cultural Heritage in Nepal and India." An earlier version of Chapter 4 appears in *Facing Globalization: Belonging and the Politics of the Self* (Gérard Toffin and Joanna Pfaff-Czarnecka, eds.), "Circular Lives: Histories and Economies of Belonging in the Transnational Thangmi Village." Chapter 8 builds upon "Agency and Resistance in the Thangmi-Newar Ritual Relationship" in *European Bulletin of Himalayan Research* 28.

My deepest gratitude goes to all of the Thangmi with whom I worked. Bir Bahadur (Lile) has been research assistant, friend, and brother all in one. In Dolakha, my hosts in Balasode/Damarang were Mangal and Dalli, and their extended family—Kedar, Pratima and Janga Bahadur, Yasoda and Krishna Bahadur, Sundar Kumar and Seti, and Jit Bahadur—made my time there pleasurable and productive. The late Rana Bahadur and Maili were the patriarch and matriarch of that family. Over the ridge in Pashelung, Kamala, Bimaya, Sita, Bimala, and Buddha Laxmi Bhojyu provided a wonderful "women's group," and Nara Bahadur often helped with crucial details. I have the gurus Lalit Bahadur (Guru Maila), Panchaman, Ram Bahadur, Uddhab, and Junkiri, along with the *pujari* Birka Bahadur and his family, and the *naris* of Dumkot and their families, to thank for my knowledge of Thangmi ritual practice. In Lapilang, Buddhiman Thami was an excellent host, while Thula Thami and his family made my stays in Alampu productive. In Charikot and Dolakha Bazaar respectively, Chiranjibi Maskey and Surya Krishna Shrestha and their families provided a broader network of support, especially during the years of conflict. In Sindhupalchok, my Chokati host Man Bahadur was a fount of knowledge, while his wife, daughters, son-in-law, and granddaughters made me wish I could have spent more time there. In Jhapa, I am grateful to Megh Raj and his family.

In Kathmandu, the Nepal Thami Samaj supported my work from the outset. I thank all of its members and officers over time: Bhabha Bahadur, Jagat Man, Kabiraj, Khumbalal, Lok Bahadur, Prakash, Tahal, Tek Raj, Tek Bahadur, and the late Singha Bahadur. The Fulbright Commission, the Centre for Nepal and Asian Studies (CNAS) and the Central Department of Sociology and Anthropology (CDSA) at Tribhuvan University, and the Cornell Nepal Study Program (CNSP) provided administrative homes in Kathmandu. I am grateful to the faculty, staff, and students at each institution, especially Mike Gill and Peter Moran at Fulbright, Nirmal Man Tuladhar at CNAS, Om Gurung at CDSA, and Banu Oja at CNSP. Traces of conversations in Kathmandu with so many colleagues and friends run through this book: my thanks to Lynn Bennett, Jessica Vantine Birkenholtz, Barbara Butterworth, Ben Campbell, Gabriel Campbell, Rhoderick Chalmers, Christina Chan, Dambar Chemjong, Tatsuro and Yasuko Fujikura, Martin Gaenszle, Krishna Hachhethu, Ian Harper, Shannon Harriman, Tina Harris, Sushma Joshi, Dipesh Kharel, Brandon Kohrt, Laura Kunreuther, Genevieve Lakier, Marie Lecomte-Tilouine, Mark Liechty, the late Bela Malik, Thomas Mathew, Don and Liesl Messerschmidt, Christina

Monson, Monica Mottin, Pratyoush Onta, Judith Pettigrew, Joanna Pfaff-Czarnecka, Dinesh Prasain, Janak Rai, Charles Ramble, Anne de Sales, Bandita Sijapati, Ajay Siwakoti, Anna Stirr, Mukta S. L. Tamang, Seira Tamang, Deepak Thapa, Sueyoshi Toba, Gérard Toffin, and Laurie Vasily. I thank Seema Chhetri, Pushpa Hamal, Hikmat Khadka, Manesh Shrestha, and the late D. B. Thapa for their translation work. Many itinerant years were spent in the households of those listed above, but Lishu and Leo Rodriguez provided the perfect spot to finally call our own. Ram Bahadur, Anita, Komin, and Shanti Thami made living there a pleasure. Finally, I thank Suren Thami and his extended family in both Nepal and India for helping me connect the dots.

In Darjeeling, the officers of the Bharatiya Thami Welfare Association opened their archives and lives to me: I thank Kala, Paras, Gautam, Shova, Rajen, and the late Basant and Gopal Singh. I am further indebted to I. B. *kaka* and the Merry Villa/Tumsong family; Nathu, Mahendra, Bishnu, Dalaman, and their extended families in Tungsung/Jawahar Basti; Bandana and her family in Tin Mile; and members of the community in Mangalpuri, Shivagram, Bauddhagram, Jorebunglow, Rangbull, Bijen Bari, and Kurseong. I am grateful to Rana Bahadur for introducing me to the Khaldo Hotel, and to Indira and Krishna for providing a safe space in which to meet its inhabitants. Sumitra provided introductions at the District Magistrate's Office, the Tribal Welfare Office, the District Agriculture Office, and the Darjeeling Gorkha Hill Council. Shariphu Bhutia, Norbu and Sangay Pelmo Dekeva, Barbara Gerke, Mary Boland, and Niraj Lama offered friendship and support. I cannot sufficiently express my gratitude to the late Latte Apa (Man Bahadur) and his family for welcoming me into their lives and opening their world to me.

Sheela Thami-Dahal and D.B. Thami made my visits to Sikkim meaningful, and Anna Balikci-Denjongpa and Director Tashi Densapa of the Namgyal Institute of Tibetology provided a base in Gangtok. Jigme Denjongpa, Ian Fitzpatrick, Saul Mullard, Arthur Pazo, Mélanie Vandenhelsken, and Pema Wangchuk shared friendship and a wealth of knowledge.

I was extremely fortunate to benefit from the guidance and warmth of David Holmberg, Kathryn March, Viranjini Munasinghe, and Shambhu Oja at Cornell. Jane Fajans, Jane-Marie Law, Palden Oshoe, Jakob Rigi, Johanna Schoss, Terry Turner, and Andrew Willford also contributed to the initial framing of the project, along with David Germano at the University of Virginia. In Ithaca, many peers shaped my thinking and made life wonderful: thanks to Nosheen Ali, Ken Bauer, Jason Cons, Sienna Craig, Steve Curtis, Gerardo Damonte, Kunga Delotsang, Jessica Falcone, Lisa Feder, Jane Ferguson, Susan Hangen, Heather Harrick, Sondra Hausner, Eric Henry, Farhana Ibrahim, Gopini Lama, Townsend Middleton, Zack Nelson, Anne Rademacher, Cabeiri Robinson, Noni Session, Jen Shannon, Amanda Snellinger, Noa Vaisman, Marcus Watson, and Abraham Zablocki.

In the Netherlands, I thank the Oorthuys family and colleagues Henk Blezer, George van Driem, Yolanda van Ede, Erik de Maaker, Heleen Plaisier, Bal Gopal Shrestha, and Peter Verhagen for making Amsterdam a warm and productive place to write. Christiane Brosius, Martin Gaenszle, Richard Handler, Karen Polit, and William (Bo) Sax provided feedback at a workshop in Heidelberg in 2007 that significantly influenced my arguments.

In the United Kingdom, I am grateful for ongoing support from Sarah Harrison, Alan Macfarlane, David Gellner, and Michael Hutt. St. Catharine's College, Cambridge, provided a wonderful post-doctoral work environment. For many illuminating conversations, my gratitude goes to Chris and Susan Bayly, Heather Bedi, Joya Chatterji, Liana Chua, Anne and Sam Cowan, Lucy Delap, Hildegard Diemberger, Beatrice Jauregui, Jonathan Mair, Nayanika Mathur, Fiona McConnell, Alpa Shah, Bimbika Sijapati Basnett, Louise Tillin, Hans van de Ven, Philippa Williams, and Harald Wydra.

Back in the United States, this book came into its final form at Yale. I am especially grateful to Kalyanakrishnan (Shivi) Sivaramakrishnan for his multifaceted engagement. Conversations with Barney Bate, Sean Brotherton, Narges Erami, Shaila Seshia Galvin, Sahana Ghosh, Phyllis Granoff, Inderpal Grewal, Erik Harms, Karen Hébert, Shafqat Hussain, Amy Johnson, Austin Lord, Mike McGovern, Gabriela Morales, Karen Nakamura, Sally Promey, Jacob Rinck, Doug Rogers, James Scott, Helen Siu, Tariq Thachil, Luke Wagner, Steven Wilkinson, and Jonathan Wyrtzen helped sharpen arguments. Amy Johnson also offered invaluable editorial precision in compiling the final product. Students in my seminar "Ethnicity and Indigeneity in a Mobile World" read the entire manuscript. Kasturi Gupta, Mary Smith, Jennifer De Chello, Francesco D'Aria, Constance Buskey and Marleen Cullen provided crucial logistical support. At the Sterling Memorial Library, Stacey Maples made the map, and Peter Leonard helped with image digitization. Andrew Quintman has been a wonderful colleague, lighting the way a few steps ahead on the path of the book. Sarah LeVine and Ajantha Subramanian offered helpful feedback at a Harvard seminar. At the University of Pennsylvania Press, I am grateful to editors Peter Agree and Noreen O'Connor-Abel for shepherding this project through many stages. Series editor Kirin Narayan offered generous suggestions that have greatly improved the book, along with Arjun Guneratne and one anonymous reviewer.

Nhima Bhuti Gurung deserves special thanks everywhere: for understanding when my research interests moved beyond Mustang, and for traveling with us first to Kathmandu, Dolakha, and Sindhapalchok, and then to India, the United Kingdom, and the United States. *Mitini*, sister, and friend, without your care and attention, the hard work of this book would have been impossible.

My parents and their partners—Nancy Shneiderman and Allan Griff, Ben Shneiderman and Jenny Preece—gave me the travel bug and encouraged me to become an anthropologist. My sister, Anna Shneiderman, has always been a steadfast sounding board. My mother-in-law Hannah Turin-Oorthuys has offered the one home that has remained constant and made many things possible. My husband, Mark Turin, introduced me to the Thangmi community and their language, encouraged me to develop this project, and experienced it with me. Mark's scholarly contribution to this book is evident from citations and notes, yet this is but one part of our shared life and work. Finally, to Samuel Ananda Turin, who traveled with me silently during the last phase of fieldwork and entered the world loudly as I began writing; and Nina Sangye Turin, whose big personality in a little package buoyed me as I finished, you have made it all worthwhile.